Herodotus: Book III

Greek Texts series

Aeschylus: Agamemnon,
Leah Himmelhoch
Aeschylus: Choephori, A. Bowen
Alcidamas, J. V. Muir
Aristophanes: Frogs, W. B. Stanford
Aristophanes: Scenes from Birds,
W. H. Oldaker
Arrian: Periplus Ponti Euxini,
Aidan Liddle
Characters of Theophrastus, R. G. Ussher
Demosthenes: De Corona,
W. W. Goodwin
Demosthenes: Olynthiacs, E. I. McQueen
Essential Hesiod, Christopher Rowe
Euripides: Cyclops, D. M. Simmonds
and R. R. Timberlake
Euripides: Hecuba, Michael Tierney
Euripides: Hippolytus, John Ferguson
*Euripides: Scenes from Iphigenia in
Aulis and Iphigenia in Tauris*,
E. C. Kennedy
Euripides: Scenes from Rhesus and Helen,
E. C. Kennedy
Four Greek Authors, E. C. Kennedy
Gorgias: Encomium of Helen,
D. M. MacDowell
Greek Lyric Poetry, David A. Campbell
The Greek Philosophers, J. H. Lesher
Herodotus: Book I, J. H. Sleeman
Herodotus: Book VI, E. I. McQueen
Herodotus: Book VIII, J. Enoch Powell
Homer: Iliad I, J. A. Harrison and
R. H. Jordan
Homer: Iliad III, J. T. Hooker
Homer: Iliad VI, J. A. Harrison and
R. H. Jordan
Homer: Iliad I–XII, M. M. Willcock

Homer: Iliad XIII–XXIV, M. M. Willcock
Homer: Odyssey VI and VII,
Janet Watson
Homer: Odyssey IX, J. V. Muir
Homer: Odyssey I–XII, W. B. Stanford
Homer: Odyssey XIII–XXIV,
M. M. Willcock
The Homeric Battle of the Frogs and Mice,
Joel P. Christensen and Erik Robinson
Lucian: Selections, Keith C. Sidwell
Lysias: Five Speeches: 1, 12, 19, 22, 30,
M. J. Edwards
Menander: Dyskolos, E. W. Handley
Plato: Crito, C. J. Emlyn-Jones
Plato: Euthyphro, C. J. Emlyn-Jones
Plato: Laches, C. J. Emlyn-Jones
Plato: Republic I, D. J. Allan
Plato: Republic X, John Ferguson
Presocratics: Main Fragments,
M. R. Wright
Protagoras, Adela Marion Adam
and James Adam
Sophocles: Ajax, W. B. Stanford
Sophocles: Oedipus Tyrannus,
Richard C. Jebb
Tales from Herodotus, G. S. Farnell
and Marie Goff
Theocritus: Select Poems, K. J. Dover
Thucydides: Book I, E. C. Marchant
Thucydides: Book II, E. C. Marchant
and Thomas Wiedemann
Thucydides: Book VI, K. J. Dover
Xenophon: Fall of Athens,
Theodore Horn
Xenophon: Oeconomicus, Ralph Doty
Xenophon: The Persian Expedition,
Stephen Usher

Herodotus: Book III

Georgina Longley

BLOOMSBURY ACADEMIC
LONDON · NEW YORK · OXFORD · NEW DELHI · SYDNEY

BLOOMSBURY ACADEMIC
Bloomsbury Publishing Plc
50 Bedford Square, London, WC1B 3DP, UK
1385 Broadway, New York, NY 10018, USA
29 Earlsfort Terrace, Dublin 2, Ireland

BLOOMSBURY, BLOOMSBURY ACADEMIC and the Diana logo are trademarks of Bloomsbury Publishing Plc

First published in Great Britain 2024

Copyright © Georgina Longley, 2024

Georgina Longley has asserted her right under the Copyright, Designs and Patents Act, 1988, to be identified as Author of this work.

Cover image: Hecte (1/6 of a stater) beaten between 560–546 BC showing foreparts of lion and bull facing each other. Illustration by Barbara Ch'en-Ling

All rights reserved. No part of this publication may be reproduced or transmitted in any form or by any means, electronic or mechanical, including photocopying, recording, or any information storage or retrieval system, without prior permission in writing from the publishers.

Bloomsbury Publishing Plc does not have any control over, or responsibility for, any third-party websites referred to or in this book. All internet addresses given in this book were correct at the time of going to press. The author and publisher regret any inconvenience caused if addresses have changed or sites have ceased to exist, but can accept no responsibility for any such changes.

A catalogue record for this book is available from the British Library.

A catalog record for this book is available from the Library of Congress.

ISBN: HB: 978-1-3502-8280-3
PB: 978-1-3502-8279-7
ePDF: 978-1-3502-8283-4
eBook: 978-1-3502-8281-0

Series: Greek Texts

Typeset by RefineCatch Limited, Bungay, Suffolk

To find out more about our authors and books visit www.bloomsbury.com and sign up for our newsletters.

Contents

Preface	vi
Introduction	1
Text	33
Translation	102
Commentary	202
Bibliography	354
Appendix – A Table of Tribute	360
Index Locorum of Greek and Latin Authors	362
General Index	365

Preface

Herodotus, the Father of History, presents us with a remarkable and rich history from a remote earlier age down to the end of the Persian Wars. So far from being a collector of fables, he has in recent decades received greater recognition for his engagement with the intellectual world around him.

Book III is, in the current author's opinion, one of the finest books in the *Histories* revealing Herodotus' interest in human nature, causation, other cultures, geography, and even medicine. It also shows him to be a talented narrator, able to create a great sense of drama in his writing.

This book aims to inform and contextualize Book III both within the *Histories* and also in Greek intellectual thought and historiography. It also hopes to excite the reader about Herodotus as an author and hopefully spur them on to delve deeper into this great work.

A central part of the work is to assist the reader in translating and understanding the Greek, and in getting to grips with Herodotus' style and language. He is not always easy to translate, but his prose attests to the rich potential of the Greek language. He is worth the effort.

I was delighted to be asked to undertake this task. Book III was a true favourite as an undergraduate. I would like to thank Alice Wright, Lily Mac Mahon and Zoe Osman at Bloomsbury for this opportunity and for all their patience and support as I put this project together. I would like to thank the reviewer for Bloomsbury for their insightful comments and recommendations. Thanks must also be given to Dr Emily Kearns for her own painstaking reading of this work. The book is stronger and more useful, thanks to their advice.

Finally, I should probably also thank Herodotus for leaving us keen Classicists such a literary treat.

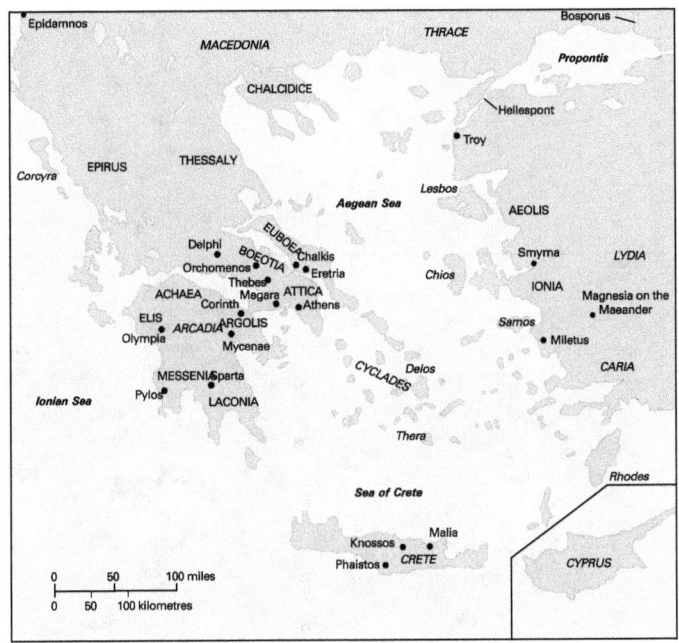

Figure 1 Greece and Asia Minor.

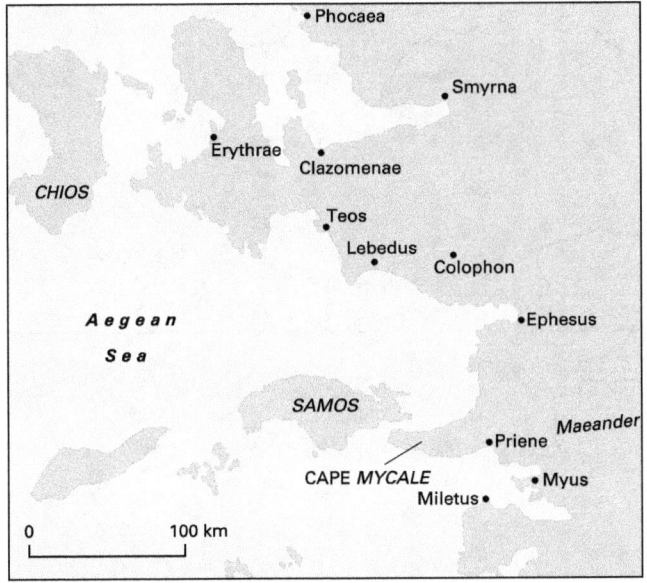

Figure 2 Samos and neighbours.

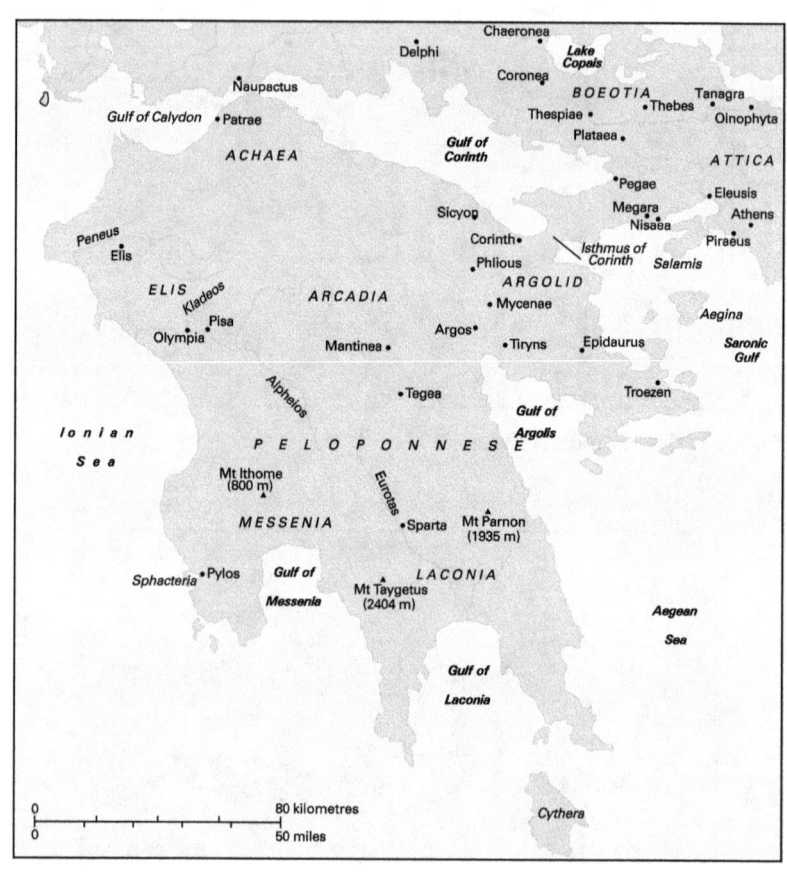

Figure 3 The Peloponnese.

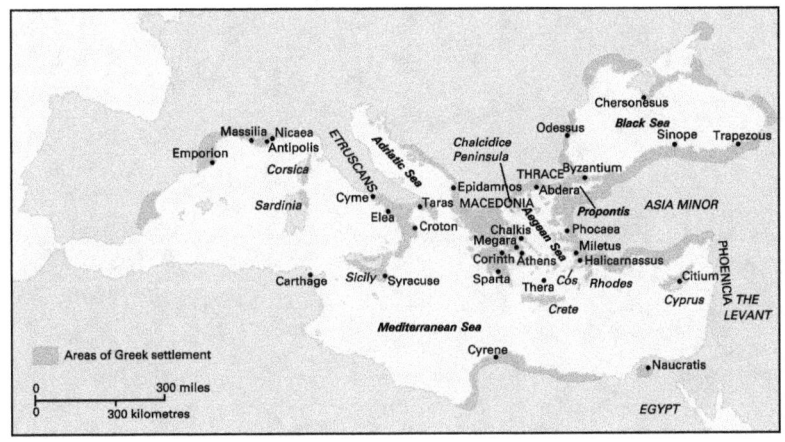

Figure 4 Greek settlements.

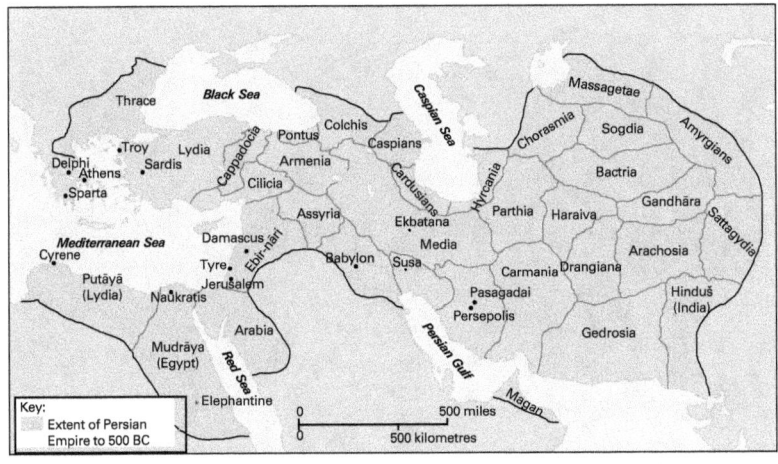

Figure 5 The Persian empire.

Introduction

Unless otherwise stated, all dates are BC. *All sections from Book III are marked* §.

I. Who was Herodotus?

Cicero dubbed Herodotus the Father of History; Plutarch branded him the 'Father of Lies'. These seemingly conflicting labels are not incompatible, but is it true that Herodotus is an historian who is not to be trusted? This is a question that has preoccupied scholars for over five decades and it is not one we shall find an answer to within the scope of this introduction. What we can certainly conclude is that Herodotus is a rich, complex, and important author worthy of modern readers' attention.

The current author's view is that, whilst sections of Herodotus are demonstrably wrong and he is certainly not free from bias, Plutarch's view that he has created a web of lies is overly cynical. Errors are, after all, not always down to deliberate falsehood. Moreover, there is more to studying an author than simply a right or wrong test, and this is perhaps particularly true for Herodotus. Into his history of vast temporal and geographical scope are woven rich themes which are explored throughout the work. Herodotus' ideas are informed by predecessors and by the contemporary milieu of ideas in which he lived.

II. Herodotus of Halicarnassus

Herodotus was from the city of Halicarnassus, located in Anatolia (modern-day Turkey). The city was originally a Doric settlement, lying at the heart of the meeting point between mainland Greece and the Persian empire. It was a rich centre of philosophy, learning and innovation in thought, and was linguistically diverse with both Carian and Greek in use. This was the region whence the Homeric poems emanated, where many of the Presocratic philosophers came from and where Greek medical thought flourished. All are palpable in the pages of the *Histories*, as we shall see. Such was Herodotus' homeland. He, however, seems to have been expelled from Halicarnassus in the 450s and may well have been related to the epic poet Panyassis (a Carian name and possibly our historian's uncle), who was killed in the political upheaval that occasioned his departure (Newmyer 1986). On his travels, we know he spent time in Athens, where his work became well known and that he very likely spent time on Samos, as his account of his Samian source suggests. If his claims are to be believed, he also visited Egypt, the Black Sea and Mesopotamia, but some modern scholars show greater scepticism towards the veracity of his claims (for example, Fehling 1994: 1–15; Armayor 1978a: 59–73) and not without some justification, given the errors that can be found in the accounts of places he claims to have visited such as Egypt. What we can say is that the work displays a rich interest in politics, ethnography, geography, and moreover an interest explaining the events he describes. It is a remarkable text, so let us look at it more closely.

III. *The Histories*

Date

It is highly likely that the *Histories*' first public appearance was not in its current nine-book form. First, the division into nine books was likely a later division made by an editor. Secondly, they may well have been originally delivered as lectures, perhaps in a series, and written up later and not necessarily in one tome all at once. A precise dating of the work is, therefore, difficult.

We certainly know that some of the work post-dates 430, since at VII.137 Herodotus refers to the execution of two Spartan ambassadors along with a Corinthian named Aristeas at Athens, which occurred in 430 (see also Thucydides, II.67).

Dewald and Munson give an excellent discussion of various ways scholars have sought to pinpoint a more precise date for publication rather than just 'the final thirty years' of the fifth century (2022: 8–9). They note that links have been made between passages in Aristophanes which could be parodying Herodotus. For example, the ambassador's description of how well he was wined and dined in Persia in *Acharnians* could be a parody of Herodotus' description of the Persian banquet at I.133. However, these links are not conclusive and may rather reflect key aspects and stereotypes of fifth-century Athenian thought.

Aims

It will become clear in this introduction that I do not see Herodotus as a Greek apologist. It is true that an aim of his work was to explain Greek, especially Athenian, victory in the Persian Wars where his work ends, but his aim was also to contextualise these events in a much wider canvas of history. There is a great deal more to the work. Compared to contemporaries such as Thucydides, he is very far from being Hellenocentric. We should not forget Herodotus' own words about his purpose from the opening of the work:

> So that the great and amazing deeds, some undertaken by Greeks, some by non-Greeks, do not pass without fame, and among other things, the reason why they went to war against one another.

The deeds of Greeks and non-Greeks alike are all worthy of the record, which Herodotus presents to us as the result of his enquiry. The word 'history' comes from the Greek verb 'to enquire', and so Herodotus' work is depicted as an active quest for knowledge and understanding (see below on the ancient historian and methods of enquiry, see below pp.4–7). What do the deeds that Herodotus records include? For the man from Halicarnassus, these were not simply about kings, leaders and battles. Customs and practices, works of art, speeches, reports (including variant versions), oracles and responses to them are all part of what people have done (see Gould 1989: 77). These deeds are mapped out onto a wide geographical scope and varied ethnographic landscape, on which Herodotus comments with varying degrees of certainty. As Katherine Clarke aptly notes, 'his historical narrative incorporates and is in turn embedded in a complex spatial framework' (Clarke 2018: 4)

This varied quilt of theme and subject-matter is masterfully woven together. Someone looking for a neat consistent argument structure is not going to find it (Dewald 1987: 147–9). Far from this being a drawback, Herodotus creates a more interesting flow of thematic, temporal, geographical, and political connections across his vast map. To see the work and its aims as a crescendo to Athenian victory, is greatly to underestimate and misunderstand it.

It is also clear from his opening words that Herodotus attached great importance to the explanation of events, their causes and how they came to be intertwined. Book III itself opens with an exploration of different explanations given for Cambyses' invasion of Egypt. In doing so, we not only see Herodotus' interest in causes, but also his awareness of their complexity.

IV. Methods and approaches

Herodotus the critic

Lateiner's masterful work (1989) on Herodotus' aims and methods as an historian remains an essential read for any keen student of the *Histories*. Since then, Herodotus' techniques and methods and how these influenced later writers have become a rich area of Herodotean scholarship. Herodotus comments extensively on the historian's task, his own efforts and on his material. In her *A Very Short Introduction to Herodotus*, Roberts (2011: 2) remarks, 'he makes some five-hundred evaluative remarks of one kind and another'.

Until Polybius appeared some three-hundred years later, it is fair to say that no other author contained quite so many methodological comments. The presence of such remarks also demonstrates that Herodotus is not the credulous teller of stories that he had previously been branded, unfavourably compared to the more obviously rationalist Thucydides. However, he often prefaces accounts with 'as *x* says', showing that inclusion of a version does not mean the reader can automatically assume his endorsement. In §116.2, Herodotus declares that he is not convinced by the tale of gold-stealing one-eyed men. The critical side to Herodotus' approach should not be overlooked. Furthermore, an examination of a passage from Book III will reveal a more critical historian aware of the difficulties one can face when seeking to access the past. In §122.3, Herodotus pauses his narrative of Oroetes' plotting to explain the ambitions of Samian tyrant Polycrates:

> For Polycrates was the first of the Greeks whom we know of who intended to become master of the sea, besides Minos of Cnossos and if there was anyone else before him who ruled the sea. Of the race that we call the human race Polycrates was the first and had great hoped that he would rule Ionia and the islands.

Minos is not classed as part of the 'what is called the human race' (τῆς δὲ ἀνθρωπηίης λεγομένης γενεῆς) and Herodotus notes that Polycrates was the first 'τῶν ἡμεῖς ἴδμεν'. Mention of Minos is, therefore, qualified. When Herodotus says 'whom we know of', he likely means those for whom eyewitnesses or more easily verifiable accounts survive. Minos clearly belongs to the much more remote past. However, what does he mean by 'what we call the human race'? This has been interpreted as referring to the 'heroic' age, denoting a race where some beings may have had divine lineage, an age very different to the 'human race.' Munson argues that the passage offers insight into Herodotus' appreciation of history's complexity and problems arising from one's sources and enquiry (Munson 2012: 200-1; see also Baragwanath and de Bakker (2012: 23-6); Williams (2004: 155-61); see the Commentary for more on this passage). In light of this, Herodotus appears more shrewd than credulous.

Enquiry

The title that Herodotus gives to his own work is as follows: 'This is the product of the enquiry of Herodotus of Halicarnassus.' The key word here is 'ἱστορίης' – enquiry, which became our own word 'history.' His writings are the results of his enquiry and so we must now ask what this involved for our historian. We have already mentioned that he had certainly ventured beyond Halicarnassus (admittedly, not willingly), although his precise itinerary is disputed. How (at least according to his own testimony) did he go about his information-gathering?

Greek historians, quite possibly starting with Herodotus, broadly distinguished two methods of enquiry: 'seeing' and 'hearing.' It was of particular value to have seen something for oneself and second best to have questioned someone who had. The term for this is αὐτοψία, an eyewitness being an αὐτόπτης (Marincola 1997: 63–85); ἀκοή (hearing) was what one heard about from others. We shall examine two passages where Herodotus deals critically with this distinction. In our current book, §115, Herodotus is discussing what he has heard about the regions that lie to the north and north-west of Europe. He makes very clear that he is only presenting what he has heard:

> Nor am I able to discover anyone who has seen for himself, despite looking into this carefully, whether there is a sea beyond Europe. I do know that we receive tin and amber from these regions.

Herodotus refuses to conjecture whether there is a sea lying beyond Europe as he has not discovered anyone who has seen it for themselves.

This does not mean of course that Herodotus was always correct, even about places he claims to have seen.. For example, his claims about the sources of the Nile at II.28 were branded 'absurd' (Wainwright 1953: 104–7; although, see Alberge 2019: 'Nile shipwreck discovery proves Herodotus right – after 2,469 years' on the discovery of a shipwreck which suggests that his accounts of the unusual Nile boats was in fact right after all).

The second passage we shall look at, which is very similar to the Book III section is IV.16. Previous to this, Herodotus has been dealing with the Cimmerian peoples, their uprooting and the mystery of the disappearing poet Aristeas. Here, he returns to the mysterious nature of the land north of Italy. Aristeas, he tells us, described this, but only from hearsay, and he has not been able to find an eyewitness. As at §115.2, the term is αὐτόπτης. Herodotus stands at the beginning of what would become a key part of a historian's rhetoric concerning accuracy and reliability.

V. Book III

Content and structure

Book III is a brilliant text and one which exemplifies many key aspects of Herodotus' thought and learning, his methods as an historian and certainly his skills as a narrator.

Following Book I, which focused on Croesus and the rise and successes of Cyrus, and Book II which focused on Egypt, Herodotus arrives again at Persia, which forms the main focus of Book III. The book opens with Cambyses, examining his conduct, his death, the rise of Darius as king, and ending with the latter's successful reconquest of Babylon. Book III also sees the empire that was to fight the Persian wars with Greece reach its mighty peak, with Persian interest in Greece already on Darius' horizon. However, this does not do justice either to the book's narrative of a large array of historical actors, peoples and places or to Herodotus' skilful handling of his multi-theatre account. Around the central thread of Persia, many other peoples and places play major roles in events, creating a complex scene of activity. The structure and content of the work is as follows:

1–38: Persian matters
    1–16: Invasion of Egypt.
    17–26: Failed expeditions and the embassy to Ethiopia.
    27–37: The Apis affair and the madness of Cambyses.
    38: *Nomos* is king.

39–60: Samian affairs
    39: The good fortune of Polycrates
    40–3: The advice of Amasis and the ring.
    43–7: Samian/Spartan relations.
    48–53: Corcyra, Corinth and Periander.
    54–6: The failed Spartan attempt to take Samos.
    57–9: The fate of the Samians exiled by Polycrates.
    60: Engineering feats of Samos.

61–97: Persian matters
    61–88: The revolt of the Magi, the death of Cambyses, the retaliation of the Seven, and the accession of Darius.
    89–97: The empire's tribute and gifts.

98–116: Remote regions and peoples
    98–107: Digression on the Indian peoples, customs, diet, gold and climate.
    106–13: Arabians, spice gathering and wondrous sheep.
    114–16: Remote regions and fine resources.

117: Realities of Persian rule (transition section)
118–60: Persian matters
    118–19: Intaphrenes' outrage.
    120–8: The death of Polycrates and revenge on Oroetes.
    129–38: Democedes and the failed *reconnaissance* of Greece.
    139–50: The Persian capture of Samos and return of the tyranny to Syloson.
    139–41: Explanation of how Persian involvement in Samos came about.
    142–3: Samian affairs after Polycrates' death.
    143–9: Persian capture of Samos and return of the tyranny to Syloson.
        (148: Maeandrius' conduct at and expulsion from Sparta.)
    151–60: Babylon in revolt and Babylon retaken.

The history of all these places is intertwined. How Herodotus navigates, steers and guides us through events and the interconnections will now be discussed.

Herodotus in control

Herodotus employs a variety of techniques for establishing the connections between different events and places in his narrative. Here we shall look at:

- Herodotus as guide – first person references and authorial comment
- Alternative versions
- Connection by place or theme
- Time management

Herodotus as guide – first person references and authorial comment

Herodotus likes to appear in his narrative, whether to highlight his own personal efforts and enquiries, make a judgement, or give an opinion (on this, see also Dewald 1987: 154–70).

We have already seen how he appears as critic at §115, stating that he cannot say anything for certain about the regions under discussion and casting doubt on whether the name of the river he mentions really is called Eridanus, saying that it sounds suspiciously Greek. There are several examples of such critical comment in Book III. I shall note a further two here. As he begins to narrate the story of the ten-year old Cambyses' proud vow to turn Egypt 'upside down', he notes that he does not find it persuasive (§3.1: ἐμοὶ μὲν οὐ πιθανός). As has already been noted, inclusion of a version does not have to signal Herodotean endorsement. At §45.3, Herodotus refutes a story some tell that a group of Samian exiles managed to conquer Polycrates by themselves, saying that 'I do not think that they are correct in saying this' (λέγοντες ἐμοὶ δοκέειν οὐκ ὀρθῶς). He goes on to give his reasons, namely that it is just not credible that a group of exiles who had called on the Spartans for assistance could alone defeat the well-equipped and highly successful Samian tyrant Polycrates.

Herodotus will also signpost something he feels to be particularly significant, as at §60 where he explains that part of his reason for recounting Samian affairs was the three great feats of engineering which they created, achievements worthy of inclusion as part of the 'remarkable deeds' he has set out to record.

Alternative versions

Throughout his work, Herodotus includes different accounts of many events, actions and motivations that he narrates and Book III contains several examples. It also contains Herodotus' explanation for why he includes them. At §9, Herodotus recounts how the Arabian king is said to have drawn water to the desert region through which Cambyses needs to pass to reach Egypt. The first version he judges to be the 'more reliable', but says:

> δεῖ δὲ καὶ τὸν ἧσσον πιθανόν, ἐπεί γε δὴ λέγεται, ῥηθῆναι.
>
> But the less convincing account must also be told, since it is indeed one that is reported.

Something that is said or reported is part of what has been done and for Herodotus it means that it must be included. It is also possible that their inclusion demonstrates the difficulty of the historian's task and the complexity of human affairs.

He does not always say which account he endorses, at times leaving his reader/listener to make the judgement. After narrating the two accounts that are given for Oroetes' motive for killing Polycrates, he says (§122.1):

> πάρεστι δὲ πείθεσθαι ὀκοτέρῃ τις βούλεται αὐτέων.
>
> ... one can believe whichever of them one wishes.

He simply noted earlier that 'fewer' people relate the second explanation (§121.1). Other alternative versions given in Book III include:

- §2 Cambyses was really Egyptian by birth.
- §3 Cambyses vows to rout Egypt.

- §9 Arabian irrigations.
- §16 It was not Amasis' body.
- §31.2 Two different versions of Smerdis' death.
- §32.1 The death of Cambyses' sister.
- §45.3 Polycrates defeated by rebels.
- §46 Spartan involvement in Samos,
- §87 On why Darius' horse whinnied first,
- §122.1 Oroetes' motive for the murder of Polycrates

Connection by place or theme

Herodotus uses various means to move between theatres or historical actors, both to create a smoother flow to his work and also to elucidate the intertwining of events and connections between peoples and places. Herodotus uses a variety of content or theme-based connections between the different theatres or stories in his work. These may be geographical. The tribute digression (§88–97) enables Herodotus to move from the Persian empire to the more remote lands of India and Arabia that lie beyond the empire's borders. The section in which he describes the coast of Palestine up to Arabia illustrates the difficult nature of the land that Cambyses has to cross, enabling him to bring the Arabians onto the stage and also include an ethnographic account of their oath-making practices (§§5-8). A nice example of a thematic link comes with Cambyses' shocking laughter at the Egyptian statues of the gods (§37). The king's disrespectful attitude towards their practices leads smoothly onto Herodotus' discussion of different people's attitude to their own customs, the famous burial practices debate of §38. Moving back from India towards Persia, Herodotus establishes both a thematic and geographical link back to his main narrative in his poignant description of the plight of the Chorasmian plain and its peoples under Persian rule (§117). The theme of the mutability of human fortune paves the way for Herodotus' explanation of the ending of the friendship between Amasis and Polycrates. When Polycrates fails to stop his own worryingly good fortune, Amasis dissolves their friendship (§43).

Time management

Herodotus also uses a variety of temporal phrases and expressions to switch between events, conveying the idea of simultaneity and the complexity of the interlacing of affairs across many theatres, or highlighting a particularly significant moment, or showing simply when an event occurred roughly in relation to another previously recounted.

Before/After: 'After a time...' (§1.4: μετὰ δὲ χρόνον).

'After/in a short time...' (§39.3: ἐν χρόνῳ δὲ ὀλίγῳ)

Simultaneity: 'At the time when [Cambyses was invading Egypt] ... (§39.1: Καμβύσεω δὲ ἐπ' Αἴγυπτον στρατευομένου)

'Around the time when... (§120.1: κατὰ δέ κου)

Significance: The following two examples indicate a moment that was carefully picked to stage an action.

> i. When Cambyses was... spending time in Egypt... (§61.1: Καμβύσῃ δὲ ... χρονίζοντι περὶ Αἴγυπτον). While the king was away, the Magi took their chance.
> ii. At the time when (§150.1: ἐν ὅσῳ... ἐν τούτῳ παντὶ τῷ χρόνῳ). The Babylonians seized the opportunity to prepare their rebellion against Persian rule. This passage also mentions how the revolt finally erupts while the fleet is away at Samos.

These demonstrate how Herodotus not only conveys events happening in parallel across different theatres, but also how he draws out the relevance of temporal connections and coincidences.

Influences on Herodotus

Herodotus' work demonstrates great engagement with his predecessors and his contemporaries in the themes of this work, and not just Athenian (Raaflaub 2002: 164). We shall look at the following important influences and themes:

- Folk tales and traditional stories
- Homer and tragedy
- Science, medicine and exploration
- Practices, politics and human beings
    Nomos versus *Physis*
    Politics and Human Nature

Folk tales and traditional stories

The influence on Herodotus' work of folktales and stories likely passed down in oral tradition has long been noticed. The text is replete with charming tales and stories that display familiar traits and recurring patterns visible in other myths. In Book I, for example, Cyrus is portrayed as abandoned to die by a jealous grandfather, king Astyages, who feared a challenge to his power, following a series of night-time dreams and visions. The general, Harpagus, charges a cowherd to ensure the baby Cyrus dies; he is threatened with death if he fails to do so (I.110.2-3). However, the kindly cowherd takes the child straight to his wife, who persuades him to exchange the child for their own stillborn baby (I.111-113). Cyrus is saved and, of course, returns to rule. The child sent to be exposed who is then not exposed, but saved for good or for ill, recurs in many Greek myths. The outcome is rather less positive in the case of Paris and Oedipus. It is highly likely that such exposures and rescues did occur and, hence, why it becomes such a familiar feature. Whether it really happened to Cyrus, of course, we cannot say.

Book III has its own story that reflects folk tale features. The story of Polycrates and his splendid ring betrays traditional hallmarks (§§39–43). The presence of a portentous item that represents Polycrates' excessive luck is a clear example. Rings appear across many different tales, both Greek and non-Greek, in relation to tales of power and success, which do not usually end well. Tolkien's *Lord of the Rings* was influenced and informed by such tales, including the great German myth, *The Song of the Niebelungen* (the 'Ring' is promoted to the title in Wagner's opera). An alternative version of the Gyges and Candaules myth (not the one told by Herodotus in Book I) involves a magic ring, which confers the power of invisibility on the bearer. Gyges wears the ring, sneaks into Lydian king Candaules' room, and kills him (Plato, *Republic*, 359a-260d). Polycrates desperately tries to 'lose' his splendid emerald ring on the urging of his ally Amasis of Egypt. Amasis fears Polycrates will suffer all the more terribly the further his success advances and advises him to try and 'end' his own good fortune. Having cast the ring into the sea, Polycrates believes it gone. By a strange twist of events the ring returns to its owner via the kind gift of a fisherman who offers Polycrates his choicest catch in tribute. The ring is found in the gutted fish. Polycrates' grim end seems assured. But he has to wait until §125.

The second element familiar from storytelling is the role of a higher power, possibly fate, possibly the divine. Upon the return of the ring, 'it occurred to him [Polycrates] that what happened was a divine sign' (§42.4). Amasis had already warned Polycrates: 'I know how jealous divine power is' (§40.2). Polycrates interprets the remarkable discovery in this light. He cannot stop his success. The notion of divine *Nemesis* coming upon the overly successful, who then fatally err, blinded by their success, is a recurring theme in Herodotus. It features particularly strongly in the story of Croesus, beginning shortly after his disrespectful rejection of Solon's warning (I.34.1), dawning upon him only as he is on the threshold of death after the fall of Sardis (I.86.6; see also II.120.6, where the destruction of Troy is taken as evidence of such retribution; IV.205 for Pheretime's grim death as retribution for a her cruel revenge on the Barcaeans). It is a recurring feature in Greek myths such as Prometheus, Sisyphys, Actaeaon and Pentheus.

The final element I shall consider here is the 'moralizing' element of the tale, namely that all good things must come to an end: success does not last forever. The story is a cautionary tale, warning mortals against excessive confidence and complacency. Human life exists in constant flux and change for reasons that are not always detectable or comprehensible. In Polycrates' case, he tried to heed the warning, but still fell victim. Like Croesus, Polycrates' judgement is coloured by his ambition and desire for success, resulting in a fatal failure to heed several portentous warnings (§123).

Homer and tragedy

The influence of epic, especially Homer, on Herodotus has long been noticed (Rawlinson 1875: 7-8). Epic also belonged to an oral tradition of stories with which Herodotus was certainly familiar

Herodotus has been described as the 'most Homeric' historian both in terms of theme and content. His interaction with the Homeric poems finds rich discussion in scholarship (see, for example, Pelling 2006: 75–104; Matijašić 2022; see also Clarke 2018: 6–8). His narrative contains many grand and significant battles and defeats of major empires and ancient cities. Book III contains the defeat of Egypt and the tragedy that follows, along with the fall of Babylon and the destruction of its walls, and it may be tempting to see Zopyrus, the fake deserter and enemy within, as a 'living' Trojan horse. The book contains quasi-mythological elements which seem to blur the boundary between myth and history, most notably the 'long-lived Ethiopians', who in Homer were the banquet-fellows of the gods (see the Commentary for more on §§17–25).

Thematically, the influence of themes familiar from Homer and Greek tragedy are plentifully in evidence. We have already met the theme of the mutability of human fortune and the tragic consequences of falls from wealth and grace in the previous section. The theme of human self-awareness or realisation of the realities of suffering and mortality, which are central themes in the *Iliad* in particular and plays such as *Persae*, *Seven Against Thebes*, *Oedipus Tyrannus*, and *Hippolytus*, are also highly significant throughout the *Histories*, with Book III containing some of the most powerful examples. Following the fall of Egypt, Psammenitus, set outside the walls by Cambyses to test the king's spirit, is forced to watch the humiliation and suffering of his children, comparable to Hecabe, Priam and Andromache watching Hector (*Iliad*, XXII.408-515). The Egyptian king casts down his head in contrast to the weeping of the leading men with him. When he then sheds tears at the sight of a former drinking companion who has fallen on hard times, his pity for the man 'now on the threshold of old age' seems directly to echo Priam's plea for Achilles to feel pity for his old father Peleas (*Iliad*,

XXIV.487). Even Cambyses seems to find wise reflection on the threshold of death as he perceives the truth of an oracle about where he would die (§64.4-5). Wisdom in the face of death is a feature of certain heroic deaths in the *Iliad*, too, and, although Cambyses does not predict anyone else's, he does curse the Persians if they do not recover the throne from the Magus. Croesus has a similar moment of 'enlightenment' about the truth of Solon's words as his pyre blazes around him. The vast tapestry of history afforded a map of rise and decline, fortune and suffering. The quest to understand and illuminate being human united the poet and the historian.

Science, medicine and exploration

Fifth-century Athens was neither the only nor the first hub for the flourishing of Greek intellectual culture. The Ionian Greeks had during the sixth century been part of a great surge in geographic and ethnographic exploration and enquiry, as well as scientific ideas and methods. This did not stop in the fifth century, as Rosalind Thomas has decisively shown (2001; see also Raaflaub 2002: 149–86; Pelling 2019: 80–105), and Herodotus experienced the parallel developments of Athens as well. The influence of this rich cultural milieu upon Herodotus is obvious looking at the scope of Book III alone. This section will consider:

- Geography and ethnography
- Science and medicine

Geography and ethnography

Interest in the wider world and its peoples had intrigued curious Greeks since at least the second half of the sixth century (Raaflaub 2002: 159). Scylax of Caryanda had explored the lands around the Indus *c.* 510 and it is quite possible that his work was an important source for Hecateus, a close predecessor of Herodotus. Hecateus' *Periegesis* recorded the customs and histories of several different peoples, quite likely influenced by the multi-ethnic character of the advancing Persian empire (D&M: 69). Herodotus' hometown also lay at the mid-point between Greece, Persia, and the eastern lands and a similar interest is abundantly evident in his work. In Book III alone, the following passages attest to Herodotus' geographical and ethnographic interests:

1. The description of the Palestinian coast and the desert region that delayed Cambyses' advance into Egypt, along with problems of irrigation (§§5–7, 9).
2. Arabian oaths and deities (§8).
3. The table of the sun and aspects of Ethiopian practices (§§17, 23–4).
4. Persian marriage customs and the royal judges (§31.2–6).
5. Cambyses' foolishness for mocking statues of deities, leading to Herodotus' demonstration that each people is wont to consider its own customs the best (§37–8).
6. Cambyses' confusion over the two Ecbatanas (§64).
7. Provinces and resources – the sheer size and variety of the Persian empire and its revenues (§§89–97).
8. The digression on the Indian peoples, description of their plants, animals, and comparison of their climate with that of Greece (§§98–106).
9. Arabian spices and the dangers of collecting them (§§107–13).
10. Fine resources, the limits of the world, and limits of human knowledge of the lands north of Europe (§§114–16).
11. The miseries of the peoples of the Chorasmian plain under Persia (§117).
12. Darius turns his ambitions to Greece and seeks to find out more (§§134.6–135).

First, these passages reveal that Herodotus is relatively even-handed in his descriptions of different customs, preferring to explain the reasons for a people's practices rather than judging them. Although cannibalism would have horrified most Greek observers, Herodotus displays no hostility in describing the Indian tribe that kill and eat those who are sick before disease destroys their flesh (§99). Could this be regarded as inconsistent with his criticism of the horror of the cannibalism that erupted in Cambyses' army on the ill-planned and ill-conceived attempt to invade Ethiopia? The answer is no. In §25 the horrific nature of the act lies in the fact that cannibalism was not part of Persian customs and also the fact that the army was reduced to this out of desperation due to poor planning. The context is quite different.

Secondly, we see an interest in the diversity of the natural world. At §106, Herodotus recounts the superior size of Indian animals compared to most of those of the Greeks and Persians, and a clear theme of §§100–16 is the resources peculiar to these more remote lands with which the Greeks are perhaps less familiar.

Herodotus is also extremely interested in the human world in terms of its highly diverse practices, relationship to the natural world and use of its resources. We meet Indians who make breastplates out of a plant similar to bamboo (§98), Indians who hunt at the hottest part of the day for gold dust to avoid menacing ants (§§104–5), and we learn about the dangerous recovery of cassia from a lake (§110). Obviously, Herodotus is not accurate in every respect about these matters. However, the fact that he reports on non-Greek peoples without any implication of their inferiority must be considered remarkable. Herodotus' interest in the different practices of different peoples will be further discussed in the next section on *Nomos versus Physis*.

Finally, we also glimpse a much darker side to human relationship to geography. Clarke writes about a 'Geographical Morality' explored by Herodotus looking at his examples of good and bad control of the landscape (2018: 171–218). One of the most poignant examples of 'bad' use of the landscape comes in Book III. As Herodotus is about to move back from the lands beyond empire to his main narrative following the accession to Darius, he describes a plain in the mountains into which flow five channels (§117). Under the Chorasmian people, this plain and its peoples were freely watered via these channels. The story under Persian control is very different. The channels were blocked off, leaving the people of the plain entirely dependent on the king's command for their water during the dry season. Only through appeals and being deemed sufficiently in need did they receive the water they needed; a grim picture of the natural landscape moulded to the behest of an imperial power.

Science and medicine

Key elements of Greek scientific and medical thought are very visible in Herodotus' work, both in terms of methods and content. The importance of enquiry, observation and verification, often with a rationalizing tendency in explanations of natural phenomena, characterized the approach of the presocratic or Milesian philosophers (Roberts 2011: 8–9). Thales (the keen astronomer who fell down the well) rejected the view that the stars were gods, arguing that they were burning globes of earth (Pseudo-Plutarch, *Placita Philosophorum*, 2.13). Xenophanes argued against the typical Greek view of vindictive, anthropomorphic gods. He did not deny their existence, but rather queried the nature of earlier depictions. This search for 'natural' or 'rational' causes was also visible in Greek medical writings as the origins of disease were increasingly looked for in the environment and nature, and interest continued to flourish in the fifth century (Thomas 2001: 8). The Hippocratic writings, particularly a treatise entitled *Airs, Waters, Places*, demonstrate the link made between human health, climate and environment. This 'rationalizing' of the causes of disease is referenced in Herodotus' account of the illness of Cambyses. At §33, he writes that the cause of Cambyses' strange behaviour has been attributed to 'a serious disease ... which some call the sacred illness'. Herodotus does not apparently endorse that this disease was in fact 'sacred'.

A famously debated and highly intriguing passage which explores the link between nature and nurture and their effect on the human condition is the comparison of Egyptian and Persian skulls (§12) on the battlefield after the fall of Egypt to Cambyses (§11). The passage also emphasizes the importance of personal enquiry. Herodotus claims to have witnessed the truth of this comparison himself. He looked to witnesses only to explain it (§12.4). He argues that Persian skulls are fragile and easily broken; they would shatter if a stone were thrown at them. However, you could not in contrast, bore through an Egyptian skull even if you wanted to (§12.1). The explanation he gives is that the Persians cover their heads with a cap from childhood, whereas Egyptians expose theirs to the sun, which strengthens and thickens the bone (§12.2). He goes on to claim that this is also the reason why one is very unlikely to see a bald Egyptian (§12.3). Whatever the accuracy of these observations, the passage reflects a very real interest in looking for natural causes and explanations, along with an emphasis on personal enquiry and verification (Thomas 2001: 21).

We also glimpse an interest in the connection between diet and longevity, as shown in the interview with the Ethiopian king, where he mocks the short lifespan of the Persians (80 years), compared with the 120 years he attributes to the Ethiopians (§22.4).

The influence of medical thought is also reflected in the importance of doctors in the narrative of Book III. Herodotus may well have been influenced here not just by Greek sources, but also by Egyptian sources. The Egyptians already had a long-established tradition of approaches to healing and medicine. Moreover, the doctors of the narrative are, even if not main characters, undeniably significant. A physician, who is disgruntled at being separated from his family in Egypt and sent to Persia, uses his feelings of resentment to engineer a situation that will make life difficult for Amasis (§1.1). Egyptian doctors fail to cure the wounded Darius, leading to the meteoric rise in influence of Crotonian doctor Democedes (§§130–2; see the Commentary for Herodotus' use of medical terminology in his narrative of this episode).

Practices, politics and human beings

Nomos versus Physis

The previous section looked at how Herodotus explores the relationship between natural factors (the sun) and human practices (cap-wearing versus exposure) in explaining a physical difference between Persian and Egyptian skulls. The debate over nature versus human practice or tradition was a very prominent theme in fifth century thought, explored by the sophists, philosophers and medical writers alike. It was a major preoccupation of political thought and speculation, which flourished in the Greek world. Which was more important in influencing human behaviour or in determining how human beings should behave, their nature or their practices? The debate's *locus classicus* is to be found in Book III, §38. Having condemned Cambyses' disrespectful mockery of Egyptian divine statues (§37), Herodotus seeks to explain why such behaviour is to be condemned. He goes on to explore how different peoples are most likely to consider their own practices the best, which he proceeds to illustrate by narrating a debate organized by Darius between some Greeks who were present and the Indian Callatiae tribe. The Greeks burn their dead, the Callatiae consume theirs. Neither side can even consider the other side's practice as valid. The Callatiae tribe are so horrified that they bid the king speak words of 'good omen', seeing the very notion of burning one's dead as impious. Herodotus has already introduced this theme at §16, where he describes the disgraceful outrage committed on Cambyses' ordes against the embalmed and entombed body of Amasis. Neither Persian nor Egyptian custom would sanction the burning of the corpse, as he eventually commands his men to do. Whilst the aim of the passage is to illustrate the shocking nature of Cambyses' deeds, it also chimes with Herodotus' key argument about peoples' attitude to their own practices. In the next section, I argue that the much-disputed political debate of Book III is closely connected to this theme.

Politics and human nature

The sixth, fifth and fourth centuries evinced a diverse range of different practices and modes of government that fuelled debate, and discussion was certainly not confined to democracy, although the success of democratic Athens certainly added a new dimension to political debate. The fifth century also witnessed the fall of the Sicilian tyrannies, and Sparta's unusual arrangement intrigued observers.

The question concerning how a city or people should be governed revolved essentially around whether one person, a few men, or the entire people governed. In Herodotus we see the beginnings of the distinction between good and bad modes of rule within each type. This is exemplified in what is quite possibly the most controversial passage of Book III – the debate between three of the Persian conspirators about which form of government Persia should now use following the overthrow of the Magus (§§80–2). Otanes, who had been one of the primary movers of the rebellion against the Magi, argues for democracy (although he does not use this actual term), Megabyzus for oligarchy, and last Darius, who argues that they should retain a monarchic government, carrying the day.

Before we explore the themes of this section, we must consider why Herodotus includes it. At the start, he confidently asserts that 'the words that were spoken which were incredible to some of the Greeks, but spoken they were' (§80.1). He knows that the scene will be sceptically received by some Greek listeners/readers, but he emphatically argues that the debate really took place. It certainly seems surprising to modern observers, too, who not unreasonably see it as reflecting thought long associated with Greek political philosophy (see Pelling 2002: 125, nn.7–8 on more cynical views). Equally, it also seems very unlikely that outside Greece there was no awareness of or debate about different forms of government among non-Greeks. So, we cannot answer the question about whether it really happened. However, we can consider why it was included, true or not. I shall suggest here that the debate showcases two important themes in the *Histories*:

- Human nature and political change
- The importance of one's own practices (closely connected to §38)

The arguments against each form of government are due primarily to the eruption of destructive traits of human nature. Otanes' argument against monarchy is that the monarch is unaccountable, liable to unchecked arrogance due to his power (of which he cites Cambyses and the Magus as an example), is cruel to his citizens, and promotes those who support his power rather than those who are truly just (§80.2-5). The circumstances of power unleash the worst aspects of human character. Megabyzus' argument against democracy is that the mob can never be stopped or held accountable, leaving government at the mercy of its violent whims. Darius argues that oligarchy degenerates because of competitive factions and rivalry among the leaders (on human nature and motivation in Book III and in the *Histories* more generally, see Baragwanath 2008; on causation, see Immerwahr 1956: 241–80).

Finally, Darius' rhetorical victory is more than just a foreshadowing of his future accession. In pointing out the merits of Persian monarchy, he, like the Greeks and Callatiae of §38, chooses his own customs as the best, even arguing that freedom could be achieved under monarchic rule. To his fellow Persians it proves persuasive.

The passage demonstrates the following:

- That political degeneration arises from within human nature and its flaws.
- That a range of possibilities exists when it comes to political arrangements.
- That valid arguments exist for and against other forms of government.
- That peoples tend to think their own practices are the best and defend them. This is the opinion of Darius and the one which triumphs, although Otanes stands aside.

Herodotus is making the point that the Athenian democratic system is not the only possible political arrangement nor the only one worthy of consideration.

VI. Herodotus and Persia

Who were the Achaemenids?

In Books I–III, we meet three kings who are traditionally regarded as members of the Achaemenid royal dynasty, founded by king

Achaemenes: Cyrus, Cambyses and Darius. This is not unproblematic and Herodotus himself does portray not the picture quite so simply. In the famous Behistun (also Bisitun, Bisotun) Inscription, commissioned by Darius himself, which details his accession and achievements, Darius firmly traces his lineage back to the same royal line as Cyrus, both being ultimately descended from the dynasty's founder Achaemenes. However, Herodotus does not mention this. Did he not know? Rollinger and Munson rather suggest that the historian is more sceptical about Darius' lineage (Rollinger 2018: 133–4; Munson 2009: 458–9). Upon Darius' arrival among the six conspirators, he arrives with a message for the king from his father Hystaspes with no mention of any familial connection to the royal dynasty (§70.3) and in the inscription on the horseman statue that Herodotus mentions at §88.3, there is likewise no mention of descent from Achaemenes. Clearly, Darius actively sought legitimacy for his power, marrying Cyrus' daughters Atossa and Artystone (§88.2). The claim that he was an Achaemenid by blood may be viewed more sceptically.

Herodotus does seem to accept that Cyrus was a true Achaemenid as suggested by his account of Prexaspes' declaration before his death, where he traces the king's lineage back to Achaemenes (§75.1). However, even this is not certain. The Cyrus Cylinder, an inscription dated to c. 539 following Cyrus' capture of Babylon, does not mention Achaemenes as an ancestor at all. Another inscription of Cyrus' that seems to have referred to Achaemenes has been called into question. Some scholars believe Darius inserted the reference. Some have even doubted Achaemenes' existence or at least whether he was the great regal predecessor that Darius suggests (see Waters 2022: Appendix C for an excellent discussion of this problem; Brosius 2021: 94). It is interesting to note that there is a very significant discrepancy between Herodotus' account of Cyrus' origins and that of later fifth-century author, Ctesias of Cnidus, who depicts Cyrus' family background as not even being royal, but rather portrays him as the son of a goat-herder (see Waters 2022: 35–47). It may, therefore, be that the name Achaemenid is misleading and may even have been 'created' by Darius. What we can say is that these three figures who are central to Herodotus' account certainly were kings of Persia and made a true impact on the empire and history. Whether they were Achaemenid or not, I leave to the reader to decide.

Herodotus and the Behistun Inscription

Despite the note of caution that we must exercise in using Darius' 'account', we are very fortunate to have the Behistun Inscription as a parallel to compare with Herodotus' account. Specific variations in the account on the inscription and that of Herodotus and possible explanations for these will be examined in the Commentary. Here, we will examine how Herodotus emerges overall when checked against the inscription. Rollinger notes: 'The parallels with the Behistun inscription are impressive, suggesting that there must have been a flow of relevant information from east to west' (2018: 126).

There are certainly discrepancies between Herodotus' account of the overthrow of the Magi and the details on the inscription, but the overall progress of events seems to cohere well. This, therefore, raises the question of whether Herodotus had seen the inscription or had read a version of it. It certainly seems fair to conclude that he had received much of the information it contains in some form. Munson concludes that:

> the similarities and discrepancies between parts of Herodotus' Book 3 and Darius' Behistun Inscription corroborate the hypothesis that Herodotus relied on genuine aristocratic Persian oral traditions that differ in interesting ways from the official tradition promulgated by the king. (2009: n.35)

Although he may have made errors, Herodotus seems at least to have tried to do his homework in gathering information about the events he describes in Book III. It should be noted, however, that Houliang has shown that Herodotus certainly 'embellished' the narrative structure that he took from the inscription (2022: 53–79). We turn now to his attitude to Persia and Persians and how 'Greek' his perspective really is.

Herodotus' attitude to Persia

As noted above, scholars are divided over whether Herodotus was a Greek apologist, hostile especially to Persia. However, Herodotus does not draw Athenians and Persians as polar opposites, one free and strong, the other weak and slavish. Llewellyn-Jones makes a good point when he argued that Darius is depicted as far too anxious about Athens than the city's pre-Persian War significance would have merited (2022: 13). This is, nevertheless, not the same as Herodotus being anti-Persian. In fact, I will suggest in this section that Persia emerges as a formidable power and future opponent of Greece in Book III.

That said, Herodotus' account is undeniably hostile to the son of Cyrus the Great, Cambyses (on his portrayal of Cambyses, see Brown (1982: 387–405) and Munson (1991: 443–465). Despite his achievement in adding Egypt to the Persian empire, a wealthy addition at that, Cambyses receives little credit for this in Herodotus' telling and instead emerges as a mad, cruel and tyrannical leader, willing to subvert or at least twist ancestral laws for his own end (§31.2-3), ruthlessly remove enemies without trial (Smerdis §30.3) and accept insincere flatteries (§34.4-5). In short, he displays many of the traits that Otanes uses in his argument against tyranny (§80.5). This is perhaps suspicious in itself. Cambyses conforms a little too closely to a stereotypical tyrant. It is possible that Herodotus was a little too accepting (willingly so?) of sources hostile to Cambyses, quite possibly Egyptian (Herodotus claims to quote Egyptian sources/accounts on the following occasions: §2.1; §12.2; §14.1; §16.7; §28.2; §30.1; §32.3). The Egyptians are visibly hostile to Cambyses, as their allegation that he went mad after his violation of the Apis calf shows (§30.1; see Commentary for a Persian source that possibly refutes this account). Herodotus can be quite sceptical regarding his Egyptian sources. Here, he prefaces his account with 'so the Egyptians say', suggesting he is not necessarily endorsing their version. Elsewhere he is even more critical. He sees, for example, that the Egyptians took their defeat badly and sees two of their less credible tales as arising from this sense of shame. He does not accept the allegation that Cambyses was really the son of Apries, whom Amasis sent to Cambyses (§2.1). Herodotus dismisses the account as impossible given Persian customs regarding succession and illegitimacy, something which the Egyptians should know. He also dismisses the claim that it was not really Amasis' body that was violated by Cambyses, but another dead Egyptian, whom Amasis had laid to rest in his place following a prophecy (§16.7). Nevertheless, a hostile Egyptian tradition may certainly have contributed to Herodotus' less than favourable depiction.

This still does not make Herodotus anti-Persian and such a mindset certainly does not emerge in his portrayal of Cyrus. Darius is undeniably ruthless, but he is capable and shrewd, as depicted in Book III. He is not responsible for drawing up the tribute system, but he certainly conducted a large-scale systematization and re-organization according to Herodotus (§88), and he does not emerge as a tyrant.

It could also be argued that Book III shows just how mighty a power the Persian empire was. The army was successful, as shown by the fall of Egypt and later by the re-taking of Babylon. The tribute digression (§§88–97) shows just how vast, diverse, and wealthy the empire was, certainly not one to be downplayed or underestimated. It is just possible that Herodotus was seeking to redress the growing Greek, especially Athenian, tradition of the fifth century to misrepresent Persian power (Hall 1989 is indispensable on this topic).

A clear and perfectly valid objection to my suggestion is that the Persians often emerge as brutal, and not just Cambyses:

- The severing of the ears of the Magus (§69.5).
- The severing of the noses and ears of the guards by Intaphrenes (§118.2).
- Zopyrus' use of the above method of mutilation to convince the Babylonians that he was a deserter (§155.4).
- Darius' impaling of the ringleaders of the Babylonian revolt (§159.1).

However, two counter arguments can be made here. Intaphrenes is punished for his rash mutilation of the guards who deny him entry. Darius is brutal, but does not punish all the citizens of Babylon following his victory, granting them their city back to live in. Such was Persian custom rather than annexing directly (§15.4). Secondly, Greeks are certainly not painted as angels. Polycrates, for example, ruthlessly expels his brothers from Samos, wishing to take sole power (§39.2). A further example from Book III is the murder of Phanes' children by the Greek mercenaries (§12). Yes, the Greeks are ultimately victorious as Herodotus draws his work to a close with the Persian wars, but to say he is a Greek or Athenian apologist, or anti-Persian, does not do justice to the far more complex portrait of human beings and different peoples that his work presents.

VII Language, composition, style

The Ionic dialect of Herodotus

Herodotus' Greek is not the Attic dialect of Thucydides. He rather uses the Ionic dialect. Halicarnassus was originally a Doric settlement, but Greek was not the only language present there. Carian was also a language found in the city. Herodotus' choice of Ionic seems to have been because this was the language which prose authors (for example, Hecateus) were using. It was also a language found on formal inscriptions in the city (for more on this and where Herodotus may have learnt Ionic Greek, see Abe (2014/2015: 145–64). There are significant differences to Attic and the key peculiarities are highlighted below with examples from Book III, although these are not exhaustive.

For those wishing for a more detailed exposition of Ionic dialect and comparison with Attic, see D&M: 85–8.

Spelling

η for α after ε, ι, ρ (normally followed by α in Attic)

ει for ε before ν, ρ, λ

ου for ο

ω for αυ, ου

ὦν = οὖν (§9.1, 3; §16.3; §44.1)

ξεῖνος for ξένος (§21.2)

μοῦνος = μόνος (§30.1; §74.1)

κούρη = κόρη (§8.3)

θῶμα = θαῦμα (§12.1; §23.2)

κ where Attic uses π:

κῶς = πῶς (§80.3; §137.3)
κότερος = πότερος (§137.3)
κοῦ = ποῦ (§6.2)
κοῖος = ποῖος (§34.2, 4; ὀκοῖος: §52.5; §103)

Unaspirated consonants, where Attic uses aspirated (*psilosis*):

π for φ (§23.1 ἀπικνέεσθαι; §25.6 ἀπικνέεται; §82.3 ἀπικνέονται)
τ for θ (αὖτις §2.2; §76.2; §157.4)
κ for χ (§51.3 δέκομαι; §115.1 ἐνδέκομαι)

Nouns

First declension

-εω = -ου for the genitive singular of masculine nouns (§2.2 – Φαρνάσπεω; § 27.1 – Καμβύσεω; § 53.2 – νεηνίεω).

-έων = -ῶν for the genitive plural of all nouns (incl. second and third declensions) (§ 9.4 – §; § 70.1 – Περσέων; §71.4 – ὑμέων).

-ῃσι = -αις for the dative plural of all nouns (§12.4 – Πέρσῃσι; §27.1 – θαλίῃσι; §120.3 – ὁπλίτῃσι).

Second declension

-οισι = -οις for the dative plural, including participles and pronouns (§12.4 – τούτοισι; §20.2 – νόμοισι; §65.7 – ἀνασωσαμένοισι).

Third declension

Uncontracted endings:

-εος = -ους (§5.3 – ὄρεος; §39.3 – Πολυκράτεος; §58.4 –ἄστεος).
-έες = -εῖς (§ 13.3 – προσεχέες; §29.3 – ἱρέες).

Pronouns

Uncontracted endings:

ἐμέο/ἐμεῦ = ἐμοῦ (§34.2 – ἐμέο; §155.6 – ἐμέο; §10.3 – ἐμεῦ; §97.3 – ἐμεῦ).
σέο/σεῦ = σοῦ (§78.4 – σέο; §36.2 – σεῦ; §85.2 – σεῦ).

τεύ = τοῦ or τίνος (§84.3 – ὅτευ).
τέῳ = τῷ or τίνι (§70.2 – ὅτεῳ).

οἱ = αὐτῷ/-η (§ 55.2; §80.3)
μιν = αὐτόν/-ήν (§28.2; §78.4; §137.1)
These forms are also found in Homer.
σφεῖς = αὐτοί/-αί
σφέας = αὐτούς /-άς (§13.3; §77.2; §143.1)
σφέων = αὐτῶν
φι = αὐτοῖς /-αῖς (§14.10; §70.2; §156.1)

Relative pronoun identical to definite article in non-nominative cases:

τόν = ὅν (§1.4)
τῷ = ᾧ (§9.2)

Reflexive third person:

ἑωυτόν = (§14.11; §125.1; §145.2)
ἑωυτοῦ = (§16.6; §61.2; §146.1)
ἑωυτῷ = (§25.1; §68.2; §142.3)
ἑωυτῶν = (§159.2)

Verbs

Omission of augment on occasion:

ἀμείβετο = ἠμείβετο (§14.9)

Uncontracted vowel stems:

αἴτεε = αἰτεῖ (§1.1)
ἀπολέεσθε = ἀπολέῖσθε (§71.4)
ἀρρωδέων = ἀρρωδῶν (§1.2)
ἐών = ὤν (§82.4)
ποιέεσθαι = (§8.1)

Third person middle/passives:

-αται = -νται
    ἐπιστέαται (§2.2) = ἐπίστανται

-ατο -ντο
γενοίατο = γένοιντο (§57.2: optative)

Miscellaneous

τὰ γινόμενα (§57.2) = τὰ γιγνόμενα (§70.6)
Note that both appear in the text.

Composition

It seems likely that Herodotus' work was originally delivered orally as lectures and possibly written up in its current form later. In *The Brill Companion to Herodotus*, Slings persuasively argued that certain features of Herodotus' prose were suggestive of original oral composition or delivery. Such features include *anacolouthon*, abrupt changes in syntax structure (see below for examples), shifts in sentence structure from complex to simple, *anaphora*, repetitions or restatements when resuming a line of argument or particular story. One could, however, argue that these repetitions of phrase reflect a deliberate structural choice designed to mark the beginnings and ends of subsections or digressions, and even highlight their importance.

Examples of these two devices include:
Anacolouthon §12.1, §153.2.
Repetition §12.1, §38.1, §80.1.
They are more fully explained in the Commentary (*ad loc.*).

Other stylistic devices in Book III

(Only one example of each is given, the list is not exhaustive)
The possible effect of the devices listed below and employed by Herodotus are dealt with in the Commentary as appropriate.

Anaphora	repetition of words at the start of successive clauses (§134.2).
Assonance	the alliteration of vowels (§1.2)
Asyndeton	the omission of connecting words such as 'and' (§80.6).

Chiasmus	a pair of balanced phrases where the word order is reversed in the second creating an ABBA pattern (§53.7).
Hendiadys	'one through two.' A concept is separated into two, for example, 'many and fine words' for 'many fine words' (§15.3).
Hyperbaton	the separation of a noun from a word that agrees with it or describes it, such as an adjective (§51.2).
Litotes	a negative statement or understatement that emphasizes the opposite to be true (§4.2: 'of no small account').
Metonymy	where a part of something symbolizes the whole, for example, a wall for a city (§155.5 Babylon).
Polyptoton	the repetition of a word in a slightly different or related form (§72.4).
Polysyndeton	a repeated use of connecting words such as 'and' (§114).
Tautology	saying the same thing twice in a slightly different way to emphasize a fact or idea (§25.2 on the madness of Cambyses).
Tmesis	the separation of a compound verb's prefix and main stem (§126.2).
Tricolon	as list of three items grouped together for a particular reason or effect (§80.5).
Variatio	saying the same thing or repeating an idea with a different mode of expression (§3.2).

A note on the text and translation

This edition of the text has been prepared by the current author, consulting Godley's *Loeb*, Hude's OCT and the more recent OCT edition by Wilson.

The translation seeks to find a medium between readability and useful reflection of the original Greek.

Text

1 ἐπὶ τοῦτον δὴ τὸν Ἄμασιν Καμβύσης ὁ Κύρου ἐστρατεύετο, ἄγων καὶ ἄλλους τε τῶν ἦρχε καὶ Ἑλλήνων Ἴωνάς τε καὶ Αἰολέας, δι' αἰτίην τοιήνδε. πέμψας Καμβύσης ἐς Αἴγυπτον κήρυκα αἴτεε Ἄμασιν θυγατέρα, αἴτεε δὲ ἐκ συμβουλῆς ἀνδρὸς Αἰγυπτίου, ὃς μεμφόμενος Ἄμασιν ἔπρηξε ταῦτα ὅτι μιν ἐξ ἁπάντων τῶν ἐν Αἰγύπτῳ ἰητρῶν ἀποσπάσας ἀπὸ γυναικός τε καὶ τέκνων ἔκδοτον ἐποίησε ἐς Πέρσας, ὅτε Κῦρος πέμψας παρὰ Ἄμασιν αἴτεε ἰητρὸν ὀφθαλμῶν ὃς εἴη ἄριστος τῶν ἐν Αἰγύπτῳ. [2] ταῦτα δὴ ἐπιμεμφόμενος ὁ Αἰγύπτιος ἐνῆγε τῇ συμβουλῇ κελεύων αἰτέειν τὸν Καμβύσεα Ἄμασιν θυγατέρα, ἵνα ἢ δοὺς ἀνιῷτο ἢ μὴ δοὺς Καμβύσῃ ἀπέχθοιτο. ὁ δὲ Ἄμασις τῇ δυνάμι τῶν Περσέων ἀχθόμενος καὶ ἀρρωδέων οὐκ εἶχε οὔτε δοῦναι οὔτε ἀρνήσασθαι· εὖ γὰρ ἠπίστατο ὅτι οὐκ ὡς γυναῖκά μιν ἔμελλε Καμβύσης ἕξειν, ἀλλ' ὡς παλλακήν. [3] ταῦτα δὴ ἐκλογιζόμενος ἐποίησε τάδε· ἦν Ἀπρίεω τοῦ προτέρου βασιλέος θυγάτηρ κάρτα μεγάλη τε καὶ εὐειδὴς μούνη τοῦ οἴκου λελειμμένη, οὔνομα δέ οἱ ἦν Νίτητις. ταύτην δὴ τὴν παῖδα ὁ Ἄμασις κοσμήσας ἐσθῆτί τε καὶ χρυσῷ ἀποπέμπει ἐς Πέρσας ὡς ἑωυτοῦ θυγατέρα. [4] μετὰ δὲ χρόνον ὥς μιν ἠσπάζετο πατρόθεν ὀνομάζων, λέγει πρὸς αὐτὸν ἡ παῖς, "Ὦ βασιλεῦ, διαβεβλημένος ὑπὸ Ἀμάσιος οὐ μανθάνεις. ὅς ἐμὲ σοὶ κόσμῳ ἀσκήσας ἀπέπεμψε ὡς ἑωυτοῦ θυγατέρα διδούς, ἐοῦσαν τῇ ἀληθείῃ Ἀπρίεω, τὸν ἐκεῖνος ἐόντα ἑωυτοῦ δεσπότεα μετ' Αἰγυπτίων ἐπαναστὰς ἐφόνευσε." [5] τοῦτο δὴ τὸ ἔπος καὶ αὕτη ἡ αἰτίη ἐγγενομένη ἤγαγε Καμβύσεα τὸν Κύρου μεγάλως θυμωθέντα ἐπ' Αἴγυπτον.

2 οὕτω μέν νυν λέγουσι Πέρσαι. Αἰγύπτιοι δὲ οἰκηιοῦνται Καμβύσεα, φάμενοί μιν ἐκ ταύτης δὲ τῆς Ἀπρίεω θυγατρὸς γενέσθαι· Κῦρον γὰρ εἶναι τὸν πέμψαντα παρὰ Ἄμασιν ἐπὶ τὴν θυγατέρα, ἀλλ' οὐ Καμβύσεα. [2] λέγοντες δὲ ταῦτα οὐκ ὀρθῶς λέγουσι. οὐ μὲν οὐδὲ λέληθε αὐτούς, εἰ γάρ τινες καὶ ἄλλοι, τὰ Περσέων νόμιμα ἐπιστέαται καὶ Αἰγύπτιοι, ὅτι πρῶτα μὲν νόθον οὔ σφι νόμος ἐστὶ βασιλεῦσαι γνησίου παρεόντος, αὖτις δὲ ὅτι Κασσανδάνης τῆς Φαρνάσπεω θυγατρὸς ἦν παῖς Καμβύσης, ἀνδρὸς Ἀχαιμενίδεω, ἀλλ' οὐκ ἐκ τῆς Αἰγυπτίης. ἀλλὰ παρατρέπουσι τὸν λόγον προσποιεύμενοι τῇ Κύρου οἰκίῃ συγγενέες εἶναι.

3 καὶ ταῦτα μὲν ὧδε ἔχει. λέγεται δὲ καὶ ὅδε λόγος, ἐμοὶ μὲν οὐ πιθανός, ὡς τῶν Περσίδων γυναικῶν ἐσελθοῦσά τις παρὰ τὰς Κύρου γυναῖκας, ὡς εἶδε τῇ Κασσανδάνῃ παρεστεῶτα τέκνα εὐειδέα τε καὶ μεγάλα, πολλῷ ἐχρᾶτο τῷ ἐπαίνῳ ὑπερθωμάζουσα, ἡ δὲ Κασσανδάνη ἐοῦσα τοῦ Κύρου γυνὴ εἶπε τάδε. [2] "Τοιῶνδε μέντοι ἐμὲ παίδων μητέρα ἐοῦσαν Κῦρος ἐν ἀτιμίῃ ἔχει, τὴν δὲ ἀπ' Αἰγύπτου ἐπίκτητον ἐν τιμῇ τίθεται." τὴν μὲν ἀχθομένην τῇ Νιτήτι εἰπεῖν ταῦτα, τῶν δέ οἱ παίδων τὸν πρεσβύτερον εἰπεῖν Καμβύσεα [3] "Τοιγάρ τοι ὦ μῆτερ, ἐπεὰν ἐγὼ γένωμαι ἀνήρ, Αἰγύπτου τὰ μὲν ἄνω κάτω θήσω, τὰ δὲ κάτω ἄνω." ταῦτα εἰπεῖν αὐτὸν ἔτεα ὡς δέκα κου γεγονότα, καὶ τὰς γυναῖκας ἐν θώματι γενέσθαι· τὸν δὲ διαμνημονεύοντα οὕτω δή, ἐπείτε ἀνδρώθη καὶ ἔσχε τὴν βασιληίην, ποιήσασθαι τὴν ἐπ' Αἴγυπτον στρατηίην.

4 συνήνεικε δὲ καὶ ἄλλο τι τοιόνδε πρῆγμα γενέσθαι ἐς τὴν ἐπιστράτευσιν ταύτην. ἦν τῶν ἐπικούρων Ἀμάσιος ἀνὴρ γένος μὲν Ἁλικαρνησσεύς, οὔνομα δέ οἱ Φάνης, καὶ γνώμην ἱκανὸς καὶ τὰ πολεμικὰ ἄλκιμος. [2] οὗτος ὁ Φάνης μεμφόμενός κού τι Ἀμάσι ἐκδιδρήσκει πλοίῳ ἐξ Αἰγύπτου, βουλόμενος Καμβύσῃ ἐλθεῖν ἐς λόγους. οἷα δὲ ἐόντα αὐτὸν ἐν τοῖσι ἐπικούροισι λόγου οὐ σμικροῦ ἐπιστάμενόν τε τὰ περὶ Αἴγυπτον ἀτρεκέστατα, μεταδιώκει ὁ Ἄμασις σπουδὴν ποιεύμενος ἑλεῖν, μεταδιώκει δὲ τῶν εὐνούχων τὸν πιστότατον ἀποστείλας τριήρεϊ κατ' αὐτόν, ὃς αἱρέει μιν ἐν Λυκίῃ, ἑλὼν δὲ οὐκ ἀνήγαγε ἐς Αἴγυπτον· σοφίῃ γάρ μιν περιῆλθε ὁ Φάνης. [3] καταμεθύσας γὰρ τοὺς φυλάκους ἀπαλλάσσετο ἐς Πέρσας. ὁρμημένῳ δὲ στρατεύεσθαι Καμβύσῃ ἐπ' Αἴγυπτον καὶ ἀπορέοντι τὴν ἔλασιν ὅκως τὴν ἄνυδρον διεκπερᾷ, ἐπελθὼν φράζει μὲν καὶ τὰ ἄλλα τὰ Ἀμάσιος πρήγματα, ἐξηγέεται δὲ καὶ τὴν ἔλασιν ὧδε παραινέων, πέμψαντα παρὰ τὸν Ἀραβίων βασιλέα δέεσθαι τὴν διέξοδόν οἱ ἀσφαλέα παρασχεῖν.

5 μούνῃ δὲ ταύτῃ εἰσὶ φανεραὶ ἐσβολαὶ ἐς Αἴγυπτον. ἀπὸ γὰρ Φοινίκης μέχρι οὔρων τῶν Καδύτιος πόλιος [ἥ] ἐστὶ Σύρων τῶν Παλαιστίνων καλεομένων· [2] ἀπὸ δὲ Καδύτιος ἐούσης πόλιος, ὡς ἐμοὶ δοκέει, Σαρδίων οὐ πολλῷ ἐλάσσονος, ἀπὸ ταύτης τὰ ἐμπόρια τὰ ἐπὶ θαλάσσης μέχρι Ἰηνύσου πόλιος ἐστὶ τοῦ Ἀραβίου, ἀπὸ δὲ Ἰηνύσου πόλιος αὖτις Σύρων μέχρι Σερβωνίδος λίμνης, παρ' ἣν δὴ τὸ Κάσιον ὄρος τείνει ἐς θάλασσαν· [3] ἀπὸ δὲ Σερβωνίδος λίμνης, ἐν τῇ δὴ λόγος τὸν Τυφῶ κεκρύφθαι, ἀπὸ ταύτης ἤδη Αἴγυπτος. τὸ δὴ μεταξὺ Ἰηνύσου πόλιος καὶ Κασίου τε ὄρεος καὶ τῆς Σερβωνίδος λίμνης, ἐὸν τοῦτο οὐκ ὀλίγον χωρίον ἀλλὰ ὅσον τε ἐπὶ τρεῖς ἡμέρας ὁδόυ, ἄνυδρον ἐστὶ δεινῶς.

6 τὸ δὲ ὀλίγοι τῶν ἐς Αἴγυπτον ναυτιλλομένων ἐννενώκασι, τοῦτο ἔρχομαι φράσων. ἐς Αἴγυπτον ἐκ τῆς Ἑλλάδος πάσης καὶ πρὸς ἐκ Φοινίκης κέραμος ἐσάγεται πλήρης οἴνου διὰ τοῦ ἔτεος ἑκάστου, καὶ ἓν κεράμιον οἰνηρὸν ἀριθμῷ κεῖνον οὐκ ἔστι ὡς λόγῳ εἰπεῖν ἰδέσθαι. [2] κοῦ δῆτα, εἴποι τις ἄν, ταῦτα ἀναισιμοῦται; ἐγὼ καὶ τοῦτο φράσω· δεῖ τὸν μὲν δήμαρχον ἕκαστον ἐκ τῆς ἑωυτοῦ πόλιος συλλέξαντα πάντα τὸν κέραμον ἄγειν ἐς Μέμφιν, τοὺς δὲ ἐκ Μέμφιος ἐς ταῦτα δὴ τὰ ἄνυδρα τῆς Συρίης κομίζειν πλήσαντας ὕδατος. οὕτω ὁ ἐπιφοιτέων κέραμος καὶ ἐξαιρεόμενος ἐν Αἰγύπτῳ ἐπὶ τὸν παλαιὸν κομίζεται ἐς Συρίην.

7 οὕτω μέν νυν Πέρσαι εἰσὶ οἱ τὴν ἐσβολὴν ταύτην παρασκευάσαντες ἐς Αἴγυπτον, κατὰ δὴ τὰ εἰρημένα σάξαντες ὕδατι, ἐπείτε τάχιστα παρέλαβον Αἴγυπτον. [2] τότε δὲ οὐκ ἐόντος κω ὕδατος ἑτοίμου, Καμβύσης πυθόμενος τοῦ Ἁλικαρνησσέος ξείνου, πέμψας παρὰ τὸν Ἀράβιον ἀγγέλους καὶ δεηθεὶς τῆς ἀσφαλείης ἔτυχε, πίστις δούς τε καὶ δεξάμενος παρ' αὐτοῦ.

8 σέβονται δὲ Ἀράβιοι πίστις ἀνθρώπων ὅμοια τοῖσι μάλιστα, ποιεῦνται δὲ αὐτὰς τρόπῳ τοιῷδε· τῶν βουλομένων τὰ πιστὰ ποιέεσθαι ἄλλος ἀνὴρ ἀμφοτέρων αὐτῶν ἐν μέσῳ ἑστεώς, λίθῳ ὀξέι τὸ ἔσω τῶν χειρῶν παρὰ τοὺς δακτύλους τοὺς μεγάλους ἐπιτάμνει τῶν ποιευμένων τὰς πίστις, καὶ ἔπειτα λαβὼν ἐκ τοῦ ἱματίου ἑκατέρου κροκύδα ἀλείφει τῷ αἵματι ἐν μέσῳ κειμένους λίθους ἑπτά· τοῦτο δὲ ποιέων ἐπικαλέει τε τὸν Διόνυσον καὶ τὴν Οὐρανίην. [2] ἐπιτελέσαντος δὲ τούτου ταῦτα, ὁ τὰς πίστις ποιησάμενος τοῖσι φίλοισι παρεγγυᾷ τὸν ξεῖνον ἢ καὶ τὸν ἀστόν, ἢν πρὸς ἀστὸν ποιέηται· οἱ δὲ φίλοι καὶ αὐτοὶ τὰς πίστις δικαιεῦσι σέβεσθαι. [3] Διόνυσον δὲ θεῶν μοῦνον καὶ τὴν Οὐρανίην ἡγέονται εἶναι καὶ τῶν τριχῶν τὴν κούρην κείρεσθαι φασὶ κατά περ αὐτὸν τὸν Διόνυσον κεκάρθαι· κείρονται δὲ περιτρόχαλα, ὑποξυρῶντες τοὺς κροτάφους. ὀνομάζουσι δὲ τὸν μὲν Διόνυσον Ὀροτάλτ, τὴν δὲ Οὐρανίην Ἀλιλάτ.

9 ἐπεὶ ὦν τὴν πίστιν τοῖσι ἀγγέλοισι τοῖσι παρὰ Καμβύσεω ἀπιγμένοισι ἐποιήσατο ὁ Ἀράβιος, ἐμηχανᾶτο τοιάδε· ἀσκοὺς καμήλων πλήσας ὕδατος ἐπέσαξε ἐπὶ τὰς ζωὰς τῶν καμήλων πάσας, τοῦτο δὲ ποιήσας ἤλασε ἐς τὴν ἄνυδρον καὶ ὑπέμενε ἐνθαῦτα τὸν Καμβύσεω στρατόν. [2] οὗτος μὲν ὁ πιθανώτερος τῶν λόγων εἴρηται, δεῖ δὲ καὶ τὸν ἧσσον πιθανόν, ἐπεί γε δὴ λέγεται, ῥηθῆναι. ποταμός ἐστι μέγας ἐν τῇ Ἀραβίῃ τῷ οὔνομα Κόρυς, ἐκδιδοῖ δὲ οὗτος ἐς τὴν Ἐρυθρὴν καλεομένην θάλασσαν· [3] ἀπὸ τούτου δὴ ὦν τοῦ ποταμοῦ λέγεται τὸν βασιλέα τῶν Ἀραβίων, ῥαψάμενον τῶν ὠμοβοέων καὶ τῶν ἄλλων δερμάτων ὀχετὸν μήκεϊ ἐξικνεύμενον ἐς τὴν ἄνυδρον, ἀγαγεῖν διὰ δὴ τούτων τὸ ὕδωρ, ἐν δὲ τῇ ἀνύδρῳ μεγάλας δεξαμενὰς ὀρύξασθαι, ἵνα δεκόμεναι τὸ ὕδωρ σώζωσι. [4] ὁδὸς δ' ἐστὶ δυώδεκα ἡμερέων ἀπὸ τοῦ ποταμοῦ ἐς ταύτην τὴν ἄνυδρον. ἄγειν δέ μιν δι' ὀχετῶν τριῶν ἐς τριξὰ χωρία.

10 ἐν δὲ τῷ Πηλουσίῳ καλεομένῳ στόματι τοῦ Νείλου ἐστρατοπεδεύετο Ψαμμήνιτος ὁ Ἀμάσιος παῖς ὑπομένων Καμβύσεα. [2] Ἄμασιν γὰρ οὐ κατέλαβε ζῶντα Καμβύσης ἐλάσας ἐπ' Αἴγυπτον, ἀλλὰ βασιλεύσας ὁ Ἄμασις τέσσερα καὶ τεσσεράκοντα ἔτεα ἀπέθανε, ἐν τοῖσι οὐδέν οἱ μέγα ἀνάρσιον πρῆγμα συνηνείχθη· ἀποθανὼν δὲ καὶ ταριχευθεὶς ἐτάφη ἐν τῇσι ταφῇσι ἐν τῷ ἱρῷ, τὰς αὐτὸς οἰκοδομήσατο. [3] ἐπὶ Ψαμμηνίτου δὲ τοῦ Ἀμάσιος βασιλεύοντος Αἰγύπτου φάσμα Αἰγυπτίοισι μέγιστον δὴ ἐγένετο· ὕσθησαν γὰρ Θῆβαι αἱ Αἰγύπτιαι, οὔτε πρότερον οὐδαμὰ ὑσθεῖσαι οὔτε ὕστερον τὸ μέχρι ἐμεῦ, ὡς λέγουσι αὐτοὶ Θηβαῖοι. οὐ γὰρ δὴ ὕεται τὰ ἄνω τῆς Αἰγύπτου τὸ παράπαν· ἀλλὰ καὶ τότε ὕσθησαν αἱ Θῆβαι ψακάδι.

11 οἱ δὲ Πέρσαι ἐπείτε διεξελάσαντες τὴν ἄνυδρον ἵζοντο πέλας τῶν Αἰγυπτίων ὡς συμβαλέοντες, ἐνθαῦτα οἱ ἐπίκουροι οἱ τοῦ Αἰγυπτίου, ἐόντες ἄνδρες Ἕλληνές τε καὶ Κᾶρες, μεμφόμενοι τῷ Φάνῃ ὅτι στρατὸν ἤγαγε ἐπ᾽ Αἴγυπτον ἀλλόθροον, μηχανῶνται πρῆγμα ἐς αὐτὸν τοιόνδε. [2] ἦσαν τῷ Φάνῃ παῖδες ἐν Αἰγύπτῳ καταλελειμμένοι, τοὺς ἀνάγοντες ἐς τὸ στρατόπεδον καὶ ἐς ὄψιν τοῦ πατρὸς κρητῆρα ἐν μέσῳ ἔστησαν ἀμφοτέρων τῶν στρατοπέδων, μετὰ δὲ ἀγινέοντες κατὰ ἕνα ἕκαστον τῶν παίδων ἔσφαζον ἐς τὸν κρητῆρα· [3] διὰ πάντων δὲ διεξελθόντες τῶν παίδων οἶνόν τε καὶ ὕδωρ ἐσεφόρεον ἐς αὐτόν, ἐμπιόντες δὲ τοῦ αἵματος πάντες οἱ ἐπίκουροι οὕτω δὴ συνέβαλον. μάχης δὲ γενομένης καρτερῆς καὶ πεσόντων ἐξ ἀμφοτέρων τῶν στρατοπέδων πλήθεϊ πολλῶν ἐτράποντο οἱ Αἰγύπτιοι.

12 θῶμα δὲ μέγα εἶδον πυθόμενος παρὰ τῶν ἐπιχωρίων· τῶν γὰρ ὀστέων περικεχυμένων χωρὶς ἑκατέρων τῶν ἐν τῇ μάχῃ ταύτῃ πεσόντων, χωρὶς μὲν γὰρ τῶν Περσέων ἐκέετο τὰ ὀστέα, ὡς ἐχωρίσθη κατ᾽ ἀρχάς, ἑτέρωθι δὲ τῶν Αἰγυπτίων, αἱ μὲν τῶν Περσέων κεφαλαί εἰσι ἀσθενέες οὕτω ὥστε, εἰ θέλεις ψήφῳ μούνῃ βαλεῖν, διατετρανέεις, αἱ δὲ τῶν Αἰγυπτίων οὕτω δή τι ἰσχυραί, μόγις ἂν λίθῳ παίσας διαρρήξειας. [2] αἴτιον δὲ τούτου τόδε ἔλεγον καὶ ἐμέ γ᾽ εὐπετέως ἔπειθον, ὅτι Αἰγύπτιοι μὲν αὐτίκα ἀπὸ παιδίων ἀρξάμενοι ξυρῶνται τὰς κεφαλὰς καὶ πρὸς τὸν ἥλιον παχύνεται τὸ ὀστέον. [3] τὠυτὸ δὲ τοῦτο καὶ τοῦ μὴ φαλακροῦσθαι αἴτιόν ἐστι· Αἰγυπτίων γὰρ ἄν τις ἐλαχίστους ἴδοιτο φαλακροὺς πάντων ἀνθρώπων. [4] τούτοισι μὲν δὴ τοῦτό ἐστι αἴτιον ἰσχυρὰς φορέειν τὰς κεφαλάς, τοῖσι δὲ Πέρσῃσι ὅτι ἀσθενέας φορέουσι τὰς κεφαλὰς αἴτιον τόδε· σκιητροφέουσι ἐξ ἀρχῆς πίλους τιάρας φορέοντες. ταῦτα μέν νυν τοιαῦτα [εἶδον]· εἶδον δὲ καὶ ἄλλα ὅμοια τούτοισι ἐν Παπρήμι τῶν ἅμα Ἀχαιμένεϊ τῷ Δαρείου διαφθαρέντων ὑπὸ Ἰνάρω τοῦ Λίβυος.

13 οἱ δὲ Αἰγύπτιοι ἐκ τῆς μάχης ὡς ἐτράποντο, ἔφευγον οὐδενὶ κόσμῳ· κατειληθέντων δὲ ἐς Μέμφιν, ἔπεμπε ἀνὰ ποταμὸν Καμβύσης νέα Μυτιληναίην κήρυκα ἄγουσαν ἄνδρα Πέρσην, ἐς ὁμολογίην προκαλεόμενος Αἰγυπτίους. [2] οἳ δὲ ἐπείτε τὴν νέα εἶδον ἐσελθοῦσαν ἐς τὴν Μέμφιν, ἐκχυθέντες ἁλέες ἐκ τοῦ τείχεος τήν τε νέα διέφθειραν καὶ τοὺς ἄνδρας κρεουργηδὸν διασπάσαντες ἐφόρεον ἐς τὸ τεῖχος. [3] καὶ Αἰγύπτιοι μὲν μετὰ τοῦτο πολιορκεύμενοι χρόνῳ παρέστησαν, οἱ δὲ προσεχέες Λίβυες δείσαντες τὰ περὶ τὴν Αἴγυπτον γεγονότα παρέδοσαν σφέας αὐτοὺς ἀμαχητὶ καὶ φόρον τε ἐτάξαντο καὶ δῶρα ἔπεμπον. ὣς δὲ Κυρηναῖοι καὶ Βαρκαῖοι, δείσαντες ὁμοίως καὶ οἱ Λίβυες, τοιαῦτα ἐποίησαν. [4] Καμβύσης δὲ τὰ μὲν παρὰ Λιβύων ἐλθόντα δῶρα φιλοφρόνως ἐδέξατο· τὰ δὲ παρὰ Κυρηναίων ἀπικόμενα μεμφθείς, ὡς ἐμοὶ δοκέει, ὅτι ἦν ὀλίγα· ἔπεμψαν γὰρ δὴ πεντακοσίας μνέας ἀργυρίου οἱ Κυρηναῖοι· ταύτας δρασσόμενος αὐτοχειρίῃ διέσπειρε τῇ στρατιῇ.

14 ἡμέρῃ δὲ δεκάτῃ ἀπ' ἧς παρέλαβε τὸ τεῖχος τὸ ἐν Μέμφι Καμβύσης, κατίσας ἐς τὸ προάστειον ἐπὶ λύμῃ τὸν βασιλέα τῶν Αἰγυπτίων Ψαμμήνιτον, βασιλεύσαντα μῆνας ἕξ, τοῦτον κατίσας σὺν ἄλλοισι Αἰγυπτίοισι διεπειρᾶτο αὐτοῦ τῆς ψυχῆς ποιέων τοιάδε· [2] στείλας αὐτοῦ τὴν θυγατέρα ἐσθῆτι δουληίῃ ἐξέπεμπε ἐπ' ὕδωρ ἔχουσαν ὑδρήιον, συνέπεμπε δὲ καὶ ἄλλας παρθένους ἀπολέξας ἀνδρῶν τῶν πρώτων, ὁμοίως ἐσταλμένας τῇ τοῦ βασιλέος. [3] ὡς δὲ βοῇ τε καὶ κλαυθμῷ παρήισαν αἱ παρθένοι παρὰ τοὺς πατέρας, οἱ μὲν ἄλλοι πάντες ἀντεβόων τε καὶ ἀντέκλαιον ὁρῶντες τὰ τέκνα κεκακωμένα, ὁ δὲ Ψαμμήνιτος προϊδὼν καὶ μαθὼν ἔκυψε ἐς τὴν γῆν. [4] παρελθουσέων δὲ τῶν ὑδροφόρων, δεύτερά οἱ τὸν παῖδα ἔπεμπε μετ' ἄλλων Αἰγυπτίων δισχιλίων τὴν αὐτὴν ἡλικίην ἐχόντων, τούς τε αὐχένας κάλῳ δεδεμένους καὶ τὰ στόματα ἐγκεχαλινωμένους· [5] ἤγοντο δὲ ποινὴν τίσοντες Μυτιληναίων τοῖσι ἐν Μέμφι ἀπολομένοισι σὺν τῇ νηί. ταῦτα γὰρ ἐδίκασαν οἱ βασιλήιοι δικασταί, ὑπὲρ ἀνδρὸς ἑκάστου δέκα Αἰγυπτίων τῶν πρώτων ἀνταπόλλυσθαι. [6] ὁ δὲ ἰδὼν παρεξιόντας καὶ μαθὼν τὸν παῖδα ἡγεόμενον ἐπὶ θάνατον, τῶν ἄλλων Αἰγυπτίων τῶν περικατημένων αὐτὸν κλαιόντων καὶ δεῖνα ποιεύντων, τὠυτὸ ἐποίησε τὸ καὶ ἐπὶ τῇ θυγατρί. [7] παρελθόντων δὲ καὶ τούτων, συνήνεικε ὥστε τῶν συμποτέων οἱ ἄνδρα ἀπηλικέστερον, ἐκπεπτωκότα ἐκ τῶν ἐόντων ἔχοντά τε οὐδὲν εἰ μὴ ὅσα πτωχὸς καὶ προσαιτέοντα τὴν στρατιήν, παριέναι Ψαμμήνιτόν τε τὸν Ἀμάσιος καὶ τοὺς ἐν τῷ προαστείῳ κατημένους Αἰγυπτίων. ὁ δὲ Ψαμμήνιτος ὡς εἶδε, ἀνακλαύσας μέγα καὶ καλέσας ὀνομαστὶ τὸν ἑταῖρον ἐπλήξατο τὴν κεφαλήν. [8] ἦσαν δ' ἄρα αὐτοῦ φύλακοι, οἳ τὸ ποιεύμενον πᾶν ἐξ ἐκείνου ἐπ' ἑκάστῃ ἐξόδῳ Καμβύσῃ ἐσήμαινον. θωμάσας δὲ ὁ Καμβύσης τὰ ποιεύμενα, πέμψας ἄγγελον εἰρώτα αὐτὸν λέγων τάδε. [9] "Δεσπότης σε Καμβύσης, Ψαμμήνιτε, εἰρώτα δι' ὅ τι δὴ τὴν μὲν θυγατέρα ὁρέων κεκακωμένην καὶ τὸν παῖδα ἐπὶ θάνατον στείχοντα οὔτε ἀνέβωσας οὔτε ἀπέκλαυσας, τὸν δὲ πτωχὸν οὐδέν σοι προσήκοντα, ὡς ἄλλων πυνθάνεται, ἐτίμησας." ὁ μὲν δὴ ταῦτα ἐπειρώτα, ὁ δ' ἀμείβετο τοῖσιδε. [10] "Ὦ παῖ Κύρου, τὰ μὲν οἰκήια ἦν μέζω κακὰ ἢ ὥστε ἀνακλαίειν, τὸ δὲ τοῦ ἑταίρου πένθος ἄξιον ἦν δακρύων, ὃς ἐκ πολλῶν τε καὶ εὐδαιμόνων ἐκπεσὼν ἐς πτωχηίην ἀπῖκται ἐπὶ γήραος οὐδῷ." [11] καὶ ταῦτα ὡς ἀπενειχθέντα ὑπὸ τούτου εὖ δοκέειν σφι εἰρῆσθαι. ὡς δὲ λέγεται ὑπ' Αἰγυπτίων, δακρύειν μὲν Κροῖσον, ἐτετεύχεε γὰρ καὶ οὗτος ἐπισπόμενος Καμβύσῃ ἐπ' Αἴγυπτον, δακρύειν δὲ Περσέων τοὺς παρεόντας· αὐτῷ τε Καμβύσῃ ἐσελθεῖν οἶκτον τινά, καὶ αὐτίκα κελεύειν τόν τε οἱ παῖδα ἐκ τῶν ἀπολλυμένων σῴζειν καὶ αὐτὸν ἐκ τοῦ προαστείου ἀναστήσαντας ἄγειν παρ' ἑωυτόν.

15 τὸν μὲν δὴ παῖδα εὗρον αὐτοῦ οἱ μετιόντες οὐκέτι περιεόντα ἀλλὰ πρῶτον κατακοπέντα, αὐτὸν δὲ Ψαμμήνιτον ἀναστήσαντες ἦγον παρὰ Καμβύσεα· [2] ἔνθα τοῦ λοιποῦ διαιτᾶτο ἔχων οὐδὲν βίαιον. εἰ δὲ καὶ ἠπιστήθη μὴ πολυπρηγμονέειν, ἀπέλαβε ἂν Αἴγυπτον ὥστε ἐπιτροπεύειν αὐτῆς, ἐπεὶ τιμᾶν ἐώθασι Πέρσαι τῶν βασιλέων τοὺς παῖδας· τῶν, εἰ καὶ σφέων ἀπεστεῶσι, ὅμως τοῖσί γε παισὶ αὐτῶν ἀποδιδοῦσι τὴν ἀρχήν. [3] πολλοῖσι μέν νυν καὶ ἄλλοισι ἐστὶ σταθμώσασθαι ὅτι τοῦτο οὕτω νενομίκασι ποιέειν, ἐν δὲ καὶ τῷ τε Ἰνάρῳ παιδὶ Θαννύρᾳ, ὃς ἀπέλαβε τήν οἱ ὁ πατὴρ εἶχε ἀρχήν, καὶ τῷ Ἀμυρταίου Παυσίρι· καὶ γὰρ οὗτος ἀπέλαβε τὴν τοῦ πατρὸς ἀρχήν. καίτοι Ἰνάρῳ γε καὶ Ἀμυρταίου οὐδαμοί κω Πέρσας κακὰ πλέω ἐργάσαντο. [4] νῦν δὲ μηχανώμενος κακὰ ὁ Ψαμμήνιτος ἔλαβε τὸν μισθόν· ἀπιστὰς γὰρ Αἰγυπτίους ἥλω· ἐπείτε δὲ ἐπάιστος ἐγένετο ὑπὸ Καμβύσεω, αἷμα ταύρου πιὼν ἀπέθανε παραχρῆμα. οὕτω δὴ οὗτος ἐτελεύτησε.

16 Καμβύσης δὲ ἐκ Μέμφιος ἀπίκετο ἐς Σάϊν πόλιν, βουλόμενος ποιῆσαι τὰ δὴ καὶ ἐποίησε. ἐπείτε γὰρ ἐσῆλθε ἐς τὰ τοῦ Ἀμάσιος οἰκία, αὐτίκα ἐκέλευε ἐκ τῆς ταφῆς τὸν Ἀμάσιος νέκυν ἐκφέρειν ἔξω· ὡς δὲ ταῦτα ἐπιτελέα ἐγένετο, μαστιγοῦν ἐκέλευε καὶ τὰς τρίχας ἀποτίλλειν καὶ κεντοῦν τε καὶ τἄλλα πάντα λυμαίνεσθαι. [2] ἐπείτε δὲ καὶ ταῦτα ἔκαμον ποιεῦντες, ὁ γὰρ δὴ νεκρὸς ἅτε τεταριχευμένος ἀντεῖχέ τε καὶ οὐδὲν διεχέετο, ἐκέλευσέ μιν ὁ Καμβύσης κατακαῦσαι, ἐντελλόμενος οὐκ ὅσια· Πέρσαι γὰρ θεὸν νομίζουσι εἶναι πῦρ. [3] τὸ ὧν κατακαίειν γε τοὺς νεκροὺς οὐδαμῶς ἐν νόμῳ οὐδετέροισι ἐστί, Πέρσῃσι μὲν δι' ὅ περ εἴρηται, θεῷ οὐ δίκαιον εἶναι λέγοντες νέμειν νεκρὸν ἀνθρώπου· Αἰγυπτίοισι δὲ νενόμισται πῦρ θηρίον εἶναι ἔμψυχον, πάντα δὲ αὐτὸ κατεσθίειν τά περ ἂν λάβῃ, πλησθὲν δὲ αὐτὸ τῆς βορῆς συναποθνῄσκειν τῷ κατεσθιομένῳ. [4] οὐκ ὦν θηρίοισι νόμος οὐδαμῶς σφι ἐστὶ τὸν νέκυν διδόναι, καὶ διὰ ταῦτα ταριχεύουσι, ἵνα μὴ κείμενος ὑπὸ εὐλέων καταβρωθῇ. οὕτω οὐδετέροισι νομιζόμενα ἐνετέλλετο ποιέειν ὁ Καμβύσης. [5] ὡς μέντοι Αἰγύπτιοι λέγουσι οὐκ Ἄμασις ἦν ὁ ταῦτα παθών, ἀλλὰ ἄλλος τις τῶν Αἰγυπτίων ἔχων τὴν αὐτὴν ἡλικίην Ἀμάσι, τῷ λυμαινόμενοι Πέρσαι ἐδόκεον Ἀμάσι λυμαίνεσθαι. [6] λέγουσι γὰρ ὡς πυθόμενος ἐκ μαντηίου ὁ Ἄμασις τὰ περὶ ἑωυτὸν ἀποθανόντα μέλλοντα γίνεσθαι, οὕτω δὴ ἀκεόμενος τὰ ἐπιφερόμενα τὸν μὲν ἄνθρωπον τοῦτον τὸν μαστιγωθέντα ἀποθανόντα ἔθαψε ἐπὶ τῇσι θύρῃσι ἐντὸς τῆς ἑωυτοῦ θήκης, ἑωυτὸν δὲ ἐνετείλατο τῷ παιδὶ ἐν μυχῷ τῆς θήκης ὡς μάλιστα θεῖναι. [7] αἱ μέν νυν ἐκ τοῦ Ἀμάσιος ἐντολαὶ αὗται αἱ ἐς τὴν ταφήν τε καὶ τὸν ἄνθρωπον ἔχουσαι οὔ μοι δοκέουσι ἀρχὴν γενέσθαι, ἄλλως δ' αὐτὰ Αἰγύπτιοι σεμνοῦν.

17 μετὰ δὲ ταῦτα ὁ Καμβύσης ἐβουλεύσατο τριφασίας στρατηίας, ἐπί τε Καρχηδονίους καὶ ἐπὶ Ἀμμωνίους καὶ ἐπὶ τοὺς μακροβίους Αἰθίοπας, οἰκημένους δὲ Λιβύης ἐπὶ τῇ νοτίῃ θαλάσσῃ· [2] βουλευομένῳ δέ οἱ ἔδοξε ἐπὶ μὲν Καρχηδονίους τὸν ναυτικὸν στρατὸν ἀποστέλλειν, ἐπὶ δὲ Ἀμμωνίους τοῦ πεζοῦ ἀποκρίναντα, ἐπὶ δὲ τοὺς Αἰθίοπας κατόπτας πρῶτον, ὀψομένους τε τὴν ἐν τούτοισι τοῖσι Αἰθίοψι λεγομένην εἶναι ἡλίου τράπεζαν εἰ ἔστι ἀληθέως, καὶ πρὸς ταύτῃ τὰ ἄλλα κατοψομένους, δῶρα δὲ τῷ λόγῳ φέροντας τῷ βασιλέι αὐτῶν.

18 ἡ δὲ τράπεζα τοῦ ἡλίου τοιηδε τις λέγεται εἶναι· λειμὼν ἐστὶ ἐν τῷ προαστείῳ ἐπίπλεος κρεῶν ἑφθῶν πάντων τῶν τετραπόδων, ἐς τὸν τὰς μὲν νύκτας ἐπιτηδεύοντας τιθέναι τὰ κρέα τοὺς ἐν τέλεϊ ἑκάστοτε ἐόντας τῶν ἀστῶν, τὰς δὲ ἡμέρας δαίνυσθαι προσιόντα τὸν βουλόμενον. φάναι δὲ τοὺς ἐπιχωρίους ταῦτα τὴν γῆν αὐτὴν ἀναδιδόναι ἑκάστοτε. ἡ μὲν δὴ τράπεζα τοῦ ἡλίου καλεομένη λέγεται εἶναι τοιηδε.

19 Καμβύσῃ δὲ ὡς ἔδοξε πέμπειν τοὺς κατασκόπους, αὐτίκα μετεπέμπετο ἐξ Ἐλεφαντίνης πόλιος τῶν Ἰχθυοφάγων ἀνδρῶν τοὺς ἐπισταμένους τὴν Αἰθιοπίδα γλῶσσαν. [2] ἐν ᾧ δὲ τούτους μετήισαν, ἐν τούτῳ ἐκέλευε ἐπὶ τὴν Καρχηδόνα πλέειν τὸν ναυτικὸν στρατόν. Φοίνικες δὲ οὐκ ἔφασαν ποιήσειν ταῦτα· ὁρκίοισι γὰρ μεγάλοισι ἐνδεδέσθαι, καὶ οὐκ ἂν ποιέειν ὅσια ἐπὶ τοὺς παῖδας τοὺς ἑωυτῶν στρατευόμενοι. Φοινίκων δὲ οὐ βουλομένων οἱ λοιποὶ οὐκ ἀξιόμαχοι ἐγίνοντο. [3] Καρχηδόνιοι μέν νυν οὕτω δουλοσύνην διέφυγον πρὸς Περσέων· Καμβύσης γὰρ βίην οὐκ ἐδικαίου προσφέρειν Φοίνιξι, ὅτι σφέας τε αὐτοὺς ἐδεδώκεσαν Πέρσῃσι καὶ πᾶς ἐκ Φοινίκων ἤρτητο ὁ ναυτικὸς στρατός. δόντες δὲ καὶ Κύπριοι σφέας αὐτοὺς Πέρσῃσι ἐστρατεύοντο ἐπ' Αἴγυπτον.

20 ἐπείτε δὲ τῷ Καμβύσῃ ἐκ τῆς Ἐλεφαντίνης ἀπίκοντο οἱ Ἰχθυοφάγοι, ἔπεμπε αὐτοὺς ἐς τοὺς Αἰθίοπας ἐντειλάμενος τὰ λέγειν χρῆν καὶ δῶρα φέροντας πορφύρεόν τε εἷμα καὶ χρύσεον στρεπτὸν περιαυχένιον καὶ ψέλια καὶ μύρου ἀλάβαστρον καὶ φοινικηίου οἴνου κάδον. [2] οἱ δὲ Αἰθίοπες οὗτοι, ἐς τοὺς ἀποπέμπει ὁ Καμβύσης, λέγονται εἶναι μέγιστοι καὶ κάλλιστοι ἀνθρώπων πάντων. νόμοισι δὲ καὶ ἄλλοισι χρᾶσθαι αὐτοὺς φασι κεχωρισμένοισι τῶν ἄλλων ἀνθρώπων καὶ δὴ καὶ κατὰ τὴν βασιληίην τοιῷδε· τὸν ἂν τῶν ἀστῶν κρίνωσι μέγιστόν τε εἶναι καὶ κατὰ τὸ μέγαθος ἔχειν τὴν ἰσχύν, τοῦτον ἀξιοῦσι βασιληίας βασιλεύειν.

21 ἐς τούτους δὴ ὦν τοὺς ἄνδρας ὡς ἀπίκοντο οἱ Ἰχθυοφάγοι, διδόντες τὰ δῶρα τῷ βασιλέϊ αὐτῶν ἔλεγον τάδε. "Βασιλεὺς ὁ Περσέων Καμβύσης, βουλόμενος φίλος καὶ ξεῖνός τοι γενέσθαι, ἡμέας τε ἀπέπεμψε ἐς λόγους τοι ἐλθεῖν κελεύων, καὶ δῶρα ταῦτά τοι διδοῖ τοῖσι καὶ αὐτὸς μάλιστα ἥδεται χρεώμενος." [2] ὁ δὲ Αἰθίοψ μαθὼν ὅτι κατόπται ἥκοιεν, λέγει πρὸς αὐτοὺς τοιάδε. "Οὔτε ὁ Περσέων βασιλεὺς δῶρα ὑμέας ἔπεμψε φέροντας προτιμῶν πολλοῦ ἐμοὶ ξεῖνος γενέσθαι, οὔτε ὑμεῖς λέγετε ἀληθέα, ἥκετε γὰρ κατόπται τῆς ἐμῆς ἀρχῆς, οὔτε ἐκεῖνος ἀνήρ ἐστι δίκαιος. εἰ γὰρ ἦν δίκαιος, οὗτος ἂν ἐπεθύμησε χώρης ἄλλης ἢ τῆς ἑωυτοῦ, οὔτ' ἂν ἐς δουλοσύνην ἀνθρώπους ἦγε ὑπ' ὧν μηδὲν ἠδίκηται. νῦν δὲ αὐτῷ τόξον τόδε διδόντες τάδε ἔπεα λέγετε. [3] 'βασιλεὺς ὁ Αἰθιόπων συμβουλεύει τῷ Περσέων βασιλέϊ, ἐπεὰν οὕτω εὐπετέως ἕλκωσι τὰ τόξα Πέρσαι ἐόντα μεγάθεϊ τοσαῦτα, τότε ἐπ' Αἰθίοπας τοὺς μακροβίους πλήθεϊ ὑπερβαλλόμενον στρατεύεσθαι· μέχρι δὲ τούτου θεοῖσι εἰδέναι χάριν, οἳ οὐκ ἐπὶ νόον τράπουσι Αἰθιόπων παισὶ γῆν ἄλλην προσκτᾶσθαί τῇ ἑωυτῶν.'"

22 ταῦτα δὲ εἴπας καὶ ἀνεὶς τὸ τόξον παρέδωκε τοῖσι ἥκουσι. λαβὼν δὲ τὸ εἷμα τὸ πορφύρεον εἰρώτα ὅ τι εἴη καὶ ὅκως πεποιημένον· εἰπόντων δὲ τῶν Ἰχθυοφάγων τὴν ἀληθείην περὶ τῆς πορφύρης καὶ τῆς βαφῆς, δολεροὺς μὲν τοὺς ἀνθρώπους ἔφη εἶναι, δολερὰ δὲ αὐτῶν τὰ εἵματα. [2] δεύτερα δὲ τὸν χρυσὸν εἰρώτα τὸν στρεπτὸν τὸν περιαυχένιον καὶ τὰ ψέλια· ἐξηγεομένων δὲ τῶν Ἰχθυοφάγων τὸν κόσμον αὐτοῦ, γελάσας ὁ βασιλεὺς καὶ νομίσας εἶναι σφέα πέδας εἶπε ὡς παρ' ἑωυτοῖσι εἰσὶ ῥωμαλεώτεραι τουτέων πέδαι. [3] τρίτον δὲ εἰρώτα τὸ μύρον· εἰπόντων δὲ τῆς ποιήσιος πέρι καὶ ἀλείψιος, τὸν αὐτὸν λόγον τὸν καὶ περὶ τοῦ εἵματος εἶπε. ὡς δὲ ἐς τὸν οἶνον ἀπίκετο καὶ ἐπύθετο αὐτοῦ τὴν ποίησιν, ὑπερησθεὶς τῷ πόματι ἐπείρετο ὅ τι τε σιτέεται ὁ βασιλεὺς καὶ χρόνον ὁκόσον μακρότατον ἀνὴρ Πέρσης ζώει. [4] οἱ δὲ σιτέεσθαι μὲν τὸν ἄρτον εἶπον, ἐξηγησάμενοι τῶν πυρῶν τὴν φύσιν, ὀγδώκοντα δὲ ἔτεα ζόης πλήρωμα ἀνδρὶ μακρότατον προκέεσθαι. πρὸς ταῦτα ὁ Αἰθίοψ ἔφη οὐδὲν θωμάζειν εἰ σιτεόμενοι κόπρον ἔτεα ὀλίγα ζώουσι· οὐδὲ γὰρ ἂν τοσαῦτα δύνασθαι ζώειν σφέας, εἰ μὴ τῷ πόματι ἀνέφερον, φράζων τοῖσι Ἰχθυοφάγοισι τὸν οἶνον· τούτῳ γὰρ ἑωυτοὺς ὑπὸ Περσέων ἑσσοῦσθαι.

23 ἀντειρομένων δὲ τὸν βασιλέα τῶν Ἰχθυοφάγων τῆς ζόης καὶ διαίτης πέρι, ἔτεα μὲν ἐς εἴκοσι καὶ ἑκατὸν τοὺς πολλοὺς αὐτῶν ἀπικνέεσθαι,

ὑπερβάλλειν δὲ τινάς καὶ ταῦτα, σίτησιν δὲ εἶναι κρέα τε ἐφθὰ καὶ πόμα γάλα. [2] θῶμα δὲ ποιευμένων τῶν κατασκόπων περὶ τῶν ἐτέων, ἐπὶ κρήνην σφι ἡγήσασθαι, ἀπ' ἧς λουόμενοι λιπαρώτεροι ἐγίνοντο, κατά περ εἰ ἐλαίου εἴη· ὄζειν δὲ ἀπ' αὐτῆς ὡς εἰ ἴων. [3] ἀσθενὲς δὲ τὸ ὕδωρ τῆς κρήνης ταύτης οὕτω δή τι ἔλεγον εἶναι οἱ κατάσκοποι ὥστε μηδὲν οἷόν τ' εἶναι ἐπ' αὐτοῦ ἐπιπλέειν, μήτε ξύλον μήτε τῶν ὅσα ξύλου ἐστὶ ἐλαφρότερα, ἀλλὰ πάντα σφέα χωρέειν ἐς βυσσόν. τὸ δὲ ὕδωρ τοῦτο εἴ σφι ἐστὶ ἀληθέως οἷόν τι λέγεται, διὰ τοῦτο ἂν εἶεν, τούτῳ τὰ πάντα χρεώμενοι, μακρόβιοι. [4] ἀπὸ τῆς κρήνης δὲ ἀπαλλασσομένων, ἀγαγεῖν σφεας ἐς δεσμωτήριον ἀνδρῶν, ἔνθα τοὺς πάντας ἐν πέδῃσι χρυσέῃσι δεδέσθαι. ἔστι δὲ ἐν τούτοισι τοῖσι Αἰθίοψι πάντων ὁ χαλκὸς σπανιώτατον καὶ τιμιώτατον. θεησάμενοι δὲ καὶ τὸ δεσμωτήριον, ἐθεήσαντο καὶ τὴν τοῦ ἡλίου λεγομένην τράπεζαν.

24 μετὰ δὲ ταύτην τελευταίας ἐθεήσαντο τὰς θήκας αὐτῶν, αἵ λέγονται σκευάζεσθαι ἐξ ὑάλου τρόπῳ τοιῷδε· [2] ἐπεὰν τὸν νεκρὸν ἰσχνήνωσι, εἴτε δὴ κατά περ Αἰγύπτιοι εἴτε ἄλλως κως, γυψώσαντες ἅπαντα αὐτὸν γραφῇ κοσμέουσι, ἐξομοιεῦντες τὸ εἶδος ἐς τὸ δυνατόν, ἔπειτα δέ οἱ περιστᾶσι στήλην ἐξ ὑάλου πεποιημένην κοίλην· ἥ δέ σφι πολλὴ καὶ εὔεργος ὀρύσσεται. [3] ἐν μέσῃ δὲ τῇ στήλῃ ἐνεὼν διαφαίνεται ὁ νέκυς, οὔτε ὀδμὴν οὐδεμίαν ἄχαριν παρεχόμενος οὔτε ἄλλο ἀεικὲς οὐδέν, καὶ ἔχει πάντα φανερὰ ὁμοίως αὐτῷ τῷ νέκυϊ. [4] ἐνιαυτὸν μὲν δὴ ἔχουσι τὴν στήλην ἐν τοῖσι οἰκίοισι οἱ μάλιστα προσήκοντες, πάντων ἀπαρχόμενοι καὶ θυσίας οἱ προσάγοντες· μετὰ δὲ ταῦτα ἐκκομίσαντες ἱστᾶσι περὶ τὴν πόλιν.

25 θεησάμενοι δὲ τὰ πάντα οἱ κατάσκοποι ἀπαλλάσσοντο ὀπίσω. ἀπαγγειλάντων δὲ ταῦτα τούτων, αὐτίκα ὁ Καμβύσης ὀργὴν ποιησάμενος ἐστρατεύετο ἐπὶ τοὺς Αἰθίοπας, οὔτε παρασκευὴν σίτου οὐδεμίαν παραγγείλας, οὔτε λόγον ἑωυτῷ δοὺς ὅτι ἐς τὰ ἔσχατα γῆς ἔμελλε στρατεύεσθαι· [2] οἷα δὲ ἐμμανής τε ἐὼν καὶ οὐ φρενήρης, ὡς ἤκουε τῶν Ἰχθυοφάγων, ἐστρατεύετο, Ἑλλήνων μὲν τοὺς παρεόντας αὐτοῦ τάξας ὑπομένειν, τὸν δὲ πεζὸν πάντα ἅμα ἀγόμενος. [3] ἐπείτε δὲ στρατευόμενος ἐγένετο ἐν Θήβῃσι, ἀπέκρινε τευ στρατοῦ ὡς πέντε μυριάδας, καὶ τούτοισι μὲν ἐνετέλλετο Ἀμμωνίους ἐξανδραποδισαμένους τὸ χρηστήριον τὸ τοῦ Διὸς ἐμπρῆσαι, αὐτὸς δὲ τὸν λοιπὸν ἄγων στρατὸν ἤιε ἐπὶ τοὺς Αἰθίοπας. [4] πρὶν δὲ τῆς ὁδοῦ τὸ πέμπτον μέρος διεληλυθέναι τὴν στρατιήν, αὐτίκα πάντα αὐτοὺς τὰ εἶχον σιτίων ἐχόμενα ἐπελελοίπεε, μετὰ δὲ τὰ σιτία καὶ τὰ ὑποζύγια ἐπέλιπε κατεσθιόμενα. [5] εἰ μέν νυν μαθὼν ταῦτα ὁ Καμβύσης ἐγνωσιμάχεε καὶ ἀπῆγε ὀπίσω τὸν στρατόν, ἐπὶ τῇ ἀρχῆθεν γενομένῃ ἁμαρτάδι ἦν ἂν ἀνὴρ σοφός· νῦν δὲ οὐδένα λόγον ποιεύμενος ἤιε αἰεὶ ἐς τὸ πρόσω. [6] οἱ δὲ στρατιῶται ἕως μέν τι εἶχον ἐκ τῆς γῆς λαμβάνειν, ποιηφαγέοντες διέζωον, ἐπεὶ δὲ ἐς τὴν ψάμμον ἀπίκοντο, δεινὸν ἔργον ἑωυτῶν αὐτῶν τινες ἐργάσαντο· ἐκ δεκάδος γὰρ ἕνα σφέων αὐτῶν ἀποκληρώσαντες κατέφαγον. πυθόμενος δὲ ταῦτα ὁ Καμβύσης, δείσας τὴν ἀλληλοφαγίην, ἀπεὶς τὸν ἐπ' Αἰθίοπας στόλον ὀπίσω ἐπορεύετο καὶ ἀπικνέεται ἐς Θήβας πολλοὺς ἀπολέσας τοῦ στρατοῦ· ἐκ Θηβέων δὲ καταβὰς ἐς Μέμφιν τοὺς Ἕλληνας ἀπῆκε ἀποπλέειν.

26 ὁ μὲν ἐπ' Αἰθίοπας στόλος οὕτω ἔπρηξε· οἱ δ' αὐτῶν ἐπ' Ἀμμωνίους ἀποσταλέντες στρατεύεσθαι, ἐπείτε ὁρμηθέντες ἐκ τῶν Θηβέων ἐπορεύοντο ἔχοντες ἀγωγούς, ἀπικόμενοι μὲν φανεροί εἰσι ἐς Ὄασιν πόλιν, τὴν ἔχουσι μὲν Σάμιοι τῆς Αἰσχριωνίης φυλῆς λεγόμενοι εἶναι, ἀπέχουσι δὲ ἑπτὰ ἡμερέων ὁδὸν ἀπὸ Θηβέων διὰ ψάμμου· ὀνομάζεται δὲ ὁ χῶρος οὗτος κατὰ Ἑλλήνων γλῶσσαν Μακάρων νῆσος. [2] ἐς μὲν δὴ τοῦτον τὸν χῶρον λέγεται ἀπικέσθαι τὸν στρατόν, τὸ ἐνθεῦτεν δέ, ὅτι μὴ αὐτοὶ Ἀμμώνιοι καὶ οἱ τούτων ἀκούσαντες, ἄλλοι οὐδένες οὐδὲν ἔχουσι εἰπεῖν περὶ αὐτῶν· οὔτε γὰρ ἐς τοὺς Ἀμμωνίους ἀπίκοντο οὔτε ὀπίσω ἐνόστησαν. [3] λέγεται δὲ κατὰ τάδε ὑπ' αὐτῶν Ἀμμωνίων· ἐπειδὴ ἐκ τῆς Ὀάσιος ταύτης ἰέναι διὰ τῆς ψάμμου ἐπὶ σφέας, γενέσθαι τε αὐτοὺς μεταξύ κου μάλιστα αὐτῶν τε καὶ τῆς Ὀάσιος, ἄριστον αἱρεομένοισι αὐτοῖσι ἐπιπνεῦσαι νότον μέγαν τε καὶ ἐξαίσιον, φορέοντα δὲ θῖνας τῆς ψάμμου καταχῶσαι σφέας, καὶ τρόπῳ τοιούτῳ ἀφανισθῆναι. Ἀμμώνιοι μὲν οὕτω λέγουσι γενέσθαι περὶ τῆς στρατιῆς ταύτης.

27 ἀπιγμένου δὲ Καμβύσεω ἐς Μέμφιν ἐφάνη Αἰγυπτίοισι ὁ Ἆπις, τὸν Ἕλληνες Ἔπαφον καλέουσι· ἐπιφανέος δὲ τούτου γενομένου αὐτίκα οἱ

Αἰγύπτιοι εἵματα ἐφόρεον τὰ κάλλιστα καὶ ἦσαν ἐν θαλίῃσι. [2] ἰδὼν δὲ ταῦτα τοὺς Αἰγυπτίους ποιεῦντας ὁ Καμβύσης, πάγχυ σφέας καταδόξας ἑωυτοῦ κακῶς πρήξαντος χαρμόσυνα ταῦτα ποιέειν, ἐκάλεε τοὺς ἐπιτρόπους τῆς Μέμφιος, ἀπικομένους δὲ ἐς ὄψιν εἴρετο ὅ τι πρότερον μὲν ἐόντος αὐτοῦ ἐν Μέμφι ἐποίευν τοιοῦτον οὐδὲν Αἰγύπτιοι, τότε δὲ ἐπεὶ αὐτὸς παρείη τῆς στρατιῆς πλῆθός τι ἀποβαλών. [3] οἳ δὲ ἔφραζον ὥς σφι θεὸς εἴη φανεὶς διὰ χρόνου πολλοῦ ἐωθὼς ἐπιφαίνεσθαι, καὶ ὡς ἐπεὰν φανῇ τότε πάντες Αἰγύπτιοι κεχαρηκότες ὀρτάζοιεν. ταῦτα ἀκούσας ὁ Καμβύσης ἔφη ψεύδεσθαι σφέας καὶ ὡς ψευδομένους θανάτῳ ἐζημίου.

28 ἀποκτείνας δὲ τούτους δεύτερα τοὺς ἱρέας ἐκάλεε ἐς ὄψιν· λεγόντων δὲ κατὰ ταὐτὰ τῶν ἱρέων, οὐ λήσειν ἔφη αὐτὸν εἰ θεός τις χειροήθης ἀπιγμένος εἴη Αἰγυπτίοισι. τοσαῦτα δὲ εἴπας ἀπάγειν ἐκέλευε τὸν Ἆπιν τοὺς ἱρέας. [2] οἱ μὲν δὴ μετήισαν ἄξοντες. ὁ δὲ Ἆπις οὗτος ὁ Ἔπαφος γίνεται μόσχος ἐκ βοός, ἥτις οὐκέτι οἵη τε γίνεται ἐς γαστέρα ἄλλον βάλλεσθαι γόνον. Αἰγύπτιοι δὲ λέγουσι σέλας ἐπὶ τὴν βοῦν ἐκ τοῦ οὐρανοῦ κατίσχειν, καί μιν ἐκ τούτου τίκτειν τὸν Ἆπιν. [3] ἔχει δὲ ὁ μόσχος οὗτος ὁ Ἆπις καλεόμενος σημήια τοιάδε ἐὼν μέλας, ἐπὶ μὲν τῷ μετώπῳ λευκόν τι τρίγωνον, ἐπὶ δὲ τοῦ νώτου αἰετὸν εἰκασμένον, ἐν δὲ τῇ οὐρῇ τὰς τρίχας διπλᾶς, ὑπὸ δὲ τῇ γλώσσῃ κάνθαρον.

29 ὡς δὲ ἤγαγον τὸν Ἆπιν οἱ ἱρέες, ὁ Καμβύσης, οἷα ἐὼν ὑπομαργότερος, σπασάμενος τὸ ἐγχειρίδιον, θέλων τύψαι τὴν γαστέρα τοῦ Ἄπιος παίει τὸν μηρόν· γελάσας δὲ εἶπε πρὸς τοὺς ἱρέας [2] "Ὦ κακαὶ κεφαλαί, τοῖσι θεοὶ γίνονται, ἔναιμοί τε καὶ σαρκώδεες καὶ ἐπαΐοντες σιδηρίων; ἄξιος μέν γε Αἰγυπτίων οὗτός γε ὁ θεός, ἀτάρ τοι ὑμεῖς γε οὐ χαίροντες γέλωτα ἐμὲ θήσεσθε." ταῦτα εἴπας ἐνετείλατο τοῖσι ταῦτα πρήσσουσι τοὺς μὲν ἱρέας ἀπομαστιγῶσαι, Αἰγυπτίων δὲ τῶν ἄλλων τὸν ἂν λάβωσι ὀρτάζοντα κτείνειν. [3] ἡ ὀρτὴ μὲν δὴ διελέλυτο Αἰγυπτίοισι, οἱ δὲ ἱρέες ἐδικαιεῦντο, ὁ δὲ Ἆπις πεπληγμένος τὸν μηρὸν ἔφθινε ἐν τῷ ἱρῷ κατακείμενος. καὶ τὸν μὲν τελευτήσαντα ἐκ τοῦ τρώματος ἔθαψαν οἱ ἱρέες λάθρῃ Καμβύσεω.

30 Καμβύσης δέ, ὡς λέγουσι Αἰγύπτιοι, αὐτίκα διὰ τοῦτο τὸ ἀδίκημα ἐμάνη, ἐὼν οὐδὲ πρότερον φρενήρης. καὶ πρῶτα μὲν τῶν κακῶν ἐξεργάσατο τὸν ἀδελφεὸν Σμέρδιν ἐόντα πατρὸς καὶ μητρὸς τῆς αὐτῆς, τὸν ἀπέπεμψε ἐς Πέρσας φθόνῳ ἐξ Αἰγύπτου, ὅτι τὸ τόξον μοῦνος Περσέων ὅσον τε ἐπὶ δύο δακτύλους εἴρυσε, τὸ παρὰ τοῦ Αἰθίοπος ἤνεικαν οἱ Ἰχθυοφάγοι, τῶν δὲ ἄλλων Περσέων οὐδεὶς οἷός τε ἐγένετο. [2] ἀποιχομένου ὡς ἐς Πέρσας τοῦ Σμέρδιος ὄψιν εἶδε ὁ Καμβύσης ἐν τῷ ὕπνῳ τοιήνδε· ἔδοξέ οἱ ἄγγελον ἐλθόντα ἐκ Περσέων ἀγγέλλειν ὡς ἐν τῷ θρόνῳ τῷ βασιληίῳ ἱζόμενος Σμέρδις τῇ κεφαλῇ τοῦ οὐρανοῦ ψαύσειε. [3] πρὸς ὧν ταῦτα δείσας περὶ ἑωυτοῦ μή μιν ἀποκτείνας ὁ ἀδελφεὸς ἄρχῃ, πέμπει Πρηξάσπεα ἐς Πέρσας, ὃς ἦν οἱ ἀνὴρ Περσέων πιστότατος, ἀποκτενέοντά μιν. ὁ δὲ ἀναβὰς ἐς Σοῦσα ἀπέκτεινε Σμέρδιν, οἱ μὲν λέγουσι ἐπ' ἄγρην ἐξαγαγόντα, οἱ δὲ ἐς τὴν Ἐρυθρὴν θάλασσαν προαγαγόντα καταποντῶσαι.

31 πρῶτον μὲν δὴ λέγουσι Καμβύσῃ τῶν κακῶν ἄρξαι τοῦτο· δεύτερα δὲ ἐξεργάσατο τὴν ἀδελφεὴν ἑσπομένην οἱ ἐς Αἴγυπτον, τῇ καὶ συνοίκεε καὶ ἦν οἱ ἀπ' ἀμφοτέρων ἀδελφεή. ἔγημε δὲ αὐτὴν ὧδε· [2] οὐδαμῶς γὰρ ἐώθεσαν πρότερον τῇσι ἀδελφεῇσι συνοικέειν Πέρσαι. ἠράσθη μιῆς τῶν ἀδελφεῶν Καμβύσης, καὶ ἔπειτα βουλόμενος αὐτὴν γῆμαι, ὅτι οὐκ ἐωθότα ἐπενόεε ποιήσειν, εἴρετο καλέσας τοὺς βασιληίους δικαστὰς εἴ τις ἐστὶ κελεύων νόμος τὸν βουλόμενον ἀδελφεῇ συνοικέειν. [3] οἱ δὲ βασιλήιοι δικασταὶ κεκριμένοι ἄνδρες γίνονται Περσέων, ἐς οὗ ἀποθάνωσι ἤ σφι παρευρεθῇ τι ἄδικον, μέχρι τούτου· οὗτοι δὲ τοῖσι Πέρσῃσι δίκας δικάζουσι καὶ ἐξηγηταὶ τῶν πατρίων θεσμῶν γίνονται, καὶ πάντα ἐς τούτους ἀνακέεται. [4] εἰρομένου ὦν τοῦ Καμβύσεω, ὑπεκρίνοντο αὐτῷ οὗτοι καὶ δίκαια καὶ ἀσφαλέα, φάμενοι νόμον οὐδένα ἐξευρίσκειν ὃς κελεύει ἀδελφεῇ συνοικέειν ἀδελφεόν, ἄλλον μέντοι ἐξευρηκέναι νόμον, τῷ βασιλεύοντι Περσέων ἐξεῖναι ποιέειν τὸ ἂν βούληται. [5] οὕτω οὔτε τὸν νόμον ἔλυσαν δείσαντες Καμβύσεα, ἵνα τε μὴ αὐτοὶ ἀπόλωνται τὸν νόμον περιστέλλοντες, παρεξεῦρον ἄλλον νόμον σύμμαχον τῷ γαμέειν ἀδελφεάς. [6] τότε μὲν δὴ ὁ Καμβύσης ἔγημε τὴν ἐρωμένην, μετὰ μέντοι οὐ πολλὸν χρόνον ἔσχε ἄλλην ἀδελφεήν. τουτέων δῆτα τὴν νεωτέρην ἐπισπομένην οἱ ἐπ' Αἴγυπτον κτείνει.

32 ἀμφὶ δὲ τῷ θανάτῳ αὐτῆς διξὸς ὥσπερ περὶ Σμέρδιος λέγεται λόγος. Ἕλληνες μὲν λέγουσι Καμβύσεα συμβαλεῖν σκύμνον λέοντος σκύλακι κυνός, θεωρέειν δὲ καὶ τὴν γυναῖκα ταύτην, νικωμένου δὲ τοῦ σκύλακος ἀδελφεὸν αὐτοῦ ἄλλον σκύλακα ἀπορρήξαντα τὸν δεσμὸν παραγενέσθαιοί, δύο δὲ γενομένους οὕτω δὴ τοὺς σκύλακας ἐπικρατῆσαι τοῦ σκύμνου. [2] καὶ τὸν μὲν Καμβύσεα ἥδεσθαι θεώμενον, τὴν δὲ παρημένην δακρύειν. Καμβύσεα δὲ μαθόντα τοῦτο ἐπειρέσθαι δι' ὅ τι δακρύει, τὴν δὲ εἰπεῖν ὡς ἰδοῦσα τὸν σκύλακα τῷ ἀδελφεῷ τιμωρήσαντα δακρύσειε, μνησθεῖσά τε Σμέρδιος καὶ μαθοῦσα ὡς ἐκείνῳ οὐκ εἴη ὁ τιμωρήσων. [3] Ἕλληνες μὲν δὴ διὰ τοῦτο τὸ ἔπος φασὶ αὐτὴν ἀπολέσθαι ὑπὸ Καμβύσεω, Αἰγύπτιοι δὲ ὡς τραπέζῃ παρακατημένων λαβοῦσαν θρίδακα τὴν γυναῖκα περιτῖλαι καὶ ἐπανειρέσθαι τὸν ἄνδρα κότερον περιτετιλμένη ἢ θρίδαξ ἢ δασέα εἴη καλλίων, καὶ τὸν φάναι δασέαν, τὴν δ' εἰπεῖν [4] "Ταύτην μέντοι κοτὲ σὺ τὴν θρίδακα ἐμιμήσαο τὸν Κύρου οἶκον ἀποψιλώσας." τὸν δὲ θυμωθέντα ἐμπηδῆσαι αὐτῇ ἐχούσῃ ἐν γαστρί, καί μιν ἐκτρώσασαν ἀποθανεῖν.

33 ταῦτα μὲν ἐς τοὺς οἰκηίους ὁ Καμβύσης ἐξεμάνη, εἴτε δὴ διὰ τὸν Ἆπιν εἴτε καὶ ἄλλως, οἷα πολλὰ ἔωθε ἀνθρώπους κακὰ καταλαμβάνειν· καὶ γὰρ τινὰ ἐκ γενεῆς νοῦσον μεγάλην λέγεται ἔχειν ὁ Καμβύσης, τὴν ἱρὴν ὀνομάζουσι τινές. οὔ νῦν τοι ἀεικὲς οὐδὲν ἦν τοῦ σώματος νοῦσον μεγάλην νοσέοντος μηδὲ τὰς φρένας ὑγιαίνειν.

34 τάδε δ' ἐς τοὺς ἄλλους Πέρσας ἐξεμάνη. λέγεται γὰρ εἰπεῖν αὐτὸν πρὸς Πρηξάσπεα, τὸν ἐτίμα τε μάλιστα καὶ οἱ τὰς ἀγγελίας ἐφόρεε οὗτος, τούτου τε ὁ παῖς οἰνοχόος ἦν τῷ Καμβύσῃ, τιμὴ δὲ καὶ αὕτη οὐ σμικρή· εἰπεῖν δὲ λέγεται τάδε. [2] "Πρήξασπες, κοῖόν με τινὰ νομίζουσι Πέρσαι εἶναι ἄνδρα τίνας τε λόγους περὶ ἐμέο ποιεῦνται;" τὸν δὲ εἰπεῖν "Ὦ δέσποτα, τὰ μὲν ἄλλα πάντα μεγάλως ἐπαινέαι, τῇ δὲ φιλοινίῃ σε φασὶ πλεόνως προσκέεσθαι." [3] τὸν μὲν δὴ λέγειν ταῦτα περὶ Περσέων, τὸν δὲ θυμωθέντα τοιάδε ἀμείβεσθαι. "Νῦν ἄρα με φασὶ Πέρσαι οἴνῳ προσκείμενον παραφρονέειν καὶ οὐκ εἶναι νοήμονα· οὐδ' ἄρα σφέων οἱ προτεροιλόγοι ἦσαν ἀληθέες." [4] πρότερον γὰρ δὴ ἄρα, Περσέων οἱ συνέδρων ἐόντων καὶ Κροίσου, εἴρετο Καμβύσης κοῖός τις δοκέοι ἀνὴρ εἶναι πρὸς τὸν πατέρα τελέσαι Κῦρον, οἱ δὲ ἀμείβοντο ὡς εἴη ἀμείνων τοῦ πατρός· τά τε γὰρ ἐκείνου πάντα ἔχειν αὐτὸν καὶ προσεκτῆσθαι Αἴγυπτόν τε καὶ τὴν θάλασσαν. [5] Πέρσαι μὲν ταῦτα ἔλεγον, Κροῖσος δὲ παρεών τε καὶ οὐκ ἀρεσκόμενος τῇ κρίσι εἶπε πρὸς τὸν Καμβύσεα τάδε. "Ἐμοὶ μέν νυν, ὦ παῖ Κύρου, οὐ δοκέεις ὅμοιος εἶναι τῷ πατρί· οὐ γάρ κώ τοι ἐστὶ υἱὸς οἷον σὲ ἐκεῖνος κατελίπετο." ἥσθη τε ταῦτα ἀκούσας ὁ Καμβύσης καὶ ἐπαίνεε τὴν Κροίσου κρίσιν.

35 τούτων δὴ ὦν ἐπιμνησθέντα ὀργῇ λέγειν πρὸς τὸν Πρηξάσπεα, "Σύ νυν μάθε εἰ λέγουσι Πέρσαι ἀληθέα εἴτε αὐτοὶ λέγοντες ταῦτα παραφρονέουσι· [2] εἰ μὲν γὰρ τοῦ παιδὸς τοῦ σοῦ τοῦδε ἑστεῶτος ἐν τοῖσι προθύροισι βαλὼν τύχοιμι μέσης τῆς καρδίης, Πέρσαι φανέονται λέγοντες οὐδέν· ἢν δὲ ἁμάρτω, φάναι Πέρσας τε λέγειν ἀληθέα καί με μὴ σωφρονέειν." [3] ταῦτα δὲ εἰπόντα καὶ διατείναντα τὸ τόξον βαλεῖν τὸν παῖδα, πεσόντος δὲ τοῦ παιδὸς ἀνασχίζειν αὐτὸν κελεύειν καὶ σκέψασθαι τὸ βλῆμα· ὡς δὲ ἐν τῇ καρδίῃ εὑρεθῆναι ἐνεόντα τὸν ὀιστόν, εἰπεῖν πρὸς τὸν πατέρα τοῦ παιδὸς γελάσαντα καὶ περιχαρέα γενόμενον [4] "Πρήξασπες, ὡς μὲν ἐγώ τε οὐ μαίνομαι Πέρσαι τε παραφρονέουσι, δῆλά τοι γέγονε. νῦν δέ μοι εἰπέ, τίνα εἶδες ἤδη πάντων ἀνθρώπων οὕτω ἐπίσκοπα τοξεύοντα;" Πρηξάσπεα δὲ ὁρῶντα ἄνδρα οὐ φρενήρεα καὶ περὶ ἑωυτῷ δειμαίνοντα εἰπεῖν "Δέσποτα, οὐδ' ἂν αὐτὸν ἔγωγε δοκέω τὸν θεὸν οὕτω ἂν καλῶς βαλεῖν." [5] τότε μὲν ταῦτα ἐξεργάσατο, ἑτέρωθι δὲ Περσέων ὁμοίους τοῖσι πρώτοισι δυώδεκα ἐπ' οὐδεμιῇ αἰτίῃ ἀξιοχρέῳ ἑλὼν ζώοντας ἐπὶ κεφαλὴν κατώρυξε.

36 ταῦτα δέ μιν ποιεῦντα ἐδικαίωσε Κροῖσος ὁ Λυδὸς νουθετῆσαι τοῖσιδε τοῖσι ἔπεσι. "Ὦ βασιλεῦ, μὴ πάντα ἡλικίῃ καὶ θυμῷ ἐπίτραπε, ἀλλ' ἴσχε καὶ καταλάμβανε σεωυτόν· ἀγαθόν τι πρόνοον εἶναι, σοφὸν δὲ ἡ προμηθίη. σὺ δὲ κτείνεις μὲν ἄνδρας σεωυτοῦ πολιήτας ἐπ' οὐδεμιῇ αἰτίῃ ἀξιοχρέῳ ἑλών, κτείνεις δὲ παῖδας. [2] ἢν δὲ πολλὰ τοιαῦτα ποιέῃς, ὅρα ὅκως μή σευ ἀποστήσονται Πέρσαι. ἐμοὶ δὲ πατὴρ σὸς Κῦρος ἐνετέλλετο πολλὰ κελεύων σε νουθετέειν καὶ ὑποτίθεσθαι ὅ τι ἂν εὑρίσκω ἀγαθόν." ὁ μὲν δὴ εὐνοίην φαίνων συνεβούλευέ οἱ ταῦτα· ὁ δ' ἀμείβετο τοῖσιδε. [3] "Σὺ καὶ ἐμοὶ τολμᾷς συμβουλεύειν, ὃς χρηστῶς μὲν τὴν σεωυτοῦ πατρίδα ἐπετρόπευσας, εὖ δὲ τῷ πατρὶ τῷ ἐμῷ συνεβούλευσας, κελεύων αὐτὸν Ἀράξεα ποταμὸν διαβάντα ἰέναι ἐπὶ Μασσαγέτας, βουλομένων ἐκείνων διαβαίνειν ἐς τὴν ἡμετέρην, καὶ ἀπὸ μὲν σεωυτὸν ὤλεσας τῆς σεωυτοῦ πατρίδος κακῶς προστάς, ἀπὸ δὲ ὤλεσας Κῦρον πειθόμενον σοί, ἀλλ' οὔτι χαίρων, ἐπεί τοι καὶ πάλαι ἐς σὲ προφάσιός τευ ἐδεόμην ἐπιλαβέσθαι." [4] ταῦτα δὲ εἴπας ἐλάμβανε τὸ τόξον ὡς κατατοξεύσων αὐτόν, Κροῖσος δὲ ἀναδραμὼν ἔθεε ἔξω. ὁ δὲ ἐπείτε τοξεῦσαι οὐκ εἶχε, ἐνετείλατο τοῖσι θεράπουσι λαβόντας μιν ἀποκτεῖναι. [5] οἱ δὲ θεράποντες ἐπιστάμενοι τὸν τρόπον αὐτοῦ κατακρύπτουσι τὸν Κροῖσον ἐπὶ τῷδε τῷ λόγῳ ὥστε, εἰ μὲν μεταμελήσῃ τῷ Καμβύσῃ καὶ ἐπιζητέῃ τὸν Κροῖσον, οἱ δὲ ἐκφήναντες αὐτὸν δῶρα λάμψονται ζωάγρια Κροίσου, ἢν δὲ μὴ μεταμέληται μηδὲ ποθέῃ μιν, τότε καταχρᾶσθαι. [6] ἐπόθησέ τε δὴ ὁ Καμβύσης τὸν Κροῖσον οὐ πολλῷ μετέπειτα χρόνῳ ὕστερον, καὶ οἱ θεράποντες μαθόντες τοῦτο ἐπηγγέλλοντο αὐτῷ ὡς περιείη. Καμβύσης δὲ Κροίσῳ μὲν συνήδεσθαι ἔφη περιεόντι, ἐκείνους μέντοι τοὺς περιποιήσαντας οὐ καταπροΐξεσθαι ἀλλ' ἀποκτενέειν· καὶ ἐποίησε ταῦτα.

37 ὁ μὲν δὴ τοιαῦτα πολλὰ ἐς Πέρσας τε καὶ τοὺς συμμάχους ἐξεμαίνετο, μένων ἐν Μέμφι καὶ θήκας τε παλαιὰς ἀνοίγων καὶ σκεπτόμενος τοὺς νεκρούς. [2] ὥς δὲ δὴ καὶ ἐς τοῦ Ἡφαίστου τὸ ἱρὸν ἦλθε καὶ πολλὰ τῷ ἀγάλματι κατεγέλασε. ἔστι γὰρ τοῦ Ἡφαίστου τὠγαλμα τοῖσι Φοινικηίοισι Παταΐκοισι ἐμφερέστατον, τοὺς οἱ Φοίνικες ἐν τῇσι πρῴρῃσι τῶν τριηρέων περιάγουσι. ὃς δὲ τούτους μὴ ὄπωπε, ὧδε σημανέω· πυγμαίου ἀνδρὸς μίμησίς ἐστιν. [3] ἐσῆλθε δὲ καὶ ἐς τῶν Καβείρων τὸ ἱρόν, ἐς τὸ οὐ θεμιτόν ἐστι ἐσιέναι ἄλλον γε ἢ τὸν ἱρέα· ταῦτα δὲ τὰ ἀγάλματα καὶ ἐνέπρησε πολλὰ κατασκώψας. ἔστι δὲ καὶ ταῦτα ὅμοια τοῖσι τοῦ Ἡφαίστου· τούτου δὲ σφεας παῖδας λέγουσι εἶναι.

38 πανταχῇ ὦν μοι δῆλα ἐστὶ ὅτι ἐμάνη μεγάλως ὁ Καμβύσης· οὐ γὰρ ἂν ἱροῖσί τε καὶ νομαίοισι ἐπεχείρησε καταγελᾶν. εἰ γάρ τις προθείη πᾶσι ἀνθρώποισι ἐκλέξασθαι κελεύων νόμους τοὺς καλλίστους ἐκ τῶν πάντων νόμων, διασκεψάμενοι ἂν ἑλοίατο ἕκαστοι τοὺς ἑωυτῶν· οὕτω νομίζουσι πολλόν τι καλλίστους τοὺς ἑωυτῶν νόμους ἕκαστοι εἶναι. [2] οὐκ ὦν οἰκός ἐστι ἄλλον γε ἢ μαινόμενον ἄνδρα γέλωτα τὰ τοιαῦτα τίθεσθαι· ὡς δὲ οὕτω νενομίκασι τὰ περὶ τοὺς νόμους οἱ πάντες ἄνθρωποι, πολλοῖσί τε καὶ ἄλλοισι τεκμηρίοισι πάρεστι σταθμώσασθαι, ἐν δὲ δὴ καὶ τῷδε. [3] Δαρεῖος ἐπὶ τῆς ἑωυτοῦ ἀρχῆς καλέσας Ἑλλήνων τοὺς παρεόντας εἴρετο ἐπὶ κόσῳ ἂν χρήματι βουλοίατο τοὺς πατέρας ἀποθνήσκοντας κατασιτέεσθαι· οἱ δὲ ἐπ᾽ οὐδενὶ ἔφασαν ἔρδειν ἂν τοῦτο. [4] Δαρεῖος δὲ μετὰ ταῦτα καλέσας Ἰνδῶν τοὺς καλεομένους Καλλατίας, οἳ τοὺς γονέας κατεσθίουσι, εἴρετο, παρεόντων τῶν Ἑλλήνων καὶ δι᾽ ἑρμηνέος μανθανόντων τὰ λεγόμενα, ἐπὶ τίνι χρήματι δεξαίατ᾽ ἂν τελευτῶντας τοὺς πατέρας κατακαίειν πυρί· οἱ δὲ ἀμβώσαντες μέγα εὐφημέειν μιν ἐκέλευον. οὕτω μέν νυν ταῦτα νενόμισται, καὶ ὀρθῶς μοι δοκέει Πίνδαρος ποιῆσαι νόμον πάντων βασιλέα φήσας εἶναι.

39 Καμβύσεω δὲ ἐπ᾽ Αἴγυπτον στρατευομένου ἐποιήσαντο καὶ Λακεδαιμόνιοι στρατηίην ἐπὶ Σάμον τε καὶ Πολυκράτεα τὸν Αἰάκεος, ὃς ἔσχε Σάμον ἐπαναστάς. [2] καὶ τὰ μὲν πρῶτα τριχῇ δασάμενος τὴν πόλιν τοῖσι ἀδελφεοῖσι Πανταγνώτῳ καὶ Συλοσῶντι ἔνειμε, μετὰ δὲ τὸν μὲν αὐτῶν ἀποκτείνας, τὸν δὲ νεώτερον Συλοσῶντα ἐξελάσας ἔσχε πᾶσαν Σάμον, σχὼν δὲ ξεινίην Ἀμάσι τῷ Αἰγύπτου βασιλέϊ συνεθήκατο, πέμπων τε δῶρα καὶ δεκόμενος ἄλλα παρ᾽ ἐκείνου. [3] ἐν χρόνῳ δὲ ὀλίγῳ αὐτίκα τοῦ Πολυκράτεος τὰ πρήγματα ηὔξετο καὶ ἦν βεβωμένα ἀνά τε τὴν Ἰωνίην καὶ τὴν ἄλλην Ἑλλάδα· ὅκου γὰρ ἰθύσειε στρατεύεσθαι, πάντα οἱ ἐχώρεε εὐτυχέως. ἔκτητο δὲ πεντηκοντέρους τε ἑκατὸν καὶ χιλίους τοξότας, ἔφερε δὲ καὶ ἦγε πάντας διακρίνων οὐδένα. [4] τῷ γὰρ φίλῳ ἔφη χαριεῖσθαι μᾶλλον ἀποδιδοὺς τὰ ἔλαβε ἢ ἀρχὴν μηδὲ λαβών. συχνὰς μὲν δὴ τῶν νήσων ἀραιρήκεε, πολλὰ δὲ καὶ τῆς ἠπείρου ἄστεα· ἐν δὲ δὴ καὶ Λεσβίους πανστρατιῇ βοηθέοντας Μιλησίοισι ναυμαχίῃ κρατήσας εἷλε, οἳ τὴν τάφρον περὶ τὸ τεῖχος τὸ ἐν Σάμῳ πᾶσαν δεδεμένοι ὤρυξαν.

40 καί κως τὸν Ἄμασιν εὐτυχέων μεγάλως ὁ Πολυκράτης οὐκ ἐλάνθανε, ἀλλά οἱ τοῦτ' ἦν ἐπιμελές. πολλῷ δὲ ἔτι πλεῦνός οἱ εὐτυχίης γινομένης γράψας ἐς βυβλίον τάδε ἐπέστειλε ἐς Σάμον. [2] " Ἄμασις Πολυκράτεϊ ὧδε λέγει. ἡδὺ μὲν πυνθάνεσθαι ἄνδρα φίλον καὶ ξεῖνον εὖ πρήσσοντα, ἐμοὶ δὲ αἱ σαὶ μεγάλαι εὐτυχίαι οὐκ ἀρέσκουσι, τὸ θεῖον ἐπισταμένῳ ὡς ἔστι φθονερόν· καί κως βούλομαι καὶ αὐτὸς καὶ τῶν ἂν κήδωμαι τὸ μέν τι εὐτυχέειν τῶν πρηγμάτων τὸ δὲ προσπταίειν, καὶ οὕτω διαφέρειν τὸν αἰῶνα ἐναλλὰξ πρήσσων ἢ εὐτυχέειν τὰ πάντα. [3] οὐδένα γάρ κω λόγῳ οἶδα ἀκούσας ὅστις ἐς τέλος οὐ κακῶς ἐτελεύτησε πρόρριζος, εὐτυχέων τὰ πάντα. σὺ νῦν ἐμοὶ πειθόμενος ποίησον πρὸς τὰς εὐτυχίας τοιάδε· [4] φροντίσας τὸ ἂν εὕρῃς ἐόν τοι πλείστου ἄξιον καὶ ἐπ' ᾧ σὺ ἀπολομένῳ μάλιστα τὴν ψυχὴν ἀλγήσεις, τοῦτο ἀπόβαλε οὕτω ὅκως μηκέτι ἥξει ἐς ἀνθρώπους· ἤν τε μὴ ἐναλλὰξ ἤδη τὠπὸ τούτου αἱ εὐτυχίαι τοι τῇσι πάθῃσι προσπίπτωσι, τρόπῳ τῷ ἐξ ἐμεῦ ὑποκειμένῳ ἀκέο."

41 ταῦτα ἐπιλεξάμενος ὁ Πολυκράτης καὶ νόῳ λαβὼν ὥς οἱ εὖ ὑπετίθετο ὁ Ἄμασις, ἐδίζητο ἐπ' ᾧ ἂν μάλιστα τὴν ψυχὴν ἀσηθείη ἀπολομένῳ τῶν κειμηλίων, διζήμενος δὲ εὕρισκε τόδε. ἦν οἱ σφρηγὶς τὴν ἐφόρεε χρυσόδετος, σμαράγδου μὲν λίθου ἐοῦσα, ἔργον δὲ ἦν Θεοδώρου τοῦ Τηλεκλέος Σαμίου. [2] ἐπεὶ ὦν ταύτην οἱ ἐδόκεε ἀποβαλεῖν, ἐποίεε τοιάδε· πεντηκόντερον πληρώσας ἀνδρῶν ἐσέβη ἐς αὐτήν, μετὰ δὲ ἀναγαγεῖν ἐκέλευε ἐς τὸ πέλαγος· ὡς δὲ ἀπὸ τῆς νήσου ἑκὰς ἐγένετο, περιελόμενος τὴν σφρηγῖδα πάντων ὁρώντων τῶν συμπλόων ῥίπτει ἐς τὸ πέλαγος. τοῦτο δὲ ποιήσας ἀπέπλεε, ἀπικόμενος δὲ ἐς τὰ οἰκία συμφορῇ ἐχρᾶτο.

42 πέμπτῃ δὲ ἢ ἕκτῃ ἡμέρῃ ἀπὸ τούτων τάδε οἱ συνήνεικε γενέσθαι. ἀνὴρ ἁλιεὺς λαβὼν ἰχθὺν μέγαν τε καὶ καλὸν ἠξίου μιν Πολυκράτεϊ δῶρον δοθῆναι· φέρων δὴ ἐπὶ τὰς θύρας Πολυκράτεϊ ἔφη ἐθέλειν ἐλθεῖν ἐς ὄψιν, χωρήσαντος δέ οἱ τούτου ἔλεγε διδοὺς τὸ ἰχθύν [2] "Ὦ βασιλεῦ, ἐγὼ τόνδε ἑλὼν οὐκ ἐδικαίωσα φέρειν ἐς ἀγορήν, καίπερ ἐὼν γε ἀποχειροβίοτος, ἀλλά μοι ἐδόκεε σεῦ τε εἶναι ἄξιος καὶ τῆς σῆς ἀρχῆς· σοὶ δή μιν φέρων δίδωμι." ὁ δὲ ἡσθεὶς τοῖσι ἔπεσι ἀμείβεται τοῖσιδε. "Κάρτα τε εὖ ἐποίησας καὶ χάρις διπλῆ τῶν τε λόγων καὶ τοῦ δώρου, καί σε ἐπὶ δεῖπνον καλέομεν." [3] ὁ μὲν δὴ ἁλιεὺς μέγα ποιεύμενος ταῦτα ἤιε ἐς τὰ οἰκία, τὸν δὲ ἰχθὺν τάμνοντες οἱ θεράποντες εὑρίσκουσι ἐν τῇ νηδύι αὐτοῦ ἐνεοῦσαν τὴν Πολυκράτεος σφρηγῖδα. [4] ὡς δὲ εἶδόν τε καὶ ἔλαβον τάχιστα, ἔφερον κεχαρηκότες παρὰ τὸν Πολυκράτεα, διδόντες δέ οἱ τὴν σφρηγῖδα ἔλεγον ὅτεῳ τρόπῳ εὑρέθη. τὸν δὲ ὡς ἐσῆλθε θεῖον εἶναι τὸ πρῆγμα, γράφει ἐς βυβλίον πάντα τὰ ποιήσαντά μιν οἷα καταλελάβηκε, γράψας δὲ ἐς Αἴγυπτον ἐπέθηκε.

43 ἐπιλεξάμενος δὲ ὁ Ἄμασις τὸ βυβλίον τὸ παρὰ τοῦ Πολυκράτεος ἧκον, ἔμαθε ὅτι ἐκκομίσαι τε ἀδύνατον εἴη ἀνθρώπῳ ἄνθρωπον ἐκ τοῦ μέλλοντος γίνεσθαι πρήγματος, καὶ ὅτι οὐκ εὖ τελευτήσειν μέλλοι Πολυκράτης εὐτυχέων τὰ πάντα, ὃς καὶ τὰ ἀποβάλλει εὑρίσκει. [2] πέμψας δέ οἱ κήρυκα ἐς Σάμον διαλύεσθαι ἔφη τὴν ξεινίην. τοῦδε δὲ εἵνεκεν ταῦτα ἐποίεε, ἵνα μὴ συντυχίης δεινῆς τε καὶ μεγάλης Πολυκράτεα καταλαβούσης αὐτὸς ἀλγήσειε τὴν ψυχὴν ὡς περὶ ξείνου ἀνδρός.

44 ἐπὶ τοῦτον δὴ ὦν τὸν Πολυκράτεα εὐτυχέοντα τὰ πάντα ἐστρατεύοντο Λακεδαιμόνιοι, ἐπικαλεσαμένων τῶν μετὰ ταῦτα Κυδωνίην τὴν ἐν Κρήτῃ κτισάντων Σαμίων. πέμψας δὲ κήρυκα λάθρῃ Σαμίων Πολυκράτης παρὰ Καμβύσεα τὸν Κύρου συλλέγοντα στρατὸν ἐπ' Αἴγυπτον, ἐδεήθη ὅκως ἂν καὶ παρ' ἑωυτὸν πέμψας ἐς Σάμον δέοιτο στρατοῦ. [2] Καμβύσης δὲ ἀκούσας τούτων προθύμως ἔπεμπε ἐς Σάμον δεόμενος Πολυκράτεος στρατὸν ναυτικὸν ἅμα πέμψαι ἑωυτῷ ἐπ' Αἴγυπτον. ὁ δὲ ἐπιλέξας τῶν ἀστῶν τοὺς ὑπώπτευε μάλιστα ἐς ἐπανάστασιν ἀπέπεμπε τεσσεράκοντα τριήρεσι, ἐντειλάμενος Καμβύσῃ ὀπίσω τούτους μὴ ἀποπέμπειν.

45 οἱ μὲν δὴ λέγουσι τοὺς ἀποπεμφθέντας Σαμίων ὑπὸ Πολυκράτεος οὐκ ἀπικέσθαι ἐς Αἴγυπτον, ἀλλ' ἐπείτε ἐγένοντο ἐν Καρπάθῳ πλέοντες, δοῦναι σφίσι λόγον, καί σφι ἁδεῖν τὸ προσωτέρω μηκέτι πλέειν· οἱ δὲ λέγουσι ἀπικομένους τε ἐς Αἴγυπτον καὶ φυλασσομένους ἐνθεῦτεν αὐτοὺς ἀποδρῆναι. [2] καταπλέουσι δὲ ἐς τὴν Σάμον Πολυκράτης νηυσὶ ἀντιάσας ἐς μάχην κατέστη· νικήσαντες δὲ οἱ κατιόντες ἀπέβησαν ἐς τὴν νῆσον, πεζομαχήσαντες δὲ ἐν αὐτῇ ἑσσώθησαν, καὶ οὕτω δὴ ἔπλεον ἐς Λακεδαίμονα. [3] εἰσὶ δὲ οἵ λέγουσι τοὺς ἀπ' Αἰγύπτου νικῆσαι Πολυκράτεα, λέγοντες ἐμοὶ δοκέειν οὐκ ὀρθῶς· οὐδὲν γὰρ ἔδει σφέας Λακεδαιμονίους ἐπικαλέεσθαι, εἴ περ αὐτοὶ ἦσαν ἱκανοὶ Πολυκράτεα παραστήσασθαι. πρὸς δὲ τούτοισι οὐδὲ λόγος αἱρέει, τῷ ἐπίκουροί τε μισθωτοὶ καὶ τοξόται οἰκήιοι ἦσαν πλήθεϊ πολλοί, τοῦτον ὑπὸ τῶν κατιόντων Σαμίων ἐόντων ὀλίγων ἑσσωθῆναι. [4] τῶν δ' ὑπ' ἑωυτῷ ἐόντων πολιητέων τὰ τέκνα καὶ τὰς γυναῖκας ὁ Πολυκράτης ἐς τοὺς νεωσοίκους συνειλήσας εἶχε ἑτοίμους, ἢν ἄρα προδιδῶσι οὗτοι πρὸς τοὺς κατιόντας, ὑποπρῆσαι αὐτοῖσι τοῖσι νεωσοίκοισι.

46 ἐπείτε δὲ οἱ ἐξελασθέντες Σαμίων ὑπὸ Πολυκράτεος ἀπίκοντο ἐς τὴν Σπάρτην, καταστάντες ἐπὶ τοὺς ἄρχοντας ἔλεγον πολλὰ οἷα κάρτα δεόμενοι· οἱ δέ σφι τῇ πρώτῃ καταστάσι ὑπεκρίναντο τὰ μὲν πρῶτα λεχθέντα ἐπιλελῆσθαι, τὰ δὲ ὕστατα οὐ συνιέναι. [2] μετὰ δὲ ταῦτα δεύτερα καταστάντες ἄλλο μὲν εἶπον οὐδέν, θύλακον δὲ φέροντες ἔφασαν τὸν θύλακον ἀλφίτων δέεσθαι. οἱ δέ σφι ὑπεκρίναντο τῷ θυλάκῳ περιεργάσθαι· βοηθέειν δ' ὦν ἔδοξε αὐτοῖσι.

47 καὶ ἔπειτα παρασκευασάμενοι ἐστρατεύοντο Λακεδαιμόνιοι ἐπὶ Σάμον, ὡς μὲν Σάμιοι λέγουσι, εὐεργεσίας ἐκτίνοντες, ὅτι σφι πρότεροι αὐτοὶ νηυσὶ ἐβοήθησαν ἐπὶ Μεσσηνίους, ὡς δὲ Λακεδαιμόνιοι λέγουσι, οὐκ οὕτω τιμωρῆσαι δεομένοισι Σαμίοισι ἐστρατεύοντο ὡς τίσασθαι βουλόμενοι τοῦ κρητῆρος τῆς ἁρπαγῆς, τὸν ἦγον Κροίσῳ, καὶ τοῦ θώρηκος, τὸν αὐτοῖσι Ἄμασις ὁ Αἰγύπτου βασιλεὺς ἔπεμπε δῶρον. [2] καὶ γὰρ θώρηκα ἐληίσαντο τῷ προτέρῳ ἔτεϊ ἢ τὸν κρητῆρα οἱ Σάμιοι, ἐόντα μὲν λίνεον καὶ ζῴων ἐνυφασμένων συχνῶν, κεκοσμημένον δὲ χρυσῷ καὶ εἰρίοισι ἀπὸ ξύλου· [3] τῶν δὲ εἵνεκα θωμάσαι ἄξιον, ἁρπεδόνη ἑκάστη τοῦ θώρηκος ποιέει· ἐοῦσα γὰρ λεπτὴ ἔχει ἁρπεδόνας ἐν ἑωυτῇ τριηκοσίας καὶ ἑξήκοντα, πάσας φανεράς. τοιοῦτος ἕτερος ἐστὶ καὶ τὸν ἐν Λίνδῳ ἀνέθηκε τῇ Ἀθηναίῃ Ἄμασις.

48 συνεπελάβοντο δὲ τοῦ στρατεύματος τοῦ ἐπὶ Σάμον ὥστε γενέσθαι καὶ Κορίνθιοι προθύμως· ὕβρισμα γὰρ καὶ ἐς τούτους εἶχε ἐκ τῶν Σαμίων γενόμενον γενεῇ πρότερον τοῦ στρατεύματος τούτου, κατὰ δὲ τὸν αὐτὸν χρόνον τοῦ κρητῆρος τῇ ἁρπάγῃ γεγονός. [2] Κερκυραίων γὰρ παῖδας τριηκοσίους ἀνδρῶν τῶν πρώτων Περίανδρος ὁ Κυψέλου ἐς Σάρδις ἀπέπεμψε παρὰ Ἀλυάττεα ἐπ' ἐκτομῇ· προσσχόντων δὲ ἐς τὴν Σάμον τῶν ἀγόντων τοὺς παῖδας Κορινθίων, πυθόμενοι οἱ Σάμιοι τὸν λόγον, ἐπ' οἷσι ἀγοίατο ἐς Σάρδις, πρῶτα μὲν τοὺς παῖδας ἐδίδαξαν ἱροῦ ἅψασθαι Ἀρτέμιδος· [3] μετὰ δὲ οὐ περιορῶντες ἀπέλκειν τοὺς ἱκέτας ἐκ τοῦ ἱροῦ, σιτίων δὲ τοὺς παῖδας ἐργόντων Κορινθίων, ἐποιήσαντο οἱ Σάμιοι ὁρτήν, τῇ καὶ νῦν ἔτι χρέωνται κατὰ ταὐτά. νυκτὸς γὰρ ἐπιγενομένης, ὅσον χρόνον ἱκέτευον οἱ παῖδες, ἵστασαν χοροὺς παρθένων τε καὶ ἠιθέων, ἱστάντες δὲ τοὺς χοροὺς τρωκτὰ σησάμου τε καὶ μέλιτος ἐποιήσαντο νόμον φέρεσθαι, ἵνα ἁρπάζοντες οἱ τῶν Κερκυραίων παῖδες ἔχοιεν τροφήν. [4] ἐς τοῦτο δὲ τόδε ἐγίνετο, ἐς ὃ οἱ Κορίνθιοι τῶν παίδων οἱ φύλακοι οἴχοντο ἀπολιπόντες· τοὺς δὲ παῖδας ἀπήγαγον ἐς Κέρκυραν οἱ Σάμιοι.

49 εἰ μέν νυν Περιάνδρου τελευτήσαντος τοῖσι Κορινθίοισι φίλα ἦν πρὸς τοὺς Κερκυραίους, οἱ δὲ οὐκ ἂν συνελάβοντο τοῦ στρατεύματος τοῦ ἐπὶ Σάμον ταύτης εἵνεκεν τῆς αἰτίης. νῦν δὲ αἰεὶ ἐπείτε ἔκτισαν τὴν νῆσον εἰσὶ ἀλλήλοισι διάφοροι, ἐόντες ἑωυτοῖσι. [2] τούτων ὦν εἵνεκεν ἀπεμνησικάκεον τοῖσι Σαμίοισι οἱ Κορίνθιοι. ἀπέπεμπε δὲ ἐς Σάρδις ἐπ' ἐκτομῇ Περίανδρος τῶν πρώτων Κερκυραίων ἐπιλέξας τοὺς παῖδας τιμωρεύμενος· πρότεροι γὰρ οἱ Κερκυραῖοι ἦρξαν ἐς αὐτὸν πρῆγμα ἀτάσθαλον ποιήσαντες.

50 ἐπείτε γὰρ τὴν ἑωυτοῦ γυναῖκα Μέλισσαν Περίανδρος ἀπέκτεινε, συμφορὴν τοιήνδε οἱ ἄλλην συνέβη πρὸς τῇ γεγονυίῃ γενέσθαι. ἦσάν οἱ ἐκ Μελίσσης δύο παῖδες, ἡλικίην ὁ μὲν ἑπτακαίδεκα ὁ δὲ ὀκτωκαίδεκα ἔτεα γεγονώς. [2] τούτους ὁ μητροπάτωρ Προκλέης ἐὼν Ἐπιδαύρου τύραννος μεταπεμψάμενος παρ' ἑωυτὸν ἐφιλοφρονέετο, ὡς οἰκὸς ἦν θυγατρὸς ἐόντας τῆς ἑωυτοῦ παῖδας. ἐπείτε δὲ σφέας ἀπεπέμπετο, εἶπε προπέμπων αὐτούς [3] "Ἆρα ἴστε, ὦ παῖδες, ὃς ὑμέων τὴν μητέρα ἀπέκτεινε;" τοῦτο τὸ ἔπος ὁ μὲν πρεσβύτερος αὐτῶν ἐν οὐδενὶ λόγῳ ἐποιήσατο· ὁ δὲ νεώτερος, τῷ οὔνομα ἦν Λυκόφρων, ἤλγησε ἀκούσας οὕτω ὥστε ἀπικόμενος ἐς τὴν Κόρινθον ἅτε φονέα τῆς μητρὸς τὸν πατέρα οὔτε προσεῖπε, διαλεγομένῳ τε οὔτε προσδιελέγετο ἱστορέοντί τε λόγον οὐδένα ἐδίδου. τέλος δέ μιν περιθύμως ἔχων ὁ Περίανδρος ἐξελαύνει ἐκ τῶν οἰκίων.

51 ἐξελάσας δὲ τοῦτον ἱστόρεε τὸν πρεσβύτερον τά σφι ὁ μητροπάτωρ διελέχθη. ὁ δέ οἱ ἀπηγέετο ὥς σφεας φιλοφρόνως ἐδέξατο· ἐκείνου δὲ τοῦ ἔπεος τό σφι ὁ Προκλέης ἀποστέλλων εἶπε ἅτε οὐ νόῳ λαβὼν οὐκ ἐμέμνητο. Περίανδρος δὲ οὐδεμίαν μηχανὴν ἔφη εἶναι μὴ οὔ σφι ἐκεῖνον ὑποθέσθαι τι, ἐλιπάρεέ τε ἱστορέων· ὁ δὲ ἀναμνησθεὶς εἶπε καὶ τοῦτο. [2] Περίανδρος δὲ νόῳ λαβὼν καὶ μαλακὸν ἐνδιδόναι βουλόμενος οὐδέν, τῇ ὁ ἐξελασθεὶς ὑπ' αὐτοῦ παῖς δίαιταν ἐποιέετο, ἐς τούτους πέμπων ἄγγελον ἀπηγόρευε μή μιν δέκεσθαι οἰκίοισι. [3] ὁ δὲ ὅκως ἀπελαυνόμενος ἔλθοι ἐς ἄλλην οἰκίην, ἀπηλαύνετ' ἂν καὶ ἀπὸ ταύτης, ἀπειλέοντός τε τοῦ Περιάνδρου τοῖσι δεξαμένοισι καὶ ἐξέργειν κελεύοντος· ἀπελαυνόμενος δ' ἂν ἤιε ἐπ' ἑτέρην τῶν ἑταίρων· οἱ δὲ ἅτε Περιάνδρου ἐόντα παῖδα καίπερ δειμαίνοντες ὅμως ἐδέκοντο.

52 τέλος δὲ ὁ Περίανδρος κήρυγμα ἐποιήσατο, ὃς ἂν ἢ οἰκίοισι ὑποδέξηταί μιν ἢ προσδιαλεχθῇ, ἱρὴν ζημίην τοῦτον τῷ Ἀπόλλωνι ὀφείλειν, ὅσην δὴ εἴπας. [2] πρὸς ὦν δὴ τοῦτο τὸ κήρυγμα οὔτε τίς οἱ διαλέγεσθαι οὔτε οἰκίοισι δέκεσθαι ἤθελε· πρὸς δὲ οὐδὲ αὐτὸς ἐκεῖνος ἐδικαίου πειρᾶσθαι ἀπειρημένου, ἀλλὰ διακαρτερέων ἐν τῇσι στοῇσι ἐκαλινδέετο. [3] τετάρτῃ δὲ ἡμέρῃ ἰδών μιν ὁ Περίανδρος ἀλουσίῃσί τε καὶ ἀσιτίῃσι συμπεπτωκότα οἴκτειρε· ὑπεὶς δὲ τῆς ὀργῆς ἤιε ἆσσον καὶ ἔλεγε [4] "Ὦ παῖ, κότερα τούτων αἱρετώτερά ἐστι, ταῦτα τὰ νῦν ἔχων πρήσσεις, ἢ τὴν τυραννίδα καὶ τὰ ἀγαθὰ τὰ νῦν ἐγὼ ἔχω, ταῦτα ἐόντα τῷ πατρὶ ἐπιτήδεον παραλαμβάνειν, ὃς ἐὼν ἐμός τε παῖς καὶ Κορίνθου τῆς εὐδαίμονος βασιλεὺς ἀλήτην βίον εἵλευ, ἀντιστατέων τε καὶ ὀργῇ χρεώμενος ἐς τὸν σε ἥκιστα ἐχρῆν. εἰ γάρ τις συμφορὴ ἐν αὐτοῖσι γέγονε, ἐξ ἧς ὑποψίην ἐς ἐμὲ ἔχεις, ἐμοί τε αὕτη γέγονε καὶ ἐγὼ αὐτῆς τὸ πλεῦν μέτοχός εἰμι, ὅσῳ αὐτὸς σφεα ἐξεργασάμην. [5] σὺ δὲ μαθὼν ὅσῳ φθονέεσθαι κρέσσον ἐστὶ ἢ οἰκτείρεσθαι, ἅμα τε ὁκοῖόν τι ἐς τοὺς τοκέας καὶ ἐς τοὺς κρέσσονας τεθυμῶσθαι, ἄπιθι ἐς τὰ οἰκία." [6] Περίανδρος μὲν τούτοισι αὐτὸν κατελάμβανε· ὁ δὲ ἄλλο μὲν οὐδὲν ἀμείβεται τὸν πατέρα, ἔφη δέ μιν ἱρὴν ζημίην ὀφείλειν τῷ θεῷ ἑωυτῷ ἐς λόγους ἀπικόμενον. μαθὼν δὲ ὁ Περίανδρος ὡς ἄπορόν τι τὸ κακὸν εἴη τοῦ παιδὸς καὶ ἀνίκητον, ἐξ ὀφθαλμῶν μιν ἀποπέμπεται στείλας πλοῖον ἐς Κέρκυραν· ἐπεκράτεε γὰρ καὶ ταύτης. [7] ἀποστείλας δὲ τοῦτον ὁ Περίανδρος ἐστρατεύετο ἐπὶ τὸν πενθερὸν Προκλέα ὡς τῶν παρεόντων οἱ πρηγμάτων ἐόντα αἰτιώτατον, καὶ εἷλε μὲν τὴν Ἐπίδαυρον, εἷλε δὲ αὐτὸν Προκλέα καὶ ἐζώγρησε.

53 ἐπεὶ δὲ τοῦ χρόνου προβαίνοντος ὁ τε Περίανδρος παρηβήκεε καὶ συνεγινώσκετο ἑωυτῷ οὐκέτι εἶναι δυνατὸς τὰ πρήγματα ἐπορᾶν τε καὶ διέπειν, πέμψας ἐς τὴν Κέρκυραν ἀπεκάλεε τὸν Λυκόφρονα ἐπὶ τὴν τυραννίδα· ἐν γὰρ δὴ τῷ πρεσβυτέρῳ τῶν παίδων οὔκων ἐνώρα, ἀλλά οἱ κατεφαίνετο εἶναι νωθέστερος. [2] ὁ δὲ Λυκόφρων οὐδὲ ἀνακρίσιος ἠξίωσε τὸν φέροντα τὴν ἀγγελίην. Περίανδρος δὲ περιεχόμενος τοῦ νεηνίεω δεύτερα ἀπέστειλε ἐπ' αὐτὸν τὴν ἀδελφεήν, ἑωυτοῦ δὲ θυγατέρα, δοκέων μιν μάλιστα ταύτῃ ἂν πείθεσθαι. [3] ἀπικομένης δὲ ταύτης καὶ λεγούσης· "Ὦ παῖ, βούλεαι τήν τε τυραννίδα ἐς ἄλλους πεσεῖν καὶ τὸν οἶκον τοῦ πατρὸς διαφορηθέντα μᾶλλον ἢ αὐτός σφεα ἀπελθὼν ἔχειν; ἄπιθι ἐς τὰ οἰκία, παῦσαι σεωυτὸν ζημιῶν. [4] ἡ φιλοτιμίη κτῆμα σκαιόν. μὴ τῷ κακῷ τὸ κακὸν ἰῶ. πολλοὶ τῶν δικαίων τὰ ἐπιεικέστερα προτιθεῖσι, πολλοὶ δὲ ἤδη τὰ μητρώια διζήμενοι τὰ πατρώια ἀπέβαλον. τυραννὶς χρῆμα σφαλερόν, πολλοὶ δὲ αὐτῆς ἐρασταί εἰσι, ὁ δὲ γέρων τε ἤδη καὶ παρηβηκώς· μὴ δῷς τὰ σεωυτοῦ ἀγαθὰ ἄλλοισι." [5] ἡ μὲν δὴ τὰ ἐπαγωγότατα διδαχθεῖσα ὑπὸ τοῦ πατρὸς ἔλεγε πρὸς αὐτόν· ὁ δὲ ὑποκρινάμενος ἔφη οὐδαμὰ ἥξειν ἐς Κόρινθον, ἔστ' ἂν πυνθάνηται περιεόντα τὸν πατέρα. [6] ἀπαγγειλάσης δὲ ταύτης ταῦτα, τὸ τρίτον Περίανδρος κήρυκα πέμπει βουλόμενος αὐτὸς μὲν ἐς Κέρκυραν ἥκειν, ἐκεῖνον δὲ ἐκέλευε ἐς Κόρινθον ἀπικόμενον διάδοχον γίνεσθαι τῆς τυραννίδος. [7] καταινέσαντος δὲ ἐπὶ τούτοισι τοῦ παιδός, ὁ μὲν Περίανδρος ἐστέλλετο ἐς τὴν Κέρκυραν, ὁ δὲ παῖς οἱ ἐς τὴν Κόρινθον. μαθόντες δὲ οἱ Κερκυραῖοι τούτων ἕκαστα, ἵνα μή σφι Περίανδρος ἐς τὴν χώρην ἀπίκηται, κτείνουσι τὸν νεηνίσκον. ἀντὶ τούτων μὲν Περίανδρος Κερκυραίους ἐτιμωρέετο.

54 Λακεδαιμόνιοι δὲ στόλῳ μεγάλῳ ὡς ἀπίκοντο, ἐπολιόρκεον Σάμον· προσβαλόντες δὲ πρὸς τὸ τεῖχος τοῦ μὲν πρὸς θαλάσσῃ ἑστεῶτος πύργου κατὰ τὸ προάστειον τῆς πόλιος ἐπέβησαν, μετὰ δὲ αὐτοῦ βοηθήσαντος Πολυκράτεος χειρὶ πολλῇ ἀπηλάσθησαν. [2] κατὰ δὲ τὸν ἐπάνω πύργον τὸν ἐπὶ τῆς ῥάχιος τοῦ ὄρεος ἐπεόντα ἐπεξῆλθον οἵ τε ἐπίκουροι καὶ αὐτῶν Σαμίων συχνοί, δεξάμενοι δὲ τοὺς Λακεδαιμονίους ἐπ' ὀλίγον χρόνον ἔφευγον ὀπίσω, οἱ δὲ ἐπισπόμενοι ἔκτεινον.

55 εἰ μέν νυν οἱ παρεόντες Λακεδαιμονίων ὅμοιοι ἐγένοντο ταύτην τὴν ἡμέρην Ἀρχίῃ τε καὶ Λυκώπῃ, αἱρέθη ἂν Σάμος. Ἀρχίης γὰρ καὶ Λυκώπης μοῦνοι συνεσπεσόντες φεύγουσι ἐς τὸ τεῖχος τοῖσι Σαμίοισι καὶ ἀποκληισθέντες τῆς ὀπίσω ὁδοῦ ἀπέθανον ἐν τῇ πόλι τῇ Σαμίων. [2] τρίτῳ δὲ ἀπ' Ἀρχίεω τούτου γεγονότι ἄλλῳ Ἀρχίῃ τῷ Σαμίου τοῦ Ἀρχίεω αὐτὸς ἐν Πιτάνῃ συνεγενόμην, δήμου γὰρ τούτου ἦν, ὃς ξείνων πάντων μάλιστα ἐτίμα τε Σαμίους καί οἱ τῷ πατρὶ ἔφη Σάμιον τοὔνομα τεθῆναι, ὅτι οἱ ὁ πατὴρ Ἀρχίης ἐν Σάμῳ ἀριστεύσας ἐτελεύτησε· τιμᾶν δὲ Σαμίους ἔφη, διότι ταφῆναί οἱ τὸν πάππον δημοσίῃ ὑπὸ Σαμίων.

56 Λακεδαιμόνιοι δέ, ὥς σφι τεσσεράκοντα ἐγεγόνεσαν ἡμέραι πολιορκέουσι Σάμον ἐς τὸ πρόσω τε οὐδὲν προεκόπτετο τῶν πρηγμάτων, ἀπαλλάσσοντο ἐς Πελοπόννησον. [2] ὡς δέ ὁ ματαιότερος λόγος ὅρμηται λεγέσθαι Πολυκράτεα ἐπιχώριον νόμισμα κόψαντα πολλὸν μολύβδου καταχρυσώσαντα δοῦναί σφι, τοὺς δὲ δεξαμένους οὕτω δὴ ἀπαλλάσσεσθαι. ταύτην πρῶτον στρατηίην ἐς τὴν Ἀσίην Λακεδαιμόνιοι Δωριέες ἐποιήσαντο.

57 οἱ δ' ἐπὶ τὸν Πολυκράτεα στρατευσάμενοι Σαμίων, ἐπεὶ οἱ Λακεδαιμόνιοι αὐτοὺς ἀπολιπεῖν ἔμελλον, καὶ αὐτοὶ ἀπέπλεον ἐς Σίφνον. [2] χρημάτων γὰρ ἐδέοντο, τὰ δὲ τῶν Σιφνίων πρήγματα ἤκμαζε τοῦτον τὸν χρόνον, καὶ νησιωτέων μάλιστα ἐπλούτεον, ἅτε ἐόντων αὐτοῖσι ἐν τῇ νήσῳ χρυσέων καὶ ἀργυρέων μετάλλων, οὕτως ὥστε ἀπὸ τῆς δεκάτης τῶν γινομένων αὐτόθεν χρημάτων θησαυρὸς ἐν Δελφοῖσι ἀνάκειται ὅμοια τοῖσι πλουσιωτάτοισι· αὐτοὶ δὲ τὰ γίνομενα τῷ ἐνιαυτῷ ἑκάστῳ χρήματα διενέμοντο. [3] ὅτε ὦν ἐποιεῦντο τὸν θησαυρόν, ἐχρέωντο τῷ χρηστηρίῳ εἰ αὐτοῖσι τὰ παρεόντα ἀγαθὰ οἷά τε ἐστὶ πολλὸν χρόνον παραμένειν· ἡ δὲ Πυθίη ἔχρησέ σφι τάδε.

[4]   ἀλλ' ὅταν ἐν Σίφνῳ πρυτανήια λευκὰ γένηται
      λεύκοφρύς τ' ἀγορή, τότε δὴ δεῖ φράδμονος ἀνδρὸς
      φράσσασθαι ξύλινόν τε λόχον κήρυκά τ' ἐρυθρόν."

τοῖσι δὲ Σιφνίοισι ἦν τότε ἡ ἀγορὴ καὶ τὸ πρυτανήιον Παρίῳ λίθῳ ἠσκημένα.

58 τοῦτον τὸν χρησμὸν οὐκ οἷοί τε ἦσαν γνῶναι οὔτε τότε εὐθὺς οὔτε τῶν Σαμίων ἀπιγμένων. ἐπείτε γὰρ τάχιστα πρὸς τὴν Σίφνον προσῖσχον οἱ Σάμιοι, ἔπεμπον τῶν νεῶν μίαν πρέσβεας ἄγουσαν ἐς τὴν πόλιν. [2] τὸ δὲ παλαιὸν ἅπασαι αἱ νέες ἦσαν μιλτηλιφέες, καὶ ἦν τοῦτο τὸ ἡ Πυθίη προηγόρευε τοῖσι Σιφνίοισι φυλάξασθαι τὸν ξύλινον λόχον κελεύουσα καὶ κήρυκα ἐρυθρόν. [3] ἀπικόμενοι ὦν οἱ ἄγγελοι ἐδέοντο τῶν Σιφνίων δέκα τάλαντά σφι χρῆσαι· οὐ φασκόντων δὲ χρήσειν τῶν Σιφνίων αὐτοῖσι, οἱ Σάμιοι τοὺς χώρους αὐτῶν ἐπόρθεον. [4] πυθόμενοι δὲ εὐθὺς ἦκον οἱ Σίφνιοι βοηθέοντες καὶ συμβαλόντες αὐτοῖσι ἐσσώθησαν, καὶ αὐτῶν πολλοὶ ἀπεκλήσθησαν τοῦ ἄστεος ὑπὸ τῶν Σαμίων καὶ αὐτοὺς μετὰ ταῦτα ἑκατὸν τάλαντα ἔπρηξαν.

59 παρὰ δὲ Ἑρμιονέων νῆσον ἀντὶ χρημάτων παρέλαβον, Ὑδρέην τὴν ἐπὶ Πελοποννήσῳ καὶ αὐτὴν Τροιζηνίοισι παρακατέθεντο· αὐτοὶ δὲ Κυδωνίην τὴν ἐν Κρήτῃ ἔκτισαν, οὐκ ἐπὶ τοῦτο πλέοντες, ἀλλὰ Ζακυνθίους ἐξελῶντες ἐκ τῆς νήσου. [2] ἔμειναν δ' ἐν ταύτῃ καὶ εὐδαιμόνησαν ἐπ' ἔτεα πέντε, ὥστε τὰ ἱρὰ τὰ ἐν Κυδωνίῃ ἐόντα νῦν οὗτοί εἰσι οἱ ποιήσαντες καὶ τὸν τῆς Δικτύνης νηόν. [3] ἕκτῳ δὲ ἔτεϊ Αἰγινῆται αὐτοὺς ναυμαχίῃ νικήσαντες ἠνδραποδίσαντο μετὰ Κρητῶν, καὶ τῶν νεῶν καπρίους ἐχουσέων τὰς πρῴρας ἠκρωτηρίασαν καὶ ἀνέθεσαν ἐς τὸ ἱρὸν τῆς Ἀθηναίης ἐν Αἰγίνῃ. [4] ταῦτα δὲ ἐποίησαν

ἔγκοτον ἔχοντες Σαμίοισι Αἰγινῆται· πρότεροι γὰρ Σάμιοι ἐπ' Ἀμφικράτεος βασιλεύοντος ἐν Σάμῳ στρατευσάμενοι ἐπ' Αἴγιναν μεγάλα κακὰ ἐποίησαν Αἰγινήτας καὶ ἔπαθον ὑπ' ἐκείνων. ἡ μὲν αἰτίη αὕτη.

60 ἐμήκυνα δὲ περὶ Σαμίων μᾶλλον, ὅτι σφι τρία ἐστὶ μέγιστα ἁπάντων Ἑλλήνων ἐξεργασμένα, ὄρεός τε ὑψηλοῦ ἐς πεντήκοντα καὶ ἑκατὸν ὀργυιάς, τούτου ὄρυγμα κάτωθεν ἀρξάμενον, ἀμφίστομον. [2] τὸ μὲν μῆκος τοῦ ὀρύγματος ἑπτὰ στάδιοί εἰσι, τὸ δὲ ὕψος καὶ εὖρος ὀκτὼ ἑκάτερον πόδες. διὰ παντὸς δὲ αὐτοῦ ἄλλο ὄρυγμα εἰκοσίπηχυ βάθος ὀρώρυκται, τρίπουν δὲ τὸ εὖρος, δι' οὗ τὸ ὕδωρ ὀχετευόμενον διὰ τῶν σωλήνων παραγίνεται ἐς τὴν πόλιν ἀγόμενον ἀπὸ μεγάλης πηγῆς. [3] ἀρχιτέκτων δὲ τοῦ ὀρύγματος τούτου ἐγένετο Μεγαρεὺς Εὐπαλῖνος Ναυστρόφου. τοῦτο μὲν δὴ ἓν τῶν τριῶν ἐστι, δεύτερον δὲ περὶ λιμένα χῶμα ἐν θαλάσσῃ, βάθος καὶ εἴκοσι ὀργυιέων· μῆκος δὲ τοῦ χώματος μέζον δύο σταδίων. [4] τρίτον δέ σφι ἐξέργασται νηὸς μέγιστος πάντων νηῶν τῶν ἡμεῖς ἴδμεν· τοῦ ἀρχιτέκτων πρῶτος ἐγένετο Ῥοῖκος Φιλέω ἐπιχώριος. τούτων εἵνεκεν μᾶλλόν τι περὶ Σαμίων ἐμήκυνα.

61 Καμβύσῃ δὲ τῷ Κύρου χρονίζοντι περὶ Αἴγυπτον καὶ παραφρονήσαντι ἐπανιστέαται ἄνδρες Μάγοι δύο ἀδελφεοί, τῶν τὸν ἕτερον καταλελοίπεε τῶν οἴκων μελεδωνὸν ὁ Καμβύσης. οὗτος δὴ ὦν οἱ ἐπανέστη μαθών τε τὸν Σμέρδιος θάνατον ὡς κρύπτοιτο γενόμενος, καὶ ὡς ὀλίγοι εἴησαν οἱ ἐπιστάμενοι αὐτὸν Περσέων, οἱ δὲ πολλοὶ περιεόντα μιν εἰδείησαν. [2] πρὸς ταῦτα βουλεύσας τάδε ἐπεχείρησε τοῖσι βασιληίοισι. ἦν οἱ ἀδελφεός, τὸν εἶπά οἱ συνεπαναστῆναι, οἰκὼς μάλιστα τὸ εἶδος Σμέρδι τῷ Κύρου, τὸν ὁ Καμβύσης ἐόντα ἑωυτοῦ ἀδελφεὸν ἀπέκτεινε· ἦν τε δὴ ὅμοιος εἶδος τῷ Σμέρδι καὶ δὴ καὶ οὔνομα τὠυτὸ εἶχε Σμέρδιν. [3] τοῦτον τὸν ἄνδρα ἀναγνώσας ὁ Μάγος Πατιζείθης ὥς οἱ αὐτὸς πάντα διαπρήξει, εἷσε ἄγων ἐς τὸν βασιλήιον θρόνον. ποιήσας δὲ τοῦτο κήρυκας τῇ τε ἄλλῃ διέπεμπε καὶ δὴ καὶ ἐς Αἴγυπτον προερέοντα τῷ στρατῷ ὡς Σμέρδιος τοῦ Κύρου ἀκουστέα εἴη τοῦ λοιποῦ ἀλλ' οὐ Καμβύσεω.

62 οἵ τε δὴ ὦν ἄλλοι κήρυκες προηγόρευον ταῦτα καὶ δὴ καὶ ὁ ἐπ' Αἴγυπτον ταχθείς, εὕρισκε γὰρ Καμβύσεα καὶ τὸν στρατὸν ἐόντα τῆς Συρίης ἐν Ἀγβατάνοισι, προηγόρευε στὰς ἐς μέσον τὰ ἐντεταλμένα ἐκ τοῦ Μάγου. [2] Καμβύσης δὲ ἀκούσας ταῦτα ἐκ τοῦ κήρυκος καὶ ἐλπίσας μιν λέγειν ἀληθέα αὐτός τε προδεδόσθαι ἐκ Πρηξάσπεος, πεμφθέντα γὰρ αὐτὸν ὡς ἀποκτενέοντα Σμέρδιν οὐ ποιῆσαι ταῦτα, βλέψας ἐς τὸν Πρηξάσπεα εἶπε· "Πρήξασπες, οὕτω μοι διεπρήξαο τό τοι προσέθηκα πρῆγμα;" ὁ δὲ εἶπε· [3] "Ὦ δέσποτα, οὐκ ἔστι ταῦτα ἀληθέα, ὅκως κοτέ σοι Σμέρδις ἀδελφεὸς σὸς ἐπανέστηκε, οὐδὲ ὅκως τι ἐξ ἐκείνου τοῦ ἀνδρὸς νεῖκός τοι ἔσται ἢ μέγα ἢ σμικρόν· ἐγὼ γὰρ αὐτός, ποιήσας τὰ σύ με ἐκέλευες, ἔθαψά μιν χερσὶ τῇσι ἐμεωυτοῦ. [4] εἰ μέν νυν οἱ τεθνεῶτες ἀνεστᾶσι, προσδέκεό τοι καὶ Ἀστυάγεα τὸν Μῆδον ἐπαναστήσεσθαι· εἰ δ' ἔστι ὥσπερ πρὸ τοῦ, οὐ μή τί τοι ἔκ γε ἐκείνου νεώτερον ἀναβλάστῃ. νῦν ὦν μοι δοκέει μεταδιώξαντας τὸν κήρυκα ἐξετάζειν εἰρωτεῦντας παρ' ὅτευ ἥκων προαγορεύει ἡμῖν Σμέρδιος βασιλέος ἀκούειν."

63 ταῦτα εἴπαντος Πρηξάσπεος, ἤρεσε γὰρ Καμβύσῃ, αὐτίκα μεταδίωκτος γενόμενος ὁ κῆρυξ ἧκε· ἀπιγμένον δέ μιν εἴρετο ὁ Πρηξάσπης τάδε. "Ὤνθρωπε, φὴς γὰρ ἥκειν παρὰ Σμέρδιος τοῦ Κύρου ἄγγελος· νῦν ὦν εἴπας τὴν ἀληθείην ἄπιθι χαίρων, κότερα αὐτός τοι Σμέρδις φαινόμενος ἐς ὄψιν ἐνετέλλετο ταῦτα ἢ τῶν τις ἐκείνου ὑπηρετέων." [2] ὁ δὲ εἶπε "Ἐγὼ Σμέρδιν μὲν τὸν Κύρου, ἐξ ὅτευ βασιλεὺς Καμβύσης ἤλασε ἐς Αἴγυπτον, οὔκω ὄπωπα· ὁ δέ μοι Μάγος τὸν Καμβύσης ἐπίτροπον τῶν οἰκίων ἀπέδεξε, οὗτος ταῦτα ἐνετείλατο, φὰς Σμέρδιν τὸν Κύρου εἶναι τὸν ταῦτα ἐπιθέμενον εἶπαι πρὸς ὑμέας." [3] ὁ μὲν δή σφι ἔλεγε οὐδὲν ἐπικατεψευσάμενος, Καμβύσης δὲ εἶπε "Πρήξασπες, σὺ μὲν οἷα ἀνὴρ ἀγαθὸς ποιήσας τὸ κελευόμενον αἰτίην ἐκπέφευγας· ἐμοὶ δὲ τίς ἂν εἴη Περσέων ὁ ἐπανεστεὼς ἐπιβατεύων τοῦ Σμέρδιος οὐνόματος;" [4] ὁ δὲ εἶπε "Ἐγώ μοι δοκέω συνιέναι τὸ γεγονὸς τοῦτο, ὦ βασιλεῦ· οἱ Μάγοι εἰσί τοι οἱ ἐπανεστεῶτες, τόν τε ἔλιπες μελεδωνὸν τῶν οἰκίων, Πατιζείθης καὶ ὁ τούτου ἀδελφεὸς Σμέρδις."

64 ἐνθαῦτα ἀκούσαντα Καμβύσεα τὸ Σμέρδιος οὔνομα ἔτυψε ἡ ἀληθείη τῶν τε λόγων καὶ τοῦ ἐνυπνίου· ὃς ἐδόκεε ἐν τῷ ὕπνῳ ἀπαγγεῖλαι τινά οἱ ὡς Σμέρδις ἱζόμενος ἐς τὸν βασιλήιον θρόνον ψαύσειε τῇ κεφαλῇ τοῦ οὐρανοῦ. [2] μαθὼν δὲ ὡς μάτην ἀπολωλεκὼς εἴη τὸν ἀδελφεόν, ἀπέκλαιε Σμέρδιν· ἀποκλαύσας δὲ καὶ περιημεκτήσας τῇ ἁπάσῃ συμφορῇ ἀναθρῴσκει ἐπὶ τὸν ἵππον, ἐν νόῳ ἔχων τὴν ταχίστην ἐς Σοῦσα στρατεύεσθαι ἐπὶ τὸν Μάγον. [3] καί οἱ ἀναθρῴσκοντι ἐπὶ τὸν ἵππον τοῦ κολεοῦ τοῦ ξίφεος ὁ μύκης ἀποπίπτει, γυμνωθὲν δὲ τὸ ξίφος παίει τὸν μηρόν· τρωματισθεὶς δὲ κατὰ τοῦτο τῇ αὐτὸς πρότερον τὸν τῶν Αἰγυπτίων θεὸν Ἆπιν ἔπληξε, ὥς οἱ καιρίη ἔδοξε τετύφθαι, εἴρετο ὁ Καμβύσης ὅ τι τῇ πόλι οὔνομα εἴη· [4] οἱ δὲ εἶπαν ὅτι Ἀγβάτανα. τῷ δὲ ἔτι πρότερον ἐκέχρηστο ἐκ Βουτοῦς πόλιος ἐν Ἀγβατάνοισι τελευτήσειν τὸν βίον. ὁ μὲν δὴ ἐν τοῖσι Μηδικοῖσι Ἀγβατάνοισι ἐδόκεε τελευτήσειν γηραιός, ἐν τοῖσί οἱ ἦν τὰ πάντα πρήγματα· τὸ δὲ χρηστήριον ἐν τοῖσι ἐν Συρίῃ Ἀγβατάνοισι ἔλεγε ἄρα. [5] καὶ δὴ ὡς τότε ἐπειρόμενος ἐπύθετο τῆς πόλιος τὸ οὔνομα, ὑπὸ τῆς συμφορῆς τῆς τε ἐκ τοῦ Μάγου ἐκπεπληγμένος καὶ τοῦ τρώματος ἐσωφρόνησε, συλλαβὼν δὲ τὸ θεοπρόπιον εἶπε " Ἐνθαῦτα Καμβύσεα τὸν Κύρου ἐστί πεπρωμένον τελευτᾶν."

65 τότε μὲν τοσαῦτα. ἡμέρῃσι δὲ ὕστερον ὡς εἴκοσι μεταπεμψάμενος Περσέων τῶν παρεόντων τοὺς λογιμωτάτους ἔλεγέ σφι τάδε. "Ὦ Πέρσαι, καταλελάβηκέ με, τὸ πάντων μάλιστα ἔκρυπτον πρηγμάτων, τοῦτο ἐς ὑμέας ἐκφῆναι. [2] ἐγὼ γὰρ ἐὼν ἐν Αἰγύπτῳ εἶδον ὄψιν ἐν τῷ ὕπνῳ, τὴν μηδαμὰ ὤφελον ἰδεῖν· ἐδόκεον δέ μοι ἄγγελον ἐλθόντα ἐξ οἴκου ἀγγέλλειν ὡς Σμέρδις ἱζόμενος ἐς τὸν βασιλήιον θρόνον ψαύσειε τῇ κεφαλῇ τοῦ οὐρανοῦ. [3] δείσας δὲ μὴ ἀπαιρεθέω τὴν ἀρχὴν πρὸς τοῦ ἀδελφεοῦ, ἐποίησα ταχύτερα ἢ σοφώτερα· ἐν τῇ γὰρ ἀνθρωπηίῃ φύσι οὐκ ἐνῆν ἄρα τὸ μέλλον γίνεσθαι ἀποτράπειν. ἐγὼ δὲ ὁ μάταιος Πρηξάσπεα ἀποπέμπω ἐς Σοῦσα ἀποκτενέοντα Σμέρδιν. ἐξεργασθέντος δὲ κακοῦ τοσούτου ἀδεῶς διαιτώμην, οὐδαμὰ ἐπιλεξάμενος μή κοτέ τίς μοι Σμέρδιος ὑπαιρημένου ἄλλος ἐπαναισταίη ἀνθρώπων. [4] παντὸς δὲ τοῦ μέλλοντος ἔσεσθαι ἁμαρτὼν ἀδελφεοκτόνος τε οὐδὲν δέον γέγονα καὶ τῆς βασιληίης οὐδὲν ἧσσον ἐστέρημαι· Σμέρδις γὰρ δὴ ἦν ὁ Μάγος τόν μοι ὁ δαίμων προέφαινε ἐν τῇ ὄψι ἐπαναστήσεσθαι. [5] τὸ μὲν δὴ ἔργον ἐξέργασταί μοι, καὶ Σμέρδιν τὸν Κύρου μηκέτι ὑμῖν ἐόντα λογίζεσθε· οἱ δὲ ὑμῖν Μάγοι κρατέουσι τῶν βασιληίων, τόν τε ἔλιπον ἐπίτροπον τῶν οἰκίων καὶ ὁ ἐκείνου ἀδελφεὸς Σμέρδις. τὸν μέν νυν μάλιστα χρῆν ἐμεῦ αἰσχρὰ πρὸς τῶν Μάγων πεπονθότος τιμωρέειν ἐμοί, οὗτος μὲν ἀνοσίῳ μόρῳ τετελεύτηκε ὑπὸ τῶν ἑωυτοῦ οἰκηιοτάτων· [6] τούτου δὲ μηκέτι ἐόντος, δεύτερα τῶν λοιπῶν ὑμῖν, ὦ Πέρσαι, γίνεταί μοι ἀναγκαιότατον ἐντέλλεσθαι τὰ θέλω μοι γενέσθαι τελευτῶν τὸν βίον· καὶ δὴ ὑμῖν τάδε ἐπισκήπτω θεοὺς τοὺς βασιληίους ἐπικαλέων καὶ πᾶσι ὑμῖν καὶ μάλιστα Ἀχαιμενιδέων τοῖσι παρεοῦσι, μὴ περιιδεῖν τὴν ἡγεμονίην αὖτις ἐς Μήδους περιελθοῦσαν, ἀλλ᾽ εἴτε δόλῳ ἔχουσι αὐτὴν κτησάμενοι, δόλῳ ἀπαιρεθῆναι ὑπὸ ὑμέων, εἴτε καὶ σθένεϊ τέῳ κατεργασάμενοι, σθένεϊ κατὰ τὸ καρτερὸν ἀνασώσασθαι. [7] καὶ ταῦτα μὲν ποιεῦσι ὑμῖν γῆ τε καρπὸν ἐκφέροι καὶ γυναῖκές τε καὶ ποῖμναι τίκτοιεν, ἐοῦσι ἐς τὸν ἅπαντα χρόνον ἐλευθέροισι· μὴ δὲ ἀνασωσαμένοισι τὴν ἀρχὴν μηδ᾽ ἐπιχειρήσασι ἀνασώζειν τὰ ἐναντία τούτοισι ἀρῶμαι ὑμῖν γενέσθαι, καὶ πρὸς ἔτι τούτοισι τὸ τέλος Περσέων ἑκάστῳ ἐπιγενέσθαι οἷον ἐμοὶ ἐπιγέγονε." ἅμα τε εἴπας ταῦτα ὁ Καμβύσης ἀπέκλαιε πᾶσαν τὴν ἑωυτοῦ πρῆξιν.

66 Πέρσαι δὲ ὡς τὸν βασιλέα εἶδον ἀνακλαύσαντα πάντες τά τε ἐσθῆτος ἐχόμενα εἶχον, ταῦτα κατηρείκοντο καὶ οἰμωγῇ ἀφθόνῳ διεχρέωντο. [2] μετὰ δὲ ταῦτα ὡς ἐσφακέλισέ τε τὸ ὀστέον καὶ ὁ μηρὸς τάχιστα ἐσάπη, ἀπήνεικε Καμβύσεα τὸν Κύρου, βασιλεύσαντα μὲν τὰ πάντα ἑπτὰ ἔτεα καὶ πέντε μῆνας, ἄπαιδα δὲ τὸ παράπαν ἐόντα ἔρσενος καὶ θήλεος γόνου. [3] Περσέων δὲ τοῖσι παρεοῦσι ἀπιστίη πολλὴ ὑπεκέχυτο τοὺς Μάγους ἔχειν τὰ πρήγματα, ἀλλ᾽ ἠπιστέατο ἐπὶ διαβολῇ εἰπεῖν Καμβύσεα τὰ εἶπε περὶ τοῦ Σμέρδιος θανάτου, ἵνα οἱ ἐκπολεμωθῇ πᾶν τὸ Περσικόν.

67 οὗτοι μέν νυν ἠπιστέατο Σμέρδιν τὸν Κύρου βασιλέα ἐνεστεῶτα· δεινῶς γὰρ καὶ ὁ Πρηξάσπης ἔξαρνος ἦν μὴ μὲν ἀποκτεῖναι Σμέρδιν· οὐ γὰρ ἦν οἱ ἀσφαλὲς Καμβύσεω τετελευτηκότος φάναι τὸν Κύρου υἱὸν ἀπολωλεκέναι αὐτοχειρίῃ. ὁ δὲ δὴ Μάγος τελευτήσαντος Καμβύσεω ἀδεῶς ἐβασίλευσε, ἐπιβατεύων τοῦ ὁμωνύμου Σμέρδιος τοῦ Κύρου, μῆνας ἑπτὰ τοὺς ἐπιλοίπους Καμβύσῃ ἐς τὰ ὀκτὼ ἔτεα τῆς πληρώσιος·

[2] ἐν τοῖσι ἀπεδέξατο ἐς τοὺς ὑπηκόους πάντας εὐεργεσίας μεγάλας, ὥστε ἀποθανόντος αὐτοῦ πόθον ἔχειν πάντας τοὺς ἐν τῇ Ἀσίῃ πάρεξ αὐτῶν Περσέων. διαπέμψας γὰρ ὁ Μάγος ἐς πᾶν ἔθνος τῶν ἦρχε προεῖπε ἀτελείην εἶναι στρατιῆς καὶ φόρου ἐπ᾽ ἔτεα τρία.

68 προεῖπε μὲν δὴ ταῦτα αὐτίκα ἐνιστάμενος ἐς τὴν ἀρχήν, ὀγδόῳ δὲ μηνὶ ἐγένετο κατάδηλος τρόπῳ τοιῷδε. Ὀτάνης ἦν Φαρνάσπεω μὲν παῖς, γένεϊ δὲ καὶ χρήμασι ὅμοιος τῷ πρώτῳ Περσέων. [2] οὗτος ὁ Ὀτάνης πρῶτος ὑπώπτευσε τὸν Μάγον ὡς οὐκ εἴη ὁ Κύρου Σμέρδις ἀλλ᾽ ὅς περ ἦν, τῇδε συμβαλόμενος, ὅτι τε οὐκ ἐξεφοίτα ἐκ τῆς ἀκροπόλιος καὶ ὅτι οὐκ ἐκάλεε ἐς ὄψιν ἑωυτῷ οὐδένα τῶν λογίμων Περσέων· ὑποπτεύσας δέ μιν ἐποίεε τάδε. [3] ἔσχε αὐτοῦ Καμβύσης θυγατέρα, τῇ οὔνομα ἦν Φαιδύμη· τὴν αὐτὴν δὴ ταύτην εἶχε τότε ὁ Μάγος καὶ ταύτῃ τε συνοίκεε καὶ τῇσι ἄλλῃσι πάσῃσι τῇσι τοῦ Καμβύσεω γυναιξί. πέμπων δὴ ὦν ὁ Ὀτάνης παρὰ ταύτην τὴν θυγατέρα ἐπυνθάνετο παρ᾽ ὅτεῳ ἀνθρώπων κοιμῷτο, εἴτε μετὰ Σμέρδιος τοῦ Κύρου εἴτε μετὰ ἄλλου τευ. [4] ἡ δέ οἱ ἀντέπεμπε φαμένη οὐ γινώσκειν· οὔτε γὰρ τὸν Κύρου Σμέρδιν ἰδέσθαι οὐδαμὰ οὔτε ὅστις εἴη ὁ συνοικέων αὐτῇ εἰδέναι. ἔπεμπε δεύτερα ὁ Ὀτάνης λέγων "Εἰ μὴ αὐτὴ Σμέρδιν τὸν Κύρου γινώσκεις, σὺ δὲ παρὰ Ἀτόσσης πύθευ ὅτεῳ τούτῳ συνοικέει αὐτή τε ἐκείνη καὶ σύ· πάντως γὰρ δή κου τόν γε ἑωυτῆς ἀδελφεὸν γινώσκει."

69 ἀντιπέμπει πρὸς ταῦτα ἡ θυγατήρ "Οὔτε Ἀτόσσῃ δύναμαι ἐς λόγους ἐλθεῖν οὔτε ἄλλην οὐδεμίαν ἰδέσθαι τῶν συγκατημενέων γυναικῶν. ἐπείτε γὰρ τάχιστα οὗτος ὥνθρωπος, ὅστις κοτέ ἐστι, παρέλαβε τὴν βασιληίην, διέσπειρε ἡμέας ἄλλην ἄλλῃ τάξας." ἀκούοντι δὲ ταῦτα τῷ Ὀτάνῃ μᾶλλον κατεφαίνετο τὸ πρῆγμα. τρίτην δὲ ἀγγελίην ἐσπέμπει παρ᾽ αὐτὴν λέγουσαν ταῦτα. [2] "Ὦ θύγατερ, δεῖ σε γεγονυῖαν εὖ κίνδυνον ἀναλαβέσθαι τὸν ἂν ὁ πατὴρ ὑποδύνειν κελεύῃ. εἰ γὰρ δὴ μή ἐστι ὁ Κύρου Σμέρδις ἀλλὰ τὸν καταδοκέω ἐγώ, οὔτοι μιν σοί τε συγκοιμώμενον καὶ τὸ Περσέων κράτος ἔχοντα δεῖ χαίροντα ἀπαλλάσσειν, ἀλλὰ δοῦναι δίκην. [3] νῦν ὦν ποίησον τάδε· ἐπεὰν σοὶ συνεύδῃ καὶ μάθῃς αὐτὸν κατυπνωμένον, ἄφασον αὐτοῦ τὰ ὦτα· καὶ ἢν μὲν φαίνηται ἔχων ὦτα, νόμιζε σεωυτὴν Σμέρδι τῷ Κύρου συνοικέειν, ἢν δὲ μὴ ἔχων, σὺ δὲ τῷ Μάγῳ Σμέρδι." [4] ἀντιπέμπει πρὸς ταῦτα ἡ Φαιδύμη φαμένη κινδυνεύσειν μεγάλως, ἢν ποιέῃ ταῦτα· εἰ γὰρ δὴ μὴ τυγχάνει τὰ ὦτα ἔχων, ἐπίλαμπτος δὲ ἀφάσσουσα ἔσται, εὖ εἰδέναι ὡς ἀϊστώσει μιν· ὅμως μέντοι ποιήσειν ταῦτα. [5] ἡ μὲν δὴ ὑπεδέξατο ταῦτα τῷ πατρὶ κατεργάσεσθαι. τοῦ δὲ Μάγου τούτου τοῦ Σμέρδιος Κῦρος ὁ Καμβύσεω ἄρχων τὰ ὦτα ἀπέταμε ἐπ' αἰτίῃ δή τινι οὐ σμικρῇ. [6] ἡ ὦν δὴ Φαιδύμη αὕτη, ἡ τοῦ Ὀτάνεω θυγάτηρ, πάντα ἐπιτελέουσα τὰ ὑπεδέξατο τῷ πατρί, ἐπείτε αὐτῆς μέρος ἐγίνετο τῆς ἀπίξιος παρὰ τὸν Μάγον, ἐν περιτροπῇ γὰρ δὴ αἱ γυναῖκες φοιτέουσι τοῖσι Πέρσῃσι, ἐλθοῦσα παρ' αὐτὸν ηὗδε, ὑπνωμένου δὲ καρτερῶς τοῦ Μάγου ἤφασε τὰ ὦτα. μαθοῦσα δὲ οὐ χαλεπῶς ἀλλ' εὐπετέως οὐκ ἔχοντα τὸν ἄνδρα ὦτα, ὡς ἡμέρη τάχιστα ἐγεγόνεε, πέμψασα ἐσήμηνε τῷ πατρὶ τὰ γενόμενα.

70 ὁ δὲ Ὀτάνης παραλαβὼν Ἀσπαθίνην καὶ Γοβρύην, Περσέων τε πρώτους ἐόντας καὶ ἑωυτῷ ἐπιτηδεοτάτους ἐς πίστιν, ἀπηγήσατο πᾶν τὸ πρῆγμα· οἱ δὲ καὶ αὐτοὶ ἄρα ὑπώπτευον οὕτω τοῦτο ἔχειν, ἀνενείκαντος δὲ τοῦ Ὀτάνεω τοὺς λόγους ἐδέξαντο. [2] καὶ ἔδοξέ σφι ἕκαστον ἄνδρα Περσέων προσεταιρίσασθαι τοῦτον ὅτεῳ πιστεύει μάλιστα. Ὀτάνης μέν νυν ἐσάγεται Ἰνταφρένεα, Γοβρύης δὲ Μεγάβυζον, Ἀσπαθίνης δὲ Ὑδάρνεα. [3] γεγονότων δὲ τούτων ἓξ παραγίνεται ἐς τὰ Σοῦσα Δαρεῖος ὁ Ὑστάσπεος ἐκ Περσέων ἥκων· τούτων γὰρ δὴ ἦν οἱ ὁ πατὴρ ὕπαρχος. ἐπεὶ ὦν οὗτος ἀπίκετο, τοῖσι ἓξ τῶν Περσέων ἔδοξε καὶ Δαρεῖον προσεταιρίσασθαι.

71 συνελθόντες δὲ οὗτοι ἐόντες ἑπτὰ ἐδίδοσαν σφίσι λόγους καὶ πίστις. ἐπείτε δὲ ἐς Δαρεῖον ἀπίκετο γνώμην ἀποφαίνεσθαι, ἔλεγέ σφι τάδε. [2] "Ἐγὼ ταῦτα ἐδόκεον μὲν αὐτὸς μοῦνος ἐπίστασθαι ὅτι τε ὁ Μάγος εἴη ὁ βασιλεύων καὶ Σμέρδις ὁ Κύρου τετελεύτηκε· καὶ αὐτοῦ τούτου εἵνεκεν ἥκω σπουδῇ ὡς συστήσων ἐπὶ τῷ Μάγῳ θάνατον. ἐπείτε δὲ συνήνεικε ὥστε καὶ ὑμέας εἰδέναι καὶ μὴ μοῦνον ἐμέ, ποιέειν αὐτίκα μοι δοκέει καὶ μὴ ὑπερβάλλεσθαι· οὐ γὰρ ἄμεινον." [3] εἶπε πρὸς ταῦτα ὁ Ὀτάνης · "Ὦ παῖ Ὑστάσπεος, εἶς τε πατρὸς ἀγαθοῦ καὶ ἐκφαίνειν ἔοικας σεωυτὸν ἐόντα τοῦ πατρὸς οὐδὲν ἥσσω· τὴν μέντοι ἐπιχείρησιν ταύτην μὴ οὕτω συντάχυνε ἀβούλως, ἀλλ' ἐπὶ τὸ σωφρονέστερον αὐτὴν λάμβανε· δεῖ γὰρ πλεῦνας γενομένους οὕτω ἐπιχειρέειν." [4] λέγει πρὸς ταῦτα Δαρεῖος· " Ἄνδρες οἱ παρεόντες, τρόπῳ τῷ εἰρημένῳ ἐξ Ὀτάνεω εἰ χρήσεσθε, ἐπίστασθε ὅτι ἀπολέεσθε κάκιστα· ἐξοίσει γάρ τις πρὸς τὸν Μάγον, ἰδίῃ περιβαλλόμενος ἑωυτῷ κέρδεα. [5] μάλιστα μέν νυν ὠφείλετε ἐπ' ὑμέων αὐτῶν βαλόμενοι ποιέειν ταῦτα· ἐπείτε δὲ ὑμῖν ἀναφέρειν ἐς πλεῦνας ἐδόκεε καὶ ἐμοὶ ὑπερέθεσθε, ἢ ποιέωμεν σήμερον ἢ ἴστε ὑμῖν ὅτι ἢν ὑπερπέσῃ ἡ νῦν ἡμέρη, ὡς οὐκ ἄλλος φθὰς ἐμεῦ κατήγορος ἔσται, ἀλλά σφεα αὐτὸς ἐγὼ κατερέω πρὸς τὸν Μάγον."

72 λέγει πρὸς ταῦτα Ὀτάνης, ἐπειδὴ ὥρα σπερχόμενον Δαρεῖον, " Ἐπείτε ἡμέας συνταχύνειν ἀναγκάζεις καὶ ὑπερβάλλεσθαι οὐκ ἐᾷς, ἴθι ἐξηγέο αὐτὸς ὅτεῳ τρόπῳ πάριμεν ἐς τὰ βασιλήια καὶ ἐπιχειρήσομεν αὐτοῖσι. φυλακὰς γὰρ δὴ διεστεώσας οἶδάς κου καὶ αὐτός, εἰ μὴ ἰδών, ἀλλ' ἀκούσας· τὰς τέῳ τρόπῳ περήσομεν;" [2] ἀμείβεται Δαρεῖος τοῖσιδε. " Ὀτάνη, πολλά ἐστι τὰ λόγῳ μὲν οὐκ οἷά τε δηλῶσαι, ἔργῳ δέ· ἄλλα δ' ἐστὶ τὰ λόγῳ μὲν οἷά τε, ἔργον δὲ οὐδὲν ἀπ' αὐτῶν λαμπρὸν γίνεται. ὑμεῖς δὲ ἴστε φυλακὰς τὰς κατεστεώσας ἐούσας οὐδὲν χαλεπὰς παρελθεῖν. [3] τοῦτο μὲν γὰρ ἡμέων ἐόντων τοιῶνδε οὐδείς ὅστις οὐ παρήσει, τὰ μέν κου καταιδεόμενος ἡμέας, τὰ δέ κου καὶ δειμαίνων· τοῦτο δὲ ἔχω αὐτὸς σκῆψιν εὐπρεπεστάτην τῇ πάριμεν, φὰς ἄρτι τε ἥκειν ἐκ Περσέων καὶ βούλεσθαί τι ἔπος παρὰ τοῦ πατρὸς σημῆναι τῷ βασιλέϊ. [4] ἔνθα γάρ τι δεῖ ψεῦδος λέγεσθαι, λεγέσθω. τοῦ γὰρ αὐτοῦ γλιχόμεθα οἵ τε ψευδόμενοι καὶ οἱ τῇ ἀληθείῃ διαχρεώμενοι. οἱ μέν γε ψεύδονται τότε ἐπεάν τι μέλλωσι τοῖσι ψεύδεσι πείσαντες κερδήσεσθαι, οἱ δ' ἀληθίζονται ἵνα τῇ ἀληθείῃ ἐπισπάσωνται κέρδος καί τι μᾶλλον σφι ἐπιτράπηται. οὕτω οὐ ταὐτὰ ἀσκέοντες τωὐτοῦ περιεχόμεθα. [5] εἰ δὲ μηδὲν κερδήσεσθαι μέλλοιεν, ὁμοίως ἂν ὅ τε ἀληθιζόμενος ψευδὴς εἴη καὶ ὁ ψευδόμενος ἀληθής. ὃς ἂν μέν νυν τῶν πυλουρῶν ἑκὼν παριῇ, αὐτῷ οἱ ἄμεινον ἐς χρόνον ἔσται· ὃς δ' ἂν ἀντιβαίνειν πειρᾶται, διαδεικνύσθω ἐνθαῦτα ἐὼν πολέμιος, καὶ ἔπειτα ὠσάμενοι ἔσω ἔργου ἐχώμεθα."

73 λέγει Γοβρύης μετὰ ταῦτα· "Ἄνδρες φίλοι, ἡμῖν κότε κάλλιον παρέξει ἀνασώσασθαι τὴν ἀρχήν, ἢ εἴ γε μὴ οἷοί τε ἐσόμεθα αὐτὴν ἀναλαβεῖν, ἀποθανεῖν; ὅτε γε ἀρχόμεθα μὲν ἐόντες Πέρσαι ὑπὸ Μήδου ἀνδρὸς Μάγου τε καὶ τούτου ὦτα οὐκ ἔχοντος. [2] ὅσοι τε ὑμέων Καμβύσῃ νοσέοντι παρεγένοντο, πάντως κου μέμνησθε τὰ ἐπέσκηψε Πέρσῃσι τελευτῶν τὸν βίον μὴ πειρωμένοισι ἀνακτᾶσθαι τὴν ἀρχήν· τὰ τότε οὐκ ἐνεδεκόμεθα, ἀλλ' ἐπὶ διαβολῇ ἐδοκέομεν εἰπεῖν Καμβύσεα. [3] νῦν ὦν τίθεμαι ψῆφον πείθεσθαι Δαρείῳ καὶ μὴ διαλύεσθαι ἐκ τοῦ συλλόγου τοῦδε ἀλλ' ἢ ἰόντας ἐπὶ τὸν Μάγον ἰθέως." ταῦτα εἶπε Γοβρύης, καὶ πάντες ταύτῃ αἴνεον.

74 ἐν ᾧ δὲ οὗτοι ταῦτα ἐβουλεύοντο, ἐγίνετο κατὰ συντυχίην τάδε. τοῖσι Μάγοισι ἔδοξε βουλευομένοισι Πρηξάσπεα φίλον προσθέσθαι, ὅτι τε ἐπεπόνθεε πρὸς Καμβύσεω ἀνάρσια, ὅς οἱ τὸν παῖδα τοξεύσας ἀπολωλέκεε, καὶ διότι μοῦνος ἠπίστατο τὸν Σμέρδιος τοῦ Κύρου θάνατον αὐτοχειρίῃ μιν ἀπολέσας, πρὸς δ' ἔτι ἐόντα ἐν αἴνῃ μεγίστῃ τὸν Πρηξάσπεα ἐν Πέρσῃσι. [2] τούτων δή μιν εἵνεκεν καλέσαντες φίλον προσεκτῶντο πίστι τε λαβόντες καὶ ὁρκίοισι, ἦ μὲν ἕξειν παρ' ἑωυτῷ μηδ' ἐξοίσειν μηδενὶ ἀνθρώπων τὴν ἀπὸ σφέων ἀπάτην ἐς Πέρσας γεγονυῖαν, ὑπισχνεύμενοι τὰ πάντα οἱ μυρία δώσειν. [3] ὑποδεκομένου δὲ τοῦ Πρηξάσπεος ποιήσειν ταῦτα, ὡς ἀνέπεισάν μιν οἱ Μάγοι, δεύτερα προσέφερον, αὐτοὶ μὲν φάμενοι Πέρσας πάντας συγκαλέειν ὑπὸ τὸ βασιλήιον τεῖχος, κεῖνον δ' ἐκέλευον ἀναβάντα ἐπὶ πύργον ἀγορεῦσαι ὡς ὑπὸ τοῦ Κύρου Σμέρδιος ἄρχονται καὶ ὑπ' οὐδενὸς ἄλλου. [4] ταῦτα δὲ οὕτω ἐνετέλλοντο ὡς πιστοτάτου δῆθεν ἐόντος αὐτοῦ ἐν Πέρσῃσι, καὶ πολλάκις ἀποδεξαμένου γνώμην ὡς περιείη ὁ Κύρου Σμέρδις, καὶ ἐξαρνησαμένου τὸν φόνον αὐτοῦ.

75 φαμένου δὲ καὶ ταῦτα ἑτοίμου εἶναι ποιέειν τοῦ Πρηξάσπεος, συγκαλέσαντες Πέρσας οἱ Μάγοι ἀνεβίβασαν αὐτὸν ἐπὶ πύργον καὶ ἀγορεύειν ἐκέλευον. ὁ δὲ τῶν μὲν ἐκεῖνοι προσεδέοντο αὐτοῦ, τούτων μὲν ἑκὼν ἐπελήθετο, ἀρξάμενος δὲ ἀπ' Ἀχαιμένεος ἐγενεηλόγησε τὴν πατριὴν τὴν Κύρου, μετὰ δὲ ὡς ἐς τοῦτον κατέβη τελευτῶν ἔλεγε ὅσα ἀγαθὰ Κῦρος Πέρσας πεποιήκοι, [2] διεξελθὼν δὲ ταῦτα ἐξέφαινε τὴν

ἀληθείην, φάμενος πρότερον μὲν κρύπτειν, οὐ γάρ οἱ εἶναι ἀσφαλὲς λέγειν τὰ γενόμενα, ἐν δὲ τῷ παρεόντι ἀναγκαίην μιν καταλαμβάνειν φαίνειν. καὶ δὴ ἔλεγε τὸν μὲν Κύρου Σμέρδιν ὡς αὐτὸς ὑπὸ Καμβύσεω ἀναγκαζόμενος ἀποκτείνειε, τοὺς Μάγους δὲ βασιλεύειν. [3] Πέρσῃσι δὲ πολλὰ ἐπαρησάμενος εἰ μὴ ἀνακτησαίατο ὀπίσω τὴν ἀρχὴν καὶ τοὺς Μάγους τεισαίατο, ἀπῆκε ἑωυτὸν ἐπὶ κεφαλὴν φέρεσθαι ἀπὸ τοῦ πύργου κάτω. Πρηξάσπης μέν νυν ἐὼν τὸν πάντα χρόνον ἀνὴρ δόκιμος οὕτω ἐτελεύτησε.

76 οἱ δὲ δὴ ἑπτὰ τῶν Περσέων ὡς ἐβουλεύσαντο αὐτίκα ἐπιχειρέειν τοῖσι Μάγοισι καὶ μὴ ὑπερβάλλεσθαι, ἤισαν εὐξάμενοι τοῖσι θεοῖσι, τῶν περὶ Πρηξάσπεα πρηχθέντων εἰδότες οὐδέν. [2] ἔν τε δὴ τῇ ὁδῷ μέσῃ στίχοντες ἐγίνοντο καὶ τὰ περὶ Πρηξάσπεα γεγονότα ἐπυνθάνοντο. ἐνθαῦτα ἐκστάντες τῆς ὁδοῦ ἐδίδοσαν αὖτις σφίσι λόγους, οἱ μὲν ἀμφὶ τὸν Ὀτάνην πάγχυ κελεύοντες ὑπερβαλέσθαι μηδὲ οἰδεόντων τῶν πρηγμάτων ἐπιτίθεσθαι, οἱ δὲ ἀμφὶ τὸν Δαρεῖον αὐτίκα τε ἰέναι καὶ τὰ δεδογμένα ποιέειν μηδὲ ὑπερβάλλεσθαι. [3] ὠθιζομένων δ' αὐτῶν ἐφάνη ἰρήκων ἑπτὰ ζεύγεα δύο αἰγυπιῶν ζεύγεα διώκοντα καὶ τίλλοντά τε καὶ ἀμύσσοντα. ἰδόντες δὲ ταῦτα οἱ ἑπτὰ τήν τε Δαρείου πάντες αἴνεον γνώμην καὶ ἔπειτα ἤισαν ἐπὶ τὰ βασιλήια τεθαρσηκότες τοῖσι ὄρνισι.

77 ἐπιστᾶσι δὲ ἐπὶ τὰς πύλας ἐγίνετο οἷόν τι Δαρείῳ ἡ γνώμη ἔφερε· καταιδεόμενοι γὰρ οἱ φύλακοι ἄνδρας τοὺς Περσέων πρώτους καὶ οὐδὲν τοιοῦτο ὑποπτεύοντες ἐξ αὐτῶν ἔσεσθαι, παρίεσαν θείῃ πομπῇ χρεωμένους, οὐδ' ἐπειρώτα οὐδείς. [2] ἐπείτε δὲ καὶ παρῆλθον ἐς τὴν αὐλήν, ἐνέκυρσαν τοῖσι τὰς ἀγγελίας ἐσφέρουσι εὐνούχοισι· οἵ σφεας ἱστόρεον ὅ τι θέλοντες ἥκοιεν, καὶ ἅμα ἱστορέοντες τούτους τοῖσι πυλουροῖσι ἀπείλεον ὅτι σφέας παρῆκαν, ἴσχόν τε βουλομένους τοὺς ἑπτὰ ἐς τὸ πρόσω παριέναι. [3] οἱ δὲ διακελευσάμενοι καὶ σπασάμενοι τὰ ἐγχειρίδια τούτους μὲν τοὺς ἴσχοντας αὐτοῦ ταύτῃ συγκεντέουσι, αὐτοὶ δὲ ἤισαν δρόμῳ ἐς τὸν ἀνδρεῶνα.

78 οἱ δὲ Μάγοι ἔτυχον ἀμφότεροι τηνικαῦτα ἐόντες τε ἔσω καὶ τὰ ἀπὸ Πρηξάσπεος γενόμενα ἐν βουλῇ ἔχοντες. ἐπεὶ ὦν εἶδον τοὺς εὐνούχους τεθορυβημένους τε καὶ βοῶντας, ἀνά τε ἔδραμον πάλιν ἀμφότεροι καὶ ὡς ἔμαθον τὸ ποιεύμενον πρὸς ἀλκὴν ἐτράποντο. [2] ὁ μὲν δὴ αὐτῶν φθάνει τὰ τόξα κατελόμενος, ὁ δὲ πρὸς τὴν αἰχμὴν ἐτράπετο. ἐνθαῦτα δὴ συνέμισγον ἀλλήλοισι. τῷ μὲν δὴ τὰ τόξα ἀναλαβόντι αὐτῶν, ἐόντων τε ἀγχοῦ τῶν πολεμίων καὶ προσκειμένων, ἦν χρηστὰ οὐδέν· ὁ δ' ἕτερος τῇ αἰχμῇ ἠμύνετο καὶ τοῦτο μὲν Ἀσπαθίνην παίει ἐς τὸν μηρόν, τοῦτο δὲ Ἰνταφρένεα ἐς τὸν ὀφθαλμόν· καὶ ἐστερήθη μὲν τοῦ ὀφθαλμοῦ ἐκ τοῦ τρώματος ὁ Ἰνταφρένης, οὐ μέντοι ἀπέθανέ γε. [3] τῶν μὲν δὴ Μάγων οὕτερος τρωματίζει τούτους· ὁ δὲ ἕτερος, ἐπείτε οἱ τὰ τόξα οὐδὲν χρηστὰ ἐγίνετο, ἦν γὰρ δὴ θάλαμος ἐσέχων ἐς τὸν ἀνδρεῶνα, ἐς τοῦτον καταφεύγει, θέλων αὐτοῦ προσθεῖναι τὰ θύρας, καί οἱ συνεσπίπτουσι τῶν ἑπτὰ δύο, Δαρεῖός τε καὶ Γοβρύης. [4] συμπλακέντος δὲ Γοβρύεω τῷ Μάγῳ ὁ Δαρεῖος ἐπεστεὼς ἠπόρεε οἷα ἐν σκότει, προμηθεόμενος μὴ πλήξῃ τὸν Γοβρύην. ὁρέων δέ μιν ἀργὸν ἐπεστεῶτα ὁ Γοβρύης εἴρετο ὅ τι οὐ χρᾶται τῇ χειρί· ὁ δὲ εἶπε· "Προμηθεόμενος σέο μὴ πλήξω." Γοβρύης δὲ ἀμείβετο· "Ὤθεε τὸ ξίφος καὶ δι' ἀμφοτέρων." Δαρεῖος δὲ πειθόμενος ὦσέ τεο ἐγχειρίδιον καὶ ἔτυχέ κως τοῦ Μάγου.

79 ἀποκτείναντες δὲ τοὺς Μάγους καὶ ἀποταμόντες αὐτῶν τὰς κεφαλάς, τοὺς μὲν τρωματίας ἑωυτῶν αὐτοῦ λείπουσι καὶ ἀδυνασίης εἵνεκεν καὶ φυλακῆς τῆς ἀκροπόλιος, οἱ δὲ πέντε αὐτῶν ἔχοντες τῶν Μάγων τὰς κεφαλὰς ἔθεον βοῇ τε καὶ πατάγῳ χρεώμενοι, καὶ Πέρσας τοὺς ἄλλους ἐπεκαλέοντο ἐξηγεόμενοί τε τὸ πρῆγμα καὶ δεικνύοντες τὰς κεφαλάς, καὶ ἅμα ἔκτεινον πάντα τινὰ τῶν Μάγων τὸν ἐν ποσὶ γινόμενον. [2] οἱ δὲ Πέρσαι μαθόντες τὸ γεγονὸς ἐκ τῶν ἑπτὰ καὶ τῶν Μάγων τὴν ἀπάτην ἐδικαίευν καὶ αὐτοὶ ἕτερα τοιαῦτα ποιέειν, σπασάμενοι δὲ τὰ ἐγχειρίδια ἔκτεινον ὅκου τινὰ Μάγον εὕρισκον· εἰ δὲ μὴ νὺξ ἐπελθοῦσα ἔσχε, ἔλιπον ἂν οὐδένα Μάγον. [3] ταύτην τὴν ἡμέρην θεραπεύουσι Πέρσαι κοινῇ μάλιστα τῶν ἡμερέων, καὶ ἐν αὐτῇ ὁρτὴν μεγάλην ἀνάγουσι, ἣ κέκληται ὑπὸ Περσέων μαγοφόνια· ἐν τῇ Μάγον οὐδένα ἔξεστι φανῆναι ἐς τὸ φῶς, ἀλλὰ κατ' οἴκους ἑωυτοὺς οἱ Μάγοι ἔχουσι τὴν ἡμέρην ταύτην.

80 ἐπείτε δὲ κατέστη ὁ θόρυβος καὶ ἐκτὸς πέντε ἡμερέων ἐγένετο, ἐβουλεύοντο οἱ ἐπαναστάντες τοῖσι Μάγοισι περὶ τῶν πάντων πρηγμάτων καὶ ἐλέχθησαν λόγοι ἄπιστοι μὲν ἐνίοισι Ἑλλήνων, ἐλέχθησαν δ' ὦν. [2] Ὀτάνης μὲν ἐκέλευε ἐς μέσον Πέρσῃσι καταθεῖναι τὰ πρήγματα, λέγων τάδε. " Ἐμοὶ δοκέει ἕνα μὲν ἡμέων μούναρχον μηκέτι γενέσθαι. οὔτε γὰρ ἡδὺ οὔτε ἀγαθόν. εἴδετε μὲν γὰρ τὴν Καμβύσεω ὕβριν ἐπ' ὅσον ἐπεξῆλθε, μετεσχήκατε δὲ καὶ τῆς τοῦ Μάγου ὕβριος. [3] κῶς δ' ἂν εἴη χρῆμα κατηρτημένον μουναρχίῃ, τῇ ἔξεστι ἀνευθύνῳ ποιέειν τὰ βούλεται; καὶ γὰρ ἂν τὸν ἄριστον ἀνδρῶν πάντων στάντα ἐς ταύτην τὴν ἀρχὴν ἐκτὸς τῶν ἐωθότων νοημάτων στήσειε. ἐγγίνεται μὲν γάρ οἱ ὕβρις ὑπὸ τῶν παρεόντων ἀγαθῶν, φθόνος δὲ ἀρχῆθεν ἐμφύεται ἀνθρώπῳ. δύο δ' ἔχων ταῦτα ἔχει πᾶσαν κακότητα· [4] τὰ μὲν γὰρ ὕβρι κεκορημένος ἔρδει πολλὰ καὶ ἀτάσθαλα, τὰ δὲ φθόνῳ. καίτοι ἄνδρα γε τύραννον ἄφθονον ἔδει εἶναι, ἔχοντά γε πάντα τὰ ἀγαθά. τὸ δὲ ὑπεναντίον τούτου ἐς τοὺς πολιήτας πέφυκε· φθονέει γὰρ τοῖσι ἀρίστοισι περιεοῦσί τε καὶ ζώουσι, χαίρει δὲ τοῖσι κακίστοισι τῶν ἀστῶν, διαβολὰς δὲ ἄριστος ἐνδέκεσθαι. [5] ἀναρμοστότατον δὲ πάντων· ἤν τε γὰρ αὐτὸν μετρίως θωμάζῃς, ἄχθεται ὅτι οὐ κάρτα θεραπεύεται, ἤν τε θεραπεύῃ τις κάρτα, ἄχθεται ἅτε θωπί. τὰ δὲ δὴ μέγιστα ἔρχομαι ἐρέων· νόμαιά τε κινέει πάτρια καὶ βιᾶται γυναῖκας κτείνει τε ἀκρίτους. [6] πλῆθος δὲ ἄρχον πρῶτα μὲν οὔνομα πάντων κάλλιστον ἔχει, ἰσονομίην, δεύτερα δὲ τούτων τῶν ὁ μούναρχος ποιέει οὐδέν· πάλῳ μὲν ἀρχὰς ἄρχει, ὑπεύθυνον δὲ ἀρχὴν ἔχει, βουλεύματα δὲ πάντα ἐς τὸ κοινὸν ἀναφέρει. τίθεμαι ὦν γνώμην μετέντας ἡμέας μουναρχίην τὸ πλῆθος ἀέξειν· ἐν γὰρ τῷ πολλῷ ἔνι τὰ πάντα."

81 Ὀτάνης μὲν δὴ ταύτην γνώμην ἐσέφερε· Μεγάβυζος δὲ ὀλιγαρχίῃ ἐκέλευε ἐπιτράπειν, λέγων τάδε. "Τὰ μὲν Ὀτάνης εἶπε τυραννίδα παύων, λελέχθω κἀμοὶ ταῦτα, τὰ δ' ἐς τὸ πλῆθος ἄνωγε φέρειν τὸ κράτος, γνώμης τῆς ἀρίστης ἡμάρτηκε· ὁμίλου γὰρ ἀχρηίου οὐδέν ἐστι ἀξυνετώτερον οὐδὲ ὑβριστότερον. [2] καίτοι τυράννου ὕβριν φεύγοντας ἄνδρας ἐς δήμου ἀκολάστου ὕβριν πεσεῖν ἐστι οὐδαμῶς ἀνασχετόν. ὁ μὲν γὰρ εἴ τι ποιέει, γινώσκων ποιέει, τῷ δὲ οὐδὲ γινώσκειν ἔνι· κῶς γὰρ

ἂν γινώσκοι ὃς οὔτ' ἐδιδάχθη οὔτε εἶδε καλὸν οὐδὲν οἰκήιον, ὠθέει τε ἐμπεσὼν τὰ πρήγματα ἄνευ νόου χειμάρρῳ ποταμῷ εἴκελος; [3] δήμῳ μέν νυν, οἳ Πέρσῃσι κακὸν νοέουσι, οὗτοι χράσθων, ἡμεῖς δὲ ἀνδρῶν τῶν ἀρίστων ἐπιλέξαντες ὁμιλίην τούτοισι περιθέωμεν τὸ κράτος· ἐν γὰρ δὴ τούτοισι καὶ αὐτοὶ ἐνεσόμεθα. ἀρίστων δὲ ἀνδρῶν οἰκὸς ἄριστα βουλεύματα γίνεσθαι."

82 Μεγάβυζος μὲν δὴ ταύτην γνώμην ἐσέφερε· τρίτος δὲ Δαρεῖος ἀπεδείκνυτο γνώμην, λέγων· " Ἐμοὶ δὲ τὰ μὲν εἶπε Μεγάβυζος ἐς τὸ πλῆθος ἔχοντα δοκέει ὀρθῶς λέξαι, τὰ δὲ ἐς ὀλιγαρχίην οὐκ ὀρθῶς. τριῶν γὰρ προκειμένων καὶ πάντων τῷ λόγῳ ἀρίστων ἐόντων, δήμου τε ἀρίστου καὶ ὀλιγαρχίης καὶ μουνάρχου, πολλῷ τοῦτο προέχειν λέγω. [2] ἀνδρὸς γὰρ ἑνὸς τοῦ ἀρίστου οὐδὲν ἄμεινον ἂν φανείη· γνώμῃ γὰρ τοιαύτῃ χρεώμενος ἐπιτροπεύοι ἂν ἀμωμήτως τοῦ πλήθεος, σιγῷτό τε ἂν βουλεύματα ἐπὶ δυσμενέας ἄνδρας οὕτω μάλιστα. [3] ἐν δὲ ὀλιγαρχίῃ πολλοῖσι ἀρετὴν ἐπασκέουσι ἐς τὸ κοινὸν ἔχθεα ἴδια ἰσχυρὰ φιλέει ἐγγίνεσθαι· αὐτὸς γὰρ ἕκαστος βουλόμενος κορυφαῖος εἶναι γνώμῃσί τε νικᾶν ἐς ἔχθεα μεγάλα ἀλλήλοισι ἀπικνέονται, ἐξ ὧν στάσιες ἐγγίνονται, ἐκ δὲ τῶν στασίων φόνος, ἐκ δὲ τοῦ φόνου ἀπέβη ἐς μουναρχίην, καὶ ἐν τούτῳ διέδεξε ὅσῳ ἐστὶ τοῦτο ἄριστον. [4] δήμου τε αὖ ἄρχοντος ἀδύνατα μὴ οὐ κακότητα ἐγγίνεσθαι· κακότητος τοίνυν ἐγγινομένης ἐς τὰ κοινὰ ἔχθεα μὲν οὐκ ἐγγίνεται τοῖσι κακοῖσι, φιλίαι δὲ ἰσχυραί· οἱ γὰρ κακοῦντες τὰ κοινὰ συγκύψαντες ποιεῦσι. τοῦτο δὲ τοιοῦτο γίνεται ἐς ὃ ἂν προστάς τις τοῦ δήμου τοὺς τοιούτους παύσῃ. ἐκ δὲ αὐτῶν θωμάζεται οὗτος δὴ ὑπὸ τοῦ δήμου, θωμαζόμενος δὲ ἀν' ὧν ἐφάνη μούναρχος ἐών, καὶ ἐν τούτῳ δηλοῖ καὶ οὗτος ὡς ἡ μουναρχίη κράτιστον. [5] ἑνὶ δὲ ἔπεϊ πάντα συλλαβόντα εἰπεῖν, κόθεν ἡμῖν ἡ ἐλευθερίη ἐγένετο καὶ τεῦ δόντος; κότερα παρὰ τοῦ δήμου ἢ ὀλιγαρχίης ἢ μουνάρχου; ἔχω τοίνυν γνώμην ἡμέας ἐλευθερωθέντας διὰ ἕνα ἄνδρα τὸ τοιοῦτο περιστέλλειν, χωρίς τε τούτου πατρίους νόμους μὴ λύειν ἔχοντας εὖ· οὐ γὰρ ἄμεινον."

83 γνῶμαι μὲν δὴ τρεῖς αὗται προεκέατο, οἱ δὲ τέσσερες τῶν ἑπτὰ ἀνδρῶν προσέθεντο ταύτῃ. ὡς δὲ ἑσσώθη τῇ γνώμῃ ὁ Ὀτάνης Πέρσῃσι ἰσονομίην σπεύδων ποιῆσαι, ἔλεξε ἐς μέσον αὐτοῖσι τάδε. [2] Ἄνδρες στασιῶται, δῆλα γὰρ δὴ ὅτι δεῖ ἕνα γε τινὰ ἡμέων βασιλέα γενέσθαι, ἤτοι κλήρῳ γε λαχόντα ἢ ἐπιτρεψάντων τῷ Περσέων πλήθεϊ τὸν ἂν ἐκεῖνο ἕληται ἢ ἄλλῃ τινὶ μηχανῇ. ἐγὼ μέν νυν ὑμῖν οὐκ ἐναγωνιεῦμαι· οὔτε γὰρ ἄρχειν οὔτε ἄρχεσθαι ἐθέλω· ἐπὶ τούτῳ δὲ ὑπεξίσταμαι τῆς ἀρχῆς, ἐπ᾽ ᾧ τε ὑπ᾽ οὐδενὸς ὑμέων ἄρξομαι, οὔτε αὐτὸς ἐγὼ οὔτε οἱ ἀπ᾽ ἐμεῦ αἰεὶ γινόμενοι." [3] τούτου εἴπαντος ταῦτα ὡς συνεχώρεον οἱ ἓξ ἐπὶ τούτοισι, οὗτος μὲν δή σφι οὐκ ἐνηγωνίζετο ἀλλ᾽ ἐκ μέσου κατῆστο, καὶ νῦν αὕτη ἡ οἰκίη διατελέει μούνη ἐλευθέρη ἐοῦσα Περσέων καὶ ἄρχεται τοσαῦτα ὅσα αὐτὴ θέλει, νόμους οὐκ ὑπερβαίνουσα τοὺς Περσέων.

84 οἱ δὲ λοιποὶ τῶν ἑπτὰ ἐβουλεύοντο ὡς βασιλέα δικαιότατα στήσονται· καί σφι ἔδοξε Ὀτάνῃ μὲν καὶ τοῖσι ἀπὸ Ὀτάνεω αἰεὶ γινομένοισι, ἢν ἐς ἄλλον τινὰ τῶν ἑπτὰ ἔλθῃ ἡ βασιληίη, ἐξαίρετα δίδοσθαι ἐσθῆτά τε Μηδικὴν ἔτεος ἑκάστου καὶ τὴν πᾶσαν δωρεὴν ἣ γίνεται ἐν Πέρσῃσι τιμιωτάτη. τοῦδε δὲ εἵνεκεν ἐβούλευσάν οἱ δίδοσθαι ταῦτα, ὅτι ἐβούλευσέ τε πρῶτος τὸ πρῆγμα καὶ συνέστησε αὐτούς. [2] ταῦτα μὲν δὴ Ὀτάνῃ ἐξαίρετα, τάδε δὲ ἐς τὸ κοινὸν ἐβούλευσαν, παριέναι ἐς τὰ βασιλήια πάντα τὸν βουλόμενον τῶν ἑπτὰ ἄνευ ἐσαγγελέος, ἢν μὴ τυγχάνῃ εὕδων μετὰ γυναικὸς βασιλεύς, γαμέειν δὲ μὴ ἐξεῖναι ἄλλοθεν τῷ βασιλέϊ ἢ ἐκ τῶν συνεπαναστάντων. [3] περὶ δὲ τῆς βασιληίης ἐβούλευσαν τοιόνδε· ὅτευ ἂν ὁ ἵππος ἡλίου ἐπανατέλλοντος πρῶτος φθέγξηται ἐν τῷ προαστείῳ αὐτῶν ἐπιβεβηκότων, τοῦτον ἔχειν τὴν βασιληίην.

85 Δαρείῳ δὲ ἦν ἱπποκόμος ἀνὴρ σοφός, τῷ οὔνομα ἦν Οἰβάρης. πρὸς τοῦτον τὸν ἄνδρα, ἐπείτε διελύθησαν, ἔλεξε Δαρεῖος τάδε. "Οἴβαρες, ἡμῖν δέδοκται περὶ τῆς βασιληίης ποιέειν κατὰ τάδε· ὅτευ ἂν ὁ ἵππος πρῶτος φθέγξηται ἅμα τῷ ἡλίῳ ἀνιόντι αὐτῶν ἐπαναβεβηκότων, τοῦτον ἔχειν τὴν βασιληίην. νῦν ὦν εἴ τινα ἔχεις σοφίην, μηχανῶ ὡς ἂν ἡμεῖς σχῶμεν τοῦτο τὸ γέρας καὶ μὴ ἄλλος τις." [2] ἀμείβεται Οἰβάρης τοῖσιδε. "Εἰ μὲν δὴ ὦ δέσποτα, ἐν τούτῳ τοι ἐστὶ ἢ βασιλέα εἶναι ἢ μή, θάρσεε τούτου εἵνεκεν καὶ θυμὸν ἔχε ἀγαθόν, ὡς βασιλεὺς οὐδεὶς ἄλλος πρὸ σεῦ ἔσται· τοιαῦτα ἔχω φάρμακα." λέγει Δαρεῖος "Εἰ τοίνυν τι τοιοῦτον ἔχεις σόφισμα, ὥρη μηχανᾶσθαι καὶ μὴ ἀναβάλλεσθαι, ὡς τῆς ἐπιούσης ἡμέρης ὁ ἀγὼν ἡμῖν ἐστί." [3] ἀκούσας ταῦτα ὁ Οἰβάρης ποιέει τοιόνδε· ὡς ἐγίνετο ἡ νύξ, τῶν θηλέων ἵππων μίαν, τὴν ὁ Δαρείου ἵππος ἔστεργε μάλιστα, ταύτην ἀγαγὼν ἐς τὸ προάστειον κατέδησε καὶ ἐπήγαγε τὸν Δαρείου ἵππον, καὶ τὰ μὲν πολλὰ περιῆγε ἀγχοῦ τῇ ἵππῳ ἐγχρίμπτων τῇ θηλέῃ, τέλος δὲ ἐπῆκε ὀχεῦσαι τὸν ἵππον.

86 ἅμ' ἡμέρῃ δὲ διαφωσκούσῃ οἱ ἓξ κατὰ συνεθήκαντο παρῆσαν ἐπὶ τῶν ἵππων· διεξελαυνόντων δὲ κατὰ τὸ προάστειον, ὡς κατὰ τοῦτο τὸ χωρίον ἐγίνοντο ἵνα τῆς παροιχομένης νυκτὸς κατεδέδετο ἡ θήλεα ἵππος, ἐνθαῦτα ὁ Δαρείου ἵππος προσδραμὼν ἐχρεμέτισε· [2] ἅμα δὲ τῷ ἵππῳ τοῦτο ποιήσαντι ἀστραπὴ ἐξ αἰθρίης καὶ βροντὴ ἐγένετο. ἐπιγενόμενα δὲ ταῦτα τῷ Δαρείῳ ἐτελέωσέ μιν ὥσπερ ἐκ συνθέτου τευ γενόμενα· οἱ δὲ καταθορόντες ἀπὸ τῶν ἵππων προσεκύνεον τὸν Δαρεῖον.

87 οἱ μὲν δή φασι τὸν Οἰβάρεα ταῦτα μηχανήσασθαι, οἱ δὲ τοιάδε, καὶ γὰρ ἐπ' ἀμφότερα λέγεται ὑπὸ Περσέων, ὡς τῆς ἵππου ταύτης τῶν ἄρθρων ἐπιψαύσας τῇ χειρὶ ἔχοι αὐτὴν κρύψας ἐν τῇσι ἀναξυρίσι· ὡς δὲ ἅμα τῷ ἡλίῳ ἀνιόντι ἀπίεσθαι μέλλειν τοὺς ἵππους, τὸν Οἰβάρεα τοῦτον ἐξείραντα τὴν χεῖρα πρὸς τοῦ Δαρείου ἵππου τοὺς μυκτῆρας προσενεῖκαι, τὸν δὲ αἰσθόμενον φριμάξασθαί τε καὶ χρεμετίσαι.

88 Δαρεῖός τε δὴ ὁ Ὑστάσπεος βασιλεὺς ἀπεδέδεκτο, καί οἱ ἦσαν ἐν τῇ Ἀσίῃ πάντες κατήκοοι πλὴν Ἀραβίων, Κύρου τε καταστρεψαμένου καὶ ὕστερον αὖτις Καμβύσεω. Ἀράβιοι δὲ οὐδαμὰ κατήκουσαν ἐπὶ δουλοσύνῃ Πέρσῃσι, ἀλλὰ ξεῖνοι ἐγένοντο παρέντες Καμβύσεα ἐπ' Αἴγυπτον· ἀκόντων γὰρ Ἀραβίων οὐκ ἂν ἐσβάλοιεν Πέρσαι ἐς Αἴγυπτον. [2] γάμους τε τοὺς πρώτους ἐγάμεε Πέρσῃσι ὁ Δαρεῖος, Κύρου μὲν δύο θυγατέρας Ἄτοσσάν τε καὶ Ἀρτυστώνην, τὴν μὲν Ἄτοσσαν προσυνοικήσασαν Καμβύσῃ τε τῷ ἀδελφεῷ καὶ αὖτις τῷ Μάγῳ, τὴν δὲ Ἀρτυστώνην παρθένον· [3] ἑτέρην δὲ Σμέρδιος τοῦ Κύρου θυγατέρα ἔγημε, τῇ οὔνομα ἦν Πάρμυς· ἔσχε δὲ καὶ τὴν

τοῦ Ὀτάνεω θυγατέρα, ἣ τὸν Μάγον κατάδηλον ἐποίησε· δυνάμιός τε πάντα οἱ ἐπιμπλέατο. πρῶτον μέν νυν τύπον ποιησάμενος λίθινον ἔστησε· ζῷον δέ οἱ ἐνῆν ἀνὴρ ἱππεύς, ἐπέγραψε δὲ γράμματα λέγοντα τάδε· "Δαρεῖος ὁ Ὑστάσπεος σύν τε τοῦ ἵππου τῇ ἀρετῇ (τὸ οὔνομα λέγων) καὶ Οἰβάρεος τοῦ ἱπποκόμου ἐκτήσατο τὴν Περσέων βασιληίην."

89 ποιήσας δὲ ταῦτα ἐν Πέρσῃσι ἀρχὰς κατεστήσατο εἴκοσι, τὰς αὐτοὶ καλέουσι σατραπηίας· καταστήσας δὲ τὰς ἀρχὰς καὶ ἄρχοντας ἐπιστήσας ἐτάξατο φορούς οἱ προσιέναι κατὰ ἔθνεά τε καὶ πρὸς τοῖσι ἔθνεσι τοὺς πλησιοχώρους προστάσσων, καὶ ὑπερβαίνων τοὺς προσεχέας τὰ ἑκαστέρω ἄλλοισι ἄλλα ἔθνεα νέμων. [2] ἀρχὰς δὲ καὶ φόρων πρόσοδον τὴν ἐπέτειον κατὰ τάδε διεῖλε. τοῖσι μὲν αὐτῶν ἀργύριον ἀπαγινέουσι εἴρητο Βαβυλώνιον σταθμὸν τάλαντον ἀπαγινέειν, τοῖσι δὲ χρυσίον ἀπαγινέουσι Εὐβοϊκόν. τὸ δὲ Βαβυλώνιον τάλαντον δύναται Εὐβοΐδας ὀκτὼ καὶ ἑβδομήκοντα μνέας. [3] ἐπὶ γὰρ Κύρου ἄρχοντος καὶ αὖτις Καμβύσεω ἦν κατεστηκὸς οὐδὲν φόρου πέρι, ἀλλὰ δῶρα ἀγίνεον. διὰ δὲ ταύτην τὴν ἐπίταξιν τοῦ φόρου καὶ παραπλήσια ταύτῃ ἄλλα λέγουσι Πέρσαι ὡς Δαρεῖος μὲν ἦν κάπηλος, Καμβύσης δὲ δεσπότης, Κῦρος δὲ πατήρ, ὁ μὲν ὅτι ἐκαπήλευε πάντα τὰ πρήγματα, ὁ δὲ ὅτι χαλεπός τε ἦν καὶ ὀλίγωρος, ὁ δὲ ὅτι ἤπιός τε καὶ ἀγαθά σφι πάντα ἐμηχανήσατο.

90 ἀπὸ μὲν δὴ Ἰώνων καὶ Μαγνήτων τῶν ἐν τῇ Ἀσίῃ καὶ Αἰολέων καὶ Καρῶν καὶ Λυκίων καὶ Μιλυέων καὶ Παμφύλων, εἷς γὰρ ἦν οἱ τεταγμένος οὗτος φόρος, προσήιε τετρακόσια τάλαντα ἀργυρίου. οὗτός μὲν δὴ πρῶτος οἱ νομὸς κατεστήκεε, ἀπὸ δὲ Μυσῶν καὶ Λυδῶν καὶ Λασονίων καὶ Καβαλέων καὶ Ὑτεννέων πεντακόσια τάλαντα· δεύτερος νομὸς οὗτος. [2] ἀπὸ δὲ Ἑλλησποντίων τῶν ἐπὶ δεξιὰ ἐσπλέοντι καὶ Φρυγῶν καὶ Θρηίκων τῶν ἐν τῇ Ἀσίῃ καὶ Παφλαγόνων καὶ Μαριανδυνῶν καὶ Συρίων ἑξήκοντα καὶ τριηκόσια τάλαντα ἦν φόρος: νομὸς τρίτος οὗτος. [3] ἀπὸ δὲ Κιλίκων ἵπποι τε λευκοὶ ἑξήκοντα καὶ τριηκόσιοι, ἑκάστης ἡμέρης εἷς γινόμενος, καὶ τάλαντα ἀργυρίου πεντακόσια· τούτων δὲ τεσσεράκοντα καὶ ἑκατὸν ἐς τὴν φρουρέουσαν ἵππον τὴν Κιλικίην χώρην ἀναισιμοῦτο, τὰ δὲ τριηκόσια καὶ ἑξήκοντα Δαρείῳ ἐφοίτα· νομὸς τέταρτος οὗτος.

91 ἀπὸ δὲ Ποσιδηίου πόλιος, τῇ Ἀμφίλοχος ὁ Ἀμφιάρεω οἴκισε ἐπ' οὔροισι τοῖσι Κιλίκων τε καὶ Συρίων, ἀρξάμενον ἀπὸ ταύτης μέχρι Αἰγύπτου, πλὴν μοίρης τῆς Ἀραβίων, ταῦτα γὰρ ἦν ἀτελέα, πεντήκοντα καὶ τριηκόσια τάλαντα φόρος ἦν. ἔστι δὲ ἐν τῷ νόμῳ τούτῳ Φοινίκη τε πᾶσα καὶ Συρίη ἡ Παλαιστίνη καλεομένη καὶ Κύπρος· νομὸς πέμπτος οὗτος. [2] ἀπ' Αἰγύπτου δὲ καὶ Λιβύων τῶν προσεχέων Αἰγύπτῳ καὶ Κυρήνης τε καὶ Βάρκης, ἐς γὰρ τὸν Αἰγύπτιον νομὸν αὗται ἐκεκοσμέατο, ἑπτακόσια προσήιε τάλαντα, πάρεξ τοῦ ἐκ τῆς Μοίριος λίμνης γινομένου ἀργυρίου, τὸ ἐγίνετο ἐκ τῶν ἰχθύων· [3] τούτου τε δὴ χωρὶς τοῦ ἀργυρίου καὶ τοῦ ἐπιμετρουμένου σίτου προσήιε ἑπτακόσια τάλαντα· σίτου γὰρ δύο καὶ δέκα μυριάδας Περσέων τε τοῖσι ἐν τῷ Λευκῷ τείχεϊ τῷ ἐν Μέμφι κατοικημένοισι καταμετρέουσι καὶ τοῖσι τούτων ἐπικούροισι. νομὸς ἕκτος οὗτος. [4] Σατταγύδαι δὲ καὶ Γανδάριοι καὶ Δαδίκαι τε καὶ Ἀπαρύται ἐς τὠυτὸ τεταγμένοι ἑβδομήκοντα καὶ ἑκατὸν τάλαντα προσέφερον· νομὸς δὲ οὗτος ἕβδομος. ἀπὸ Σούσων δὲ καὶ τῆς ἄλλης Κισσίων χώρης τριηκόσια· νομὸς ὄγδοος οὗτος.

92 ἀπὸ Βαβυλῶνος δὲ καὶ τῆς λοιπῆς Ἀσσυρίης χίλιά οἱ προσήιε τάλαντα ἀργυρίου καὶ παῖδες ἐκτομίαι πεντακόσιοι· νομὸς εἴνατος οὗτος. ἀπὸ δὲ Ἀγβατάνων καὶ τῆς λοιπῆς Μηδικῆς καὶ Παρικανίων καὶ Ὀρθοκορυβαντίων πεντήκοντά τε καὶ τετρακόσια τάλαντα· νομὸς δέκατος οὗτος. [2] Κάσπιοι δὲ καὶ Παυσίκαι καὶ Παντίμαθοί τε καὶ Δαρεῖται ἐς τὠυτὸ συμφέροντες διηκόσια τάλαντα ἀπαγίνεον· νομὸς ἑνδέκατος οὗτος.

93 ἀπὸ Βακτριανῶν δὲ μέχρι Αἰγλῶν ἑξήκοντα καὶ τριηκόσια τάλαντα φόρος ἦν· νομὸς δυωδέκατος οὗτος. ἀπὸ Πακτυϊκῆς δὲ καὶ Ἀρμενίων καὶ τῶν προσεχέων μέχρι τοῦ πόντου τοῦ Εὐξείνου τετρακόσια τάλαντα· νομὸς τρίτος καὶ δέκατος οὗτος. [2] ἀπὸ δὲ Σαγαρτίων καὶ Σαραγγέων καὶ Θαμαναίων καὶ Οὐτίων καὶ Μύκων καὶ τῶν ἐν τῇσι νήσοισι οἰκεόντων τῶν ἐν τῇ Ἐρυθρῇ θαλάσσῃ, ἐν τῇσι τοὺς ἀνασπάστους καλεομένους κατοικίζει βασιλεύς, ἀπὸ τούτων πάντων ἑξακόσια τάλαντα ἐγίνετο φόρος· νομὸς τέταρτος καὶ δέκατος οὗτος. [3] Σάκαι δὲ καὶ Κάσπιοι πεντήκοντα καὶ διηκόσια ἀπαγίνεον τάλαντα· νομὸς πέμπτος καὶ δέκατος οὗτος. Πάρθοι δὲ καὶ Χοράσμιοι καὶ Σόγδοι τε καὶ Ἄρειοι τριηκόσια τάλαντα· νομὸς ἕκτος καὶ δέκατος οὗτος.

94 Παρικάνιοι δὲ καὶ Αἰθίοπες οἱ ἐκ τῆς Ἀσίης τετρακόσια τάλαντα ἀπαγίνεον· νομὸς ἕβδομος καὶ δέκατος οὗτος. Ματιηνοῖσι δὲ καὶ Σάσπειρσι καὶ Ἀλαροδίοισι διηκόσια ἐπετέτακτο τάλαντα· νομὸς ὄγδοος καὶ δέκατος οὗτος. [2] Μόσχοισι δὲ καὶ Τιβαρηνοῖσι καὶ Μάκρωσι καὶ Μοσσυνοίκοισι καὶ Μαρσὶ τριηκόσια τάλαντα προείρητο· νομὸς εἴνατος καὶ δέκατος οὗτος. Ἰνδῶν δὲ πλῆθός τε πολλῷ πλεῖστον ἐστὶ πάντων τῶν ἡμεῖς ἴδμεν ἀνθρώπων καὶ φόρον ἀπαγίνεον πρὸς πάντας τοὺς ἄλλους ἑξήκοντα καὶ τριηκόσια τάλαντα ψήγματος· νομὸς εἰκοστὸς οὗτος.

95 τὸ μὲν δὴ ἀργύριον τὸ Βαβυλώνιον πρὸς τὸ Εὐβοϊκὸν συμβαλλόμενον τάλαντον γίνεται ὀγδώκοντα καὶ ὀκτακόσια καὶ εἰνακισχίλια τάλαντα· τὸ δὲ χρυσίον τρισκαιδεκαστάσιον λογιζόμενον, τὸ ψῆγμα εὑρίσκεται ἐὸν Εὐβοϊκῶν ταλάντων ὀγδώκοντα καὶ ἑξακοσίων καὶ τετρακισχιλίων. [2] τούτων ὦν πάντων συντιθεμένων τὸ πλῆθος Εὐβοϊκὰ τάλαντα συνελέγετο ἐς τὸν ἐπέτειον φόρον Δαρείῳ μύρια καὶ τετρακισχίλια καὶ πεντακόσια καὶ ἑξήκοντα· τὸ δ' ἔτι τούτων ἔλασσον ἀπιεὶς οὐ λέγω.

96 οὗτος Δαρείῳ προσήιε φόρος ἀπὸ τῆς τε Ἀσίης καὶ τῆς Λιβύης ὀλιγαχόθεν. προϊόντος μέντοι τοῦ χρόνου καὶ ἀπὸ νήσων προσήιε ἄλλος φόρος καὶ τῶν ἐν τῇ Εὐρώπῃ μέχρι Θεσσαλίης οἰκημένων. [2] τοῦτον τὸν φόρον θησαυρίζει βασιλεὺς τρόπῳ τοιῷδε· ἐς πίθους κεραμίνους τήξας καταχέει, πλήσας δὲ τὸ ἄγγος περιαιρέει τὸν κέραμον· ἐπεὰν δὲ δεηθῇ χρημάτων, κατακόπτει τοσοῦτον ὅσον ἂν ἑκάστοτε δέηται.

97 αὗται μὲν νῦν ἀρχαί τε ἦσαν καὶ φόρων ἐπιτάξιες. ἡ Περσὶς δὲ χώρη μούνη μοι οὐκ εἴρηται δασμοφόρος· ἀτελέα γὰρ Πέρσαι νέμονται χώρην. [2] οἵδε δὲ φορὸν μὲν οὐδένα ἐτάχθησαν φέρειν, δῶρα δὲ ἀγίνεον· Αἰθίοπες οἱ πρόσουροι Αἰγύπτῳ, τοὺς Καμβύσης ἐλαύνων ἐπὶ τοὺς μακροβίους Αἰθίοπας κατεστρέψατο, οἵ τε περί τε Νύσην τὴν ἱρὴν κατοίκηνται καὶ τῷ Διονύσῳ ἀνάγουσι τὰς ὁρτάς· [οὗτοι οἱ Αἰθίοπες καὶ οἱ πλησιόχωροι τούτοισι σπέρματι μὲν χρέωνται τῷ αὐτῷ τῷ καὶ οἱ Καλλαντίαι Ἰνδοί, οἰκήματα δὲ ἔκτηνται κατάγαια.] [3] οὗτοι συναμφότεροι διὰ τρίτου ἔτεος ἀγίνεον, ἀγινέουσι δὲ καὶ τὸ μέχρι ἐμεῦ, δύο χοίνικας ἀπύρου χρυσίου καὶ διηκοσίας φάλαγγας ἐβένου καὶ πέντε παῖδας Αἰθίοπας καὶ ἐλέφαντος ὀδόντας μεγάλους εἴκοσι. [4] Κόλχοι δὲ ἐτάξαντο ἐς τὴν δωρεὴν καὶ οἱ προσεχέες μέχρι Καυκάσιος ὄρεος, ἐς τοῦτο γὰρ τὸ ὄρος ὑπὸ Πέρσῃσι ἄρχεται, τὰ δὲ πρὸς βορέην ἄνεμον τοῦ Καυκάσιος Περσέων οὐδὲν ἔτι φροντίζει. οὗτοι ὦν δῶρα τὰ ἐτάξαντο ἔτι καὶ ἐς ἐμὲ διὰ πεντετηρίδος ἀγίνεον, ἑκατὸν παῖδας καὶ ἑκατὸν παρθένους. [5] Ἀράβιοι δὲ χίλια τάλαντα ἀγίνεον λιβανωτοῦ ἀνὰ πᾶν ἔτος. ταῦτα μὲν οὗτοι δῶρα πάρεξ τοῦ φόρου βασιλέϊ ἐκόμιζον.

98 τὸν δὲ χρυσὸν τοῦτον τὸν πολλὸν οἱ Ἰνδοί, ἀπ' οὗ τὸ ψῆγμα τῷ βασιλέϊ τὸ εἰρημένον κομίζουσι, τρόπῳ τοιῷδε κτῶνται. [2] ἔστι τῆς Ἰνδικῆς χώρης τὸ πρὸς ἥλιον ἀνίσχοντα ψάμμος· τῶν γὰρ ἡμεῖς ἴδμεν, τῶν καὶ πέρι ἀτρεκές τι λέγεται, πρῶτοι πρὸς ἠῶ καὶ ἡλίου ἀνατολὰς οἰκέουσι ἀνθρώπων τῶν ἐν τῇ Ἀσίῃ Ἰνδοί· Ἰνδῶν γὰρ τὸ πρὸς τὴν ἠῶ ἐρημίη ἐστὶ διὰ τὴν ψάμμον. [3] ἔστι δὲ πολλὰ ἔθνεα Ἰνδῶν καὶ οὐκ ὁμόφωνα σφίσι, καὶ οἱ μὲν αὐτῶν νομάδες εἰσί, οἱ δὲ οὔ, οἱ δὲ ἐν τοῖσι ἕλεσι οἰκέουσι τοῦ ποταμοῦ καὶ ἰχθύας σιτέονται ὠμούς, τοὺς αἱρέουσι ἐκ πλοίων καλαμίνων ὁρμώμενοι· καλάμου δὲ ἓν γόνυ πλοῖον ἕκαστον ποιέεται. [4] οὗτοι μὲν δὴ τῶν Ἰνδῶν φορέουσι ἐσθῆτα φλοΐνην· ἐπεὰν ἐκ τοῦ ποταμοῦ φλοῦν ἀμήσωσι καὶ κόψωσι, τὸ ἐνθεῦτεν φορμοῦ τρόπον καταπλέξαντες ὡς θώρηκα ἐνδύνουσι.

99 ἄλλοι δὲ τῶν Ἰνδῶν πρὸς ἠῶ οἰκέοντες τούτων νομάδες εἰσί, κρεῶν ἐδεσταὶ ὠμῶν, καλέονται δὲ Παδαῖοι, νομαίοισι δὲ τοιοῖσιδε λέγονται χρᾶσθαι· ὃς ἂν κάμῃ τῶν ἀστῶν, ἤν τε γυνὴ ἤν τε ἀνήρ, τὸν μὲν ἄνδρα ἄνδρες οἱ μάλιστά οἱ ὁμιλέοντες κτείνουσι, φάμενοι αὐτὸν τηκόμενον τῇ νούσῳ τὰ κρέα σφίσι διαφθείρεσθαι· ὁ δὲ ἄπαρνος ἐστὶ μὴ μὲν νοσέειν, οἱ δὲ οὐ συγγινωσκόμενοι ἀποκτείναντες κατευωχέονται. [2] ἢ δὲ ἂν γυνὴ κάμῃ, ὡσαύτως αἱ ἐπιχρεώμεναι μάλιστα γυναῖκες ταὐτὰ τοῖσι ἀνδράσι ποιεῦσι. τὸν γὰρ δὴ ἐς γῆρας ἀπικόμενον θύσαντες κατευωχέονται· ἐς δὲ τούτου λόγον οὐ πολλοί τινες αὐτῶν ἀπικνέονται· πρὸ γὰρ τοῦ τὸν ἐς νοῦσον πίπτοντα πάντα κτείνουσι.

100 ἑτέρων δὲ ἐστὶ Ἰνδῶν ὅδε ἄλλος τρόπος· οὔτε κτείνουσι οὐδὲν ἔμψυχον οὔτε τι σπείρουσι οὔτε οἰκίας νομίζουσι ἐκτῆσθαι, ποιηφαγέουσί δέ καὶ αὐτοῖσι ἐστὶ ὅσον κέγχρος τὸ μέγαθος ἐν κάλυκι αὐτόματον ἐκ τῆς γῆς γινόμενον, τὸ συλλέγοντες αὐτῇ τῇ κάλυκι ἕψουσί τε καὶ σιτέονται. ὃς δ᾽ ἂν ἐς νοῦσον αὐτῶν πέσῃ, ἐλθὼν ἐς τὴν γῆν ἔρημον κεῖται· φροντίζει δὲ οὐδεὶς οὔτε ἀποθανόντος οὔτε κάμνοντος.

101 μίξις δὲ τούτων τῶν Ἰνδῶν τῶν κατέλεξα πάντων ἐμφανής ἐστι κατὰ περ τῶν προβάτων, καὶ τὸ χρῶμα φορέουσι ὅμοιον πάντες καὶ παραπλήσιον Αἰθίοψι. [2] ἡ γονὴ δὲ αὐτῶν, τὴν ἀπίενται ἐς τὰς γυναῖκας, οὐ κατὰ περ τῶν ἄλλων ἀνθρώπων ἐστὶ λευκή, ἀλλὰ μέλαινα κατὰ περ τὸ χρῶμα. τοιαύτην δὲ καὶ Αἰθίοπες ἀπίενται θορήν. οὗτοι μὲν τῶν Ἰνδῶν ἑκαστέρω τῶν Περσέων οἰκέουσι καὶ πρὸς νότου ἀνέμου καὶ Δαρείου βασιλέος οὐδαμὰ ὑπήκουσαν.

102 ἄλλοι δὲ τῶν Ἰνδῶν Κασπατύρῳ τε πόλι καὶ τῇ Πακτυϊκῇ χώρῃ εἰσὶ πρόσουροι, πρὸς ἄρκτου τε καὶ βορέω ἀνέμου κατοικημένοι τῶν ἄλλων Ἰνδῶν, οἳ Βακτρίοισι παραπλησίην ἔχουσι δίαιταν. οὗτοι καὶ μαχιμώτατοι εἰσὶ Ἰνδῶν καὶ οἱ ἐπὶ τὸν χρυσὸν στελλόμενοι εἰσὶ οὗτοι· κατὰ γὰρ τοῦτο ἐστὶ ἐρημίη διὰ τὴν ψάμμον. [2] ἐν δὴ ὦν τῇ ἐρημίῃ ταύτῃ καὶ τῇ ψάμμῳ γίνονται μύρμηκες μεγάθεα ἔχοντες κυνῶν μὲν ἐλάσσονα ἀλωπέκων δὲ μέζονα· εἰσὶ γὰρ αὐτῶν καὶ παρὰ βασιλέϊ τῷ Περσέων ἐνθεῦτεν θηρευθέντες. οὗτοι ὦν οἱ μύρμηκες ποιεύμενοι οἴκησιν ὑπὸ γῆν ἀναφορέουσι τὴν ψάμμον κατὰ περ οἱ ἐν τοῖσι Ἕλλησι μύρμηκες κατὰ τὸν αὐτὸν τρόπον, εἰσὶ δὲ καὶ αὐτοὶ τὸ εἶδος ὁμοιότατοι· ἡ δὲ ψάμμος ἡ ἀναφερομένη ἐστὶ χρυσῖτις. [3] ἐπὶ δὴ ταύτην τὴν ψάμμον στέλλονται ἐς τὴν ἔρημον οἱ Ἰνδοί, ζευξάμενος ἕκαστος καμήλους τρεῖς, σειρηφόρον μὲν ἑκατέρωθεν ἔρσενα παρέλκειν, θήλεαν δὲ ἐς μέσον· ἐπὶ ταύτην δὴ αὐτὸς ἀναβαίνει, ἐπιτηδεύσας ὅκως ἀπὸ τέκνων ὡς νεωτάτων ἀποσπάσας ζεύξει. αἱ γάρ σφι κάμηλοι ἵππων οὐκ ἥσσονες ἐς ταχυτῆτα εἰσί, χωρὶς δὲ ἄχθεα δυνατώτεραι πολλὸν φέρειν.

103 τὸ μὲν δὴ εἶδος ὁκοῖόν τι ἔχει ἡ κάμηλος ἐπισταμένοισι τοῖσι Ἕλλησι οὐ συγγράφω· τὸ δὲ μὴ ἐπιστέαται αὐτῆς, τοῦτο φράσω· κάμηλος ἐν τοῖσι ὀπισθίοισι σκέλεσι ἔχει τέσσερας μηροὺς καὶ γούνατα τέσσερα, τά τε αἰδοῖα διὰ τῶν ὀπισθίων σκελέων πρὸς τὴν οὐρὴν τετραμμένα.

104 οἱ δὲ δὴ Ἰνδοὶ τρόπῳ τοιούτῳ καὶ ζεύξι τοιαύτῃ χρεώμενοι ἐλαύνουσι ἐπὶ τὸν χρυσὸν λελογισμένως ὅκως καυμάτων τῶν θερμοτάτων ἐόντων ἔσονται ἐν τῇ ἁρπάγῃ· ὑπὸ γὰρ τοῦ καύματος οἱ μύρμηκες ἀφανέες γίνονται ὑπὸ γῆν. [2] θερμότατος δὲ ἐστὶ ὁ ἥλιος τούτοισι τοῖσι ἀνθρώποισι τὸ ἑωθινόν, οὐ κατά περ τοῖσι ἄλλοισι μεσαμβρίης, ἀλλ' ὑπερτείλας μέχρι οὗ ἀγορῆς διαλύσιος. τοῦτον δὲ τὸν χρόνον καίει πολλῷ μᾶλλον ἢ τῇ μεσαμβρίῃ τὴν Ἑλλάδα, οὕτως ὥστ' ἐν ὕδατι λόγος αὐτούς ἐστι βρέχεσθαι τηνικαῦτα. [3] μέσουσα δὲ ἡ ἡμέρη σχεδὸν παραπλησίως καίει τούς τε ἄλλους ἀνθρώπους καὶ τοὺς Ἰνδούς. ἀποκλινομένης δὲ τῆς μεσαμβρίης γίνεταί σφι ὁ ἥλιος κατά περ τοῖσι ἄλλοισι ὁ ἑωθινός, καὶ τὸ ἀπὸ τούτου ἀπιὼν ἐπὶ μᾶλλον ψύχει, ἐς ὃ ἐπὶ δυσμῇσι ἐὼν καὶ τὸ κάρτα ψύχει.

105 ἐπεὰν δὲ ἔλθωσι ἐς τὸν χῶρον οἱ Ἰνδοὶ ἔχοντες θυλάκια, ἐμπλήσαντες ταῦτα τῆς ψάμμου τὴν ταχίστην ἐλαύνουσι ὀπίσω· αὐτίκα γὰρ οἱ μύρμηκες ὀδμῇ, ὡς δὴ λέγεται ὑπὸ Περσέων, μαθόντες διώκουσι. εἶναι δὲ ταχυτῆτα οὐδενὶ ἑτέρῳ ὅμοιον, οὕτω ὥστε, εἰ μὴ προλαμβάνειν τοὺς Ἰνδοὺς τῆς ὁδοῦ ἐν ᾧ τοὺς μύρμηκας συλλέγεσθαι, οὐδένα ἂν σφέων ἀποσώζεσθαι. [2] τοὺς μέν νυν ἔρσενας τῶν καμήλων, εἶναι γὰρ ἥσσονας θέειν τῶν θηλέων, παραλύεσθαι ἐπελκομένους, οὐκ ὁμοῦ ἀμφοτέρους· τὰς δὲ θηλέας ἀναμιμνησκομένας τῶν ἔλιπον τέκνων ἐνδιδόναι μαλακὸν οὐδέν. τὸν μὲν δὴ πλέω τοῦ χρυσοῦ οὕτω οἱ Ἰνδοὶ κτῶνται, ὡς Πέρσαι φασί· ἄλλος δὲ σπανιώτερος ἐστι ἐν τῇ χώρῃ ὀρυσσόμενος.

106 αἱ δ' ἐσχατιαί κως τῆς οἰκεομένης τὰ κάλλιστα ἔλαχον, κατά περ ἡ Ἑλλὰς τὰς ὥρας πολλόν τι κάλλιστα κεκρημένας ἔλαχε. [2] τοῦτο μὲν γὰρ πρὸς τὴν ἠῶ ἐσχάτη τῶν οἰκεομενέων ἡ Ἰνδική ἐστι, ὥσπερ ὀλίγῳ πρότερον εἴρηκα· ἐν ταύτῃ τοῦτο μὲν τὰ ἔμψυχα, τετράποδά τε καὶ τὰ πετεινά, πολλῷ μέζω ἢ ἐν τοῖσι ἄλλοισι χωρίοισι ἐστί, πάρεξ τῶν ἵππων, οὗτοι δὲ ἐσσοῦνται ὑπὸ τῶν Μηδικῶν Νησαίων δὲ καλευμένων ἵππων, τοῦτο δὲ χρυσὸς ἄπλετος αὐτόθι ἐστί, ὁ μὲν ὀρυσσόμενος, ὁ δὲ καταφορεύμενος ὑπὸ ποταμῶν, ὁ δὲ ὥσπερ ἐσήμηνα ἀρπαζόμενος. [3] τὰ δὲ δένδρεα τὰ ἄγρια αὐτόθι φέρει καρπὸν εἴρια καλλονῇ τε προφέροντα καὶ ἀρετῇ τῶν ἀπὸ τῶν ὀίων· καὶ ἐσθῆτι Ἰνδοὶ ἀπὸ τούτων τῶν δενδρέων χρέωνται.

107 πρὸς δ' αὖ μεσαμβρίης ἐσχάτη Ἀραβίη τῶν οἰκεομενέων χωρέων ἐστί, ἐν δὲ ταύτῃ λιβανωτός τε ἐστι μούνῃ χωρέων πασέων φυόμενος καὶ σμύρνη καὶ κασίη καὶ κινάμωμον καὶ λήδανον. ταῦτα πάντα πλὴν τῆς σμύρνης δυσπετέως κτῶνται οἱ Ἀράβιοι. [2] τὸν μέν γε λιβανωτὸν συλλέγουσι τὴν στύρακα θυμιῶντες, τὴν ἐς Ἕλληνας Φοίνικες ἐξάγουσι· ταύτην θυμιῶντες λαμβάνουσι· τὰ γὰρ δένδρεα ταῦτα τὰ λιβανωτοφόρα ὄφιες ὑπόπτεροι, σμικροὶ τὰ μεγάθεα, ποικίλοι τὰ εἴδεα, φυλάσσουσι πλήθεϊ πολλοὶ περὶ δένδρον ἕκαστον. οὗτοι οἵ περ ἐπ' Αἴγυπτον ἐπιστρατεύονται, οὐδενὶ δὲ ἄλλῳ ἀπελαύνονται ἀπὸ τῶν δενδρέων ἢ τῆς στύρακος τῷ καπνῷ.

108 λέγουσι δὲ καὶ τόδε Ἀράβιοι, ὡς πᾶσα ἂν γῆ ἐπίμπλατο τῶν ὀφίων τούτων, εἰ μὴ γίνεσθαι κατ' αὐτοὺς οἷόν τι κατὰ τὰς ἐχίδνας ἠπιστάμην γίνεσθαι. [2] καί κως τοῦ θείου ἡ προνοίη, ὥσπερ καὶ οἰκὸς ἐστι, ἐοῦσα σοφή, ὅσα μὲν ψυχήν τε δειλὰ καὶ ἐδώδιμα, ταῦτα μὲν πάντα πολύγονα πεποίηκε, ἵνα μὴ ἐπιλίπῃ κατεσθιόμενα, ὅσα δὲ σχέτλια καὶ ἀνιηρά, ὀλιγόγονα. [3] τοῦτο μέν, ὅτι ὁ λαγὸς ὑπὸ παντὸς θηρεύεται θηρίου καὶ ὄρνιθος καὶ ἀνθρώπου, οὕτω δή τι πολύγονος ἐστί· ἐπικυΐσκεται μοῦνον πάντων θηρίων, καὶ τὸ μὲν δασὺ τῶν τέκνων ἐν τῇ γαστρὶ, τὸ δὲ ψιλόν, τὸ δὲ ἄρτι ἐν τῇσι μήτρῃσι πλάσσεται, τὸ δὲ ἀναιρέεται. [4] τοῦτο μὲν δὴ τοιοῦτο ἐστί· ἡ δὲ δὴ λέαινα ἐὸν ἰσχυρότατον καὶ θρασύτατον ἅπαξ ἐν τῷ βίῳ τίκτει ἕν· τίκτουσα γὰρ συνεκβάλλει τῷ τέκνῳ τὰς μήτρας. τὸ δὲ αἴτιον τούτου τόδε ἐστί· ἐπεὰν ὁ σκύμνος ἐν τῇ μητρὶ ἐὼν ἄρχηται διακινεόμενος, ὁ δὲ ἔχων ὄνυχας θηρίων πολλὸν πάντων ὀξυτάτους ἀμύσσει τὰς μήτρας, αὐξόμενός τε δὴ πολλῷ μᾶλλον ἐσικνέεται καταγράφων· πέλας τε δὴ ὁ τόκος ἐστί καὶ τὸ παράπαν λείπεται αὐτέων ὑγιὲς οὐδέν.

109 ὡς δὲ καὶ οἱ ἔχιδναί τε καὶ οἱ ἐν Ἀραβίοισι ὑπόπτεροι ὄφιες εἰ ἐγίνοντο ὡς ἡ φύσις αὐτοῖσι ὑπάρχει, οὐκ ἂν ἦν βιώσιμα ἀνθρώποισι · νῦν δ' ἐπεὰν θορνύωνται κατὰ ζεύγεα καὶ ἐν αὐτῇ ᾖ ὁ ἔρσην τῇ ἐκποιήσι, ἀπιεμένου αὐτοῦ τὴν γονὴν ἡ θήλεα ἅπτεται τῆς δειρῆς, καὶ ἐμφῦσα οὐκ ἀνίει πρὶν ἂν διαγάγῃ. [2] ὁ μὲν δὴ ἔρσην ἀποθνήσκει τρόπῳ τῷ εἰρημένῳ, ἡ δὲ θήλεα τίσιν τοιήνδε ἀποτίνει τῷ ἔρσενι· τῷ γονέϊ τιμωρέοντα ἔτι ἐν τῇ γαστρὶ ἐόντα τὰ τέκνα διεσθίει τὴν μητέρα, διαφαγόντα δὲ τὴν νηδὺν αὐτῆς οὕτω τὴν ἔκδυσιν ποιέεται. [3] οἱ δὲ ἄλλοι ὄφιες ἐόντες ἀνθρώπων οὐ δηλήμονες τίκτουσί τε ᾠὰ καὶ ἐκλέπουσι πολλόν τι χρῆμα τῶν τέκνων. αἱ μέν νυν ἔχιδναι κατὰ πᾶσαν γῆν εἰσί, οἱ δὲ ὑπόπτεροι ὄφιες ἀθρόοι εἰσὶ ἐν τῇ Ἀραβίῃ καὶ οὐδαμῇ ἄλλῃ· κατὰ τοῦτο δοκέουσι πολλοὶ εἶναι.

110 τὸν μὲν δὴ λιβανωτὸν τοῦτον οὕτω κτῶνται Ἀράβιοι, τὴν δὲ κασίην ὧδε. ἐπεὰν καταδήσωνται βύρσῃσι καὶ δέρμασι ἄλλοισι πᾶν τὸ σῶμα καὶ τὸ πρόσωπον πλὴν αὐτῶν τῶν ὀφθαλμῶν, ἔρχονται ἐπὶ τὴν κασίην· ἡ δὲ ἐν λίμνῃ φύεται οὐ βαθέῃ, περὶ δὲ αὐτὴν καὶ ἐν αὐτῇ αὐλίζεταί κου θηρία πτερωτά, τῇσι νυκτερίσι προσείκελα μάλιστα, καὶ τέτριγε δεινόν, καὶ ἐς ἀλκὴν ἄλκιμα· τὰ δεῖ ἀπαμυνομένους ἀπὸ τῶν ὀφθαλμῶν οὕτω δρέπειν τὴν κασίην.

111 τὸ δὲ δὴ κιναμώμον ἔτι τούτων θωμαστότερον συλλέγουσι. ὅκου μὲν γὰρ γίνεται καὶ ἥτις μιν γῆ ἡ τρέφουσα ἐστί, οὐκ ἔχουσι εἰπεῖν, πλὴν ὅτι λόγῳ οἰκότι χρεώμενοι ἐν τοῖσιδε χωρίοισι φασὶ τινες αὐτὸ φύεσθαι ἐν τοῖσι ὁ Διόνυσος ἐτράφη· [2] ὄρνιθας δὲ λέγουσι μεγάλας φορέειν ταῦτα τὰ κάρφεα τὰ ἡμεῖς ἀπὸ Φοινίκων μαθόντες κινάμωμον καλέομεν, φορέειν δὲ τὰς ὄρνιθας ἐς νεοσσιὰς προσπεπλασμένας ἐκ πηλοῦ πρὸς ἀποκρήμνοισι ὄρεσι, ἔνθα πρόσβασιν ἀνθρώπῳ οὐδεμίαν εἶναι. [3] πρὸς ὦν δὴ ταῦτα τοὺς Ἀραβίους σοφίζεσθαι τάδε· βοῶν τε καὶ ὄνων τῶν ἀπογινομένων καὶ τῶν ἄλλων ὑποζυγίων τὰ μέλεα διαταμόντας ὡς μέγιστα κομίζειν ἐς ταῦτα τὰ χωρία, καί σφεα θέντας ἀγχοῦ τῶν νεοσσιέων ἀπαλλάσσεσθαι ἑκὰς αὐτέων· τὰς δὲ ὄρνιθας καταπετομένας τὰ μέλεα τῶν ὑποζυγίων ἀναφορέειν ἐπὶ τὰς νεοσσιάς, τὰς δὲ οὐ δυναμένας ἴσχειν καταρρήγνυσθαι ἐπὶ γῆν, τοὺς δὲ ἐπιόντας συλλέγειν. οὕτω μὲν τὸ κινάμωμον συλλεγόμενον ἐκ τούτων ἀπικνέεσθαι ἐς τὰς ἄλλας χώρας.

112 τὸ δὲ δὴ λήδανον, τὸ καλέουσι Ἀράβιοι λάδανον, ἔτι τούτου θωμασιώτερον γίνεται· ἐν γὰρ δυσοδμοτάτῳ γινόμενον εὐωδέστατον ἐστί· τῶν γὰρ αἰγῶν τῶν τράγων ἐν τοῖσι πώγωσι εὑρίσκεται ἐγγινόμενον οἷον γλοιὸς ἀπὸ τῆς ὕλης. χρήσιμον δ' ἐς πολλὰ τῶν μύρων ἐστί, θυμιῶσί τε μάλιστα τοῦτο Ἀράβιοι.

113 τοσαῦτα μὲν θυωμάτων πέρι εἰρήσθω, ἀπόζει δὲ τῆς χώρης τοὺς Ἀραβίης θεσπέσιον ὡς ἡδύ. δύο δὲ γένεα ὀίων σφι ἐστὶ θώματος ἄξια, τὰ οὐδαμόθι ἑτέρωθι ἐστί. τὸ μὲν αὐτῶν ἕτερον ἔχει τὰς οὐρὰς μακράς, τριῶν πηχέων οὐκ ἐλάσσονας, τὰς εἴ τις ἐπείη σφι ἐπέλκειν, ἕλκεα ἂν ἔχοιεν ἀνατριβομενέων πρὸς τῇ γῇ τῶν οὐρέων· [2] νῦν δ' ἅπας τις τῶν ποιμένων ἐπίσταται ξυλουργέειν ἐς τοσοῦτο· ἁμαξίδας γὰρ ποιεῦντες ὑποδέουσι αὐτὰς τῇσι οὐρῇσι, ἑνὸς ἑκάστου κτήνεος τὴν οὐρὴν ἐπὶ ἁμαξίδα ἑκάστην καταδέοντες. τὸ δὲ ἕτερον γένος τῶν οἴων τὰς οὐρὰς πλατέας φορέουσι καὶ ἐπὶ πῆχυν πλάτος.

114 ἀποκλινομένης δὲ μεσαμβρίης παρήκει πρὸς δύνοντα ἥλιον ἡ Αἰθιοπίη χώρη ἐσχάτη τῶν οἰκεομενέων· αὕτη δὲ χρυσόν τε φέρει πολλὸν καὶ ἐλέφαντας ἀμφιλαφέας καὶ δένδρεα πάντα ἄγρια καὶ ἔβενον καὶ ἄνδρας μεγίστους καὶ καλλίστους καὶ μακροβιωτάτους.

115 αὗται μέν νυν ἔν τε τῇ Ἀσίῃ ἐσχατιαί εἰσι καὶ ἐν τῇ Λιβύῃ. περὶ δὲ τῶν ἐν τῇ Εὐρώπῃ τῶν πρὸς ἑσπέρην ἐσχατιέων ἔχω μὲν οὐκ ἀτρεκέως λέγειν· οὔτε γὰρ ἔγωγε ἐνδέκομαι Ἠριδανὸν καλέεσθαι πρὸς βαρβάρων ποταμὸν ἐκδιδόντα ἐς θάλασσαν τὴν πρὸς βορέην ἄνεμον, ἀπ' ὅτευ τὸ ἤλεκτρον φοιτᾶν λόγος ἐστί, οὔτε νήσους οἶδα Κασσιτερίδας ἐούσας, ἐκ τῶν ὁ κασσίτερος ἡμῖν φοιτᾷ. [2] τοῦτο μὲν γὰρ ὁ Ἠριδανὸς αὐτὸ κατηγορέει τὸ οὔνομα ὡς ἔστι Ἑλληνικὸν καὶ οὐ βάρβαρον, ὑπὸ ποιητέω δὲ τινὸς ποιηθέν· τοῦτο δὲ οὐδενὸς αὐτόπτεω γενομένου δύναμαι ἀκοῦσαι, τοῦτο μελετῶν, ὅκως θάλασσά ἐστι τὰ ἐπέκεινα Εὐρώπης. ἐξ ἐσχάτης δ' ὦν ὁ κασσίτερος ἡμῖν φοιτᾷ καὶ τὸ ἤλεκτρον.

116 πρὸς δὲ ἄρκτου τῆς Εὐρώπης πολλῷ τι πλεῖστος χρυσὸς φαίνεται ἐών· ὅκως μὲν γινόμενος, οὐκ ἔχω οὐδὲ τοῦτο ἀτρεκέως εἶπαι, λέγεται δὲ ὑπὲκ τῶν γρυπῶν ἁρπάζειν Ἀριμασποὺς ἄνδρας μουνοφθάλμους. [2] πείθομαι δὲ οὐδὲ τοῦτο ὅκως μουνόφθαλμοι ἄνδρες φύονται, φύσιν ἔχοντες τὴν ἄλλην ὁμοίην τοῖσι ἄλλοισι ἀνθρώποισι· [3] αἱ δὲ ὦν ἐσχατιαὶ οἴκασι, περικληίουσαι τὴν ἄλλην χώρην καὶ ἐντὸς ἀπέργουσαι, τὰ κάλλιστα δοκέοντα ἡμῖν εἶναι καὶ σπανιώτατα ἔχειν αὐτά.

117 ἔστι δὲ πεδίον ἐν τῇ Ἀσίῃ περικεκλημένον ὄρεϊ πάντοθεν, διασφάγες δὲ τοῦ ὄρεος εἰσί πέντε. τοῦτο τὸ πεδίον ἦν μέν κοτε Χορασμίων, ἐν οὔροισι ἐὸν Χορασμίων τε αὐτῶν καὶ Ὑρκανίων καὶ Πάρθων καὶ Σαραγγέων καὶ Θαμαναίων, ἐπείτε δὲ Πέρσαι ἔχουσι τὸ κράτος, ἐστὶ τοῦ βασιλέος. [2] ἐκ δὴ ὦν τοῦ περικληίοντος ὄρεος τούτου ῥέει ποταμὸς μέγας, οὔνομα δέ οἱ ἐστὶ Ἄκης. οὗτος πρότερον μὲν ἄρδεσκε διαλελαμμένος πενταχοῦ τούτων τῶν εἰρημένων τὰς χώρας, διὰ διασφάγος ἀγόμενος ἑκάστης ἑκάστοισι· ἐπείτε δὲ ὑπὸ τῷ Πέρσῃ εἰσί, πεπόνθασι τοιόνδε· [3] τὰς διασφάγας τῶν ὀρέων ἐνδείμας ὁ βασιλεὺς πύλας ἐπ' ἑκάστῃ διασφάγι ἔστησε· ἀποκεκλημένου δὲ τοῦ ὕδατος τῆς ἐξόδου τὸ πεδίον τὸ ἐντὸς τῶν ὀρέων πέλαγος γίνεται, ἐνδιδόντος μὲν τοῦ ποταμοῦ, ἔχοντος δὲ οὐδαμῇ ἐξήλυσιν. [4] οὗτοι ὦν οἵ περ ἔμπροσθε ἐώθεσαν χρᾶσθαι τῷ ὕδατι, οὐκ ἔχοντες αὐτῷ χρᾶσθαι συμφορῇ μεγάλῃ διαχρέωνται. τὸν μὲν γὰρ χειμῶνα ὕει σφι ὁ θεὸς ὥσπερ καὶ τοῖσι ἄλλοισι ἀνθρώποισι, τοῦ δὲ θέρεος σπείροντες μελίνην καὶ σήσαμον χρηίσκονται τῷ ὕδατι. [5] ἐπεὰν ὦν μηδέν σφι παραδιδῶται τοῦ ὕδατος, ἐλθόντες ἐς τοὺς Πέρσας αὐτοί τε καὶ γυναῖκες, στάντες κατὰ τὰς θύρας τοῦ βασιλέος βοῶσι ὠρυόμενοι, ὁ δὲ βασιλεὺς τοῖσι δεομένοισι αὐτῶν μάλιστα ἐντέλλεται ἀνοίγειν τὰς πύλας τὰς ἐς τοῦτο φερούσας. [6] ἐπεὰν δὲ διάκορος ἡ γῆ σφεων γένηται πίνουσα τὸ ὕδωρ, αὗται μὲν αἱ πύλαι ἀποκληίονται, ἄλλας δ' ἐντέλλεται ἀνοίγειν ἄλλοισι τοῖσι δεομένοισι μάλιστα τῶν λοιπῶν. ὡς δ' ἐγὼ οἶδα ἀκούσας, χρήματα μεγάλα πρησσόμενος ἀνοίγει πάρεξ τοῦ φόρου. ταῦτα μὲν δὴ ἔχει οὕτω.

118 τῶν δὲ τῷ Μάγῳ ἐπαναστάντων ἑπτὰ ἀνδρῶν ἕνα αὐτῶν Ἰνταφρένεα κατέλαβε ὑβρίσαντα τάδε ἀποθανεῖν αὐτίκα μετὰ τὴν ἐπανάστασιν. ἤθελε ἐς τὰ βασιλήια ἐσελθὼν χρηματίσασθαι τῷ βασιλέϊ· καὶ γὰρ δὴ καὶ ὁ νόμος οὕτω εἶχε, τοῖσι ἐπαναστᾶσι τῷ Μάγῳ ἔσοδον εἶναι παρὰ βασιλέα ἄνευ ἀγγέλου, ἢν μὴ γυναικὶ τυγχάνῃ μισγόμενος βασιλεύς. [2] οὔκων δὴ ὁ Ἰνταφρένης ἐδικαίου οὐδένα οἱ ἐσαγγεῖλαι, ἀλλ' ὅτι ἦν τῶν ἑπτά, ἐσιέναι ἤθελε. ὁ δὲ πυλουρὸς καὶ ὁ ἀγγελιηφόρος οὐ περιώρων, φάμενοι τὸν βασιλέα γυναικὶ μίσγεσθαι. ὁ δὲ Ἰνταφρένης δοκέων σφέας ψευδέα λέγειν ποιέει τοιάδε· σπασάμενος τὸν ἀκινάκεα ἀποτάμνει αὐτῶν τά τε ὦτα καὶ τὰς ῥῖνας, καὶ ἀνείρας περὶ τὸν χαλινὸν τοῦ ἵππου περὶ τοὺς αὐχένας σφέων ἔδησε καὶ ἀπῆκε.

119 οἱ δὲ τῷ βασιλέϊ δεικνύουσι ἑωυτοὺς καὶ τὴν αἰτίην εἶπον δι' ἣν πεπονθότες εἴησαν. Δαρεῖος δὲ ἀρρωδήσας μὴ κοινῷ λόγῳ οἱ ἓξ πεποιηκότες ἔωσι ταῦτα, μεταπεμπόμενος ἕνα ἕκαστον ἀπεπειρᾶτο γνώμης, εἰ συνέπαινοί εἰσι τῷ πεποιημένῳ. [2] ἐπείτε δὲ ἐξέμαθε ὡς οὐ σὺν κείνοισι εἴη ταῦτα πεποιηκώς, ἔλαβε αὐτόν τε τὸν Ἰνταφρένεα καὶ τοὺς παῖδας αὐτοῦ καὶ τοὺς οἰκηίους πάντας, ἐλπίδας πολλὰς ἔχων μετὰ τῶν συγγενέων μιν ἐπιβουλεύειν οἱ ἐπανάστασιν, συλλαβὼν δὲ σφέας ἔδησε τὴν ἐπὶ θανάτῳ. [3] ἡ δὲ γυνὴ τοῦ Ἰνταφρένεος φοιτῶσα ἐπὶ τὰς θύρας τοῦ βασιλέος κλαίεσκε ἂν καὶ ὀδυρέσκετο· ποιεῦσα δὲ αἰεὶ τὠυτὸ τοῦτο τὸν Δαρεῖον ἔπεισε οἰκτεῖραί μιν. πέμψας δὲ ἄγγελον ἔλεγε τάδε· "Ὦ γύναι, βασιλεύς τοι Δαρεῖος διδοῖ ἕνα τῶν δεδεμένων οἰκηίων ῥύσασθαι τὸν βούλεαι ἐκ πάντων." [4] ἡ δὲ βουλευσαμένη ὑπεκρίνετο τάδε· "Εἰ μὲν δή μοι διδοῖ βασιλεὺς ἑνὸς τὴν ψυχήν, αἱρέομαι ἐκ πάντων τὸν ἀδελφεόν." [5] πυθόμενος δὲ Δαρεῖος ταῦτα καὶ θωμάσας τὸν λόγον, πέμψας ἠγόρευε· "Ὦ γύναι, εἰρωτᾷ σε βασιλεὺς τίνα ἔχουσα γνώμην, τὸν ἄνδρα τε καὶ τὰ τέκνα ἐγκαταλιποῦσα, τὸν ἀδελφεὸν εἵλευ περιεῖναί τοι, ὃς καὶ ἀλλοτριώτερός τοι τῶν παίδων καὶ ἧσσον κεχαρισμένος τοῦ ἀνδρός ἐστι." [6] ἡ δ' ἀμείβετο τοῖσιδε. "Ὦ βασιλεῦ, ἀνὴρ μέν μοι ἂν ἄλλος γένοιτο, εἰ δαίμων ἐθέλοι, καὶ τέκνα ἄλλα, εἰ ταῦτα ἀποβάλοιμι· πατρὸς δὲ καὶ μητρὸς οὐκέτι μευ ζωόντων ἀδελφεὸς ἂν ἄλλος οὐδενὶ τρόπῳ γένοιτο. ταύτῃ τῇ γνώμῃ χρεωμένη ἔλεξα ταῦτα." [7] εὖ τε δὴ ἔδοξε τῷ Δαρείῳ εἰπεῖν ἡ γυνή, καί οἱ ἀπῆκε τοῦτόν τε τὸν παραιτέετο καὶ τῶν παίδων τὸν πρεσβύτατον ἡσθεὶς αὐτῇ, τοὺς δὲ ἄλλους ἀπέκτεινε πάντας. τῶν μὲν δὴ ἑπτὰ εἷς αὐτίκα τρόπῳ τῷ εἰρημένῳ ἀπολώλεε.

120 κατὰ δέ κου μάλιστα τὴν Καμβύσεω νοῦσον ἐγίνετο τάδε. ὑπὸ Κύρου κατασταθεὶς ἦν Σαρδίων ὕπαρχος Ὀροίτης ἀνὴρ Πέρσης· οὗτος ἐπεθύμησε πρήγματος οὐκ ὁσίου· οὔτε γάρ τι παθὼν οὔτε ἀκούσας μάταιον ἔπος πρὸς Πολυκράτεος τοῦ Σαμίου, οὐδὲ ἰδὼν πρότερον ἐπεθύμεε λαβὼν αὐτὸν ἀπολέσαι, ὡς μὲν οἱ πλεῦνες λέγουσι, διὰ τοιήνδε τινὰ αἰτίην. [2] ἐπὶ τῶν βασιλέος θυρέων κατήμενον τόν τε Ὀροίτεα καὶ ἄλλον Πέρσην τῷ οὔνομα εἶναι Μιτροβάτεα, νόμου ἄρχοντα τοῦ ἐν Δασκυλείῳ, τούτους ἐκ λόγων ἐς νείκεα συμπεσεῖν, κρινομένων δὲ περὶ ἀρετῆς εἰπεῖν τὸν Μιτροβάτεα τῷ Ὀροίτῃ προφέροντα [3] "Σὺ γὰρ ἐν ἀνδρῶν λόγῳ, ὃς βασιλέϊ νῆσον Σάμον πρὸς τῷ σῷ νόμῳ προσκειμένην οὐ προσεκτήσαο, ὧδε δή τι ἐοῦσαν εὐπετέα χειρωθῆναι, τὴν τῶν τις ἐπιχωρίων πεντεκαίδεκα ὁπλίτῃσι ἐπαναστὰς ἔσχε καὶ νῦν αὐτῆς τυραννεύει." [4] οἱ μὲν δή μιν φασὶ τοῦτο ἀκούσαντα καὶ ἀλγήσαντα τῷ ὀνείδεϊ ἐπιθυμῆσαι οὐκ οὕτω τὸν εἴπαντα ταῦτα τίσασθαι ὡς Πολυκράτεα πάντως ἀπολέσαι, δι' ὅντινα κακῶς ἤκουσε.

121 οἱ δὲ ἐλάσσονες λέγουσι πέμψαι Ὀροίτεα ἐς Σάμον κήρυκα ὅτευ δὴ χρήματος δεησόμενον, οὐ γὰρ ὧν δὴ τοῦτό γε λέγεται, καὶ τὸν Πολυκράτεα τυχεῖν κατακείμενον ἐν ἀνδρεῶνι, παρεῖναι δέ οἱ καὶ

Ἀνακρέοντα τὸν Τήιον· [2] καί κως εἴτ᾽ ἐκ προνοίης αὐτὸν κατηλογέοντα τὰ Ὀροίτεω πρήγματα, εἴτε καὶ συντυχίη τις τοιαύτη ἐπεγένετο· τόν τε γὰρ κήρυκα τὸν Ὀροίτεω παρελθόντα διαλέγεσθαι, καὶ τὸν Πολυκράτεα τυχεῖν γὰρ ἀπεστραμμένον πρὸς τὸν τοῖχον, οὔτε τι μεταστραφῆναι οὔτε ὑποκρίνασθαι.

122 αἰτίαι μὲν δὴ αὗται διφάσιαι λέγονται τοῦ θανάτου τοῦ Πολυκράτεος γενέσθαι, πάρεστι δὲ πείθεσθαι ὁκοτέρῃ τις βούλεται αὐτέων. ὁ δὲ ὢν Ὀροίτης ἱζόμενος ἐν Μαγνησίῃ τῇ ὑπὲρ Μαιάνδρου ποταμοῦ οἰκημένῃ ἔπεμπε Μύρσον τὸν Γύγεω ἄνδρα Λυδὸν ἐς Σάμον ἀγγελίην φέροντα, μαθὼν τοῦ Πολυκράτεος τὸν νόον. [2] Πολυκράτης γὰρ ἐστὶ πρῶτος τῶν ἡμεῖς ἴδμεν Ἑλλήνων ὃς θαλασσοκρατέειν ἐπενοήθη, πάρεξ Μίνωός τε τοῦ Κνωσσίου καὶ εἰ δή τις ἄλλος πρότερος τούτου ἦρξε τῆς θαλάσσης· τῆς δὲ ἀνθρωπηίης λεγομένης γενεῆς Πολυκράτης πρῶτος, ἐλπίδας πολλὰς ἔχων Ἰωνίης τε καὶ νήσων ἄρξειν. [3] μαθὼν ὦν ταῦτά μιν διανοεύμενον ὁ Ὀροίτης πέμψας ἀγγελίην ἔλεγε τάδε. "Ὀροίτης Πολυκράτεϊ ὧδε λέγει. πυνθάνομαι ἐπιβουλεύειν σε πρήγμασι μεγάλοισι, καὶ χρήματά δέ τοι οὐκ εἶναι κατὰ τὰ φρονήματα. σύ νυν ὧδε ποιήσας ὀρθώσεις μὲν σεωυτόν, σώσεις δὲ καὶ ἐμέ· ἐμοὶ γὰρ βασιλεὺς Καμβύσης ἐπιβουλεύει θάνατον, καί μοι τοῦτο ἐξαγγέλλεται σαφηνέως. [4] σύ νυν ἐμὲ ἐκκομίσας αὐτὸν καὶ χρήματα, τὰ μὲν αὐτῶν αὐτὸς ἔχε, τὰ δὲ ἐμὲ ἔα ἔχειν· εἵνεκέν τε χρημάτων ἄρξεις ἁπάσης τῆς Ἑλλάδος. εἰ δέ μοι ἀπιστέες τὰ περὶ τῶν χρημάτων, πέμψον ὅστις τοι πιστότατος τυγχάνει ἐών, τῷ ἐγὼ ἀποδέξω."

123 ταῦτα ἀκούσας Πολυκράτης ἥσθη τε καὶ ἐβούλετο· καί κως ἱμείρετο γὰρ χρημάτων μεγάλως, ἀποπέμπει πρῶτα κατοψόμενον Μαιάνδριον Μαιανδρίου ἄνδρα τῶν ἀστῶν, ὅς οἱ ἦν γραμματιστής· ὃς χρόνῳ οὐ πολλῷ ὕστερον τούτων τὸν κόσμον τὸν ἐκ τοῦ ἀνδρεῶνος τοῦ Πολυκράτεος ἐόντα ἀξιοθέητον ἀνέθηκε πάντα ἐς τὸ Ἥραιον. [2] ὁ δὲ Ὀροίτης μαθὼν τὸν κατάσκοπον ἐόντα προσδόκιμον ἐποίεε τοιάδε· λάρνακας ὀκτὼ πληρώσας λίθων πλὴν κάρτα βραχέος τοῦ περὶ αὐτὰ τὰ χείλεα, ἐπιπολῆς τῶν λίθων χρυσὸν ἐπέβαλε, καταδήσας δὲ τὰς λάρνακας εἶχε ἑτοίμας. ἐλθὼν δὲ ὁ Μαιάνδριος καὶ θεησάμενος ἀπήγγελλε τῷ Πολυκράτεϊ.

124 ὁ δὲ πολλὰ μὲν τῶν μαντίων ἀπαγορευόντων πολλὰ δὲ τῶν φίλων ἐστέλλετο αὐτόσε, πρὸς δὲ καὶ ἰδούσης τῆς θυγατρὸς ὄψιν ἐνυπνίου τοιήνδε· ἐδόκεέ οἱ τὸν πατέρα ἐν τῷ ἠέρι μετέωρον ἐόντα λοῦσθαι μὲν ὑπὸ τοῦ Διός, χρίεσθαι δὲ ὑπὸ τοῦ ἡλίου. [2] ταύτην ἰδοῦσα τὴν ὄψιν παντοίη ἐγίνετο μὴ ἀποδημῆσαι τὸν Πολυκράτεα παρὰ τὸν Ὀροίτεα, καὶ δὴ καὶ ἰόντος αὐτοῦ ἐπὶ τὴν πεντηκόντερον ἐπεφημίζετο. ὁδέ οἱ ἠπείλησε, ἢν σῶς ἀπονοστήσῃ, πολλόν μιν χρόνον παρθενεύεσθαι. ἡ δὲ ἠρήσατο ἐπιτελέα ταῦτα γενέσθαι· βούλεσθαι γὰρ παρθενεύεσθαι πλέω χρόνον ἢ τοῦ πατρὸς ἐστερῆσθαι.

125 Πολυκράτης δὲ πάσης συμβουλίης ἀλογήσας ἔπλεε παρὰ τὸν Ὀροίτεα, ἅμα ἀγόμενος ἄλλους τε πολλοὺς τῶν ἑταίρων, ἐν δὲ δὴ καὶ Δημοκήδεα τὸν Καλλιφῶντος Κροτωνιήτην ἄνδρα, ἰητρόν τε ἐόντα καὶ τὴν τέχνην ἀσκέοντα ἄριστα τῶν κατ' ἑωυτόν. [2] ἀπικόμενος δὲ ἐς τὴν Μαγνησίην ὁ Πολυκράτης διεφθάρη κακῶς, οὔτε ἑωυτοῦ ἀξίως οὔτε τῶν ἑωυτοῦ φρονημάτων· ὅτι γὰρ μὴ οἱ Συρηκοσίων γενόμενοι τύραννοι οὐδὲ εἷς τῶν ἄλλων Ἑλληνικῶν τυράννων ἄξιος ἐστὶ Πολυκράτεϊ μεγαλοπρεπείην συμβληθῆναι. [3] ἀποκτείνας δέ μιν οὐκ ἀξίως ἀπηγήσιος Ὀροίτης ἀνεσταύρωσε· τῶν δέ οἱ ἑπομένων ὅσοι μὲν ἦσαν Σάμιοι, ἀπῆκε, κελεύων σφέας ἑωυτῷ χάριν εἰδέναι ἐόντας ἐλευθέρους, ὅσοι δὲ ἦσαν ξεῖνοί τε καὶ δοῦλοι τῶν ἑπομένων, ἐν ἀνδραπόδων λόγῳ ποιεύμενος εἶχε. Πολυκράτης δὲ ἀνακρεμάμενος ἐπετέλεε πᾶσαν τὴν ὄψιν τῆς θυγατρός· ἐλοῦτο μὲν γὰρ ὑπὸ τοῦ Διὸς ὅκως ὕοι, ἐχρίετο δὲ ὑπὸ τοῦ ἡλίου, ἀνιεὶς αὐτὸς ἐκ τοῦ σώματος ἰκμάδα. [4] Πολυκράτεος μὲν δὴ αἱ πολλαὶ εὐτυχίαι ἐς τοῦτο ἐτελεύτησαν τῇ οἱ Ἄμασις ὁ Αἰγύπτου βασιλεὺς προεμαντεύσατο.

126 χρόνῳ δὲ οὐ πολλῷ ὕστερον καὶ Ὀροίτεα Πολυκράτεος τίσιες μετῆλθον. μετὰ γὰρ τὸν Καμβύσεω θάνατον καὶ τῶν Μάγων τὴν βασιληίην μένων ἐν τῇσι Σάρδισι Ὀροίτης ὠφέλεε μὲν οὐδὲν Πέρσας ὑπὸ Μήδων ἀπαραιρημένους τὴν ἀρχήν· [2] ὁ δὲ ἐν ταύτῃ τῇ ταραχῇ κατὰ μὲν ἔκτεινε Μιτροβάτεα τὸν ἐκ Δασκυλείου ὕπαρχον, ὅς οἱ ὠνείδισε τὰ ἐς Πολυκράτεα ἔχοντα, κατὰ δὲ τοῦ Μιτροβάτεω τὸν παῖδα Κρανάσπην, ἄνδρας ἐν Πέρσῃσι δοκίμους, ἄλλα τε ἐξύβρισε παντοῖα καί τινα ἀγγελιηφόρον ἐλθόντα Δαρείου παρ' αὐτόν, ὡς οὐ πρὸς ἡδονήν οἱ ἦν τὰ ἀγγελλόμενα, κτείνει μιν ὀπίσω κομιζόμενον, ἄνδρας οἱ ὑπείσας κατ' ὁδόν, ἀποκτείνας δέ μιν ἠφάνισε αὐτῷ ἵππῳ.

127 Δαρεῖος δὲ ὡς ἔσχε τὴν ἀρχήν, ἐπεθύμεε τὸν Ὀροίτεα τίσασθαι πάντων τῶν ἀδικημάτων εἵνεκεν καὶ μάλιστα Μιτροβάτεω καὶ τοῦ παιδός. ἐκ μὲν δὴ τῆς ἰθέης στρατὸν ἐπ' αὐτὸν οὐκ ἐδόκεε πέμπειν ἅτε οἰδεόντων ἔτι τῶν πρηγμάτων καὶ νεωστὶ ἔχων τῇ ἀρχὴν καὶ τὸν Ὀροίτεα μεγάλην τὴν ἰσχὺν πυνθανόμενος ἔχειν, τὸν χίλιοι μὲν Περσέων ἐδορυφόρεον, εἶχε δὲ νομὸν τόν τε Φρύγιον καὶ Λύδιον καὶ Ἰωνικόν. [2] πρὸς ταῦτα δὴ ὦν ὁ Δαρεῖος τάδε ἐμηχανήσατο. συγκαλέσας Περσέων τοὺς δοκιμωτάτους ἔλεγέ σφι τάδε. "Ὦ Πέρσαι, τίς ἄν μοι τοῦτο ὑμέων ὑποστὰς ἐπιτελέσειε σοφίῃ καὶ μὴ βίῃ τε καὶ ὁμίλῳ; ἔνθα γὰρ σοφίης δέει, βίης ἔργον οὐδέν· [3] ὑμέων δὲ ὦν τίς μοι Ὀροίτεα ἢ ζώοντα ἀγάγοι ἢ ἀποκτείνειε; ὅς ὠφέλησε μέν κω Πέρσας οὐδέν, κακὰ δὲ μεγάλα ἔοργε· τοῦτο μὲν δύο ἡμέων ἤιστωσε, Μιτροβάτεά τε καὶ τὸν παῖδα αὐτοῦ, τοῦτο δὲ τοὺς ἀνακαλέοντας αὐτὸν καὶ πεμπομένους ὑπ' ἐμεῦ κτείνει, ὕβριν οὐκ ἀνασχετὸν φαίνων. πρίν τι ὦν μέζον ἐξεργάσασθαί μιν Πέρσας κακόν, καταλαμπτέος ἐστὶ ἡμῖν θανάτῳ."

128 Δαρεῖος μὲν ταῦτα ἐπειρώτα, τῷ δὲ ἄνδρες τριήκοντα ὑπέστησαν, αὐτὸς ἕκαστος ἐθέλων ποιέειν ταῦτα. ἐρίζοντας δὲ Δαρεῖος κατελάμβανε κελεύων πάλλεσθαι· παλλομένων δὲ λαγχάνει ἐκ πάντων Βαγαῖος ὁ Ἀρτόντεω· [2] λαχὼν δὲ ὁ Βαγαῖος ποιέει τάδε· βυβλία γραψάμενος πολλὰ καὶ περὶ πολλῶν ἔχοντα πρηγμάτων σφρηγίδά σφι ἐπέβαλε τὴν Δαρείου, μετὰ δὲ ἤιε ἔχων ταῦτα ἐς τὰς Σάρδις. [3] ἀπικόμενος δὲ καὶ Ὀροίτεω ἐς ὄψιν ἐλθών, τῶν βυβλίων ἓν ἕκαστον περιαιρεόμενος ἐδίδου τῷ γραμματιστῇ τῷ βασιληίῳ ἐπιλέγεσθαι· γραμματιστὰς δὲ βασιληίους οἱ πάντες ὕπαρχοι ἔχουσι· ἀποπειρώμενος δὲ τῶν δορυφόρων ἐδίδου τὰ βυβλία ὁ Βαγαῖος, εἰ ἐνδεξαίατο ἀπόστασιν ἀπὸ Ὀροίτεω. [4] ὀρέων δὲ σφέας τά τε βυβλία σεβομένους μεγάλως καὶ τὰ λεγόμενα ἐκ τῶν βυβλίων ἔτι μεζόνως, διδοῖ ἄλλο ἐν τῷ ἐνῆν ἔπεα τάδε· "Ὦ Πέρσαι, βασιλεὺς Δαρεῖος ἀπαγορεύει ὑμῖν μὴ δορυφορέειν Ὀροίτεα." οἱ δὲ ἀκούσαντες τούτων μετῆκάν οἱ τὰς αἰχμάς. [5] ἰδὼν δὲ τοῦτό σφεας ὁ Βαγαῖος πειθομένους τῷ βυβλίῳ, ἐνθαῦτα δὴ θαρσήσας τὸ τελευταῖον τῶν βυβλίων διδοῖ τῷ γραμματιστῇ, ἐν τῷ ἐγέγραπτο "Βασιλεὺς Δαρεῖος Πέρσῃσι τοῖσι ἐν Σάρδισι ἐντέλλεται κτείνειν Ὀροίτεα." οἱ δὲ δορυφόροι ὡς ἤκουσαν ταῦτα, σπασάμενοι τοὺς ἀκινάκεας κτείνουσι παραυτίκα μιν. οὕτω δὴ Ὀροίτεα τὸν Πέρσην Πολυκράτεος τοῦ Σαμίου τίσιες μετῆλθον.

129 ἀπικομένων δὲ καὶ ἀνακομισθέντων τῶν Ὀροίτεω χρημάτων ἐς τὰ Σοῦσα, συνήνεικε χρόνῳ οὐ πολλῷ ὕστερον βασιλέα Δαρεῖον ἐν ἄγρῃ θηρῶν ἀποθρώσκοντα ἀπ' ἵππου στραφῆναι τὸν πόδα. [2] καί κως ἰσχυροτέρως ἐστράφη· ὁ γάρ οἱ ἀστράγαλος ἐξεχώρησε ἐκ τῶν ἄρθρων. νομίζων δὲ καὶ πρότερον περὶ ἑωυτὸν ἔχειν Αἰγυπτίων τοὺς δοκέοντας εἶναι πρώτους τὴν ἰητρικήν, τούτοισι ἐχρᾶτο. οἱ δὲ στρεβλοῦντες καὶ βιώμενοι τὸν πόδα κακὸν μέζον ἐργάζοντο. [3] ἐπ' ἑπτὰ μὲν δὴ ἡμέρας καὶ ἑπτὰ νύκτας ὑπὸ τοῦ παρεόντος κακοῦ ὁ Δαρεῖος ἀγρυπνίῃσι εἴχετο, τῇ δὲ δὴ ὀγδόῃ ἡμέρῃ ἔχοντί οἱ φλαύρως, παρακούσας τις πρότερον ἔτι ἐν Σάρδισι τοῦ Κροτωνιήτεω Δημοκήδεος τὴν τέχνην ἐσαγγέλλει τῷ Δαρείῳ· ὁ δὲ ἄγειν μιν τὴν ταχίστην παρ' ἑωυτὸν ἐκέλευσε· τὸν δὲ ὡς ἐξεῦρον ἐν τοῖσι Ὀροίτεω ἀνδραπόδοισι ὅκου δὴ ἀπημελημένον, παρῆγον ἐς μέσον πέδας τε ἕλκοντα καὶ ῥάκεσι ἐσθημένον.

130 σταθέντα δὲ ἐς μέσον εἰρώτα ὁ Δαρεῖος τὴν τέχνην εἰ ἐπίσταιτο· ὁ δὲ οὐκ ὑπεδέκετο, ἀρρωδέων μὴ ἑωυτὸν ἐκφήνας τὸ παράπαν τῆς Ἑλλάδος ᾖ ἀπεστερημένος· [2] κατεφάνη δέ τῷ Δαρείῳ τεχνάζειν ἐπιστάμενος, καὶ τοὺς ἀγαγόντας αὐτὸν ἐκέλευσε μάστιγάς τε καὶ κέντρα παραφέρειν ἐς τὸ μέσον. ὁ δὲ ἐνθαῦτα δὴ ὦν ἐκφαίνει, φὰς ἀτρεκέως μὲν οὐκ ἐπίστασθαι, ὁμιλήσας δὲ ἰητρῷ φλαύρως ἔχειν τὴν τέχνην. [3] μετὰ δέ, ὥς οἱ ἐπέτρεψε, Ἑλληνικοῖσι ἰήμασι χρεώμενος καὶ ἤπια μετὰ τὰ ἰσχυρὰ προσάγων ὕπνου τέ μιν λαγχάνειν ἐποίεε καὶ ἐν χρόνῳ ὀλίγῳ ὑγιέα μιν ἀπέδεξε, οὐδαμὰ ἔτι ἐλπίζοντα ἀρτίπουν ἔσεσθαι. [4] δωρέεται δή μιν μετὰ ταῦτα ὁ Δαρεῖος πεδέων χρυσέων δύο ζεύγεσι· ὁ δέ μιν ἐπείρετο εἴ οἱ διπλήσιον τὸ κακὸν ἐπίτηδες νέμει ὅτι μιν ὑγιέα ἐποίησε. ἡσθεὶς δὲ τῷ ἔπεϊ ὁ Δαρεῖος ἀποπέμπει μιν παρὰ τὰς ἑωυτοῦ γυναῖκας· παράγοντες δὲ οἱ εὐνοῦχοι ἔλεγον πρὸς τὰς γυναῖκας ὡς βασιλέϊ οὗτος εἴη ὃς τὴν ψυχὴν ἀπέδωκε. [5] ὑποτύπτουσα δὲ αὐτέων ἑκάστη φιάλῃ τοῦ χρυσοῦ ἐς θήκην ἐδωρέετο Δημοκήδεα οὕτω δή τι δαψιλέϊ δωρεῇ ὡς τοὺς ἀποπίπτοντας ἀπὸ τῶν φιαλέων στατῆρας ἑπόμενος ὁ οἰκέτης, τῷ οὔνομα ἦν Σκίτων, ἀνελέγετο καί οἱ χρῆμα πολλόν τι χρυσοῦ συνελέχθη.

131 ὁ δὲ Δημοκήδης οὗτος ὧδε ἐκ Κρότωνος ἀπιγμένος Πολυκράτεϊ ὡμίλησε· πατρὶ συνείχετο ἐν τῇ Κρότωνι ὀργὴν χαλεπῷ· τοῦτον ἐπείτε οὐκ ἐδύνατο φέρειν, ἀπολιπὼν οἴχετο ἐς Αἴγιναν. καταστὰς δὲ ἐς ταύτην πρώτῳ ἔτεϊ ὑπερεβάλετο τοὺς ἄλλους ἰητρούς, ἀσκευής περ ἐὼν καὶ ἔχων οὐδὲν τῶν ὅσα περὶ τὴν τέχνην ἐστὶ ἐργαλήια. [2] καί μιν δευτέρῳ ἔτεϊ ταλάντου Αἰγινῆται δημοσίῃ μισθοῦνται, τρίτῳ δὲ ἔτεϊ Ἀθηναῖοι ἑκατὸν μνέων, τετάρτῳ δὲ ἔτεϊ Πολυκράτης δυῶν ταλάντων. οὕτω μὲν ἀπίκετο ἐς τὴν Σάμον, καὶ ἀπὸ τούτου τοῦ ἀνδρὸς οὐκ ἥκιστα Κροτωνιῆται ἰητροὶ εὐδοκίμησαν. [3] ἐγένετο γὰρ ὦν τοῦτο ὅτε πρῶτοι μὲν Κροτωνιῆται ἰητροὶ ἐλέγοντο ἀνὰ τὴν Ἑλλάδα εἶναι, δεύτεροι δὲ Κυρηναῖοι. [κατὰ τὸν αὐτὸν δὲ τοῦτον χρόνον καὶ Ἀργεῖοι ἤκουον μουσικὴν εἶναι Ἑλλήνων πρῶτοι.]

132 τότε δὴ ὁ Δημοκήδης ἐν τοῖσι Σούσοισι ἐξιησάμενος Δαρεῖον οἶκόν τε μέγιστον εἶχε καὶ ὁμοτράπεζος βασιλέϊ ἐγεγόνεε, πλήν τε ἑνὸς τοῦ ἐς Ἕλληνας ἀπιέναι πάντα τἄλλά οἱ παρῆν. [2] καὶ τοῦτο μὲν τοὺς Αἰγυπτίους ἰητρούς, οἳ βασιλέα πρότερον ἰῶντο, μέλλοντας ἀνασκολοπιεῖσθαι διότι ὑπὸ Ἕλληνος ἰητροῦ ἑσσώθησαν, τούτους βασιλέα παραιτησάμενος ἐρρύσατο· τοῦτο δὲ μάντιν Ἠλεῖον Πολυκράτεϊ ἐπισπόμενον καὶ ἀπημελημένον ἐν τοῖσι ἀνδραπόδοισι ἐρρύσατο. ἦν δὲ μέγιστον πρῆγμα Δημοκήδης παρὰ βασιλέϊ.

133 ἐν χρόνῳ δὲ ὀλίγῳ μετὰ ταῦτα τάδε ἄλλα συνήνεικε γενέσθαι. Ἀτόσσῃ τῇ Κύρου μὲν θυγατρὶ Δαρείου δὲ γυναικὶ ἐπὶ τοῦ μαστοῦ ἔφυ φῦμα, μετὰ δὲ ἐκραγὲν ἐνέμετο πρόσω. ὅσον μὲν δὴ χρόνον ἦν ἔλασσον, ἡ δὲ κρύπτουσα καὶ αἰσχυνομένη ἔφραζε οὐδενί· [2] ἐπείτε δὲ ἐν κακῷ ἦν, μετεπέμψατο τὸν Δημοκήδεα καί οἱ ἐπέδεξε. ὁ δὲ φὰς ὑγιέα ποιήσειν ἐξορκοῖ μιν ἦ μέν οἱ ἀντυπουργήσειν ἐκείνην τοῦτο τὸ ἂν αὐτῆς δεηθῇ· δεήσεσθαι δὲ οὐδενὸς τῶν ὅσα ἐς αἰσχύνην ἐστὶ φέροντα.

134 ὡς δὲ ἄρα μιν μετὰ ταῦτα ἰώμενος ὑγιέα ἀπέδεξε, ἐνθαῦτα δὴ διδαχθεῖσα ὑπὸ τοῦ Δημοκήδεος ἡ Ἄτοσσα προσέφερε ἐν τῇ κοίτῃ Δαρείῳ λόγον τοιόνδε. "Ὦ βασιλεῦ, ἔχων δύναμιν τοσαύτην κάτησαι οὔτε τι ἔθνος προσκτώμενος οὔτε δύναμιν Πέρσῃσι. [2] οἰκὸς δὲ ἐστὶ ἄνδρα καὶ νέον καὶ χρημάτων μεγάλων δεσπότην φαίνεσθαί τι ἀποδεικνύμενον ἵνα καὶ Πέρσαι ἐκμάθωσι ὅτι ὑπ' ἀνδρὸς ἄρχονται. ἐπ' ἀμφότερα δέ τοι συμφέρει ταῦτα ποιεῖν, καὶ ἵνα σφέων Πέρσαι ἐπίστωνται ἄνδρα εἶναι τὸν προεστεῶτα, καὶ ἵνα τρίβωνται πολέμῳ μηδὲ σχολὴν ἄγοντες ἐπιβουλεύωσί τοι. [3] νῦν γὰρ ἄν τι καὶ ἀποδέξαιο ἔργον, ἕως νέος εἰς ἡλικίην· αὐξομένῳ γὰρ τῷ σώματι συναύξονται καὶ αἱ φρένες, γηράσκοντι δὲ συγγηράσκουσι καὶ ἐς τὰ πρήγματα πάντα ἀπαμβλύνονται." [4] ἡ μὲν δὴ ταῦτα ἐκ διδαχῆς ἔλεγε, ὁ δ' ἀμείβετο τοῖσιδε. "Ὦ γύναι, πάντα ὅσα περ αὐτὸς ἐπινοέω ποιήσειν εἴρηκας· ἐγὼ γὰρ βεβούλευμαι ζεύξας γέφυραν ἐκ τῆσδε τῆς ἠπείρου ἐς τὴν ἑτέρην ἤπειρον ἐπὶ Σκύθας στρατεύεσθαι· καὶ ταῦτα ὀλίγου χρόνου ἔσται τελεύμενα." [5] λέγει Ἄτοσσα τάδε. "Ὅρα νυν, ἐπὶ Σκύθας μὲν τὴν πρώτην ἰέναι ἔασον· οὗτοι γάρ, ἐπεὰν σὺ βούλῃ, ἔσονταί τοι· σὺ δέ μοι ἐπὶ τὴν Ἑλλάδα στρατεύεσθαι. ἐπιθυμέω γὰρ λόγῳ πυνθανομένη Λακαίνας τέ μοι γενέσθαι θεραπαίνας καὶ Ἀργείας καὶ Ἀττικὰς καὶ Κορινθίας. ἔχεις δὲ ἄνδρα ἐπιτηδεότατον ἀνδρῶν πάντων δέξαι τε ἕκαστα τῆς Ἑλλάδος καὶ κατηγήσασθαι, τοῦτον ὅς σεῦ τὸν πόδα ἐξιήσατο." [6] ἀμείβεται Δαρεῖος "Ὦ γύναι, ἐπεὶ τοίνυν τοι δοκέει τῆς Ἑλλάδος ἡμέας πρῶτα ἀποπειρᾶσθαι, κατασκόπους μοι δοκέει Περσέων πρῶτον ἄμεινον εἶναι ὁμοῦ τούτῳ τῷ σὺ λέγεις πέμψαι ἐς αὐτούς, οἳ μαθόντες καὶ ἰδόντες ἐξαγγελέουσι ἕκαστα αὐτῶν ἡμῖν· καὶ ἔπειτα ἐξεπιστάμενος ἐπ' αὐτοὺς τρέψομαι.

135 ταῦτα εἶπε καὶ ἅμα ἔπος τε καὶ ἔργον ἐποίεε. ἐπείτε γὰρ τάχιστα ἡμέρη ἐπέλαμψε, καλέσας Περσέων ἄνδρας δοκίμους πεντεκαίδεκα ἐνετέλλετό σφι ἑπομένους Δημοκήδεϊ διεξελθεῖν τὰ παραθαλάσσια τῆς Ἑλλάδος, ὅκως τε μὴ διαδρήσεταί σφεας ὁ Δημοκήδης, ἀλλά μιν πάντως ὀπίσω ἀπάξουσι. [2] ἐντειλάμενος δὲ τούτοισι ταῦτα, δεύτερα καλέσας αὐτὸν Δημοκήδεα ἐδέετο αὐτοῦ ὅκως ἐξηγησάμενος πᾶσαν καὶ ἐπιδέξας τὴν Ἑλλάδα τοῖσι Πέρσῃσι ὀπίσω ἥξει· δῶρα δέ μιν τῷ πατρὶ καὶ τοῖσι ἀδελφεοῖσι ἐκέλευε πάντα τὰ ἐκείνου ἔπιπλα λαβόντα ἄγειν, φὰς ἄλλα οἱ πολλαπλήσια ἀντιδώσειν· πρὸς δὲ ἐς τὰ δῶρα ὁλκάδα οἱ ἔφη συμβαλέεσθαι πλήσας ἀγαθῶν παντοίων, τὴν ἅμα οἱ πλεύσεσθαι. [3] Δαρεῖος μὲν δή, δοκέειν ἐμοί, ἀπ' οὐδενὸς δολεροῦ νόου ἐπαγγέλλετό οἱ ταῦτα. Δημοκήδης δὲ δείσας μὴ εὖ ἐκπειρῷτο Δαρεῖος, οὔτι ἐπιδραμὼν πάντα τὰ διδόμενα ἐδέκετο, ἀλλὰ τὰ μὲν ἑωυτοῦ κατὰ χώρην ἔφη καταλείψειν ἵνα ὀπίσω σφέα ἀπελθὼν ἔχοι, τὴν μέντοι ὁλκάδα, τὴν οἱ Δαρεῖος ἐπαγγέλλετο, ἐς τὴν δωρεὴν τοῖσι ἀδελφεοῖσι δέκεσθαι ἔφη. ἐντειλάμενος δὲ καὶ τούτῳ ταὐτὰ ὁ Δαρεῖος ἀποστέλλει αὐτοὺς ἐπὶ θάλασσαν.

136 καταβάντες δὲ οὗτοι ἐς Φοινίκην καὶ Φοινίκης ἐς Σιδῶνα πόλιν αὐτίκα μὲν τριήρεας δύο ἐπλήρωσαν, ἅμα δὲ αὐτῇσι καὶ γαῦλον μέγαν παντοίων ἀγαθῶν· παρασκευάσμενοι δὲ πάντα ἔπλεον ἐς τὴν Ἑλλάδα, προσίσχοντες δὲ αὐτῆς τὰ παραθαλάσσια ἐθηεῦντο καὶ ἀπεγράφοντο, ἐς ὃ τὰ πολλὰ αὐτῆς καὶ ὀνομαστὰ θεησάμενοι ἀπίκοντο τῆς Ἰταλίης ἐς Τάραντα. [2] ἐνθαῦτα δὲ ἐκ ῥηϊστώνης τῆς Δημοκήδεος Ἀριστοφιλίδης τῶν Ταραντίνων ὁ βασιλεὺς τοῦτο μὲν τὰ πηδάλια παρέλυσε τῶν Μηδικέων νεῶν, τοῦτο δὲ αὐτοὺς τοὺς Πέρσας εἷρξε ὡς κατασκόπους δῆθεν ἐόντας. ἐν ᾧ δὲ οὗτοι ταῦτα ἔπασχον, ὁ Δημοκήδης ἐς τὴν Κρότωνα ἀπικνέεται· ἀπιγμένου δὲ ἤδη τούτου ἐς τὴν ἑωυτοῦ ὁ Ἀριστοφιλίδης ἔλυσε τοὺς Πέρσας καὶ τὰ παρέλαβε τῶν νεῶν ἀπέδωκέ σφι.

137 πλέοντες δὲ ἐνθεῦτεν οἱ Πέρσαι καὶ διώκοντες Δημοκήδεα ἀπικνέονται ἐς τὴν Κρότωνα, εὑρόντες δέ μιν ἀγοράζοντα ἅπτοντο αὐτοῦ. [2] τῶν δὲ Κροτωνιητέων οἱ μὲν καταρρωδέοντες τὰ Περσικὰ πρήγματα προϊέναι ἕτοιμοι ἦσαν, οἱ δὲ ἀντάπτοντο καὶ τοῖσι σκυτάλοισι ἔπαιον τοὺς Πέρσας προϊσχομένους ἔπεα τάδε. " Ἄνδρες Κροτωνιῆται, ὁρᾶτε τὰ ποιέετε· ἄνδρα βασιλέος δρηπέτην γενόμενον ἐξαιρέεσθε. [3] κῶς ταῦτα βασιλέϊ Δαρείῳ ἐκχρήσει περιυβρίσθαι; κῶς δὲ ὑμῖν τὰ ποιεύμενα ἕξει καλῶς, ἢν ἀπέλησθε ἡμέας; ἐπὶ τίνα δὲ τῆσδε προτέρην στρατευσόμεθα πόλιν; τίνα δὲ προτέρην ἀνδραποδίζεσθαι περιησόμεθα;" [4] ταῦτα λέγοντες τοὺς Κροτωνιήτας οὔκων ἔπειθον, ἀλλ᾽ ἐξαιρεθέντες τε τὸν Δημοκήδεα καὶ τὸν γαῦλον τὸν ἅμα ἤγοντο ἀπαιρεθέντες ἀπέπλεον ὀπίσω ἐς τὴν Ἀσίην, οὐδ᾽ ἔτι ἐζήτησαν τὸ προσωτέρω τῆς Ἑλλάδος ἀπικόμενοι ἐκμαθεῖν, ἐστερημένοι τοῦ ἡγεμόνος. [5] τοσόνδε μέντοι ἐνετείλατό σφι Δημοκήδης ἀναγομένοισι, κελεύων εἰπεῖν σφεας Δαρείῳ ὅτι ἅρμοσται τὴν Μίλωνος θυγατέρα Δημοκήδης γυναῖκα. τοῦ γὰρ δὴ παλαιστέω Μίλωνος ἦν οὔνομα πολλὸν παρὰ βασιλέϊ· κατὰ δὲ τοῦτό μοι δοκέει σπεῦσαι τὸν γάμον τοῦτον τελέσας χρήματα μεγάλα Δημοκήδης, ἵνα φανῇ πρὸς Δαρείου ἐὼν καὶ ἐν τῇ ἑωυτοῦ δόκιμος.

138 ἀναχθέντες δὲ ἐκ τῆς Κρότωνος οἱ Πέρσαι ἐκπίπτουσι τῇσι νηυσὶ ἐς Ἰηπυγίην, καί σφεας δουλεύοντας ἐνθαῦτα Γίλλος ἀνὴρ Ταραντῖνος φυγὰς ῥυσάμενος ἀπήγαγε παρὰ βασιλέα Δαρεῖον. ὁ δὲ ἀντὶ τούτων ἕτοιμος ἦν διδόναι τοῦτο ὅ τι βούλοιτο αὐτός. [2] Γίλλος δὲ αἱρέεται κάτοδόν οἱ ἐς Τάραντα γενέσθαι, προαπηγησάμενος τὴν συμφορήν· ἵνα δὲ μὴ συνταράξῃ τὴν Ἑλλάδα, ἢν δι᾽ αὐτὸν στόλος μέγας πλέῃ ἐπὶ τὴν Ἰταλίην, Κνιδίους μούνους ἀποχρᾶν οἱ ἔφη τοὺς κατάγοντας γίνεσθαι, δοκέων ἀπὸ τούτων ἐόντων τοῖσι Ταραντίνοισι φίλων μάλιστα τὴν κάτοδόν οἱ ἔσεσθαι. [3] Δαρεῖος δὲ ὑποδεξάμενος ἐπετέλεε· πέμψας γὰρ ἄγγελον ἐς Κνίδον κατάγειν σφέας ἐκέλευε Γίλλον ἐς Τάραντα. πειθόμενοι δὲ Δαρείῳ Κνίδιοι Ταραντίνους οὔκων ἔπειθον, βίην δὲ ἀδύνατοι ἦσαν προσφέρειν. ταῦτα μέν νυν οὕτω ἐπρήχθη· οὗτοι δὲ πρῶτοι ἐκ τῆς Ἀσίης ἐς τὴν Ἑλλάδα ἀπίκοντο Πέρσαι, καὶ οὗτοι διὰ τοιόνδε πρῆγμα κατάσκοποι ἐγένοντο.

139 μετὰ δὲ ταῦτα Σάμον βασιλεὺς Δαρεῖος αἱρέει πολίων πασέων πρώτην Ἑλληνίδων καὶ βαρβάρων διὰ τοιήνδε τινὰ αἰτίην. Καμβύσεω τοῦ Κύρου στρατευομένου ἐπ' Αἴγυπτον ἄλλοι τε συχνοὶ ἐς τὴν Αἴγυπτον ἀπίκοντο Ἑλλήνων, οἱ μέν, ὡς οἰκός, κατ' ἐμπορίην στρατευόμενοι, οἱ δὲ τινὲς καὶ αὐτῆς τῆς χώρης θεηταί· τῶν ἦν καὶ Συλοσῶν ὁ Αἰακέος, Πολυκράτεός τε ἐὼν ἀδελφεὸς καὶ φεύγων ἐκ Σάμου. [2] τοῦτον τὸν Συλοσῶντα κατέλαβε εὐτυχίη τις τοιήδε. λαβὼν χλανίδα καὶ περιβαλόμενος πυρρὴν ἠγόραζε ἐν τῇ Μέμφι· ἰδὼν δὲ αὐτὸν Δαρεῖος, δορυφόρος τε ἐὼν Καμβύσεω καὶ λόγου οὐδενός κω μεγάλου, ἐπεθύμησε τῆς χλανίδος καὶ αὐτὴν προσελθὼν ὠνέετο. [3] ὁ δὲ Συλοσῶν ὁρέων τὸν Δαρεῖον μεγάλως ἐπιθυμέοντα τῆς χλανίδος, θείῃ τύχῃ χρεώμενος λέγει "Ἐγὼ ταύτην πωλέω μὲν οὐδενὸς χρήματος, δίδωμι δὲ ἄλλως, εἴ περ οὕτω δεῖ γενέσθαι πάντως τοι." αἰνέσας ταῦτα ὁ Δαρεῖος παραλαμβάνει τὸ εἷμα.

140 ὁ μὲν δὴ Συλοσῶν ἠπίστατο τοῦτό οἱ ἀπολωλέναι δι' εὐηθείην. ὡς δὲ τοῦ χρόνου προβαίνοντος Καμβύσης τε ἀπέθανε καὶ τῷ Μάγῳ ἐπανέστησαν οἱ ἑπτὰ καὶ ἐκ τῶν ἑπτὰ Δαρεῖος τὴν βασιληίην ἔσχε, πυνθάνεται ὁ Συλοσῶν ὡς ἡ βασιληίη περιεληλύθοι ἐς τοῦτον τὸν ἄνδρα τῷ κοτὲ αὐτὸς ἔδωκε ἐν Αἰγύπτῳ δεηθέντι τὸ εἷμα. ἀναβὰς δὲ ἐς τὰ Σοῦσα ἵζετο ἐς τὰ πρόθυρα τῶν βασιλέος οἰκίων καὶ ἔφη Δαρείου εὐεργέτης εἶναι. [2] ἀγγελλεῖ ταῦτα ἀκούσας ὁ πυλουρὸς τῷ βασιλέϊ· ὁ δὲ θωμάσας λέγει πρὸς αὐτόν "Καὶ τίς ἐστὶ Ἑλλήνων εὐεργέτης τῷ ἐγὼ προαιδεῦμαι, νεωστὶ μὲν τὴν ἀρχὴν ἔχων; ἀναβέβηκε δ' ἤ τις ἢ οὐδείς κω παρ' ἡμέας αὐτῶν, ἔχω δὲ χρέος εἰπεῖν οὐδὲν ἀνδρὸς Ἕλληνος. ὅμως δὲ αὐτὸν παράγετε ἔσω, ἵνα εἰδέω τί θέλων λέγει ταῦτα." [3] παρῆγε ὁ πυλουρὸς τὸν Συλοσῶντα, στάντα δὲ ἐς μέσον εἰρώτων οἱ ἑρμηνέες τίς τε εἴη καὶ τί ποιήσας εὐεργέτης φησὶ εἶναι βασιλέος. εἶπε ὦν ὁ Συλοσῶν πάντα τὰ περὶ τὴν χλανίδα γενόμενα, καὶ ὡς αὐτὸς εἴη κεῖνος ὁ δούς. [4] ἀμείβεται πρὸς ταῦτα Δαρεῖος· "Ὦ γενναιότατε ἀνδρῶν, σὺ κεῖνος εἷς ὃς ἐμοὶ οὐδεμίαν ἔχοντί κω δύναμιν ἔδωκας εἰ καὶ σμικρά, ἀλλ' ὦν ἴση γε ἡ χάρις ὁμοίως ὡς εἰ νῦν κοθέν τι μέγα λάβοιμι· ἀντ' ὧν τοι χρυσὸν καὶ ἄργυρον ἄπλετον δίδωμι, ὡς μή κοτέ τοι μεταμελήσῃ Δαρείῳ τὸν Ὑστάσπεος εὖ ποιήσαντι." [5] λέγει πρὸς ταῦτα ὁ Συλοσῶν· "Ἐμοὶ μήτε χρυσόν, ὦ βασιλεῦ, ἤτε ἄργυρον δίδου, ἀλλ' ἀνασωσάμενός μοι δὸς τὴν πατρίδα Σάμον, τὴν νῦν ἀδελφεοῦ τοῦ ἐμοῦ Πολυκράτεος ἀποθανόντος ὑπὸ Ὀροίτεω ἔχει δοῦλος ἡμέτερος· ταύτην μοι δὸς ἄνευ τε φόνου καὶ ἐξανδραποδίσιος."

141 ταῦτα ἀκούσας Δαρεῖος ἀπέστελλε στρατιήν τε καὶ στρατηγὸν Ὀτάνεα ἀνδρῶν τῶν ἑπτὰ γενόμενον, ἐντειλάμενος ὅσων ἐδεήθη ὁ Συλοσῶν ταῦτά οἱ ποιέειν ἐπιτελέα. καταβὰς δὲ ἐπὶ τὴν θάλασσαν ὁ Ὀτάνης ἔστελλε τὴν στρατιήν.

142 τῆς δὲ Σάμου Μαιάνδριος ὁ Μαιανδρίου εἶχε τὸ κράτος, ἐπιτροπαίην παρὰ Πολυκράτεος λαβὼν τὴν ἀρχήν· τῷ δικαιοτάτῳ ἀνδρῶν βουλομένῳ γενέσθαι οὐκ ἐξεγένετο. [2] ἐπειδὴ γάρ οἱ ἐξαγγέλθη ὁ Πολυκράτεος θάνατος, ἐποίεε τοιάδε· πρῶτα μὲν Διὸς Ἐλευθερίου βωμὸν ἱδρύσατο καὶ τέμενος περὶ αὐτὸν οὔρισε τοῦτο τὸ νῦν ἐν τῷ προαστείῳ ἐστί· μετὰ δέ, ὥς οἱ ἐπεποίητο, ἐκκλησίην συναγείρας πάντων τῶν ἀστῶν ἔλεξε τάδε. [3] "Ἐμοί, ὡς ἴστε καὶ ὑμεῖς, σκῆπτρον καὶ δύναμις πᾶσα ἡ Πολυκράτεος ἐπιτέτραπται, καί μοι παρέχει νῦν ὑμέων ἄρχειν. ἐγὼ δὲ τὰ τῷ πέλας ἐπιπλήσσω, αὐτὸς κατὰ δύναμιν οὐ ποιήσω· οὔτε γάρ μοι Πολυκράτης ἤρεσκε δεσπόζων ἀνδρῶν ὁμοίων ἑωυτῷ οὔτε ἄλλος ὅστις τοιαῦτα ποιέει. Πολυκράτης μέν νυν ἐξέπλησε μοῖραν τὴν ἑωυτοῦ, ἐγὼ δὲ ἐς μέσον τὴν ἀρχὴν τιθεὶς ἰσονομίην ὑμῖν προαγορεύω. [4] τοσάδε μέντοι δικαιῶ γέρεα ἐμεωυτῷ γενέσθαι, ἐκ μέν γε τῶν Πολυκράτεος χρημάτων ἐξαίρετα ἓξ τάλαντά μοι γενέσθαι, ἱερωσύνην δὲ πρὸς τούτοισι αἱρεῦμαι αὐτῷ τέ μοι καὶ τοῖσι ἀπ' ἐμεῦ αἰεὶ γινομένοισι τοῦ Διὸς τοῦ Ἐλευθερίου· τῷ αὐτός τε ἱρὸν ἱδρυσάμην καὶ τὴν ἐλευθερίην ὑμῖν περιτίθημι." [5] ὁ μὲν δὴ ταῦτα τοῖσι Σαμίοισι ἐπηγγέλλετο· τῶν δέ τις ἐξαναστὰς εἶπε "Ἀλλ' οὐδ' ἄξιος εἶς σύ γε ἡμέων ἄρχειν, γεγονώς τε κακῶς καὶ ἐὼν ὄλεθρος· ἀλλὰ μᾶλλον ὅκως λόγον δώσεις τῶν μετεχείρισας χρημάτων."

143 ταῦτα εἶπε ἐὼν ἐν τοῖσι ἀστοῖσι δόκιμος, τῷ οὔνομα ἦν Τελέσαρχος. Μαιάνδριος δὲ νόῳ λαβὼν ὡς εἰ μετήσει τὴν ἀρχήν, ἄλλος τις ἀντ' αὐτοῦ τύραννος καταστήσεται, οὐ δή τί ἐν νόῳ εἶχε μετιέναι αὐτήν, ἀλλ' ὡς ἀνεχώρησε ἐς τὴν ἀκρόπολιν, μεταπεμπόμενος ἕνα ἕκαστον ὡς δὴ λόγον τῶν χρημάτων δώσων, συνέλαβε σφέας καὶ κατέδησε. [2] οἱ μὲν δὴ ἐδεδέατο, Μαιάνδριον δὲ μετὰ ταῦτα κατέλαβε νοῦσος. ἐλπίζων δέ μιν ἀποθανέεσθαι ὁ ἀδελφεός, τῷ οὔνομα ἦν Λυκάρητος, ἵνα εὐπετεστέρως κατάσχῃ τὰ ἐν τῇ Σάμῳ πρήγματα, κατακτείνει τοὺς δεσμώτας πάντας· οὐ γὰρ δή, οἴκασι, ἐβούλοντο εἶναι ἐλεύθεροι.

144 ἐπειδὴ ὦν ἀπίκοντο ἐς τὴν Σάμον οἱ Πέρσαι κατάγοντες Συλοσῶντα, οὔτε τίς σφι χεῖρας ἀνταείρεται, ὑπόσπονδοί τε ἔφασαν εἶναι ἕτοιμοι οἱ τοῦ Μαιανδρίου στασιῶται καὶ αὐτὸς Μαιάνδριος ἐκχωρῆσαι ἐκ τῆς νήσου. καταινέσαντος δ' ἐπὶ τούτοισι Ὀτάνεω καὶ σπεισαμένου, τῶν Περσέων οἱ πλείστου ἄξιοι θρόνους θέμενοι κατεναντίον τῆς ἀκροπόλιος κατέατο.

145 Μαιανδρίῳ δὲ τῷ τυράννῳ ἦν ἀδελφεὸς ὑπομαργότερος, τῷ οὔνομα ἦν Χαρίλεως· οὗτος ὅ τι δὴ ἐξαμαρτὼν ἐν γοργύρῃ ἐδέδετο. καὶ δὴ τότε ἐπακούσας τε τὰ πρησσόμενα καὶ διακύψας διὰ τῆς γοργύρης, ὡς εἶδε τοὺς Πέρσας εἰρηναίως κατημένους, ἐβόα τε καὶ ἔφη λέγων Μαιανδρίῳ θέλειν ἐλθεῖν ἐς λόγους. [2] ἐπακούσας δὲ ὁ Μαιάνδριος λύσαντας αὐτὸν ἐκέλευε ἄγειν παρ' ἑωυτόν· ὡς δὲ ἄχθη τάχιστα, λοιδορέων τε καὶ κακίζων μιν ἀνέπειθε ἐπιθέσθαι τοῖσι Πέρσῃσι, λέγων τοιάδε. " Ἐμέ μέν, ὦ κάκιστε ἀνδρῶν, ἐόντα σεωυτοῦ ἀδελφεὸν καὶ ἀδικήσαντα οὐδὲν ἄξιον δεσμοῦ δήσας γοργύρης ἠξίωσας· ὀρέων δὲ τοὺς Πέρσας ἐκβάλλοντάς τέ σε καὶ ἄνοικον ποιέοντας οὐ τολμᾷς τίσασθαι, οὕτω δή τι ἐόντας εὐπετέας χειρωθῆναι. [3] ἀλλ' εἴ τοι σὺ σφέας καταρρώδηκας, ἐμοὶ δὸς τοὺς ἐπικούρους, καί σφεας ἐγὼ τιμωρήσομαι τῆς ἐνθάδε ἀπίξιος· αὐτὸν δέ σε ἐκπέμψαι ἐκ τῆς νήσου ἕτοιμος εἰμί."

146 ταῦτα δὲ ἔλεξε ὁ Χαρίλεως· Μαιάνδριος δὲ ὑπέλαβε τὸν λόγον, ὡς μὲν ἐγὼ δοκέω, οὐκ ἐς τοῦτο ἀφροσύνης ἀπικόμενος ὡς δόξαι τὴν ἑωυτοῦ δύναμιν περιέσεσθαι τῆς βασιλέος, ἀλλὰ φθονήσας μᾶλλον Συλοσῶντι εἰ ἀπονητὶ ἔμελλε ἀπολάμψεσθαι ἀκέραιον τὴν πόλιν. [2] ἐρεθίσας ὦν τοὺς Πέρσας ἤθελε ὡς ἀσθενέστατα ποιῆσαι τὰ Σάμια πρήγματα καὶ οὕτω παραδιδόναι, εὖ ἐξεπιστάμενος ὡς παθόντες οἱ Πέρσαι κακῶς προσεμπικρανέεσθαι ἔμελλον τοῖσι Σαμίοισι, εἰδώς τε ἑωυτῷ ἀσφαλέα ἔκδυσιν ἐοῦσαν ἐκ τῆς νήσου τότε ἐπεὰν αὐτὸς βούληται· ἐπεποίητο γάρ οἱ κρυπτὴ διῶρυξ ἐκ τῆς ἀκροπόλιος φέρουσα ἐπὶ θάλασσαν. [3] αὐτὸς μὲν δὴ ὁ Μαιάνδριος ἐκπλέει ἐκ τῆς Σάμου· τοὺς δ' ἐπικούρους πάντας ὁπλίσας ὁ Χαρίλεως, καὶ ἀναπετάσας τὰς πύλας ἐξῆκε ἐπὶ τοὺς Πέρσας οὔτε προσδεκομένους τοιοῦτον οὐδὲν δοκέοντάς τε δὴ πάντα συμβεβάναι. ἐμπεσόντες δὲ οἱ ἐπίκουροι τῶν Περσέων τοὺς διφροφορευμένους τε καὶ λόγου πλείστου ἐόντας ἔκτεινον. [4] καὶ οὗτοι μὲν ταῦτα ἐποίευν, ἡ δὲ ἄλλη στρατιὴ ἡ Περσικὴ ἐπεβοήθεε· πιεζεύμενοι δὲ οἱ ἐπίκουροι ὀπίσω κατειλήθησαν ἐς τὴν ἀκρόπολιν.

147 Ὀτάνης ὁ στρατηγὸς ἰδὼν πάθος μέγα Πέρσας πεπονθότας, ἐντολὰς μὲν τὰς Δαρεῖός οἱ ἀποστέλλων ἐνετέλλετο μήτε κτείνειν μηδένα Σαμίων μήτε ἀνδραποδίζεσθαι ἀπαθέα τε κακῶν ἀποδοῦναι τὴν νῆσον Συλοσῶντι, τουτέων μὲν τῶν ἐντολέων μεμνημένος ἐπελανθάνετο, ὁδὲ παρήγγειλε τῇ στρατιῇ πάντα τὸν ἂν λάβωσι καὶ ἄνδρα καὶ παῖδα ὁμοίως κτείνειν. ἐνθαῦτα τῆς στρατιῆς οἱ μὲν τὴν ἀκρόπολιν ἐπολιόρκεον, οἱ δὲ ἔκτεινον πάντα τὸν ἐμποδὼν γινόμενον ὁμοίως ἔν τε ἱρῷ καὶ ἔξω ἱροῦ.

148 Μαιάνδριος δὲ ἀποδρὰς ἐκ τῆς Σάμου ἐκπλέει ἐς Λακεδαίμονα· ἀπικόμενος δὲ ἐς αὐτὴν καὶ ἀνενεικάμενος τὰ ἔχων ἐξεχώρησε, ἐποίεε τοιάδε· ὅκως ποτήρια ἀργύρεά τε καὶ χρυσέα προθεῖτο, οἱ μὲν θεράποντες αὐτοῦ ἐξέσμων αὐτά, ὁ δ' ἂν τὸν χρόνον τοῦτον τῷ Κλεομένεϊ τῷ Ἀναξανδρίδεω ἐν λόγοισι ἐών, βασιλεύοντι Σπάρτης, προῆγέ μιν ἐς τὰ οἰκία· ὅκως δὲ ἴδοιτο Κλεομένης τὰ ποτήρια, ἀπεθώμαζέ τε καὶ ἐξεπλήσσετο· ὁ δὲ ἂν ἐκέλευε αὐτὸν ἀποφέρεσθαι αὐτῶν ὅσα βούλοιτο. [2] τοῦτο καὶ δὶς καὶ τρὶς εἴπαντος Μαιανδρίου ὁ Κλεομένης δικαιότατος ἀνδρῶν γίνεται, ὃς λαβεῖν μὲν διδόμενα οὐκ ἐδικαίου, μαθὼν δὲ ὡς ἄλλοισι διδοὺς τῶν ἀστῶν εὑρήσεται τιμωρίην, βὰς ἐπὶ τοὺς ἐφόρους ἄμεινον εἶναι ἔφη τῇ Σπάρτῃ τὸν ξεῖνον τὸν Σάμιον ἀπαλλάσσεσθαι ἐκ τῆς Πελοποννήσου, ἵνα μὴ ἀναπείσῃ ἢ αὐτὸν ἢ ἄλλον τινὰ Σπαρτιητέων κακὸν γενέσθαι. οἱ δ' ὑπακούσαντες ἐξεκήρυξαν Μαιάνδριον.

149 τὴν δὲ Σάμον σαγηνεύσαντες οἱ Πέρσαι παρέδοσαν Συλοσῶντι ἔρημον ἐοῦσαν ἀνδρῶν. ὑστέρῳ μέντοι χρόνῳ καὶ συγκατοίκισε αὐτὴν ὁ στρατηγὸς Ὀτάνης ἔκ τε ὄψιος ὀνείρου καὶ νούσου ἥ μιν κατέλαβε νοσῆσαι τὰ αἰδοῖα.

150 ἐπὶ δὲ Σάμον στρατεύματος ναυτικοῦ οἰχομένου Βαβυλώνιοι ἀπέστησαν, κάρτα εὖ παρεσκευασμένοι· ἐν ὅσῳ γὰρ ὅ τε Μάγος ἦρχε καὶ οἱ ἑπτὰ ἐπανέστησαν, ἐν τούτῳ παντὶ τῷ χρόνῳ καὶ τῇ ταραχῇ ἐς τὴν πολιορκίην παρεσκευάζοντο. καί κως ταῦτα ποιεῦντες ἐλάνθανον. [2] ἐπείτε δὲ ἐκ τοῦ ἐμφανέος ἀπέστησαν, ἐποίησαν τοιόνδε· τὰς μητέρας ἐξελόντες γυναῖκα ἕκαστος μίαν προσεξαιρέετο τὴν ἐβούλετο ἐκ τῶν ἑωυτοῦ οἰκίων, τὰς δὲ λοιπὰς ἁπάσας συναγαγόντες ἀπέπνιξαν· τὴν δὲ μίαν ἕκαστος σιτοποιὸν ἐξαιρέετο· ἀπέπνιξαν δὲ αὐτάς, ἵνα μὴ σφεων τὸν σῖτον ἀναισιμώσωσι.

151 πυθόμενος δὲ ταῦτα ὁ Δαρεῖος καὶ συλλέξας πᾶσαν τὴν ἑωυτοῦ δύναμιν ἐστρατεύετο ἐπ᾽ αὐτούς, ἐπελάσας δὲ ἐπὶ τὴν Βαβυλῶνα ἐπολιόρκεε φροντίζοντας οὐδὲν τῆς πολιορκίης. ἀναβαίνοντες γὰρ ἐπὶ τοὺς προμαχεῶνας τοῦ τείχεος οἱ Βαβυλώνιοι κατωρχέοντο καὶ κατέσκωπτον Δαρεῖον καὶ τὴν στρατιὴν αὐτοῦ, καί τις αὐτῶν εἶπε τοῦτο τὸ ἔπος. [2] "Τί κάτησθε, ὦ Πέρσαι, ἐνθαῦτα, ἀλλ᾽ οὐκ ἀπαλλάσσεσθε; τότε γὰρ αἱρήσετε ἡμέας, ἐπεὰν ἡμίονοι τέκωσι." τοῦτο εἶπε τῶν τις Βαβυλωνίων οὐδαμὰ ἐλπίζων ἂν ἡμίονον τεκεῖν.

152 ἑπτὰ δὲ μηνῶν καὶ ἐνιαυτοῦ διεληλυθότος ἤδη ὁ Δαρεῖός τε ἤσχαλλε καὶ ἡ στρατιὴ πᾶσα οὐ δυνατὴ ἐοῦσα ἑλεῖν τοὺς Βαβυλωνίους. καίτοι πάντα σοφίσματα καὶ πάσας μηχανὰς ἐπεποιήκεε ἐς αὐτοὺς Δαρεῖος· ἀλλ᾽ οὐδ᾽ ὣς ἐδύνατο ἑλεῖν σφεας, ἄλλοισί τε σοφίσμασι πειρησάμενος, καὶ δὴ καὶ τῷ Κῦρος εἷλε σφεας, καὶ τούτῳ ἐπειρήθη. ἀλλὰ γὰρ δεινῶς ἦσαν ἐν φυλακῇσι οἱ Βαβυλώνιοι, οὐδὲ σφέας οἷός τε ἦν ἑλεῖν.

153 ἐνθαῦτα εἰκοστῷ μηνὶ Ζωπύρῳ τῷ Μεγαβύζου, τούτου ὃς τῶν ἑπτὰ ἀνδρῶν ἐγένετο τῶν τὸν Μάγον κατελόντων, τούτου τοῦ

Μεγαβύζου παιδὶ Ζωπύρῳ ἐγένετο τέρας τόδε· τῶν οἱ σιτοφόρων ἡμιόνων μία ἔτεκε. ὡς δέ οἱ ἐξαγγέλθη καὶ ὑπὸ ἀπιστίης αὐτὸς ὁ Ζώπυρος εἶδε τὸ βρέφος, ἀπείπας τοῖσι ἰδοῦσι μηδενὶ φράζειν τὸ γεγονὸς ἐβουλεύετο. [2] καί οἱ πρὸς τὰ τοῦ Βαβυλωνίου ῥήματα, ὃς κατ᾽ ἀρχὰς ἔφησε, ἐπεάν περ ἡμίονοι τέκωσι, τότε τὸ τεῖχος ἁλώσεσθαι, πρὸς ταύτην τὴν φήμην Ζωπύρῳ ἐδόκεε εἶναι ἁλώσιμος ἡ Βαβυλών· σὺν γὰρ θεῷ ἐκεῖνόν τε εἰπεῖν καὶ ἑωυτῷ τεκεῖν τὴν ἡμίονον.

154 ὡς δέ οἱ ἐδόκεε μόρσιμον εἶναι ἤδη τῇ Βαβυλῶνι ἁλίσκεσθαι, προελθὼν Δαρείου ἀπεπυνθάνετο εἰ περὶ πολλοῦ κάρτα ποιέεται τὴν Βαβυλῶνα ἑλεῖν. πυθόμενος δὲ ὡς πολλοῦ τιμῷτο, ἄλλο ἐβουλεύετο, ὅκως αὐτός τε ἔσται ὁ ἑλὼν αὐτὴν καὶ ἑωυτοῦ τὸ ἔργον ἔσται· κάρτα γὰρ ἐν τοῖσι Πέρσῃσι αἱ ἀγαθοεργίαι ἐς τὸ πρόσω μεγάθεος τιμῶνται. [2] ἄλλῳ μέν νυν οὐκ ἐφράζετο ἔργῳ δυνατὸς εἶναί μιν ὑποχειρίην ποιῆσαι, εἰ δ᾽ ἑωυτὸν λωβησάμενος αὐτομολήσειε ἐς αὐτούς. ἐνθαῦτα ἐν ἐλαφρῷ ποιησάμενος ἑωυτὸν λωβᾶται λώβην ἀνήκεστον· ἀποταμὼν γὰρ ἑωυτοῦ τὴν ῥῖνα καὶ τὰ ὦτα καὶ τὴν κόμην κακῶς περικείρας καὶ μαστιγώσας ἦλθε παρὰ Δαρεῖον.

155 Δαρεῖος δὲ κάρτα βαρέως ἤνεικε ἰδὼν ἄνδρα δοκιμώτατον λελωβημένον, ἔκ τε τοῦ θρόνου ἀναπηδήσας ἀνέβωσέ τε καὶ εἴρετό μιν ὅστις εἴη ὁ λωβησάμενος καὶ ὅ τι ποιήσαντα. [2] ὁ δὲ εἶπε, "Οὐκ ἔστι οὗτος ἀνήρ, ὅτι μὴ σύ, τῷ ἐστὶ δύναμις τοσαύτη ἐμὲ δὴ ὧδε διαθεῖναι· οὐδέ τις ἀλλοτρίων, ὦ βασιλεῦ, τάδε ἔργασται, ἀλλ᾽ αὐτὸς ἐγὼ ἐμεωυτόν, δεινόν τι ποιεύμενος Ἀσσυρίους Πέρσῃσι καταγελᾶν." [3] ὁ δ᾽ ἀμείβετο "Ὦ σχετλιώτατε ἀνδρῶν, ἔργῳ τῷ αἰσχίστῳ οὔνομα τὸ κάλλιστον ἔθευ, φὰς διὰ τοὺς πολιορκεομένους σεωυτὸν ἀνηκέστως διαθεῖναι. τί δ᾽, ὦ μάταιε, λελωβημένου σεῦ θᾶσσον οἱ πολέμιοι παραστήσονται; κῶς οὐκ ἐξέπλωσας τῶν φρενῶν σεωυτὸν διαφθείρας;" [4] ὁ δὲ εἶπε· "Εἰ μέν τοι ὑπερετίθεα τὰ ἔμελλον ποιήσειν, οὐκ ἄν με περιεῖδες· νῦν δ᾽ ἐπ᾽ ἐμεωυτοῦ βαλόμενος ἔπρηξα. ἤδη ὦν ἢν μὴ τῶν σῶν δεήσῃ, αἱρέομεν Βαβυλῶνα. ἐγὼ μὲν γὰρ ὡς ἔχω αὐτομολήσω ἐς τὸ τεῖχος καὶ φήσω πρὸς αὐτοὺς ὡς ὑπὸ σεῦ τάδε ἔπαθον· καὶ δοκέω, πείσας σφέας ταῦτα ἔχειν οὕτω, τεύξεσθαι στρατιῆς. [5] σὺ δέ, ἀπ᾽ ἧς ἂν ἡμέρης ἐγὼ ἐσέλθω ἐς τὸ τεῖχος, ἀπὸ ταύτης ἐς δεκάτην ἡμέρην τῆς σεωυτοῦ στρατιῆς, τῆς οὐδεμία ἔσται ὥρη ἀπολλυμένης, ταύτης χιλίους τάξον κατὰ τὰς Σεμιράμιος καλεομένας πύλας· μετὰ δὲ αὖτις ἀπὸ τῆς δεκάτης ἐς ἑβδόμην ἄλλους μοι τάξον δισχιλίους κατὰ τὰς Νινίων καλεομένας πύλας· ἀπὸ δὲ τῆς ἑβδόμης διαλείπειν εἴκοσι ἡμέρας καὶ ἔπειτα ἄλλους κάτισον ἀγαγὼν κατὰ τὰς Χαλδαίων καλεομένας πύλας τετρακισχιλίους. ἐχόντων δὲ μήτε οἱ πρότεροι μηδὲν τῶν ἀμυνεύντων μήτε οὗτοι, πλὴν ἐγχειριδίων· τοῦτο δὲ ἐᾶν ἔχειν. [6] μετὰ δὲ τὴν εἰκοστὴν ἡμέρην ἰθέως τὴν μὲν ἄλλην στρατιὴν κελεύειν πέριξ προσβάλλειν πρὸς τὸ τεῖχος, Πέρσας δέ μοι τάξον κατά τε τὰς Βηλίδας καλεομένας καὶ Κισσίας πύλας. ὡς γὰρ ἐγὼ δοκέω, ἐμέο μεγάλα ἔργα ἀποδεξαμένου, τά τε ἄλλα ἐπιτρέψονται ἐμοὶ Βαβυλώνιοι καὶ δὴ καὶ τῶν πυλέων τὰς βαλανάγρας· τὸ δὲ ἐνθεῦτεν ἐμοί τε καὶ Πέρσῃσι μελήσει τὰ δεῖ ποιέειν."

156 ταῦτα ἐντειλάμενος ἤιε ἐπὶ τὰς πύλας, ἐπιστρεφόμενος ὡς δὴ ἀληθέως αὐτόμολος. ὁρῶντες δὲ ἀπὸ τῶν πύργων οἱ κατὰ τοῦτο τεταγμένοι κατέτρεχον κάτω καὶ ὀλίγον τι παρακλίναντες τὴν ἑτέρην πύλην εἰρώτων τίς τε εἴη καὶ ὅτευ δεόμενος ἥκοι. ὁ δέ σφι ἠγόρευε ὡς εἴη τε Ζώπυρος καὶ αὐτομολέοι ἐς ἐκείνους. [2] ἦγον δή μιν οἱ πυλουροί, ταῦτα ὡς ἤκουσαν, ἐπὶ τὰ κοινὰ τῶν Βαβυλωνίων· καταστὰς δὲ ἐπ᾽ αὐτὰ κατοικτίζετο, φὰς ὑπὸ Δαρείου πεπονθέναι τὰ ἐπεπόνθεε ὑπ᾽ ἑωυτοῦ, παθεῖν δὲ ταῦτα διότι συμβουλεύσαι οἱ ἀπανιστάναι τὴν στρατιήν, ἐπείτε δὴ οὐδεὶς πόρος ἐφαίνετο τῆς ἁλώσιος. [3] "Νῦν τε" ἔφη λέγων "ἐγὼ ὑμῖν ὦ Βαβυλώνιοι ἥκω μέγιστον ἀγαθόν, Δαρείῳ δὲ καὶ τῇ στρατιῇ καὶ Πέρσῃσι μέγιστον κακόν· οὐ γὰρ δὴ ἐμέ γε ὧδε λωβησάμενος καταπροΐξεται· ἐπίσταμαι δ᾽ αὐτοῦ πάσας τὰς διεξόδους τῶν βουλευμάτων." τοιαῦτα ἔλεγε.

157 οἱ δὲ Βαβυλώνιοι ὁρῶντες ἄνδρα τὸν ἐν Πέρσῃσι δοκιμώτατον ῥινός τε καὶ ὤτων ἐστερημένον, μάστιξί τε καὶ αἵματι ἀναπεφυρμένον, πάγχυ ἐλπίσαντες λέγειν μιν ἀληθέα καί σφι ἥκειν σύμμαχον, ἐπιτράπεσθαι ἕτοιμοι ἦσαν τῶν ἐδέετο σφέων· [2] ἐδέετο δὲ στρατιῆς. ὁ δὲ ἐπείτε αὐτῶν τοῦτο παρέλαβε, ἐποίεε τά περ τῷ Δαρείῳ συνεθήκατο·

ἐξαγαγὼν γὰρ τῇ δεκάτῃ ἡμέρῃ τὴν στρατιὴν τῶν Βαβυλωνίων καὶ κυκλωσάμενος τοὺς χιλίους τοὺς πρώτους ἐνετείλατο Δαρείῳ τάξαι, τούτους κατεφόνευσε. [3] μαθόντες δέ μιν οἱ Βαβυλώνιοι τοῖσι ἔπεσι τὰ ἔργα παρεχόμενον ὅμοια, πάγχυ περιχαρέες ἐόντες πᾶν δὴ ἕτοιμοι ἦσαν ὑπηρετέειν. ὁ δὲ διαλιπὼν ἡμέρας τὰς συγκειμένας, αὖτις ἐπιλεξάμενος τῶν Βαβυλωνίων ἐξήγαγε καὶ κατεφόνευσε τῶν Δαρείου στρατιωτέων τοὺς δισχιλίους. ἰδόντες δὲ καὶ τοῦτο τὸ ἔργον οἱ Βαβυλώνιοι πάντες Ζώπυρον εἶχον ἐν στόμασι αἰνέοντες. [4] ὁ δὲ αὖτις διαλιπὼν τὰς συγκειμένας ἡμέρας ἐξήγαγε ἐς τὸ προειρημένον, καὶ κυκλωσάμενος κατεφόνευσε τοὺς τετρακισχιλίους. ὡς δὲ καὶ τοῦτο κατέργαστο, πάντα δὴ ἦν ἐν τοῖσι Βαβυλωνίοισι Ζώπυρος, καὶ στρατάρχης τε οὗτός σφι καὶ τειχοφύλαξ ἀπεδέδεκτο.

158 προσβολὴν δὲ Δαρείου κατὰ τὰ συγκείμενα ποιευμένου πέριξ τὸ τεῖχος, ἐνθαῦτα δὴ πάντα τὸν δόλον ὁ Ζώπυρος ἐξέφαινε. οἱ μὲν γὰρ Βαβυλώνιοι ἀναβάντες ἐπὶ τὸ τεῖχος ἠμύνοντο τὴν Δαρείου στρατιὴν προσβάλλουσαν, ὁ δὲ Ζώπυρος τάς τε Κισσίας καὶ Βηλίδας καλεομένας πύλας ἀναπετάσας ἐσῆκε τοὺς Πέρσας ἐς τὸ τεῖχος. [2] τῶν δὲ Βαβυλωνίων οἱ μὲν εἶδον τὸ ποιηθέν, οὗτοι μὲν ἔφευγον ἐς τοῦ Διὸς τοῦ βήλου τὸ ἱρόν, οἱ δὲ οὐκ εἶδον, ἔμενον ἐν τῇ ἑωυτοῦ τάξι ἕκαστος, ἐς ὃ δὴ καὶ οὗτοι ἔμαθον προδεδομένοι.

159 Βαβυλὼν μέν νυν οὕτω τὸ δεύτερον αἱρέθη. Δαρεῖος δὲ ἐπείτε ἐκράτησε τῶν Βαβυλωνίων, τοῦτο μὲν σφέων τὸ τεῖχος περιεῖλε καὶ τὰς πύλας πάσας ἀπέσπασε· τὸ γὰρ πρότερον ἑλὼν Κῦρος τὴν Βαβυλῶνα ἐποίησε τούτων οὐδέτερον· τοῦτο δὲ ὁ Δαρεῖος τῶν ἀνδρῶν τοὺς κορυφαίους μάλιστα ἐς τρισχιλίους ἀνεσκολόπισε, τοῖσι δὲ λοιποῖσι Βαβυλωνίοισι ἀπέδωκε τὴν πόλιν οἰκέειν. [2] ὡς δ' ἕξουσι γυναῖκας οἱ Βαβυλώνιοι ἵνα σφι γενεὴ ὑπογινῆται, τάδε Δαρεῖος προϊδὼν ἐποίησε, τὰς γὰρ ἑωυτῶν, ὡς καὶ κατ' ἀρχὰς δεδήλωται, ἀπέπνιξαν οἱ Βαβυλώνιοι τοῦ σίτου προορέοντες· ἐπέταξε τοῖσι περιοίκοισι ἔθνεσι γυναῖκας ἐς Βαβυλῶνα κατιστάναι, ὅσας δὴ ἑκάστοισι ἐπιτάσσων, ὥστε πέντε μυριάδων τὸ κεφαλαίωμα τῶν γυναικῶν συνῆλθε· ἐκ τουτέων δὲ τῶν γυναικῶν οἱ νῦν Βαβυλώνιοι γεγόνασι.

160 Ζωπύρου δὲ οὐδεὶς ἀγαθοεργίην Περσέων ὑπερεβάλετο παρὰ Δαρείῳ κριτῇ οὔτε τῶν ὕστερον γενομένων οὔτε τῶν πρότερον, ὅτι μὴ Κῦρος μοῦνος· τούτῳ γὰρ οὐδεὶς Περσέων ἠξίωσέ κω ἑωυτὸν συμβαλεῖν. πολλάκις δὲ Δαρεῖον λέγεται γνώμην τήνδε ἀποδέξασθαι, ὡς βούλοιτο ἂν Ζώπυρον εἶναι ἀπαθέα τῆς ἀεικείης μᾶλλον ἢ Βαβυλῶνάς οἱ εἴκοσι πρὸς τῇ ἐούσῃ προσγενέσθαι. ἐτίμησε δέ μιν μεγάλως· [2] καὶ γὰρ δῶρά οἱ ἀνὰ πᾶν ἔτος ἐδίδου ταῦτα τὰ Πέρσῃσι ἐστὶ τιμιώτατα καὶ τὴν Βαβυλῶνά οἱ ἔδωκε ἀτελέα νέμεσθαι μέχρι τῆς ἐκείνου ζόης καὶ ἄλλα πολλὰ ἐπέδωκε. Ζωπύρου δὲ τούτου γίνεται Μεγάβυζος, ὃς ἐν Αἰγύπτῳ ἀντία Ἀθηναίων καὶ τῶν συμμάχων ἐστρατήγησε· Μεγαβύζου δὲ τούτου γίνεται Ζώπυρος, ὃς ἐς Ἀθήνας ηὐτομόλησε ἐκ Περσέων.

Translation

1

1.1 It was against this man Amasis that Cambyses son of Cyrus made an expedition leading an army composed of the different men over whom he ruled, among whom were Ionian and Aeolian Greeks, for the following reason. Cambyses had sent a herald to Egypt and asked Amasis for his daughter, and he made this request on the advice of an Egyptian man, who did this because he used to blame Amasis for the fact that out of all the doctors in Egypt, he had dragged him away from his wife and children and delivered him up to the Persians, at the time when Cyrus sent to Amasis and asked for whoever was the best eye-doctor in Egypt.

1.2 And because the Egyptian blamed Amasis for this, in their shared counsel he urged on and encouraged Cambyses to ask Amasis for his daughter so that either he would be distressed after handing her over, or, if he did not hand her over, he would be hated by Cambyses. Amasis, anxious about the power of the Persians and frightened, could neither hand over his daughter nor refuse to do so. For he knew well that Cambyses did not intend to keep her as a wife, but as a concubine.

1.3 After reflecting upon these issues, he took the following course of action. There was a daughter of the former king Apries, who was especially tall and beautiful. She alone remained from his household and her name was Nitetis. Amasis dressed this girl up in gold raiment and sent her off to the Persians as his daughter.

1.4 But after a time when he [Cambyses] embraced her while addressing her by her father's name, the girl spoke to him: 'Oh, king, you do not realize how you have been wronged by Amasis. After clothing me in fine raiment, he sent me away giving me to you as if I were his own daughter, but in fact I am the daughter of Apries, the ruler against whom that man revolted along with the Egyptians and killed.'

1.5 And this speech was then the very reason that drove Cambyses son of Cyrus against Egypt, since he was extremely angry.

2

2.1 This is what the Persians say now. The Egyptians, however, appropriate Cambyses as their own, claiming that he was born from this daughter of Apries: for it was Cyrus who had sent to Amasis for his daughter, but not Cambyses.

2.2 However, in saying this they do not speak correctly. It has certainly has not escaped their notice, for if there is anyone who knows the customs of the Persians it is the Egyptians, that firstly, it is not their custom for an illegitimate son to be king when there is a legitimate child, and secondly because Cambyses was the son of Cassandane daughter of Pharnaspes, an Achaemenid man, but not of the Egyptian woman. But they twist the story pretending kinship with the house of Cyrus.

3

3.1 And that's the way it is. But the following story is also told, which I do not find persuasive, that when one of the Persian women came to visit the wives of Cyrus, upon seeing the handsome and tall children standing by Cassandane, she heaped praise upon them, expressing her great admiration, but Cassandane, who was the wife of Cyrus, spoke as follows:

3.2 'Cyrus, however, although I am the mother of such children, dishonours me, and instead honours his newly acquired woman from Egypt.' So she spoke in her hatred towards Nitetis, and Cambyses, the elder of her sons said:

3.3 'Because of this, Mother, when I am a grown man, I shall turn the affairs of Egypt entirely upside down.' He was about ten years old when he made this speech, and the women were astonished: and because he remembered this very clearly, when he grew up and became king, he made the campaign against Egypt.

4

4.1 It also happened that another occurrence contributed to this expedition, and it happened like this. There was among the mercenaries of Amasis, a man whose name was Phanes and who was a Halicarnassian by birth, a clever man and a skilled soldier.

4.2 This man Phanes, because he blamed Amasis for something or other, fled Egypt desiring to speak with Cambyses. Because he was so well-regarded among the mercenaries and possessed a very accurate knowledge of Egyptian affairs, Amasis, making haste to capture him, pursued him closely and sent out against him the most trusted of his eunuchs in a trireme, who captured him in Lycia; but he did not bring him back to Egypt after capturing him: for Phanes surpassed him in cleverness.

4.3 For, after getting his guards drunk, he escaped to Persia. After he met Cambyses, who was eager to make his expedition against Egypt, but was at a loss as to how he would march through the waterless desert, Phanes explained the state of Amasis' affairs to him, giving guidance about his march and advising him to send word to the king of the Arabians and ask him to provide a safe passage.

5

5.1 Clear entrance into Egypt is by this route alone. For it runs from Phoenicia all the way up to the borders of the city of Cadytis, which belongs to the Syrians who are known as the Palestinians.

5.2 From the city of Cadytis which is, as it seems to me, a city not much smaller than Sardis, right up to the city of Ienysus, the seaports belong to Arabia, and from Ienysus as far as the Serbonian marsh, the ports once again belong to the Syrians, and alongside these the Casian Mountain stretches towards the sea.

5.3 But from the Serbonian marsh, where according to one story Typhon was hidden, Egypt is from that point. Between the city of Ienysus and the Casian Mountain and the Serbonian marsh, there lies a space, which is not small but is around three days' journey in distance, and it is terribly dry.

6

6.1 There is something which few of those who have sailed to Egypt have realized, which I am going to explain. Throughout the year ceramic jars full of wine are brought to Egypt from all over Greece and also from Phoenicia, and it is not possible in short to count one single empty wine jar.

6.2 But I suppose someone might say, 'how then are these being used up?' I will also explain this. Each of the demarchs must gather every jar from his own city and take them to Memphis, and those from Memphis must take them to these dry lands in Syria once they have filled them with water. And so, each jar that comes in and is used up in Egypt is carried off to Syria and added to the old stock.

7

7.1 Thus the Persians are the ones who guarded this entry into Egypt, which they watered in the manner mentioned above as soon as they took possession of Egypt.

7.2 But at that point there was as yet no water ready and Cambyses, having learnt this from the stranger from Halicarnassus, sent messengers to the Arabian and obtained his request for safe passage, having granted and received pledges from him.

8

8.1 The Arabians especially of mortals respect pledges, and they make them in the following manner: a different man stands in between both of the parties who wish to make the pledge, and with a sharp stone cuts the inside of their hands along the big fingers of those giving pledges; and he then takes a piece of wool from the cloak of each man and smears with the blood seven stones lying in between them. While doing this he calls upon Dionysus and the Heavenly Goddess.

8.2 When he has completed this, the man who has given the pledge entrusts to his friends a stranger or fellow citizen, if he is making it with a citizen. And his friends themselves deem it just to honour the pledge.

8.3 They consider only Dionysus and the Heavenly Goddess to be gods and they say that they cut the hair on their head, just as Dionysus cuts it; they clip all around the head, shaving the temples. They call Dionysus Orotalt and the Heavenly Goddess Alilat.

9

9.1 When, therefore, the Arabian (king) gave his pledge to the ambassadors who arrived from Cambyses, he contrived the following means: he filled camel-skins and loaded them onto all his camels, and once he had done this, he drove them to the waterless region and waited there for Cambyses' army.

9.2 This is the more convincing of the accounts given, but the less convincing account must be told, since it is indeed one that is reported. There is a great river in Arabia which is called Corys, and it runs out to the sea known as The Red.

9.3 From this river, the story goes, the king of the Arabians, after he had a water-pipe made of raw ox-hide and other skins stitched together that was long enough to reach the dry region, he drew water to it through these; and in this desert area he had large tanks dug to receive and store the water.

9.4 The journey from the river to this dry region is twelve days. It is also said that he drew water to three different areas via these pipes.

10

10.1 At the mouth of the Nile that is called Pelusium, Psammenitus, son of Amasis, was encamped waiting for Cambyses.

10.2 For when he invaded Egypt, Cambyses did not capture Amasis while he was alive, but Amasis had died having been king for forty-four years, during which time no significant misfortune befell him; after he had died and had been embalmed, he was buried in the burial places that he had had built for him in the temple.

10.3 When Psammenitus, son of Amasis was ruling Egypt, the greatest natural phenomenon happened to the Egyptians: there was rain in

Egyptian Thebes, and, so the Thebans say, it had neither rained before nor after this point right down to my own time. For indeed, it does not rain at all in the upper parts of Egypt. But at that time, a light sprinkling fell on Thebes.

11

11.1 When the Persians had driven through the desert region, and once they settled close to the Egyptians intending to engage them, the mercenaries of Egypt, who were both Greeks and Carians, because they bore a grudge against Phanes for leading a foreign army against Egypt, hatched the following plan against him.

11.2 Phanes had children, who had been left behind in Egypt; after they had led them to the camp and had before their father's eyes set down a mixing bowl between both camps, they then led each of the children up to it one at a time and slit their throats into the bowl.

11.3 Having gone through all of the children, they were pouring water and wine into the bowl, and once they had all drunk from the bowl, the mercenaries thus engaged in battle. Although the fighting was fierce and many fell in great numbers from both camps, the Egyptians were turned to flight.

12

12.1 I saw a very strange thing, which I had [also] learnt from the natives. For with the bones of those who fell in the battle on either side lying scattered separately, since those of the Persians lay in one place, as they had been separate at the start, and those of the Egyptians in a different spot, the skulls of the Persians are so brittle that, if you wished to cast a single pebble at them, you will pierce them through, but those of the Egyptians are in fact so strong, that you would scarcely even break them if you struck them with a stone.

12.2 They used to give the following reason for this, and they certainly convinced me easily; the reason is that the Egyptians, starting right from when they are children, shave their heads and this thickens the bone through exposure to the sun.

12.3 And this is the very reason why they do not go bald. For one is least likely to see a bald man among the Egyptians of all men.

12.4 And so this is the reason that these men sport strong skulls, and the reason that the Persians on the other hand bear weak skulls is as follows: from the beginning they cover their heads by wearing felt tiara caps. Such are the things I saw: and I saw other things similar to this with the skulls of those who were killed at Papremis alongside Achaemenes son of Darius by Inaros the Libyan.

13

13.1 When the Egyptians were turned in flight from the battle, they were fleeing in no order. When they were cut off at Memphis, Cambyses sent along the river to Memphis a Mytilenean ship carrying a Persian man, a herald, to ask the Egyptians to make an agreement.

13.2 When they saw the ship coming into Memphis, they poured out of the walls *en masse* and destroyed the ship, tearing the men to pieces like a butcher and carried them back to the city.

13.3 After this the Egyptians were then besieged and after a time they surrendered; and the neighbouring Libyans, frightened at what had happened in Egypt, surrendered themselves without a fight and even drew up their own tribute and sent gifts. The Cyreneans and Barcaeans also did this since like the Libyans they were scared.

13.4 Cambyses kindly received the gifts that came from the Libyans, but rebuked those from the Cyreneans, because, I think, they were small: for the Cyreneans sent precisely five hundred mina of silver and having grasped hold of these, he scattered them among the army with his own hand.

14

14.1 On the tenth day after Cambyses took the wall in Memphis, he set Psammenitus king of the Egyptians, who had reigned for six months, outside the city for the purpose of an outrageous act; and having made him sit there with other Egyptians, he tested his spirit in the following way:

14.2 After dressing his daughter up in slave's clothing, he sent her out carrying a bucket to fetch water, and with her he also sent other maiden daughters that he had chosen from the families of the leading men, who were dressed like the daughter of the king.

14.3 When the maidens went past with weeping and shouting before the eyes of their fathers, all the other men raised cries and lamented in response, when they saw their children mistreated, but Psammenitus upon seeing this and taking it in, bowed his head to the ground.

14.4 After the water carriers had passed by Cambyses then sent out Psammenitus' son with two thousand other Egyptian men of the same age, bound with rope around their necks and with bridle bits placed in their mouths.

14.5 They were led out to pay the penalty for the Mytileneans who were destroyed with their ship at Memphis; for this was what the Royal Judges deemed just: that for the death of each man ten leading Egyptians would be killed in return.

14.6 And Psammenitus having seen them passing by and realised that his son was being led to his death, while the other Egyptians who were sitting around him were weeping and making clear their sufferings, he did the same as he had done in the case of his daughter.

14.7 When these too had gone past, it happened that a man, one of his drinking companions who was rather past his prime and who had fallen from fortune, having nothing except as much as a beggar did, was pleading to the army for alms and then came round to Psammenitus, son of Amasis, and the Egyptians sitting outside the city. When he saw him, Psammenitus wept loudly, called on his companion by name and struck his head.

14.8 Now there were guards with him, who informed Cambyses of everything that man had done as each came out. Cambyses, astonished at his actions, sent a messenger who questioned him as follows:

14.9 'Lord Cambyses, Psammenitus, asks why upon seeing your daughter abused and your son going to his death you neither shouted not cried out, yet when you saw the beggar who was not related to you at all, as he learnt from others, you show your esteem for him.' This is what the messenger asked, and Psammenitus answered as follows:

14.10 'Oh, son of Cyrus, the sufferings of my family are too great for tears, but the distress of my companion is worthy of tears, because after he has fallen from owning a lot and having good fortune to begging, he has arrived at the threshold of old age.'

14.11 When what he had said was reported back, they thought Psammenitus had spoken well. And it is also said by the Egyptians that Croesus wept, for this man happened to have accompanied Cambyses to Egypt, and that those of the Persians who were present also wept: some pity also came over Cambyses, and he immediately gave orders for Psammenitus' son to be saved from those who were being killed, and that they bring Psammenitus himself in before him from outside the city.

15

15.1 Those who went to fetch his son discovered that he was no longer alive but had been the first who had been butchered. However, they fetched Psammenitus and led him to Cambyses.

15.2 He then passed the rest of his life without any violence. And if he had known not to be meddlesome, he could have recovered Egypt to govern, since the Persians are accustomed to honour the sons of kings; even if the kings have revolted from them, they give power back to their sons.

15.3 It can also be judged from many other examples that they have become accustomed to do this, among them to Thannyras son of Inaros, who received back the power which his father held, and also to Pausiris son of Amyrtaeus: for he recovered his father's power; and yet no one ever did greater harm to the Persians than Inaros and Amyrtaeus.

15.4 But Psammenitus then earned his payment for contriving evils: for he was caught stirring the Egyptians to revolt: when he was discovered by Cambyses, he drank bull's blood and died immediately. Such was the way this man died.

16

16.1 Cambyses arrived from Memphis at the city of Sais, wanting to do exactly what he then did do. For when he entered the palace of Amasis, he immediately gave orders for Amasis' body to be carried out of his tomb: when these orders had been fulfilled, he gave orders to flog it, rip its hair out, prick it with spurs and defile it in every other way.

16.2 And when they were wearied by doing this, because the corpse had in fact been embalmed it endured and was not liquefied in any way, Cambyses gave orders to burn it, instructing them to commit impious acts: for the Persians consider fire to be a god.

16.3 Burning corpses is therefore in no way a customary practice on either side, to the Persians for the reason I have just mentioned, because they say that it is not just to apportion the body of a man to a god: and fire is considered by the Egyptians to be a living beast, and one which consumes everything that it seizes, and that once it is full of food, it dies along with what it has eaten.

16.4 It is, therefore, in no way their custom to give a corpse to beasts, and it is for these reasons that they embalm it, so that it is not devoured by worms when it is laid out. Cambyses was thus instructing them to do things which were customary to neither side.

16.5 However, the Egyptians say that it was not Amasis who suffered this, but that it was some other Egyptian man who was of the same age as Amasis whom the Persians defiled, thinking that they were abusing Amasis.

16.6 For they say that because Amasis had learnt from a seer what was going to happen to him after he had died, and thus to remedy the impending threats he buried this man the one who was flogged after he had died near the doors just within his own vault, but gave orders to his son that he himself be placed in the innermost part of the tomb.

16.7 I do not think that these commands regarding the burial and the man were ever initiated, but that the Egyptians are magnifying the affair to no purpose.

17

17.1 After this Cambyses planned three expeditions, against the Carthaginians, the Ammonians, and the long-lived Ethiopians who inhabit the part of Libya on the southern sea.

17.2 While deliberating he decided to send his fleet against the Carthaginians, a select part of his land army against the Ammonians and spies initially to the Ethiopians to see if there was any truth in the story of the Table of the Sun that was told among the Ethiopians, and to observe other things in addition, but under the pretext of bringing gifts to their king.

18

18.1 The Table of the Sun is said to be like this: there is a meadow outside the city full of the boiled flesh of all four-footed creatures, where at night those citizens who are in power take care on each occasion to set out the meat, and by day anyone who wishes to can come and feast. Such is what the Table of the Sun is said to be like.

19

19.1 When Cambyses had decided to send spies, he immediately sent for the Fish-eater men who were from the city of Elephantine because they knew the Ethiopian language.

19.2 While they went to fetch these men, he meanwhile ordered the fleet to sail against Carthage. But the Phoenicians said that they would not do this: for they were bound by strong oaths and would commit impious acts if they made an expedition against their own children. With the Phoenicians not being willing, the rest were not battle-worthy.

19.3 Thus, the Carthaginians escaped slavery at the hands of the Persians: for Cambyses did not consider it right to use force against the Phoenicians, because they had surrendered themselves to the Persians and the entire fleet was dependent upon the Phoenicians. The Cyprians also, after surrendering to the Persians, made an expedition against Egypt.

20

20.1 When the Fish-eaters arrived from Elephantine for Cambyses, he sent them to the Ethiopians instructing them as to what they should say, and carrying as gifts a red cloak, necklace of twisted gold, bracelets, a pot of myrrh and a jar of Phoenician wine.

20.2 The Ethiopians, to whom Cambyses sent these, are said to be the tallest and fairest of all men. And they say that these men employ customs that are different and distinct from those of other men particularly with regard to their kingship: they deem worthy to be king, the man whom they judge to be the tallest of the citizens and who possesses strength proportional to his size.

21

21.1 It was thus before these men that the Fish-eaters arrived, giving gifts to their king, to whom they spoke as follows: 'The king of the Persians, Cambyses, wishes to become your friend and ally, and he has sent us with orders to speak to you and he offers to you these gifts which he especially delights in using himself.'

21.2 But the Ethiopian king had realised that they were spies and gave them the following reply: 'neither did the Persian king send you bringing gifts because he greatly values becoming my ally, nor do you speak the truth: for you have come as spies of my kingdom. And he is not a just man. For if he were he a just man, he would not have coveted any land other than his own, nor would seek to lead into slavery men by whom he has never been wronged. Now give him this bow and deliver this message.

21.3 'The king of the Ethiopians advises the king of the Persians that, whenever the Persians can draw back a bow of such a size in length as easily as I can, to then bring an expedition of superior number against the long-lived Ethiopians: but that until then he should acknowledge his thanks to the gods that they do not turn the minds of the sons of the Ethiopians to acquiring land in addition to their own.'

22

22.1 Having said this, he unstrung the bow and handed it over to the men who had come. Then, taking up the red cloak, he asked what it was and how it had been made. When the Fish-eaters spoke the truth about the red colour and the dyeing process, he said that the men were deceitful and that their clothes were deceitful.

22.2 Secondly, he asked about the twisted gold necklace and the bracelets. When the Fish-eaters explained how it was fashioned, the king laughed and because he thought they were chains, he said that they possessed stronger fetters than these.

22.3 Thirdly, he asked about the myrrh. When they told him how it was made and how it was applied to the skin, he said exactly the same thing as he had said about the cloak. When he came to the wine and asked about its production, he was very pleased with the drink and asked in addition what the king ate and the greatest age to which a Persian man lived.

22.4 The men replied that their king ate bread, explaining the nature of wheat, and that the longest full number of years for the life of a man was eighty. To this the Ethiopian king replied that it was no wonder they lived for so few years if they ate dung. For they would not be able to live that long, unless they were refreshed by the drink, indicating the wine to the Fish-eaters. In this respect, he said, they themselves were beaten by the Persians.

23

23.1 When the Fish-eaters asked the king in return about their length of life and way of life, he said that many of them reached one hundred and twenty years, and some exceeded this, and their food was boiled meat and their drink milk.

23.2 When the spies expressed their surprise about the number of years they lived to, he led them to a spring, which made people more radiant when they washed in it, just as if it were olive oil. And the aroma from it was like violets.

23.3 The spies said that the water from this spring was indeed so soft that nothing was able to float upon it, neither wood nor anything that was lighter than wood, but it all went to the bottom. If this water is truly as reported, it is because of this that they are so long-lived, by using it for everything.

23.4 After they left the spring, he led them to the prison where everyone was bound in golden chains. And copper is the rarest and most valuable substance of all among these Ethiopians. Having seen the prison, they saw the so-called Table of the Sun.

24

24.1 After this, the final thing they saw was their coffins, which are said to be made out of a transparent stone in the following manner.

24.2 Whenever they embalm a body, either just as the Egyptians do or by some other method, after rubbing the entire body with gypsum they decorate it with drawing, making it look as much like the person as possible, and then they set around it the hollow pillar made from the clear stone: this is dug by them from the ground in great quantity and is easy to work.

24.3 The corpse, which is in the centre of the pillar, is clearly visible and it does not give off any kind of unpleasant smell nor anything else unseemly, and everything that is visible bears the likeness to the dead man himself.

24.4 Close relatives keep the pillar in their homes for a year, bringing to it offerings from all the first fruits and conducting sacrifices: after this they carry them outside and set them up around the city.

25

25.1 When they had seen everything the spies went back. When these men had reported this, Cambyses immediately became angry and made an expedition against the Ethiopians, having given no instruction either regarding the provision of food, nor having himself given any consideration to the fact that he was about to send an expedition to the furthest points of the earth.

25.2 But being quite mad and not in his right mind, once he had listened to the Fish-eaters, and after instructing the Greeks with him to remain behind, he marched out leading with him his entire land army.

25.3 When on the march he arrived in Thebes, he detached around fifty thousand men from his army, and ordered these men to enslave the Ammonians and burn the oracle of Zeus, while he himself leading the rest of the army went against the Ethiopians.

25.4 Before the army had completed a fifth of the journey, already all the food that they had had been used up, and after the grain the pack animals were consumed and used up.

25.5 Had Cambyses, once he understood the situation, at that point changed his mind and led the army back, he would have been a wise man as a result of his initial fault. But he now gave it no consideration and pressed on ever further.

25.6 The soldiers, while they were able to get anything from the land, survived by eating grass, but when they arrived at the desert, some of them committed a dreadful act: for after choosing one man out of every ten of them by lot, they ate them. Cambyses upon learning of this and being afraid of their cannibalism, abandoned the expedition against the Ethiopians, marched back to Thebes and arrived after losing many from his army. From Thebes, he went down to Memphis and let the Greeks sail away.

26

26.1 This is how the expedition against the Ethiopians fared. Those who were dispatched to march against the Ammonians, after they set out from Thebes and were on the march with their guides, were known to have arrived at the city of Oasis, which the Samians hold who are said to be of the Aeschrione tribe, and they are seven days' journey from Thebes across the desert. In the Greek language this place is called the 'Island of the Blessed'.

26.2 It is said that the army arrived at this region, but from there, apart from the Ammonians and those who heard it from them, no one else can say anything about them; for they neither reached the Ammonians nor returned.

26.3 The following is what the Ammonians themselves say. When they were going out of this oasis through the desert against them and were at a point between themselves and the oasis, while they were taking their breakfast a great and extraordinarily violent south wind blew up before them and buried them in the masses of sand that it stirred up, and they vanished in such a manner. Such is what the Ammonians say about this army.

27

27.1 When Cambyses had arrived at Memphis, Apis, whom the Greeks call Epaphus, appeared to the Egyptians,. With his appearance, the Egyptians immediately began wearing their finest cloaks and held a festival.

27.2 When he saw the Egyptians doing this, Cambyses, firmly convinced that they were doing this because he had fared badly, summoned the governors of Memphis, and when they came before him, he asked why the Egyptians had done nothing like this when he was previously in Memphis, but were doing so then when he was present after losing a large number of his army.

27.3 These men explained that a god had appeared, and one who was accustomed to appear after a long time, and that at the very moment when he appeared all the Egyptians then rejoiced and celebrated a festival. When he heard this, Cambyses said that they were lying and put them to death on the grounds that they were lying.

28

28.1 After he killed these men, he then summoned the priests to come before him. When the priests said the same things, he said that it would not escape his notice if some tame god had arrived among the Egyptians. Having spoken thus, he bid the priests lead Apis to him.

28.2 They then went off to bring him to him. Now this Apis Epaphus is a calf born from a cow which is no longer capable of conceiving another offspring in its womb. The Egyptians say that a ray of moonlight from heaven impregnates the cow and that as a result it gives birth to Apis.

28.3 This calf called Apis is black and bears the following marks, a three-cornered white mark on its forehead, one shaped like an eagle on its back, double hairs on its tail, and a knot under its tongue.

29

29.1 When the priests brought in Apis, Cambyses, because he was beyond mad, drew his dagger, and wishing to strike Apis in the chest he struck his thigh. He laughed and said to the priests:

29.2 'Oh you blockheads, are your gods made of flesh and blood and able to feel the blow of iron? This god is indeed worthy of the Egyptians, but you will certainly not get away with making me a laughing stock by your rejoicing.' Having said this, he gave orders to those whose task it was to perform such actions to flog the priests, and to kill any Egyptian they came across celebrating the festival.

29.3 The festival therefore came to an end for the Egyptians, the priests were condemned, and Apis, after being struck in the thigh, lay down in the temple and died. And after he had died from the wound, the priests buried him in secret without Cambyses' knowledge.

30

30.1 Cambyses, so the Egyptians say, immediately went mad because of this unjust action, although he was not even in his right mind before. The first of his wicked acts was to achieve the ruin of his brother Smerdis of the same father and mother, whom he had sent away from Egypt out of envy, because he alone of the Persians could draw back the bow, which the Fish-eaters brought back from the Ethiopian king, to a width of two fingers, but none of the other Persians were able to.

30.2 When Smerdis had gone away to Persia, Cambyses saw the following vision in sleep. It seemed to him that a messenger came from the Persians to announce that Smerdis was sitting on the royal throne and that he touched the heaven with his head.

30.3 Being afraid as a result that his brother would kill him and take power, he sent to Persia Prexaspes, who was his most trusted man among the Persians, to kill him. He, after going up to Susa, killed Smerdis; some say that he took him out on a hunt, and others that he led him to the Red Sea and drowned him.

31

31.1 This then, they say, was the first of Cambyses' wicked acts. The second he committed against his sister who had followed him to Egypt, and with whom he also lived as his wife and who was his full sister from both sides. He married her in the following way.

31.2 For the Persians had in no way been previously accustomed to marry their sisters. Cambyses was in love with one of his sisters and then wishing to marry her, because he knew that he would not be acting according to custom, he summoned those called the Royal Judges and asked them if there was any law that permitted someone who wished to do so to marry his sister.

31.3 The Royal Judges are men chosen from the Persians until they either die or some wrongdoing of theirs is discovered. These men judge lawsuits for the Persians and are the interpreters of the ancestral laws, and all other matters that are laid before them.

31.4 When, therefore, Cambyses posed his question, these men gave him an answer that was both just and safe, saying that they did not find any law which bid a brother take his sister as a wife, but that they had, however, found another law which permitted whoever was king of the Persians to do whatever he wanted.

31.5 Thus, they did not break the law out of fear of Cambyses, and so that should not be killed for protecting custom, they found another law as an ally for someone wishing to marry his sisters.

31.6 Then of course Cambyses married the woman who was the object of his desire; not long after, however, he took another sister. It was the younger of these who followed him to Egypt and whom he killed.

32

32.1 Just as in the case of Smerdis, there are two versions of the story about her death. The Greeks say that Cambyses pitted a lion cub against a puppy, and that this woman was watching, and when the puppy was being defeated, another puppy which was its brother broke its tether and came to help; and thus, the two puppies overpowered the lion cub.

32.2 Cambyses was pleased while he watched, but the woman sitting beside him was crying. Cambyses, when he realized this, asked her why she was crying; and she said that she was crying after seeing the puppy exacting revenge for its brother, since she was reminded of Smerdis and realized that there was no one to take revenge for him.

32.3 The Greeks say it was for this utterance that she was killed by Cambyses, but the Egyptians say that while they were sitting at the table, his wife picked up a lettuce and she stripped off its leaves and asked her husband whether the lettuce was more beautiful stripped of its leaves or with its leaves; he said with its leaves, and she said:

32.4 'You have made the house of Cyrus just like this lettuce then because you have stripped that bare.' He was angered by this and jumped on her while she was pregnant, and she miscarried and died.

33

33.1 Such were the actions Cambyses inflicted on his relatives in his madness, whether because of Apis or some other reason through which evils are accustomed to grip men. For Cambyses is said to have suffered from a serious illness from birth, the one which some call sacred. It is not indeed unlikely that if he had a serious disease in his body, his mind also would not be healthy.

34

34.1 He also vented his madness on the rest of the Persians. For it is said that he spoke to Prexaspes, whom he especially honoured, and this man used to bring him his messages, and his son was cupbearer to Cambyses, and this was no small honour. It is said that he spoke as follows:

34.2 'Prexaspes, what sort of man do the Persians consider me to be and what sort of things do they say about me?' And Prexaspes said, 'Lord, in every respect, they praise you greatly, but they do say that you are rather too fond of your wine.'

34.3 This was what Prexaspes said about the Persians, and an angered Cambyses answered as follows: 'So, given the Persians now say that I am mad because I am too fond of wine and that I am out of my mind, then their earlier words were therefore in no way truthful.'

34.4 For on a previous occasion, when some of the Persians and Croesus were sitting with him in council, Cambyses asked what sort of man he seemed to be in comparison to his father Cyrus, and they replied that he was a better man than his father; for he held everything that that man had and had also acquired both Egypt and the sea in addition.

34.5 This was what the Persians said, but Croesus, who was present and who was not at all pleased with their judgement, spoke as follows to Cambyses: 'Child of Cyrus, you do not seem to be to be like your father; for as yet you have no son, such as that man left in you.' Having heard this, Cambyses was pleased and praised Croesus' judgement.

35

35.1 And, therefore, after recalling this occasion, he spoke angrily to Prexaspes: 'you, learn now whether the Persians spoke the truth or whether they were out of their minds in saying this.

35.2 For I if I were to take a shot at your son who is standing in the doorway and were to strike him through the middle of his heart, the Persians will seem to be talking nonsense. But if I miss, then the Persians seem to speak the truth and it is I who am not in my right mind.'

35.3 Having said this, he drew back his bow and shot at the boy, and when the boy fell down, he gave orders to cut him open and examine the wound. When it was found that the shaft was lodged in the boy's heart, he laughed and spoke with excessive glee to the boy's father:

35.4 'Prexaspes, it is indeed clear both that I am not mad and that the Persians are out of their wits. And now tell me, who of all men have you seen shoot so precisely on the mark?' Prexaspes, because he saw that the man was not at all sane and because he was afraid for himself, said: 'Lord, I do not even think that a god would shoot so well.'

35.5 This was what he did on that occasion, and on another, for no worthy reason, he arrested twelve Persians who were the equals of the leading men and buried them up to their necks.

36

36.1 Croesus the Lydian thought it right to rebuke him for acting like this in the following words: 'King, do not entrust everything to your youthful anger, but restrain and control yourself! For it is good to be prudent, and forethought is wise. You are arresting and killing your own citizens for no justifiable reason, and you are killing children.

36.2 'If you commit many acts like this, take care that the Persians do not revolt from you. Your father Cyrus gave me many instructions ordering me to admonish you and counsel you about whatever I considered good.' Croesus gave him this advice to show his goodwill. But Cambyses replied as follows:

36.3 'Do you dare to give me advice, you who governed his own fatherland well, you who counselled my father well, bidding him cross the Araxes river and attack the Massagetae, when those men were wishing to cross against our land, and you who destroyed your own fatherland with your bad leadership, and who destroyed Cyrus because he obeyed you, but you won't get away with it, since I have long been looking for a pretext to take care of you.'

36.4 Having spoken thus, he took up his bow intending to shoot at him, but Croesus leapt up and ran outside. Cambyses was not then able to shoot him, but he ordered his attendants to arrest him and kill him.

36.5 But his attendants, because they knew his manner, hid Croesus on the following reasoning that, if any feeling of regret should come over Cambyses and he missed Croesus, they would reveal him and would receive rewards for saving Croesus' life, but if he did not change his mind nor want him, they would then make away with him.

36.6 And not long afterwards Cambyses did indeed long for Croesus, and when his attendants learnt this, they announced that he was alive. Cambyses said he was very pleased that Croesus was alive, but that the men who had kept him safe, however, would not get off scot-free, but would be killed. This was what he did.

37

37.1 Such were the many actions he inflicted on both the Persians and his allies in his madness, and while remaining at Memphis he used to open the ancient tombs and examine the corpses.

37.2 In fact, when he came to the temple of Hephaestus he even laughed loudly at the statue. For it is this statue of Hephaestus that most resembles the Phoenician Pataeci, which the Phoenicians carry on the prows of their triremes. For anyone who has not seen these, I will describe them. They resemble a dwarf.

37.3 He also entered the temple of the Cabeirians, which it is entirely unlawful for anyone else to enter save the priest. After mocking these statues loudly, he set them on fire. There is a resemblance between these statues and those of Hephaestus. They say that they are his children.

38

38.1 It is therefore clear to me that Cambyses was completely mad in every respect; for otherwise he would not have undertaken to jeer at sacred matters and customs. For if someone were to pose the question to all men, bidding them choose the finest laws from all laws, each would, after consideration, choose his own customs. For every people considers their own customs to be the finest by far.

38.2 It is not, therefore, likely that anyone other than someone who was mad would consider such things laughable. That all men have this belief about their customs can be concluded from many different pieces of evidence, and especially from this example.

38.3 Darius, when he was in power, summoned the Greeks who were present and asked them for what price they would be willing to consume their ancestors. These men replied that they would not do this for any price.

38.4 After this, Darius summoned the Indian tribe called the Callatiae, who do consume their ancestors, and asked them, with the Greeks who were present learning what they said through an interpreter, for what amount of money they would undertake to burn their relatives with fire. They cried out in response and ordered him to speak words of good omen. So established have these customs become, and Pindar, I think, was quite correct when he said that custom was king of all.

39

39.1 At the time when Cambyses was waging war against Egypt, the Spartans made an expedition against Samos and Polycrates son of Aeaces, who held Samos at that time after stirring up a rebellion.

39.2 At first, after dividing the city into three, he distributed a share to his brothers Pantagnotus and Syloson; but after he had killed the former and driven out the younger one Syloson, he held all of Samos; and he had a tie of guest-friendship and made a treaty with Amasis king of Egypt, both sending him gifts and receiving other gifts from him.

39.3 In a short time Polycrates' power immediately grew and was loudly spoken of throughout Ionia and the rest of Greece; for wherever he directed his expeditions, everything turned out successfully for him. He had acquired one hundred fifty-oared ships and one thousand archers, and he carried off and led away all men alike making no distinction.

39.4 For he said that he would receive greater thanks by giving back to a friend what he had taken than if he had not taken it from the start. He had in fact taken many of the islands and many of the cities on the mainland. Among them he subdued and captured in full force the people of Lesbos who had come to the aid of the Milesians in a sea battle, who as captives dug the trench all the way round the fortification at Samos.

40

40.1 And somehow Polycrates' great success did not escape Amasis' notice, but it became a matter of concern for him. When Polycrates became still more successful, he wrote him the following letter which he sent to Samos.

40.2 'Amasis addresses Polycrates as follows: it is a pleasant thing to learn of a friend and guest-friend enjoying success; but your great successes also do not please me, since I know how jealous divine power is. And I myself somehow wish that those about whom I care could succeed in some of their affairs but fail in others and thus spend life with alternating fortunes rather than being successful in everything.

40.3 'For I do not as yet know from what I have heard of anyone who succeeded in everything, who did not meet a terrible end in utter ruin. Now, if you are persuaded by me, do as follows with regards to your successes.

40.4 'Think about what you consider to be the most valuable of your possessions and for which you would grieve most deeply in your soul if you lost it and throw it away so that it will never again return to the sight of men. And conversely, if as a result of this your successes do not meet alternately with sufferings, remedy the situation in the manner I set out.'

41

41.1 After he had read this and realized that Amasis was giving him good advice, he was divided as to which of his treasured possessions it would most deeply upset him to lose, but while pondering he decided upon the following item. He owned a seal-ring, which was an emerald set-in gold, and which was the creation of Theodorus son of Telecles of Samos.

41.2 When he had decided to throw this away, he acted as follows: after manning a fifty-oared ship with a crew, he boarded it, and then gave orders for them to set sail to the open sea. When he was far away from the island, he removed the ring with all the sailors watching and hurled it into the sea. When he had done this and after arriving back home, he mourned his loss.

42

42.1 But on the fifth or sixth day after this, the following events befell him. A fisherman caught a large and fine fish, and he considered it worthy to be given as a gift to Polycrates; he brought it do the door and said that he would like to see Polycrates, and when he came to him, he gave him the fish and said:

42.2 'O king, when I caught this fish I did not think it right to take it to the market, although I make my living by my own hands' work, but I decided that it was worthy of you and your power; so I bring it and offer it to you.' Polycrates was pleased with what he said and replied as follows: 'you have done very well, and your favour is twofold both because of your words and your gift, and I invite you to dinner.'

42.3 The fisherman was delighted with this and went home, but the servants while cutting up the fish found Polycrates' ring inside its belly.

42.4 When they saw it, they seized it as quickly as possible, and rejoicing they brought it to Polycrates, and as they gave him the ring, they told him how it had been found. When it occurred to him that what happened was a divine sign, he wrote everything that he had done and what had befallen him in a letter which he despatched to Egypt once he had written it.

43

43.1 Amasis, when he read the letter that had come from Polycrates, realized that it was impossible for a man to protect a fellow mortal from whatever circumstance was going to happen to him, and that Polycrates was not going to meet a good end while he was successful in all matters, since he had even found what he threw away.

43.2 He send a herald to Samos to dissolve their friendship. And he did this for the following reason, so that he himself should not be deeply aggrieved for a friend when some terrible and serious misfortune befell Polycrates.

44

44.1 It was indeed against this man Polycrates who was successful in every way that the Lacedaemonians made an expedition, when the Samians, who later founded Cydonia in Greece, called on them for help. And Polycrates, after secretly sending a herald to Cambyses son of Cyrus, who was gathering his army against Egypt, and asked Cambyses, after he had sent to him at Samos, to request an army from him.

44.2 When he heard this, Cambyses eagerly sent word to Samos at the same time asking Polycrates to send a fleet against Egypt. Polycrates chose those of his citizens whom he most suspected of rebellion and sent them off in forty triremes, instructing Cambyses not to send these men back.

45

45.1 Some in fact say that the Samian men sent away by Polycrates did not arrive in Egypt, but that when they were sailing around Carpathus, they were talking among themselves, and it pleased them no longer to sail on any further. Others say that they arrived at Egypt and ran away from those who were guarding them there.

45.2 As they were sailing back to Samos Polycrates met them with his ships and engaged them in battle. The men who were returning were victorious and disembarked onto the island, but when they fought on land they were beaten in this battle, and so it was that then they sailed to Sparta.

45.3 There are those who say that the Samians returning from Egypt conquered Polycrates, but I do not think they are correct in saying so. For they would not have needed to call upon the Spartans, if by themselves there were enough of them to bring Polycrates to terms. What's more, the story is not even convincing, that the man who had both hired mercenaries and his own archers in great numbers, would be beaten by a few returning Samians.

45.4 Polycrates gathered together the children and wives of the citizens subject to him into houseboats and, if their men betrayed him to those returning, he was ready to burn them along with the houseboats.

46

46.1 When the Samians, who had been driven out by Polycrates, arrived at Sparta, after they came to the leaders, they spoke at length about their great need. But at the first sitting the Spartan leaders replied to them that they had forgotten what they had said first and did not understand what they had said later.

46.2 After they came before them a second time, they were carrying a sack and said nothing except that the sack needed meal. And the leaders replied that the sack was excessive. But they decided to help them.

47

47.1 Then after they had made their preparations, the Spartans made an expedition against Samos, so the Samians say, in repayment of benefactions, because they were the first to come to the Spartans' aid with ships against the Messenians; but the Spartans say that they sent an army not so much to avenge the Samians in their need as because they wanted to exact retribution for the theft of a bowl, which they were taking to Croesus, and of a breastplate, which Amasis king of Egypt sent to them as a gift.

47.2 For the Samians stole the breastplate the year before they took the bowl; the breastplate was made of linen and there were many figures embroidered on it, and it was adorned with gold and cotton threads.

47.3 But what made it worthy of admiration is each individual thread from which the breastplate is made; for each fine thread is itself composed of three hundred and sixty threads, all clear to see. This is the pair of the one which Amasis dedicated to Athena at Lindus.

48

48.1 The Corinthians also enthusiastically took part in furthering the expedition against Samos; for an outrageous act had been committed against them by the Samians a generation before this expedition, about the same time that the robbery of the bowl had occurred.

48.2 Periander son of Cypselus had sent to Alyattes at Sardis three hundred sons of the leading men of Corcyra to be castrated: when the Corinthians who were escorting the boys put in at Samos, the Samians, upon learning their reason for conducting the boys to Sardis, first instructed the boys to attach themselves to the temple of Artemis.

48.3 Afterwards since they did not allow the suppliants to be dragged from the temple and because the Corinthians were withholding food from the boys, the Samians created a festival, which they still now celebrate in the following manner. For when night-time arrived, as long as the boys were seeking refuge, they set up dances of unmarried girls and youths, and by establishing the dances they made it customary for sesame and honey cakes to be brought to them, so that the Corcyrean boys could snatch these and take nourishment.

48.4 This went on until the boys' Corinthian guards went away and left them behind. The Samians led the boys back to Corcyra.

49

49.1 If after Periander died the Corinthians had been friendly towards the Corcyreans, they would not have taken part in the expedition against Samos for this reason. But in fact, ever since they colonized the island, they have been at odds with one another, although they are their own.

49.2 For these reasons the Corinthians bore a grudge against the Samians. Periander chose the sons of the leading Corcyreans and sent them off to Sardis for castration as an act of revenge. For the Corcyreans first had started it after they committed an intolerable act against him.

50

50.1 When Periander murdered his wife Melissa, it happened that another misfortune befell him in addition to what had already happened. He had two sons by Melissa, one being seventeen years of age, the other eighteen.

50.2 Procles the boys' maternal grandfather, who was tyrant ruler of Epidaurus, sent for them to come to him and welcomed them kindly, as was reasonable given that they were his own daughter's sons. When he was sending them back, before he did so, he told them:

50.3 'Do you know, boys, who killed your mother?' To this utterance the elder of them gave no attention. But the younger, whose name was

Lycophron, was so upset when he heard this, that, when he arrived at Corinth, he would neither address his father, nor conversed with him when he addressed him, nor gave any response to him when he questioned him, on the grounds that he was his mother's killer. Finally, because he was extremely angry with him, Periander drove him out of his house.

51

51.1 After driving him out, he questioned his elder son about what his maternal grandfather had said. The boy explained that he had welcomed them kindly. But he made no mention of what Procles said as he was sending them away because he had not given it any attention. Periander said that there was no way that man had not suggested something to them, and he persisted in questioning him. The boy then remembered and told him.

51.2 Periander understood and wishing to give no hint of weakness, he sent a messenger to the places where the son, who had been driven out by him, was spending his life, and ordered people there not to receive him in their homes.

51.3 The son was then driven out and whenever he came to a different household, he would be driven out of this one, since Periander was threatening those who took him in and ordering them to shut him out. Driven out, he went to another of his companions' households. They, despite being afraid, received him as the son of Periander.

52

52.1 Finally, Periander made a proclamation that whoever either received him into their home or spoke to him, would owe a sacred fine to Apollo, having stated how much this would be.

52.2 In response to the proclamation, therefore, no one was willing either to address him or to receive him in their homes. In response, the young man himself did not think it right to attempt what had been forbidden but endured it and curled up in open porticoes.

52.3 When Periander saw him on the fourth day in a wretched state from being unwashed and through lack of food, he pitied him. Letting go of his anger, he went towards him and addressed him.

52.4 'My son, which is the more preferable of these, that you carry on in the state you are in now, or that you take over the power and good things which I now have, being helpful to your father? You who are my son and king of prosperous Corinth have chosen a vagabond's life, by being hostile to and harbouring anger towards the man about whom you should least feel like this. For if in these matters some misfortune has occurred, as a result of which you harbour suspicion towards me, this same thing has befallen me, too, and I have a greater share in it, in as much as I myself brought it about.

52.5 Once you have understood how much better it is to be envied than it is to be pitied, and what it is like to have been angry at your parents and your superiors, come back home.'

52.6 With these words Periander sought to win him over. But the boy made no other reply to his father, except to tell him that he owed a sacred fine to the god himself because he had come to talk to him. Periander realized how implacable and immoveable his son's ill-feeling was, and so he sent him away from his sight in a ship to Corcyra.

52.7 After he sent him away, Periander made an expedition against his father-in-law Procles as the man most to blame for the current state of affairs, and he took Epidaurus, and Procles himself he arrested and imprisoned.

53

53.1 With time advancing, Periander had now passed his prime and was conscious that he was no longer capable of seeing and managing his affairs; he sent to Corcyra and called Lycophron back to take over his power. For in the elder of his sons he saw nothing, but he seemed to him rather stupid.

53.2 But Lycophron did not deem the man who brought the message worthy of a reply. Periander continued to press the young man a second time and sent his sister to him, his own daughter, thinking that she especially would be able to persuade him.

53.3 When the girl arrived, she said: 'Child, do you wish the tyranny to fall into another's hands and for our father's household to be ruined rather than you yourself holding it once you have come back? Come back home and stop punishing yourself.

53.4 'Pride is an unhappy possession. Do not cure evil with evil. Many elevate things that are more fair sounding above what is just, and many already by looking out for their mother's affairs, cast away their father's. Power is a slippery thing; many covet it and our father is already an old man and past his prime. Do not give away the goods you have to others.'

53.5 And thus she addressed him conveying her father's most attractive arguments; but he replied that he would never come to Corinth, while he learned that his father was still alive.

53.6 When this was reported back, Periander sent a herald for a third time saying that he was willing to come to Corcyra, and he ordered that man to come back to Corinth and take over as successor to his power.

53.7 Since the boy approved these conditions, Periander prepared to go to Corcyra, his son to Corinth. But when the Corcyreans learnt the details of the matter, they killed the young man so that Periander would not come to their land. It was for this that Periander was taking revenge on the Corcyreans.

54

54.1 When the Lacedaemonians arrived with a large fleet, they began besieging Samos. And when they advanced to the wall, they mounted the tower which stands beside the sea in the outer region of the city, but when Polycrates then attacked them with a great force they were driven back.

54.2 The mercenaries and many of the Samians themselves sallied forth near the upper tower on the ridge of the mountain and, after they had withstood the Spartans for a little while, they fled back, and the Spartans killed them as they went in pursuit.

55

55.1 Had the Spartans present that day been like Archias and Lycopas, Samos would have been taken: Archias and Lycopas alone fell upon the Samians who were fleeing to the wall and, after being cut off from behind, they died in the city of Samos.

55.2 I myself met another Archias in Pitane, for he was from this area, who was the grandson of this Archias; he himself was the son of Samius who was Archias' son, who particularly honoured the Samians above all his guest-friends and said that his father was given the name Samius, because his father Archias had died at Samos having shown the highest bravery. He said that he honoured the Samians because his grandfather had been given a public burial by them.

56

56.1 The Spartans, when they had been besieging Samos for forty days and no progress had been made in their situation, they went back to the Peloponnese.

56.2 And there is a rather foolish tale that is spreading abroad which says that Polycrates minted a considerable amount of native coinage made out of lead, which he covered in gold and gave to them, and that they accepted this and thus left. This was the first expedition that the Dorian Spartans made to Asia.

57

57.1 The Samians who had made the expedition against Polycrates sailed away to Siphnus when the Spartans were about to abandon them.

57.2 For they were in need of money, and at that time Siphnian affairs were prosperous, and of the islanders they were the wealthiest, because they owned the gold and silver mines on the island; they were so wealthy that the treasury dedicated by them at Delphi, which is equal to the richest there, comprises a tenth of their income: they used to divide the revenues that came in each year among themselves.

57.3 When they were setting up the treasury, they consulted the oracle as to whether their current good fortunes could continue for a long time. Then the Pythia gave them the following reply.

57.4 'But whenever the walls of the town hall turn white at Siphnus,

And the marketplace white-browed, there is then need of a wise man
to recognize the wooden force and the red herald.'

The Siphnians' marketplace and town hall were at this time with white Parian marble.

58

58.1 They were not able to understand this oracle, either straightaway at the time or later when the Samians arrived. For as soon as the Samians put in at Siphnus, they sent one of their ships carrying ambassadors to the city.

58.2 For in ancient times all ships were painted red, and this was what the Pythia meant when she addressed the Siphnians urging them to be on their guard against the wooden force and the red herald.

58.3 Therefore, when the messengers arrived, they asked the Siphnians to lend them ten talents. When the Siphnians replied that they would not lend this to them, the Samians began laying waste to their lands.

58.4 After they learnt this, the Siphnians immediately came to help and after engaging in battle were defeated, and many were cut off from the city by their Samians, and after this they exacted one hundred talents from them.

59

59.1 Then from the people of Hermione instead of money they took the island of Hydrea in the Peloponnese and entrusted it to the Troezenians. They themselves founded Cydonia on Crete, although it was not for this reason that they sailed there, but in fact to drive the Zacynthians out of the island.

59.2 They remained there and flourished for five years, and they were the ones who built the temples that are now in Cydonia, including the shrine at Dictyne.

59.3 But in the sixth year the Aeginetans conquered them in a sea battle and enslaved them with the help of the Cretans, and they cut off the prows from their ships which were shaped like boars' heads and dedicated them at the temple of Athena at Aegina.

59.4 The Aeginetans did this because they harboured spiteful feelings towards the Samians. For previously, at the time when Amphicrates was king in Samos, the Samians made an expedition against Aegina and inflicted great evils on the Aeginetans and suffered at the hands of those men. This then was the cause.

60

60.1 I have spoken about the Samians at such length because the three greatest works of all the Greeks were constructed by them; the first of these is a double-mouthed tunnel that starts from below and runs for nine hundred feet through a high mountain.

60.2 The length of the tunnel is four thousand two hundred feet, and the width and height are both eight feet. Throughout its entire length there is another channel that is dug to a depth of two cubits, three feet in width, through which water is conducted via pipes and carried to the city from a great spring.

60.3 The designer of the tunnel was the Megarian Eupalenus son of Naustrophus. This is one of the three works. The second is a bank in the sea which encloses the harbour; it has a depth of one hundred and twenty feet and the length is greater than twelve hundred feet.

60.4 The third is the temple that was constructed by them which is the greatest of all the temples that we have seen. Its first architect was Rhoecus son of Phileus, a native Samian. These then are the reasons that I have discussed the Samians at length.

61

61.1 It was at this time when he was in Egypt and had gone quite mad that the two Magi brothers rebelled against Cambyses son of Cyrus, the one of whom Cambyses had left behind as steward of his household. This man in fact rebelled against him after he learned of the death of Smerdis and that it was being concealed and also that few of the Persians knew about it, but that many believed that he was alive.

61.2 In response to this, he made the following plot with a view to seizing royal power. He had a brother, whom I mentioned was his partner in the rebellion, who was very like Smerdis son of Cyrus in appearance, the brother whom Cambyses had murdered. He was in fact both like Smerdis in appearance and also bore the same name of Smerdis.

61.3 After the Magus Patizeithes had persuaded this man he himself would take care of everything, he led his brother to the throne and sat him upon it. After he did this, he sent heralds to various places and also in fact one to Egypt to announce to the army that in future they must listen to Smerdis son of Cyrus, but not Cambyses.

62

62.1 The rest of these heralds, therefore, made this announcement, but the one appointed to go to Egypt, for he found Cambyses and the army at Ecbatana in Syria, stood in their midst and announced the instructions given by the Magus.

62.2 When Cambyses heard this from the herald and because he believed that he was speaking the truth and that he himself had been betrayed by Prexaspes, and that, when he had been sent him to kill Smerdis, he had not done this, he looked at Prexaspes and said:

'Prexaspes, did you carry out the task that I entrusted to you?' Prexaspes said:

62.3 'Lord, this is not the truth that somehow your brother Smerdis has rebelled against you, nor that you will have any trouble from that man either great or small. For I myself did exactly what you ordered me to, and I buried him with my own hands.

62.4 'If the dead have now risen up, expect Astyages the Mede to rise up against you. But if things are as before, no fresh harm will rise up against you from that man. Now, it is, therefore, my opinion that we should go after this herald and interrogate him thoroughly, asking from whom he has come to announce that we should listen to Smerdis as king.'

63

63.1 When Prexaspes said this, because it pleased Cambyses, the herald was immediately pursued, and he came. When he arrived, Prexaspes questioned him as follows: 'Sir, you say then that you have come as a messenger from Smerdis son of Cyrus. Tell me the truth now and go away unpunished, did Smerdis himself appear to you in person when he issued these instructions or one of his servants?'

63.2 The herald replied: 'I have not seen Smerdis the son of Cyrus at all, since king Cambyses marched out to Egypt. But the Magus, whom Cambyses appointed to be guardian of his household, this is the man who gave these instructions saying that Smerdis son of Cyrus set down these orders and to relay them to you.'

63.3 The herald spoke feeding them no lies, and Cambyses said 'Prexaspes, like a good man you did what I ordered and have escaped blame. But which of the Persians has rebelled against me usurping the name of Smerdis?'

63.4 Prexaspes said: 'I think, oh king, what has happened is this. It is the Magi who have rebelled against you, the man your left as steward of your household, Patizeithes, and this man's brother Smerdis.'

64

64.1 Then when Cambyses heard the name of Smerdis the truth of the words of the dream struck him. He thought in his sleep that someone had declared that Smerdis was sitting on the royal throne and that he touched the heaven with his head.

64.2 Upon realizing that he had killed his brother in vain, he wept for Smerdis. And after weeping loudly and grieving at his whole misfortune, he leapt up onto his horse intending very soon to launch an expedition against the Magus.

64.3 And as he was jumping onto his horse the cap fell from the sheath of his sword and the sword struck his naked thigh. He was wounded in exactly the same place as he had previously struck Apis, god of the Egyptians. Since he thought he had been struck with a fatal blow, Cambyses asked the name of the city where he was.

64.4 They said it was Ecbatana. It had formerly been prophesied to him from the city of Buto that he would die in Ecbatana. Cambyses had thought that he would die an old man in Median Ecbatana, where all his affairs were located. But in fact, the oracle meant he would die in Ecbatana in Syria.

64.5 And at that moment when he learnt the name of the city from his enquiry, he was shocked by the misfortune caused by the Magus and also by his wound, he came to his senses, and because he understood the prophecy he said: 'it has been prophesied that here Cambyses son of Cyrus is to die.'

65

65.1 At that point, he said just this. Twenty days later, he sent for the most notable of the Persians present and addressed them as follows: 'Persians, I am compelled to reveal to you something, which I have above all else been keeping hidden.

65.2 'For when I was in Egypt, I saw a dream while I was asleep, and one which I wish I had never seen. It seemed to me that a messenger came from my house to announce that Smerdis was sitting on the royal throne and touched the heaven with his head.

65.3 'Fearing that I might be deprived of my power by my brother, I acted with greater haste than wisdom. For it is not in human nature to be able to turn away what is going to happen. But I foolishly sent Prexaspes to Susa to kill Smerdis. When such an evil deed had been carried out, I lived without fear, never considering that any other man might rise against me with Smerdis removed from the scene.

65.4 'But since I was mistaken about everything that was to be I became my brother's killer unnecessarily and have been deprived no less of my kingship. It was Smerdis the Magus whom the god showed me would rebel against me in the dream.

65.5 'I did in fact carry out this deed, and you realize that Smerdis son of Cyrus is no longer among you. The Magi are your rulers and masters of my kingdom, the man whom I left as guardian of my household and his brother Smerdis. He who now ought to be taking revenge for the disgraceful acts that I have suffered at the hands of the Magi; this man has died an impious death at the hands of his own relatives.

65.6 Since he is here no longer, in second place out of those who remain, the greatest necessity compels me, Persians, to instruct you regarding what I wish once I am dead; and calling upon the royal gods as witnesses, I charge you all, and especially those of you of the Achaemenids who are present, not to allow the leadership to pass again to the Medes, but if they hold it after taking possession of it by trickery, take it away from them by trickery, and if they have achieved it by force, recover it by strength with even greater force.

65.7 'If you do this, may the land bear fruit for you and your wives and flocks produce offspring, and may you be free for all time. But if you neither recover my power nor attempt to recover it, I pray that opposite happens to you, and in addition that each of the Persians meet a similar end to me.' As soon as he had said this, Cambyses bewailed his entire situation.

66

66.1 When the Persians saw their king weeping, all of them tore at the clothing they were wearing and engaged in unsparing cries of lamentation.

66.2 After this the bone became infected and his thigh became putrid and it carried off Cambyses son of Cyrus, who had ruled for a total of seven years and five months and was entirely childless, having neither male nor female offspring.

66.3 The Persians present were full of great disbelief that the Magi were controlling affairs, but distrustfully thought that Cambyses spoke slanderously about the death of Smerdis so that the whole of Persia would make war against him. These men believed that Smerdis son of Cyrus was now their king. For Prexaspes fiercely denied that he had killed Smerdis. For it was not safe once Cambyses was dead for him to say that he had destroyed Smerdis son of Cyrus by his own hand.

67

67.1 After Cambyses' death, the Magus, taking the name of Smerdis son of Cyrus, ruled without fear for the seven months by which Cambyses' reign had fallen short of a full eight years.

67.2 During this period he conferred such great benefits on all his subjects that, when he died, all those in Asia longed for him, with the exception of the Persians. For the Magus sent to every people over whom he ruled and proclaimed them to be exempt from military service and tribute for three years.

68

68.1 Such was the proclamation he made immediately upon coming to power, but in the eighth month was exposed in the following manner. There was a man named Otanes son of Pharnaspes, equal in birth and wealth to the first of the Persians.

68.2 This man Otanes was the first to suspect who the Magus really was and that he was not Smerdis the son of Cyrus, a conclusion he came to for the reason that he never ventured outside of acropolis nor summoned any of the foremost Persians to his presence. Because he suspected him, he took the following action.

68.3 Cambyses had married his daughter whose name was Phaedyme. And the Magus had now married this same girl and lived with her and also with all the other wives of Cambyses. Therefore, when Otanes sent for her, he enquired of his daughter with what man she was sleeping, namely whether it was Cyrus' son Smerdis or someone else.

68.4 She sent back to him her reply which said that she did not know. For she had neither ever seen Smerdis son of Cyrus, nor did she know who it was that was sleeping with her. Otanes sent to her a second time saying: 'if you do not know Smerdis the son of Cyrus, ask Atossa with whom she and you are living; for I suppose she surely recognizes her own brother.'

69

69.1 To this his daughter replied: 'I am able neither to converse with Atossa nor to see any other of the women who dwell with us. For as soon as this man took over royal power, he separated us, appointing each to a different place.' When he heard this, the matter was even clearer to Otanes. He sent to her a third message, which said this:

69.2 'Daughter, it is necessary for you as you are of noble birth to undertake whatever danger your father commands you to shoulder. For if in fact, he is not Smerdis the son of Cyrus but who I think he is, he must not get away unpunished for sleeping with you and holding power over the Persians but must pay the penalty.

69.3 Now, therefore, do as follows: whenever he sleeps with you and you perceive that he is fast asleep, touch his ears; and if he clearly has ears, know that you are sleeping with Smerdis son of Cyrus, but if he does not, it is Smerdis the Magus.

69.4 Phaedyme sent a reply saying that she would be taking a great risk if she did this. For if he turned out not to have ears and she were caught touching them, she knew well that he would kill her. But that she would nevertheless do this.

69.5 She undertook to fulfil this for her father. For Cyrus, son of Cambyses, while he was in power had cut off the ears of Smerdis the Magus for what was in fact no trivial reason.

69.6 This girl Phaedyme the daughter of Otanes, therefore, carried out everything she promised her father. When her turn came to approach the Magus, for wives sleep with their Persian husbands in rotation, she came and lay with him. When the Magus was sleeping deeply, she touched his ears and upon realizing easily and without difficulty that the man had no ears, as soon as day came, she sent word to inform him about what had happened.

70

70.1 Otanes, after he took aside Aspathines and Gobryas, leading Persians whom he deemed most worthy to be trusted, he explained the whole matter to them; these men it seems also suspected that this was the case, and they readily believed what Otanes said.

70.2 They decided that each take as his ally the man he trusted most. Otanes then brought in Intaphrenes, Gobryas brought in Megabyzus, and Aspathines brought in Hydranes.

70.3 When there were six of them, Darius, son of Hystaspes, arrived at Susa from the Persians; for his father was their governor. When this man arrived the six Persians decided to make Darius their ally.

71

71.1 When these seven men came together, they exchanged pledges and words. When it came to Darius' turn to give his opinion, he addressed them as follows:

71.2 'I used to think I was alone in knowing that the Magus was ruling as king and that Smerdis son of Cyrus was dead. It is for this very reason that I have come with haste to arrange death for the Magus. But since it turned out that you also know, and it is not just me, I think we should act immediately and not put it off. For that is not the better option.'

71.3 To this Otanes replied: 'son of Hystaspes, you are the son of a good father, and you seem to show yourself to be in no way inferior to him. However, do not hasten the attempt without consideration, but take it on more prudently. For it is necessary for there to be more of us to undertake this.'

71.4 Darius said in response: 'you gentlemen who are present, if you act as Otanes says, know that you will die most horribly. For someone will tip off the Magus looking out for his own private gain.

71.5 'You ought indeed to have done this kind of thing on your own responsibility; but since you decided to include me in your number and let me in on it, either let us act today or know that if the present moment passes you by, no other man will be your accuser before me, but I myself will denounce you to the Magus.'

72

72.1 When Otanes saw that Darius was of a hasty temper he spoke in response: 'since you compel us to speed things up and do not allow us to put it off, come, tell us how we are going to pass into the palace and attack them. For I suppose you yourself know from what you have heard, even if you have not seen them, that guards are stationed all around. How are we going to get past them?' Darius replied with these words:

72.2 'Otanes, there are many things which are made clear not by one's speech, but by one's actions; but there are also some things that can be put into words, from which no shining deed can come. You men know that the appointed guards are not difficult to slip by.

72.3 'For on the one hand given the sort of men we are, there is no one who will not let us pass, either because they respect us or because they fear us. On the other hand, I myself have a very plausible pretext by which we can pass, saying that I have lately arrived from the Persians and wish to convey a message to the king from my father.

72.4 'For when it is necessary to tell a lie, let it be told. After all we are striving after the same thing, either by lying or by telling the truth. For some lie when they are convinced that they are about to make some profit from their lies, some tell the truth so that they might profit and so that more might be entrusted to them. And so, although we practise differently, we work for the same end.

72.5 'But if they were not going to profit in any way, he who tells the truth would be as likely to be the liar, as the liar could become the truth teller. If any of the gate guards willingly let us pass, it will be better for him in the long term; but anyone who tries to bar our path, let him be shown to be an enemy, and once we have forced our way in, let us get to work.'

73

73.1 Afterwards Gobryas said this: 'Friends, when will there ever be a finer chance for us to recover power, or if we are not going to be able to take it back, to die? When we who are Persians are ruled by the Magus, a Mede, who does not have any ears.

73.2 'And those of us who were present with Cambyses when he was sick, you remember well I suppose that he called down curses upon the Persians when he died if they did not try to recover his power. We did not then accept what he said but thought that Cambyses was speaking slanderously.

73.3 'Now, therefore, I vote that we obey Darius and do not dissolve this meeting for any other reason than to attack the Magus.' So spoke Gobryas and all approved.

74

74.1 While these men were in deliberations, the following occurred quite by chance. After taking counsel that the Magi decided to win Prexaspes over as a friend, because he had suffered terrible things at the hands of Cambyses, who shot and killed his son, and also because he alone knew about the death of Smerdis son of Cyrus, because he had killed him with his own hand, and in addition because Prexaspes enjoyed great praise among the Persians.

74.2 For these reasons they summoned him and sought to win him over as a friend by a pledge of good faith and by taking oaths that he would keep it to himself and would not tell any mortal about their deception of the Persians, promising they would grant him everything in abundance.

74.3 When Prexaspes promised that he would do this, since the Magi convinced him, they made a second proposal, saying that they were going to summon the Persians to come below the palace wall, and ordered him to go up to the tower and announce that they were being ruled by Smerdis son of Cyrus and not anyone else.

74.4 Such were the instructions that they gave him as truly the most trustworthy among the Persians, and because he often expressed the opinion that Smerdis son of Cyrus was alive and denied his murder.

75

75.1 With Prexaspes saying that he was ready to do this, the Magi summoned together the Persians beneath the wall and made him go up to the tower and ordered him to speak. Then he willingly forgot what those men had demanded of him, but beginning with Achaemenes, he traced the lineage of Cyrus from that point, and after he had finally got to that man, he spoke about the many good things that Cyrus had done for the Persians.

75.2 And after he had explained this, he revealed the truth, saying that he had formerly concealed it for it had not been safe for him to say what happened, but in the present situation necessity forced him to reveal it. And he in fact said that he killed Smerdis son of Cyrus since he was forced to do so by Cambyses, and that the Magi were in power.

75.3 After calling many curses down on the Persians if they did not take back power and take revenge on the Magi, he flung himself headlong down from the top of the tower. And so Prexaspes, a man always well-esteemed in his time, died like this.

76

76.1 The seven Persians, when they had decided to attack the Magi immediately and not to delay, they set off praying to the gods knowing nothing of what had happened to Prexaspes.

76.2 They were in fact in the middle of their journey when they found out what had happened to Prexaspes. Whilst standing there beside the road they began to quarrel again, some in favour of Otanes ordering that they should entirely delay and not to attack while the situation was till simmering, whereas those on Darius' side said that they should go and do immediately what they had decided and not delay.

76.3 While they were arguing, seven pairs of hawks appeared chasing and tearing at and ripping to pieces two pairs of vultures. Upon seeing this, all the seven praised the opinion of Darius and then emboldened by the birds set off towards the palace.

77

77.1 When they came to stand the gates, it turned out just as Darius had expected. For the guards showed respect for the leading men of the Persians and suspecting nothing of the sort would follow from these men, they let them pass acting under divine guidance and no one questioned them.

77.2 When they arrived at the court, they met the eunuchs who carried his messages. These men asked them what they had come in search of, and while questioning them, they were threatening the gate guards for letting them pass and were hindering the seven who were wanting to advance further.

77.3 But the seven gave their orders and drew their daggers and together stabbed those who were blocking their path, but the eunuchs went running to the men's quarters.

78

78.1 At that moment both the Magi happened to be inside and were in deliberations as a result of what happened to Prexaspes. When they saw the eunuchs in uproar and shouting out, they both jumped up and when they realised what was happening turned to their defence.

78.2 One snatched up his bow before they arrived, and the other went for his spear. There they engaged one another in battle. Since the enemy were nearby and pressing on them, the bow proved of no use to the one who had grabbed his. The other was defending himself with his spear and struck Aspathines in the thigh and Intaphrenes in the eye. Although Intaphrenes lost his eye as a result of the wound, he did not die.

78.3 It was the other of the Magi that wounded them. The other one, when his bow proved useless, since there was a room which opened onto the men's apartment, he fled there, aiming to shut the doors, but two of the seven Darius and Gobryas pressed hard upon him.

78.4 Since Gobryas was locked in close fight with the Magus, Darius was standing in a quandary about what he should do in the darkness taking care not to strike Gobryas. Gobryas upon seeing him standing there asked why he did not take action. Darius said, 'taking care I do not stab you.' And Gobryas answered 'thrust your sword, even if it goes through us both.' Darius obeyed him, thrust his sword and somehow struck the Magus.

79

79.1 After killing the Magi and cutting off their heads, they left their wounded there because of their incapacity and also for the purpose of guarding the acropolis. The five of them carrying the heads of the Magi ran outside shouting and making a clamour and called the other Persians to witness explaining that they had done, displaying the heads and at the same time killing every Magus who crossed their path.

79.2 When the Persians learnt from the seven what had happened and about the deception of the Magi, they thought it right to act as they did, and drawing their daggers they killed a Magus wherever they found one. Had the approaching night not stopped them, they would have left no Magus alive.

79.3 This day especially of all days the Persians revere in common, and they hold a great festival on this day which the Persians call 'the Massacre of the Magi'. On this day it is impossible for any Magus to appear out of doors, but the Magi keep to their own homes for the duration of the day.

80

80.1 When the unrest had settled down and five days had passed, the rebels against the Magi were discussing the entire state of affairs, and the words that were spoken are incredible to some of the Greeks, but spoken they were.

80.2 Otanes urged them to hand over affairs to the Persian people and he spoke as follows: 'I think that one man should no longer rule over us. It is something that is neither pleasant nor good. You saw the arrogance of Cambyses and how far it went, and you had your share of the Magus' arrogance.

80.3 'How can the rule of a single person be suitable, when it is possible for that person to do whatever he likes without accountability? For were the best of men appointed to such power, it would stir up even in him thoughts beyond what was customary. For arrogance is bred in him as a result of the good things around him, and envy is born in men from the outset.

80.4 'And because he harbours these two things, he harbours all wickedness: for having satisfied his desires he carries out many reckless actions, some due to arrogance, some because of envy. And yet an absolute ruler should be free of envy and have every good thing. But he is by nature the opposite of this towards his citizens: for he envies the best men who surpass him and live, and delights in the most wicked of his citizens, and he is the best at giving his approval to slanders.

80.5 'He is the most inconsistent of all men: for if you give him moderate admiration, he hates the fact that he is not flattered excessively, and if someone flatters him excessively, he hates them for being a false friend. But I come now to the most important point I am going to make: he overturns the ancestral laws and violates women and kills people without trial. But first, the people as the ruling power has the finest name of them all, equality in law, and secondly, the single ruler does none of these things: it determines offices by lot, it holds power that is subject to accountability and it refers all decisions to the public. Therefore, I give you my opinion that we abandon one-man-rule and glorify the multitude: for all things exist among the majority.'

81

81.1 This then was the opinion that Otanes brought forward. Megabyzus urged them to entrust matters to oligarchy, speaking as follows: 'I agree with what Otanes said about doing away with tyranny, but when he urges us to hand power over to the masses, he has fallen short of the best judgement. For than a useless mob, there is nothing more foolish and violent.

81.2 'It is hardly tolerable that men who have fled the violence of a tyrant fall into the violence of the unpunishable mob. For whatever the former does, he does so with understanding, but the other has no knowledge. For how could someone, who has neither been taught nor who knows neither what is noble or fitting, show knowledge? Instead, he rushes headlong throwing himself into affairs without sense, just like a river swollen with the melted snow.

81.3 'Now let those who show ill-will to the Persians employ the power of the people, but let us, after choosing a group of the best men and invest them with power. For we ourselves should of course be among them; it is likely that the best counsels arise from the best men.'

82

82.1 This is the opinion that Megabyzus put forward. Darius was the third to lay out his judgement and he said: 'Concerning what he says about the mob, I think Megabyzus is right, but not with regards to what he said about oligarchy. For since the three forms have been proposed that are all in theory the best, I say that out of the best rule of the people, the best oligarchy and the best monarchy, this last is superior by far.

82.2 For nothing would seem better than the rule of the one best man. On the basis of this opinion, he would govern the masses faultlessly, and would be discreet particularly about his plans against his enemies.

82.3 'Under an oligarchy among the many who strive virtuously for the common good strong personal feelings of hostility are wont to develop. For because each man wishes to be the best and to be victorious in his judgments, they end up feeling great hatred towards one another, and from these arise factions, and from factions arises murder. From the slaughter monarchy results, and this shows just how far it is the best.

82.4 'When the people are in power the absence of wicked acts are impossible; when an evil against the state arises, hatred does not arise among wicked men, but rather strong friendships. For those who cause harm to the public good, do so by banding together. Such a state of affairs continues until a someone as leader of the people puts a stop to such men. As a result, this man is admired by the people, and because he is admired, he therefore now shows himself to be a monarch, and also in this way this man shows monarchy to be the strongest.

82.5 'And so to sum it all up in a word, where has our freedom come from and who granted it? Has it come from the people, an oligarchy, or one-man rule? In fact, I hold the opinion that we have been freed through the agency of one man and that we should defend such a system, and not to overthrow our ancestral laws for they are sound. For there is nothing better.'

83

83.1 These then were the three opinions set before them, and four of the seven agreed with that of Darius. Since Otanes was defeated in his judgement, urging them to grant equal power to the Persians, he addressed them publicly as follows.

83.2 'Fellow partisans, since it is clear that one of us at least must become king, whether chosen by lot, or by the majority of the Persians entrusting affairs to whomsoever they choose, or by some other means. I myself will not now compete with you. For I wish neither to rule nor be ruled. But I give up my claim to power on this condition, namely that I shall be ruled by none of you, neither I myself nor any of those born from me for all time.'

83.3 When he said this and the other six agreed to his conditions, this man did not compete but sat apart from their meeting, and now this household alone achieved its aim in being free from the Persians and being self-governing only so far as it is itself willing and as long as it does not overstep the laws of the Persians.

84

84.1 The rest of the seven then deliberated as to how they would most justly appoint a king. They decided that, if the kingship came to any of the seven of them, each year they would give to Otanes and those descended from him for all time choice gifts of Median clothing and every sort of gift that was most prized among the Persians. They decided to grant him these gifts for the very reason that he was the first of them to begin deliberations about the matter and gather them together.

84.2 These then were the gifts they decided upon for Otanes, but with regard to the other matter that concerned them all, they decided as follows: that it would be possible for any of the seven wishing to enter the royal palace to do so without announcement, unless the king was sleeping with a woman, and also that it would not be possible for the king to marry anyone except women from the households of the conspirators.

84.3 Concerning the kingship, they made the following decision. Whoever's horse first whinnied at the moment of sunrise, once they had all mounted their horses outside the city, this man would hold the kingship.

85

85.1 Darius had a groom who was a clever man, named Oebares. When they dispersed, Darius addressed this man as follows: 'Oebares, we have decided to act as follows regarding the kingship. Once we have mounted our horses, whoever's horse is the first to whinny at sunrise, this man will be king. Now therefore, if you are indeed clever, figure out how we may take this prize and no one else.'

85.2 Oebares gave the following reply: 'If, master, this is about whether you become king or not, have courage and take good heart because no one else shall be king before you; such are the tricks that I have.' Darius said, 'if you really do know such a clever trick, now is the time to use it and not put it off, since the contest is set for tomorrow.'

85.3 Upon hearing this, Oebares acted as follows: when night came, he led out one of the mares of whom Darius' horse was particularly fond, tied her up just outside the city, and led Darius' horse to her, repeatedly leading him around near the mare so he brushed against her. Finally, he let the horse mount the female.

86

86.1 Just as the dawn was shining through, as they agreed, the six were present on their horses. They drove them out to the area outside the city when they came to the place where the mare had been tied up on the previous night. Darius' horse trotted to that spot and whinnied.

86.2 At the very moment that the horse did this, lightning came out of a clear sky and there was thunder. These events confirmed matters for

Darius as though they had occurred by the agency of a god. They immediately leapt from their horses and bowed to Darius.

87

87.1 Some say that Oebares planned this way, but others say his plan was as follows, for both versions are told by the Persians, namely that he touched the genitals of the mare with his hand, which he kept hidden in his trousers. When he was about to send forth the horses at sunrise, Oebares removed his hand and held it near the nostrils of Darius' horse, and when the horse smelt this, he snorted and whinnied.

88

88.1 And so, Darius, son of Hystaspes, succeeded as king, and all the peoples in Asia except for the Arabians were subject to him, after first Cyrus and then later Cambyses had conquered them. The Arabians were in no way subject to slavery under the Persians but became their friends after letting Cambyses pass into Egypt. For had the Arabians been unwilling, the Persians would not have invaded Egypt.

88.2 Darius made his first marriages from among the Persians Cyrus' two daughters Atossa and Artystone, Atossa had been wife to her brother Cambyses and then to the Magus, whereas Artystone was a virgin.

88.3 He married the daughter of Smerdis son of Cyrus as another wife, whose name was Parmys. And he also took as his wife the daughter of Otanes, who had exposed the Magus. Everything was filled with his power. Firstly, he had made and set up a stone carving; on this was the image of a horseman, and he inscribed on it a message which declared the following : 'Darius son of Hystaspes obtained the kingship over the Persians aided by the excellence of his horse (giving the name of the horse) and of his groom Oebares.'

89

89.1 Having done this in Persia, he arranged his lands into twenty regions, which they call satrapies. After organizing these regions and appointing governors, he drew up the tribute to be paid to him people by people, attaching together neighbouring peoples and, as he went beyond those lands nearest, he assigned the more remote peoples to various regions.

89.2 He divided up the regions and annual revenue from tribute as follows: those who brought silver as their tribute were ordered to bring a Babylonian talent in weight, those who brought gold were ordered to bring the weight of a Euboic talent. A Babylonian talent is worth seventy-eight Euboic minas.

89.3 For during Cyrus' reign and again under Cambyses there was nothing established concerning tribute, but they used to bring gifts. Because of his organization of the tribute and other similar measures, the Persians say that Darius was the shopkeeper, Cambyses the despot, and Cyrus the father, because the former made all thing purchasable, Cambyses was difficult and insolent, and Cyrus was merciful and devised for all things that were good.

90

90.1 From the Ionians and the Magnesians in Asia, the Aeolians, the Carians, the Lycians, the Milyans and the Pamphylians, for this was drawn up as a single tribute payment, came revenue of four hundred talents of silver. This then was established as the first province. From the Mysians, Lydians, the Lasonians, Cabalians, and the Hytennians came five hundred talents: this was the second province.

90.2 From the Hellespontine peoples to the right of the entrance to the straits, from the Phrygians, the Thracians in Asia, the Paphlagonians, the Mariandynians and the Syrians came tribute of three hundred and sixty talents. These made up the third province.

90.3 From the Cilicians came three hundred and sixty white horses, one for each day, and five hundred talents of silver; one hundred and forty of these were spent on the horse which guarded the country of Cilicia, the remaining three hundred and sixty came to Darius. This was the fourth province.

91

91.1 From the city of Posideia, which Amphilochus son of Amphiareus founded on the borders between Cilicia and Syria, the area which begins from this city right up to Egypt, except the part that belongs to Arabia, for they are exempt from tribute, came three hundred and fifty talents in tribute. Also in this region is the whole of Phoenicia, the part of Syria that is called Palestine, and Cyprus. This is the fifth province.

91.2 From Egypt and the Libyans who neighbour Egypt, from Cyrene, and Barca, for these were assigned to the Egyptian province, came seven hundred talents, besides the silver from lake Moeris, income which comes from fish.

91.3 Apart from this silver, and the grain that was measured out as payment, came seven hundred talents, for they measured out one hundred and twenty thousand measures of grain for those Persians and their allies appointed to guard the White Wall at Memphis. This was the sixth province.

91.4 The Sattagydae, the Gandarii, the Dadicae, and the Aparytae were drawn up together and used to pay one hundred and seventy talents. This was the seventh province. From Susa and the rest of the country of the Cissians came three hundred. They formed the eighth province.

92

92.1 From Babylon and the rest of Assyria came one thousand talents of silver and five hundred castrated boys. This was the ninth province. From Ecbatana and the rest of Media, from the Paricanians and the Orthocorybantians came four hundred and fifty talents. This was the tenth province.

92.2 The Caspians, the Pausicae, the Pantimathi, and the Dareitae, paid two hundred talents as their collective contribution. They formed the eleventh province.

93

93.1 From the Bactria up to the land of the Aegli the revenue was three hundred and sixty talents. This is the twelfth province. From Pactyae and the Armenians and their neighbours as far as the Euxine Sea came four hundred talents. These form the thirteenth province.

93.2 From the Sagariti, the Saranges, the Thamanaei, the Outii, the Mycii and those who inhabit the islands in the Red Sea, on which the king settled those known as the uprooted peoples, from all of these came tribute of six hundred talents. This is the fourteenth province.

93.3 The Sakae and the Caspians used to pay two hundred and fifty talents. They form the fifteenth province. The Parthians, the Chorasmians, the Sogdi, and the Areii pay three hundred talents. This was the sixteenth province.

94

94.1 The Paricanians and the Ethiopians of Asia pay four hundred talents. This is the seventeenth province. To the Matieni, the Saspeiri, and the

Alarodians tribute of two hundred talents was assigned. These make up the eighteenth province.

94.2 The Moschi, Tibareni, Macrones and Mossynoeci were ordered to contribute three hundred talents: this is the nineteenth province. The total number of Indian peoples is by far the most numerous of all men that we know about, and they paid a tribute that was proportionately more compared to all the other peoples, namely three hundred and sixty talents of gold dust. This is the twentieth province.

95

95.1 Babylonian silver when converted to the Euboic talent brings the total to nine thousand nine hundred and eighty talents. As regards gold, which is reckoned at thirteen times the value, the dust is found to have the value of four thousand six hundred and eighty Euboic talents.

95.2 When all this is taken together the amount of tribute gathered yearly for Darius is fourteen thousand five hundred and sixty talents. I do not mention those that contribute less than these.

96

96.1 This then was the tribute that came to Darius from Asia and a few parts of Libya. However, as time went on further tribute came in from the islands and those who inhabited Europe as far as Thessaly.

96.2 The king stores this tribute in the following manner. After melting it down he pours it into clay jars, and having filled the vessel, he removes the clay around it. Whenever he needs money, he strikes has much as he needs for each occasion.

97

97.1 These then were the provinces and the arrangements for the tributes. It is only Persia that I have not mentioned as tribute-paying, for the Persians possess a land exempt from tribute.

97.2 These following peoples were not assigned to pay tribute but gifts: the Ethiopians that border Egypt, whom Cambyses conquered while marching against the long-lived Ethiopians, who inhabit the area around sacred Nysa and hold festivals for Dionysus. [These Ethiopians and those who border them use the same seed as the Callantiae Indians and their buildings are located underground].

97.3 Both of these together every three years used to bring and still bring right down to my own time two *choinixes* of unsmelted gold, two hundred logs of ebony, five Ethiopian boys and twenty large elephant tusks.

97.4 The Colchians were also assigned to bring gifts as were their neighbours as far as the Caucasian Mountain, for the region as far as the mountain is ruled by the Persians, but the region to the north of the Caucasus as yet pays no regard to Persian power. These men therefore were assigned to bring gifts and up to my own time every five years they bring one hundred boys and one hundred virgins.

97.5 The Arabians used to bring one thousand talents worth of frankincense every year. Such were the gifts these men used to bring for the king instead of tribute.

98

98.1 The Indians obtain their plentiful supply of gold, from which they get the previously mentioned dust that they bring to the king, in the following manner.

98.2 Towards the east of the Indian land there is a sandy region: for of those regions we know about and about which something certain can be said, of the peoples in Asia, the Indians dwell the nearest to the dawn and the rising sun. For east of the Indians on account of the sand it is desert.

98.3 There are many Indian tribes and they do not speak the same language, some are nomads, some are not, some dwell in the marshes along the river and feed on raw fish, which they catch setting out on reed boats. Each boat is made from one knee of reed.

98.4 These Indians wear clothes made of rushes: whenever they harvest rush from the river and beat it down, they then weave it together like a mat and wear it as a breastplate.

99

99.1 Other Indian peoples who dwell to the east of these are nomads and are consumers of raw flesh; they are called the Padaeans and are said to practise the following customs. If any of the citizens, either man or woman, is wearied by disease, if a man, those men closest to him kill him, saying his flesh would be ruined for them because he is wasted by disease. The man protests that he is not sick, but they are not forgiving and, once they have killed him, they feast upon him.

99.2 If a woman is sick, her close female friends do exactly the same to her as are done to the men. And as for the man who has reached old age, they sacrifice him and feed on him. Not many of them reach the point where this matters. For before this they kill everyone who falls ill.

100

100.1 Other Indians have the following different practice. They neither kill any living creature, nor do they plant anything, nor are they accustomed to have houses, and they eat grass. They also have a grain similar in size to the millet seed in its husk which grows naturally from the earth, and they gather it, boil it in its husk, and feed on it. Whenever one of them becomes ill, he goes to the desert and lies down. No one thinks either about whether he has died or whether he is sick.

101

101.1 Among those Indians whom I have described sexual intercourse is in the open just as cattle do, and they are all dark-skinned very similar to the Ethiopians.

101.2 Their semen, which they ejaculate into their women, is not white like that of other men, but black like their skin. The Ethiopians emit just such semen. These Indians dwell far from the Persians and to the south and are not subjects of king Darius in any way.

102

102.1 The rest of the Indians share their borders with the city of Caspatyrus and the Pactyan land, having settled to both the north and north-east of the rest of the Indians, and they have a way of life very similar to that of the Bactrians. These men are the most warlike of the Indians and it is they who are sent to get the gold. For this region is desert on account of the sand.

102.2 And in this sandy desert area are ants which are smaller than dogs in size, but larger than foxes: for the Persian king has some which were hunted from their natural habitat. These ants make their dwelling under the ground and carry up sand exactly as ants in Greece do, and they are very like these in appearance. The sand that they bring up contains gold.

102.3 The Indians then are sent to the desert region for this sand, after each of them has yoked three camels, one male on either side to draw the yoke by reins, and the female in the middle. The man himself rides the female, once he has equipped and yoked her, after he has removed her from the youngest offspring possible. For their camels are no less swift than horses, and apart from this are much more capable in bearing loads.

103

103.1 Since Greeks know what a camel looks like I am not going to describe it. But there is something that they are not aware of, which I will describe. A camel has four thighbones on its hind legs and four knee-joints, and its genitals are turned towards the tail behind the hind legs.

104

104.1 By using them in this manner and yoking them in this way, the Indians drive them to the gold carefully calculating that they will be engaged in its seizure right at the point when the burning heat is at its very hottest. For the ants disappear under the ground because of the heat.

104.2 For these men the sun is at its very hottest in the morning, not at midday as for other people, but from the sunrise until the close of the market. For during this time, it burns far hotter than at midday in Greece, so much so that there is a story that they drench themselves with water at that time.

104.3 At midday, the heat is very similar for the Indians as for other men. When midday is passing, the sun for them is like the early morning sun elsewhere, and from this point as the sun departs that it becomes cooler, and right up to sunset when it becomes especially cold.

105

105.1 Whenever they come to the place carrying seed capsules, they fill these with sand and drive back as fast as they can: for, so the Persians say, once the ants have detected them by smell they give chase immediately. And that their speed is equal to no other so that, unless the Indians get a head start on their journey while the ants gather, none of them would get away safely.

105.2 Then, because they are slower at running than the females, they release the male camels as they begin to lag but not at the same time; but the females, because they are mindful of the children they left behind, show no weakness. The Indians, so the Persians say, obtain most of their gold in this way. It is also mined in their country, but less plentifully.

106

106.1 The furthest nations of the world have somehow drawn as their lot the finest goods, just as Greece happens to have by far the finest combination of seasons.

106.2 As I said a little earlier, the Indian land lies at the furthest point of the inhabited lands towards the East: and living there are beings both four-footed and winged, that are far bigger than those in other lands, apart from the horses, for these are surpassed by the horses called Nasaeans by the Medes, and there gold is unlimited, some is mined, some is carried down by the river, and some is seized in the manner I have shown.

106.3 There the trees bring forth wool as their fruit and this surpasses the wool that comes from sheep in its fineness and quality. The Indians also make their clothing from these trees.

107

107.1 To the south, Arabia is the most distant of the inhabited lands, and it is there alone of all lands that frankincense is produced as well as myrrh, cassia, cinnamon and gum-mastic. The Arabians obtain all of these with difficulty apart from myrrh.

107.2 They gather the frankincense by burning the storax, which the Phoenicians export to Greece. The extract it by burning this. For winged snakes that are small in size and multi-coloured in appearance guard the trees that bear frankincense in great numbers around each tree. These attack Egypt, and they cannot be driven away from the trees by anything other than the smoke of the storax.

108

108.1 And this is what the Arabians say: that every land would be full of these snakes, unless similar occurred among them, as I know happens among vipers.

108.2 And since the forethought of the divine is wise, as is reasonable, it has made prolific all living creatures that are cowardly and edible prey, so that they do not die out through being eaten, and has made it that those animals which are hardy and troublesome produce few offspring.

108.3 On the one hand, the hare, because it is hunted by every beast and bird and man, is indeed prolific. Of all beasts, it alone become can become pregnant while already pregnant, and part of its offspring in the womb are hairy, part are bare, some are being recently formed in the womb, others are being conceived.

108.4 On the other hand, this sort of thing occurs. The lioness being the strongest and boldest creature gives birth once in her lifetime: for while giving birth, she casts out her womb with her cub. The reason for this is as follows: when the cub begins stirring inside the mother, it tears the womb because it possesses by far the sharpest claws of all beasts, and the more it grows, the more it pierces it by scratching.

And when the birth is near there is almost no healthy part of the womb remaining.

109

109.1 Thus, if vipers and the winged serpents among the Arabians were born as is natural for their kind, it would not be possible for men to live there. Now when they are engaged in mating, and the male is impregnating her, once he has ejaculated his seed, the female seizes him by the neck and bites him, and she does not let go until she has bitten right through.

109.2 The male dies in the aforementioned manner, but the female pays the following penalty for the suffering of the male: the offspring avenge their father while they are still in the womb, they eat through their mother and make their way out after eating through her womb.

109.3 But other snakes which are not harmful to humans lay eggs and hatch out many young. There are to be sure vipers in every land, but the winged snakes are located in Arabia and nowhere else. It is for this reason that they seem to be so numerous.

110

110.1 This is how the Arabians obtain the frankincense and they obtain the cassia in the following way. After binding their entire body and face except for their eyes with ox hides and skins, they go after the cassia: it grows in a lake that is not deep, but around which live winged beasts, which are very like bats; they squeal terribly and are strong in their defence. They have to keep these away from their eyes in order to get the cassia.

111

111.1 The way they collect the cinnamon is even more remarkable than this. For they are not able to say where it comes from or which land produces it, except that some give a plausible account that it grows in those places which reared Dionysus.

111.2 They say that large birds carry these dry stalks, which we have learnt from the Phoenicians to call cinnamon, and that these birds carry them to their nests, which are formed of clay and are attached to steep cliffs, where there is no means of approach for a man.

111.3 As a result, the Arabians have devised the following solution: when they have cut up dead oxen, asses, and other beasts of burden into pieces that are as large as possible, they take them to these places, and after setting them near the nests, they withdraw far away: the birds then fly down and carry the slices of these beasts back up to their nests, which break and fall to the ground, because they are not strong enough to hold them. The Arabians then move in and gather them up. This is how the cinnamon is said to be gathered from these places and arrive in other lands.

112

112.1 Regarding the gum-mastic or ledanon, which the Arabians call ladanon, its production is even stranger than this. For something that is so fragrant grows in the most foul-smelling place. For it is found in the beard of he-goats, forming in them just as gum does in wood. It is used in many perfumes, and it is especially this that the Arabians burn.

113

113.1 I have said enough about these marvels, which it is said result in a sweet scent emanating from the Arabian land. There are two kinds of sheep that they have that are worthy of wonder and which do not exist in any other place. One type has long tails, no less than three forearms in length, but if someone were to allow them to drag these along, they would injure themselves with their tails rubbing on the ground.

113.2 Now every single shepherd knows how to do carpentry for such a purpose. For they make little carts and bind the sheep to these by their tails, tying the tail of each beast to its own cart. The other type of sheep have wide tails which are the width of a forearm.

114

114.1 Where the south turns towards the west, the land of the inhabited world that is furthest towards the setting sun is Ethiopia: this produces gold in abundance, huge elephants, all sorts of wild trees, including ebony, and men that are the tallest and fairest and longest-lived of all.

115

115.1 These then are the most remote lands of Asia and Libya. Concerning the furthest places of Europe towards the west, I am not able to say anything with certainty. For I do not believe that there is a river that is called Eridanus by the barbarians which flows into the sea towards the north and there is a story that amber is washed down from there; nor do I know about the Tin islands where our tin comes from.

115.2 For by its very name the Eridanus shows that it is Greek and not barbarian and has been made up by some poet. Nor am I able to discover anyone who has seen for himself, despite looking into this carefully, as to whether there is a sea beyond Europe. I do know that we receive tin and amber from these regions.

116

116.1 In the north of Europe there seems to be a very plentiful supply of gold: how it is produced, I am not able to say with certainty, but it is said that one-eyed men called Arimaspi steal it from griffins.

116.2 But I am not convinced by the notion that somehow there exist one-eyed men who have the same nature as other men.

116.3 These, since they hem in another land and shut them off inside, are likely the furthest lands, to have those things that we consider to be the finest and are rarest.

117

117.1 There is a plain in Asia, enclosed on all sides by a mountain, through which there are five passes. This plain once belonged to the Chorasmians, since it lies on the boundaries between the Chorasmians, the Hyrcanii, the Saranges, and the Thamanaei, but since the Persians took power, it belongs to the king.

117.2 From this surrounding mountain there in fact flows a great river called the Akes. This river which is divided into five channels formerly used to water the lands of the aforementioned peoples, leading its path to each people through each of its passes, but since they have been under Persian rule, they suffer as follows:

117.3 When the king walled up the mountain passes, he set gates at each: with the outflow of the water shut off, the plain between the mountains became a lake, since the river pours into it, because there is no outlet.

117.4 These peoples, therefore, that had previously been accustomed to use the water, because they were now not able to do so, meet with great misfortune. For during the winter god rains for them as for the rest of mortals, but in the summer when they sow their millet and sesame seed, they are greatly in need of water.

117.5 So whenever no water is given to them, they and their women come to Persia, and, standing at the king's doors, they cry and wail, and the king gives the order for the gates to be opened for those who need it the most.

117.6 Whenever their land has drunk its fill of water, the gates are shut, and he gives orders for the other gates to be opened for the people who are most in need next out of the rest; and he makes a lot of money when he opens the gates alongside the tribute. This I know from hearsay. This is the situation here.

118

118.1 When the seven had risen up against the Magus, it befell Intaphrenes to be put to death for the following outrage that he committed immediately after the rebellion. He wanted to enter the palace and speak to the king; for, it was indeed the rule that access to the king's presence was permitted to the other rebels without announcement, unless the king was sleeping with one of his wives.

118.2 Therefore, Intaphrenes thought it right for him not to make any announcement that he wished to enter because he was one of the seven. But the gate guard and the messenger did not allow him, saying that the king was having sex with one of his wives. But Intaphrenes, because he believed them to be lying, acted as follows: he drew his short sword and cut off their ears and noses, and having fastened these to his horse's bridle, he tied them around the necks of the men and let them go.

119

119.1 These men presented themselves to the king and told him the reason why they had suffered this. Darius, fearing that the other six might have done this together, sent for each one of them and asked their opinion, as to whether each approved of what had been done.

119.2 When he fully understood that Intaphrenes had not acted in cahoots with them, he arrested Intaphrenes himself, his sons and all his relatives, harbouring a strong expectation that he was plotting a rebellion against him with his kinsmen, and after arresting them, he imprisoned them for execution.

119.3 Intaphrenes' wife kept on coming to the doors of the palace and would weep and lament: by continuously doing so she convinced Darius to take pity on her. He sent a messenger who spoke as follows: 'Lady, king Darius grants that you may save one of your imprisoned relatives, whichever one you wish out of them all.'

119.4 After she had given the matter some thought, she gave the following reply: 'If the king grants me the life of one of them, out of them all I choose my brother.'

119.5 Upon learning this Darius was surprised at what she said, and sent someone to address her: 'Lady, the king asks you on what reasoning you leave behind your husband and children and chose your brother to survive, who is less close to you than your children and less dear to you than your husband.'

119.6 She replied as follows: 'King, I may have another husband, if god is willing, and other children, if I lose these. But since my father and mother are no longer living it is in no way possible that I could get another brother. Following this reasoning, I made this choice.'

119.7 Darius thought the woman spoke well and released to her the man whom she had asked for and the oldest of her sons, because he was impressed with her, but he killed all the others. And so, one of the seven perished immediately in the manner I have related.

120

120.1 At just about the same time that Cambyses was ill, the following events occurred. The governor of Sardis, who had been appointed by Cyrus, was Oroetes, a Persian man: this man conceived a desire for something in no way pious. For he had neither suffered at the hands of Polycrates of Samos, nor had he been insulted by him, nor had he even seen him before conceiving the desire to kill him for, as many say, the following reason.

120.2 That when Oroetes was sitting at the king's doors along with another Persian by the name of Mitrobates, who governed the region at Dascyleium, they started quarrelling verbally, and that while comparing themselves in terms of their prowess, Mitrobates reproachfully said to Oroetes:

120.3 'You are a man in word only, you who did not acquire for the king the island of Samos although it lies next to your province, which would, therefore, thus be so easy to subdue, and which some native took control of and now rules alone after rebelling with fifteen hoplites.'

120.4 Some say that after hearing this and because he was pained by the reproach, he desired not so much to take revenge on the man who had said this, but rather to destroy Polycrates entirely, on account of whom he had been insulted.

121

121.1 Fewer say that Oroetes sent a herald to Samos to ask for something or other, for what this was is not in fact told, and that the herald found Polycrates lying in the men's quarters, and that Anacreon of Teos was present with him.

121.2 And this was how it happened, either because he was deliberately belittling Oroetes' affairs, or it was a coincidence. For they say that when Oroetes' herald arrived and was conversing with him, Polycrates happened to be turned away facing the wall, but neither turned round nor made any reply.

122

122.1 These then are the two reasons given for the death of Polycrates, and one can believe whichever of them one wishes. Oroetes, therefore, who was then settled at Magnesia which lies above the river Maeander, sent Myrsus son of Gyges, a Lydian man, to Samos carrying a message, having ascertained Polycrates' intention.

122.2 For Polycrates was the first of the Greeks whom we know of who intended to become master of the sea, besides Minos of Cnossos and if there was anyone else before him who ruled the sea. Of the race that is called the human race, Polycrates was the first and had great hopes that he would rule Ionia and the islands.

122.3 Therefore, after learning that this was what he was intending, Oroetes sent a message addressing him as follows: 'Oroetes addresses Polycrates as follows. I understand that you have plans for great deeds, but that you do not have the money for your designs. If you now act as follows, you will bring yourself success and you will save me. For king Cambyses is plotting my death, and this has been clearly made known to me.

122.4 'Now, once you have taken me and my money to safety, take some yourself and let me have the rest. Thanks to this money, you will rule all of Greece. But if you don't believe me about the money, send whoever you trust most, and I will prove it to him.'

123

123.1 When Polycrates heard this, he was both pleased and willing. For since he greatly desired money, first of all he sent Maeandrius son of Maeandrius one of the citizens, who was his scribe, to explore. It was he who not long afterwards dedicated the furnishings of Polycrates' men's quarters, which are well worth seeing, at the Heraeum.

123.2 Oroetes upon learning that a spy was expected took the following action. After he filled eight chests up with stones except for a small space around the rim, he placed gold on top of the stones, and after securing the chests, he kept them ready. When Maeandrius came and saw them, he reported back to Polycrates.

124

124.1 Polycrates was preparing to go there despite the seers and his friends seeking to dissuade him in many ways, and also so was his daughter who had seen the following vision in a dream: it seemed to her that her father was up high in the air and was being washed by Zeus and anointed by the sun.

124.2 After she saw this vision, she tried every means to persuade Polycrates not to travel to Oroetes, and she was uttering words of ill-omen even as he approached his fifty-oared ship. He threatened her that, if he came home safe, she would remain a virgin for a long time. She prayed that this might be fulfilled. For she said that she would more willingly remain unmarried for a long time than be deprived of her father.

125

125.1 But Polycrates paid no attention to any advice and set sail to Oroetes, bringing with him many of his companions, among whom was Democedes of Croton son of Calliphon, who was a physician and who of those in his own time was the very best at practising his skill.

125.2 When he arrived at Magnesia, Polycrates perished horribly, in a way worthy neither of him nor his aims. For, except for the rulers of Syracuse, none of the other Greek tyrants is worthy to be compared to Polycrates in magnificence.

125.3 After killing him, Oroetes crucified him in a manner in no way worthy to be recounted. As for those who had accompanied him, he let go those who were Samians bidding them acknowledge their thanks to him because they were free, but those who were foreigners or who were slaves among those who accompanied him, he kept among his own slaves.

125.4 Being hung up in the air, Polycrates completely fulfilled his daughter's vision. For he was washed by Zeus whenever it rained and was anointed by the sun, exuding sweat from his body. So, the many good fortunes of Polycrates met this end just as Amasis king of Egypt had prophesied.

126

126.1 But not much later, the avengers of Polycrates came after Oroetes. For after the death of Cambyses and during the rule of the Magi, Oroetes stayed in Sardis where he gave no help at all to the Persians regarding the power taken from them by the Medes.

126.2 In fact, during this troubled period, he killed Mitrobates the governor of Dascyleium, who had taunted him regarding Polycrates, and also Mitrobates' son Carnaspes, men who were well-esteemed among the Persians. And he committed many other violent acts of all kinds including any messenger who came to him from Darius. When the announcements displeased him, he killed the messenger as he was travelling back, after laying a trap for the men on their journey, and having killed him, he concealed him along with his horse.

127

127.1 When Darius came to power, he very much desired that Oroetes pay for all his wrongdoings and especially for Mitrobates and his son. But he decided not to send an army directly against him since affairs were still in a state of turmoil, and also because he had only recently come to power and had learnt that Oroetes possessed great strength. A thousand Persians served as his bodyguard, and he held the Phrygian, Lydian and Ionian province.

127.2 Concerning this matter, Darius contrived the following plan. He summoned the most noble of the Persians and addressed them as follows: 'Persians, which of you would undertake to carry this out by means of your cleverness, and not by means of force or numbers? For where cleverness is needed, it is no task for force.

127.3 'Which of you would either lead Oroetes to me alive or kill him? He who has given no benefit to the Persians but has rather committed great evils. For he has slain two of our own, Mitrobates and his son, and also kills those sent me my to recall him, showing intolerable arrogance. Therefore, before he does any greater evil to the Persians, we must arrest him to be put to death.'

128

128.1 This was what Darius asked, and thirty gave him their promise, each wanting to carry it out himself. Darius stopped them quarrelling and bid them decide by lot. They drew lots and from all of them the lot fell to Bagaeus son of Artontes.

128.2 Having obtained the lot, Bagaeus acted as follows. After he had many letters written on many matters, he stamped them with the seal of Darius, and after this he took them to Sardis.

128.3 When he arrived and came to Oroetes, he opened each letter one at a time and gave it to the royal scribe to read. All the governors have royal scribes. He then tested the spearmen and gave them the letters to see if they would agree to revolt from Oroetes.

128.4 Upon seeing that they showed great respect for the letters and still greater for what they said, he gave them another which contained the following words: 'Persians, king Darius forbids you to act as bodyguards for Oroetes.' When they heard this, they let go of their spears.

128.5 When Bagaeus saw that they were convinced by the letter, he was emboldened and gave the last of the letters to the scribe, in which it was written, 'King Darius instructs the Persians in Sardis to kill Oroetes.' When they heard this, the bodyguards drew their daggers and killed him immediately. And so, vengeance for Polycrates of Samos caught up with the Persian Oroetes.

129

129.1 When Oroetes' possessions were transported to and then arrived at Susa, it happened not long after that king Darius twisted his foot while jumping from his horse while hunting.

129.2 And he somehow twisted it quite violently; for the ankle bone came out of its socket. Because he thought previously that the Egyptians around him seemed to be the best regarding medicine, he employed them. But by twisting and forcing the foot, they made it worse.

129.3 For seven days and seven nights Darius was gripped by insomnia because of his current pain. On the eighth day when he was doing poorly, someone who had heard previously about the skill of Democedes of Croton who was still in Sardis announced this to Darius. He gave orders for this man to be brought to him as quickly as possible. When they found him among the slaves of Oroetes where he had been completely neglected, they brought him along dragging his chains and dressed in rags.

130

130.1 And as he stood in their midst, Darius asked him if he knew his trade well. But Democedes did not admit it, fearing that, if he revealed himself, he would be forever deprived of Greece.

130.2 He demonstrated to Darius that he knew how to show his cunning, and Darius gave orders for those who had led him in to bring in whips and scourges. As a result, he then revealed all saying that he did not know exactly, but had a scant knowledge of the craft because he had been acquainted with a physician.

130.3 Afterwards, when Darius entrusted the matter to him, by using Greek remedies and by treating it gently after the violent application, he enabled him to get some sleep and in a short time made him healthy, although he still did not hope that his foot would ever be right again.

130.4 After this, Darius rewarded him with two golden fetters. In response Democedes asked if he was deliberately awarding him a double evil for making him well. Pleased with what he said, Darius sent him off to his own wives. The eunuchs who accompanied him told the women that this was the man who had given the king his life back.

130.5 Each of them dipped a bowl into a chest of gold and presented it to Democedes with such a plentiful reward that the servant who accompanied him, called Sciton, collected a considerable quantity of gold for himself once he had gathered for himself the staters which fell from the bowls.

131

131.1 This was how Democedes formed his acquaintance with Polycrates after he came from Croton. In Croton, he quarrelled with his father who had a harsh temper. When he could no longer endure him, he left and went away to Aegina. After settling there, he surpassed the other physicians in his first year, although he was not equipped with the necessary tools and did not possess the instruments needed for his art.

131.2 And in his second year the Aeginetans paid him a talent at public expense, his third year the Athenians hired him for one hundred minas, and in his fourth year Polycrates hired him for two talents. And so, he came to Samos and the Crotonian physicians became highly respected not least because of this man.

131.3 For it was the case at the time that the Crotonians were said throughout Greece to be the best physicians, and the Cyreneans the second best. [At about the same time, the Argives were said to be the best at music.]

132

132.1 Then Democedes, because he had healed Darius at Susa, possessed a very large house and ate at the same table as the king, and every other thing was possible for him except for the one thing: to go back to Greece.

132.2 For example, when the Egyptian physicians, who had previously treated the king, were about to be impaled because they had been surpassed by a Greek physician, after pleading with the king, Democedes rescued them. He also rescued a seer from Elis who had accompanied Polycrates and who was also left neglected among the slaves. For Democedes possessed very great influence with the king.

133

133.1 A short time after this, something else occurred. Atossa, the daughter of Cyrus and wife of Darius had a swelling growing on her breast, and it later broke out and spread further. While it was smaller, she concealed it as she felt embarrassed and told no one.

133.2 But when it was serious, she sent for Democedes and showed it to him. He said that he would restore her to health but exacted from her an oath that she would repay him whatever he requested from her. But he said that it would be nothing that would bring her any shame.

134

134.1 And so, after he treated and cured her, Atossa, when she had been instructed by Democedes, addressed Darius as follows in their chamber. 'King, although you have such great power, you sit idle acquiring neither an additional people nor power for the Persians.

134.2 'It is right for a young man who is master of great wealth to be seen to be proving himself so that the Persians realize that they are governed by a man. From both angles it is in your interest to do this, both so that the Persians know that their leader is a man, and also so that they may be kept busy in war and do not have the leisure time to plot against you.

134.3 'For you should show off your work now while you are still young in age. For the wits grow alongside the growing body, but they also grow old along with it and they lose their edge in all matters.'

134.4 She spoke in accordance with her instruction, and Darius replied as follows: 'Lady, I am intending to do everything you have just said. For I have planned to build a bridge which yokes this continent to the other to make an expedition against the Scythians. And it will be achieved in a short time.'

134.5 Atossa spoke as follows: 'Now look, allow yourself to give up your plan against the Scythians for the present. These men will be yours whenever you wish. Make your expedition against Greece for me. For having heard reports, I desire Spartan, Argive, Attic and Corinthian women as my attendants. And you have a man most suitable of all men to inform you all about Greece and to guide you, namely the man who healed your foot.'

134.6 Darius answered, 'Since, lady, it seems to you a good idea that we make an attempt on Greece first, I think that it is better in the first instance nevertheless to send Persian spies to them along with this man that you mention, who will report to me in detail what they have learnt and seen. And, once I am fully informed, I will direct my efforts against them.'

135

135.1 So he spoke and acted at once upon what he said. For as soon as the day dawned, he summoned fifteen esteemed men of the Persians and instructed them to accompany Democedes and travel along the coast of Greece and see to it that Democedes did not escape from them, but to lead him back by all means.

135.2 After giving the men these instructions, he then summoned Democedes himself and asked him to come back to the Persians, once he had explained and shown to him the whole of Greece. He bid him take gifts to his father and siblings and to take all his moveable goods with him, saying that he would give many times as much in return. In addition, he said that he would send a ship to meet him which he would fill with every sort of good thing and in which he would make his journey.

135.3 Darius, it seems to me, did not make this promise to him as a result of any deceitful intent. But Democedes, because he feared that Darius was testing him, did not rush in to accept everything that he was offering, but said that he would leave his possessions in place so that he might have them when he came back; the ship which Darius promised, however, he said he accepted for the gifts for his siblings. After giving him these instructions, Darius dispatched them to the sea.

136

136.1 When these men came to the city of Sidon in Phoenicia, they immediately equipped two triremes, and alongside these filled a great galleon with all sorts of goods. After getting them all ready, they sailed to Greece, and after landing there they observed and recorded the areas along the coast, until, after viewing many of the most famous regions, they arrived at Tarentum in Italy.

136.2 Here out of friendly feeling towards Democedes the king of the Tarentines Aristophilides disabled the rudders of the Persian ships, and then put the Persians under guard on the grounds that they were actually spies. While they suffered this, Democedes arrived at Croton. When he arrived at his own city, Aristophilides released the Persians and gave back to them the ships which he had seized.

137

137.1 From there the Persians set sail in pursuit of Democedes and arrived at Croton, where they seized him after finding him wandering around openly.

137.2 Some of the Crotonians greatly feared Persian power and were ready to let him go, but others tried to snatch him back and were striking the Persians with sticks when they spoke out as follows: 'Men of Croton, see what you're doing? You are taking away a man who is the king's runaway slave.

137.3 How will it please Darius that he has been insulted in this way? How can what you have done turn out well for you, if you take him from us? Against what city in this land shall we first march? Which shall we try to enslave first?'

137.4 In saying this they did not persuade the Crotonians at all, but Democedes was wrested from them and at the same time they put to sea the galleon that had brought them there and sailed away back to Asia, and no longer sought to come and learn anything further about Greece, having been robbed of their guide.

137.5 However as they were setting sail, Democedes gave to them the following instruction, bidding them tell Darius that Democedes was betrothed to take the daughter of Milon as his wife. For the name of the wrestler Milon was much revered by the king. And I think that it was for this reason that Democedes eagerly sought out this marriage and paid a great deal of money for it, so that he could show that he was esteemed both by Darius and in his own country.

138

138.1 After setting sail from Croton the Persians were driven ashore with their ships to Iapygia, and there Gillus a Tarentine man who was an exile rescued them serving there as slaves and led them back to king Darius. In return for these men, Darius was ready to give him whatever he wanted.

138.2 Gillus chose to return to Tarentum, after recounting his misfortune. But so that he should not cause any disturbance to Greece, if a great fleet were to sail against Italy because of him, he said that it was enough for him that Cnidians alone escort him back, thinking that this would make his return better for the Tarentines since the Cnidians were their friends.

138.3 Darius fulfilled his promise. For having sent a messenger to Cnidus he ordered them to escort Gillus back to Tarentum. The Cnidians obeyed Darius but did not persuade the Tarentines and were unable to use force. This then was what happened. And these Persians were the first to arrive in Greece from Asia, and these men acted as spies for this very reason.

139

139.1 Following these events Darius chose Samos as the first out of all the Greek and barbarian cities for the following reason. When

Cambyses son of Cyrus was making his expedition against Egypt, many Greeks arrived in Egypt, some, as was reasonable, came with the army for trade, some came as observers of the country. Among these was Syloson son of Aeaces, who was brother of Polycrates and in exile from Samos.

139.2 To this Syloson fell the following stroke of good fortune. He was wandering through the marketplace in Memphis wearing a red cloak, when Darius, then a bodyguard of Cambyses and as yet a man of no great importance, saw him and wanted the cloak, so he came over and tried to buy it.

139.3 Syloson, seeing that Darius really wanted the cloak, guided by his divine fortune said, 'I am not selling this for any money, but I give it to you free, if it is absolutely necessary for you to have it.' Darius praised his words and accepted the cloak.

140

140.1 Syloson knew that he had lost this item on account of his good nature. But when in time, Cambyses died, the seven revolted against the Magus, and from the seven Darius became king, Syloson learned that the kingship had passed to the very man to whom he had once given his cloak in Egypt when he wanted it. After he went up to Susa, he sat by the porticoes of the king's palace and said that he was a benefactor of Darius.

140.2 Upon hearing this, the guard announced him to the king. Darius was amazed and said to him, 'And which of the Greeks is my benefactor to whom I am already obliged, having so recently taken power, hardly anyone has come up to see us yet and I have no debt to any Greek man. Nevertheless, bring him in so that I can understand what he wants in saying this.'

140.3 The gatekeeper brought in Syloson and as he stood in their midst the interpreters asked him who he was and on the basis of what act he claimed to be the king's benefactor. Syloson, therefore, told him the entire course of events surrounding the cloak, and how he was the very man who gave it to him.

140.4 Darius gave this reply to what he said: 'Oh, noblest of men, you are the one man who gave me a gift when I did not as yet possess any power, even if it was a small one, yet indeed my gratitude then was equal to what I should feel now if I were to receive something big. In return for this, I give you limitless gold and silver so that you may never regret that you treated Darius, son of Hystaspes, well.

140.5 In response, Syloson said, 'Give me neither gold, nor silver, king, but grant me my homeland of Samos after you have recovered it for me, which our slave holds: now that my brother Polycrates has died at the hands of Oroetes, and grant me this without any killing and enslavement.'

141

141.1 When Darius heard this, he despatched an army and Otanes, who had been one of the seven, as its general, having instructed him to fulfil the tasks just as Syloson requested. Otanes went down to the shore and prepared the army.

142

142.1 At Samos, Maeandrius son of Maeandrius held power, who had authority that had been entrusted to him by Polycrates. Although he wanted to be the most just of men, it was impossible for him.

142.2 When the death of Polycrates was announced to him, he did as follows: first, he set up an altar to Zeus the Liberator and marked out a sanctuary around it, and it is still there now outside the city; then when this had been done, he summoned an assembly of the citizens and addressed it as follows:

142.3 'As you know, the sceptre and all the power have been entrusted to me by Polycrates, and it is in my power to govern you. But to the best of my ability, I shall not do those things that I would rebuke in my neighbour. For it did not please me that Polycrates ruled absolutely over men who were like himself, nor does anyone else who does the same. Now that Polycrates has fulfilled his lot, I publicly lay down my authority and declare equal sharing in power for you.

142.4 'However, I claim this much as a prize for myself, that six talents be taken from Polycrates' money and kept for myself, and in addition to this, I also claim the priesthood of Zeus the Liberator for me and my descendants. To him, I myself established the temple and now I bestow freedom upon you.'

142.5 Such was the announcement that he made to the Samians, and one of them stood up and said: 'But you are not worthy of ruling us, since you are of low birth and you're a pest. But it is better that you render account of the money you have handled.'

143

143.1 This was spoken by a man named Telesarchus who was well esteemed among the citizens. Maeandrius, realizing that if he relinquished his power, someone would be appointed to rule as tyrant in his place, he in fact did not intend to let it go, and retreated to the acropolis, and, sending for each one individually on the pretext of giving account of the money, he arrested and imprisoned them.

143.2 These men were imprisoned and following these events a disease befell Maeandrius. His brother, whose name was Lycaretus, because he was hoping that he would die so that he could seize control of Samian affairs more easily, put all the prisoners to death. For they did not, as it seems, wish to be free.

144

144.1 When, therefore, the Persians escorting Syloson arrived at Samos, no one raised a hand against them, but Maeandrius himself and his supporters said that they were ready to leave the island under a truce. When Otanes had given approval on these terms and the treaty made, the most worthy of the Persians set up and sat on thrones facing the acropolis.

145

145.1 The tyrant Maeandrius had a brother who was quite mad, whose name was Charileos. This man was in prison for committing some offence. And then having heard what was going on and peeped through the dungeon window and, when he saw the Persians sitting peacefully, he started shouting out and saying that he wished to speak with Maeandrius.

145.2 When Maeandrius heard him, he bid them release his brother and bring him to him. As soon as he was led in, by railing and cursing he attempted to persuade his brother to attack the Persians, speaking as follows: 'Oh you most cowardly of men, although I am your brother and did nothing worthy of imprisonment, you bound me and deemed me worthy of the dungeon. But when you see the Persians throwing you out and making you homeless, you do not dare to take revenge, even though in fact they could be so easily beaten.

145.3 'But if you yourself are afraid of them, give me your mercenaries, and I will take revenge on them for coming here. You, I am prepared to send away from the island.'

146

146.1 This was what Charileos said. Maeandrius accepted his argument, as I think, not because he had come to such a point of foolishness as to think his forces would defeat the king, but more because he refused to make it possible for Syloson to take the city intact without difficulty.

146.2 Having angered the Persians he wished, therefore, to render Samian affairs as weak as possible and to hand it over in this state, knowing well that if the Persians suffered badly, they would be even more bitterly angry with the Samians, being well aware that he had the means for a safe departure from the island whenever he wished. For a secret tunnel had been dug for him leading from the acropolis to the sea.

146.3 In fact, Maeandrius himself sailed away from Samos. But Charileos, after equipping all the hoplites and flinging open the gates, sent them out against the Persians who were not expecting anything of the sort thinking that an agreement had been reached on all matters. The mercenaries fell upon and killed the most distinguished of the Persians who were riding in their sedan chairs.

146.4 Such were the actions of these men, but the rest of the Persian army came up to assist. Hard pressed, the mercenaries were driven back to the Acropolis.

147

147.1 When the general Otanes saw the great suffering experienced by the Persians, he deliberately forgot the instructions which Darius gave to him as he set out, which were neither to kill nor to enslave any of the Samians and to give the island untouched to Syloson. He ordered the army to kill everyone they laid hold of, man and child alike. Then some of the army were besieging the acropolis, others were killing everyone who crossed their path both inside and outside the temples.

148

148.1 After running away from Samos, Maeandrius sailed to Sparta. When he arrived there and after he had brought up all the possessions he left with, he used to do as follows: whenever he set out his silver and gold drinking cups, his attendants used to clean them, and he would be talking at the same time to Cleomenes son of Anaxandrides, who was king of Sparta, and he would lead him to his house. Whenever Cleomenes saw the drinking cups, he marvelled at them and was struck by them. Maeandrius used to bid him carry away as many of them as he wished.

148.2 After Maeandrius had said this a second and third time, Cleomenes was the most just of men, for he did not think it right to accept what was offered, and upon learning that he would find assistance by giving gifts to other citizens, he went to the ephors and said that it would be better for Sparta if the Samian stranger left the Peloponnese so that he would not persuade either himself or another of the Spartiates to become wicked. Upon hearing what he said, they banished Maeandrius by proclamation.

149

149.1 After sweeping Samos clean, the Persians handed it over to Syloson bereft of men. However, general Otanes later helped to colonize it as a result of a vision he had and a disease which attacked his genitals.

150

150.1 When the naval expedition was going against Samos, the Babylonians revolted, heaving prepared themselves especially well. For at the time when the Magus was in power and the seven revolted, it was during this entire period of confusion that they were preparing for the siege. And they somehow managed to evade notice while doing so.

150.2 When they openly revolted, they took the following action. After driving out their mothers, each man chose one woman whom he wanted from his household, but the rest they gathered together and strangled. Each man chose a single woman to be the bread maker. They strangled the rest so that they would not eat their grain.

151

151.1 When Darius learnt of this and had gathered together his entire force, he led the expedition against them, and after marching out in force against Babylon, he besieged them, but they thought nothing of the siege. For the Babylonians, going up onto the battlements of the wall, used to dance triumphantly and mock Darius and his army, and one of them made the following remark:

151.2 'Why do you sit about Persians, but don't leave? For you will take us, whenever mules give birth.' One of the Babylonians said this in no way expecting that a mule would give birth.

152

152.1 When a year and seven months had passed, Darius and his whole army were already vexed at their not being able to capture the Babylonians. And yet Darius had tried every trick and device against them: but he was not able to take them with other strategies that he tried, even making an attempt employing the very same method Cyrus had used when he took them. For the Babylonians were keeping a very keen watch and he was not able to take them.

153

153.1 Then during the twentieth month, the following portent happened to Zopyrus son of Megabyzus, the very one who was one of the seven who destroyed the Magus. One of his grain carrying mules gave birth. When it was announced to him, Zopyrus was in disbelief, but when he saw the foal, he forbade those who had seen it to tell anyone and pondered what had happened.

153.2 And to his mind came the words of the Babylonian, who at the beginning had said that, whenever mules gave birth, then the wall would be captured, and it seemed to Zopyrus, in response to this utterance, that Babylon could be taken. For it seemed to him that it was with divine inspiration that that man had spoken and also that his mule had given birth.

154

154.1 Since he decided that it was fated for Babylon to be taken, he approached Darius and enquired whether it was especially important for him to take Babylon. Upon learning that considered it extremely important, he made another plan, so that he himself would be the one to take the city and that the deed would be his. For among the Persians good services are honoured with the increase of one's prestige.

154.2 He now considered that he would not be able to take the city by any other method other than by mutilating himself and deserting to them. Then making light of it he inflicted irremediable mutilation upon himself. For having cut off his nose and his ears and also having badly shorn off his hair and even having scourged himself, he came before Darius.

155

155.1 Darius reacted very badly upon seeing a man so esteemed mutilated, and leaping up from his throne and cried out and asked him who it was that had mutilated him and for doing what.

155.2 He said: 'There is no such man, except you, who has it in their power to make me like this. No stranger, oh king, has done this to me, but I have done this to myself, because I thought it dreadful that Assyrians are laughing at the Persians.'

155.3 Darius replied, 'Oh most wretched of men, you attach the noblest of labels to the most shameful of deeds, in claiming that you have done something irremediable to yourself on account of the besieged. How, foolish man, will the enemy surrender more quickly because you have mutilated yourself? How could you have taken leave of your senses to destroy yourself?'

155.4 Zopyrus said, 'If I had told you what I was intending to do, you would not have let me. But I have done it now and I inflicted it on myself. Now then, if you do not neglect what you need to do, we will take Babylon. For I will go just as I am to the city wall as a deserter and tell them that I have suffered this at your hands; and I think that, having persuaded them that this is the case, I will obtain command of an army.

155.5 'You, on the tenth day after I enter the city, post one thousand men from that part of the army about which you have no concern for losing, at the gate called the Semiramis. And then again on the seventh day after this, post another two thousand at the gates known as the Ninevites; and from the seventh day allow another twenty to pass, and then lead out and set four thousand at the gates of the Chaldaeans. Let neither the previous group nor these men have any means of defending themselves except their daggers. Allow them to have these.

155.6 'But after the twentieth day, immediately order the rest of the army to launch an assault all around the walls and post the Persians for me at the Belian and Kissian gates. For I think that, once I have performed great deeds, the Babylonians will entrust to me other matters and even the keys of the city gates. It will then be the concern of myself and the Persians to do what is necessary.'

156

156.1 Having given these instructions, he went to the gates, constantly turning back as if he truly were a deserter. When the men stationed there saw him from the towers, they ran down and setting the other gate ajar, asked him who he was and in search of what he had come. He explained that he was Zopyrus and that he was deserting to them.

156.2 The gate guards, when they heard this, led him before the general assembly of the Babylonians. Standing before them he was full of lament for what happened, saying that he had suffered at Darius' hands what he had suffered at his own hand, and that he had suffered this way because he had counselled him to send away the army, since there indeed seemed to be no way of capturing the city.

156.3 'Now,' he said, 'I come to you men of Babylon as your greatest benefit, and to Darius and his entire army and the Persians, their greatest curse. For he will not get away with having mutilated me in this way. I know well all the ins and outs of his plans.' Such were his words.

157

157.1 The Babylonians, upon seeing a man who was most highly esteemed among the Persians deprived of his nose and ears, and defiled by scourge marks and blood, because they entirely expected that he was telling them the truth and had come as an ally, they were ready to entrust to him whatever he asked for.

157.2 He asked for an army. When he had received this from them, he did exactly as he had agreed with Darius. For on the tenth day, when he led out the army of Babylonians and surrounded the thousand men, which he had ordered Darius to draw up first, he slaughtered them.

157.3 The Babylonians, upon realizing that he made his deeds match his words, and being exceedingly pleased, were ready to serve him in every way. Having let the agreed number of days pass, again, after selecting some of the Babylonians, led them out and slaughtered the two thousand men from Darius' soldiers. When they saw this act, the Babylonians all held words of praise for Zopyrus on their lips.

157.4 After once again letting the agreed number of days pass, he led them out to the agreed place, and surrounded and slaughtered the four thousand. When he had accomplished this act, Zopyrus meant truly everything to the Babylonians, and this man was accepted as their army commander and wall guard.

158

158.1 When Darius made his attack all around the wall as agreed, it was indeed then that Zopyrus revealed the complete deception. For the Babylonians went up onto the wall and resisted Darius' attacking army, but Zopyrus flung open the Belian and Kissian gates and let the Persians into the city.

158.2 When some of the Babylonians saw what had been done, they fled to the temple of Belian Zeus. Those who did not see what was going on, each remained at their post, until they realized how they had in fact been betrayed.

159

159.1 This was how Babylon was captured for the second time. When Darius became master of Babylon, one thing he did was to pull down their wall and tear down the gates. For when he previously took the city Cyrus had not done either of these things. Then Darius impaled around three thousand of the leading men, but to the remaining Babylonians he gave back them back their city to live in.

159.2 So that the Babylonians would have wives in order for a future generation to grow, Darius made provision and did as follows. For as I showed at the start of the account, the Babylonians had strangled their own women to take provision for their grain. He arranged for the neighbouring peoples to send women to Babylon, as many as he assigned for each one, so that a total of fifty thousand women assembled. And it is from these women that the Babylonians of today were born.

160

160.1 Not one Persian surpassed the great service of Zopyrus in the judgement of Darius, either of those who came before or after, except Cyrus alone. For none of the Persians deemed himself to be worthy of comparison to that man. It is said that Darius often expressed the opinion that he would rather have wished that Zopyrus had not suffered his injury than have twenty Babylons in addition to the one he already had. He honoured him greatly.

160.2 For every year he gave him gifts of those things most highly valued among the Persians, and he granted that he govern Babylon for the rest of his life without tribute and gave him many other things besides. Megabyzus was the son of this Zopyrus who served as general in Egypt against the Athenians and their allies. This Megabyzus' son was Zopyrus, who deserted to Athens from the Persians.

Commentary

The end of Book II detailed the offerings made by Amasis and the origins of the friendship formed between him and Polycrates of Samos.

1

1.1: τοῦτον ... τὸν Ἄμασιν: 'this man ... Amasis'. τοῦτον links back to the end of Book II (but note that it is unlikely that these divisions were made by Herodotus; see Introduction, p. 2), which ends with Amasis' dedications at Cyrene, Lindus (see §47.3), and Samos.

ἄγων καί ἄλλους ... τε καὶ Αἰολέας: 'composed of the different men over whom he ruled, among whom were Ionian and Aeolian Greeks.' Ἴωνάς and Αἰολέας are in apposition to ἄλλους.

δι' αἰτίην τοιήνδε: Herodotus often carefully signposts his account. He will explain the reason for the expedition in the section that follows.

αἴτεε Ἄμασιν θυγατέρα: 'he asked Amasis for his daughter'. αἰτέω takes a double object. See below, §31.2: αἰτέειν τὸν Καμβύσεα Ἄμασιν θυγατέρα.

ἐκ συμβουλῆς: 'on the advice of'.

μεμφόμενος: 'because he used to blame'. Present participle of μέμφομαι.

ἀποσπάσας: lit. 'having dragged him away from'. The choice of verb is significant, suggesting a violent or forced separation. Is this Herodotus telling us that Amasis exerted undue pressure in sending the physician off to Persia? Or is he reflecting the anger and unwillingness of the physician himself at being sent away?

γυναικός τε καὶ τέκνων: τε καὶ stresses the separation from his family and consequent resentment felt by the physician.

μιν ... ἔκδοτον: *hyperbaton*, stressing the cause of the unnamed doctor's resentment against Amasis.

ὅτι μιν ... ἔκδοτον ἐποίησε ἐς Πέρσας: 'because he ... delivered him up to the Persians'.

πέμψας παρὰ Ἄμασιν: lit. 'having sent to Amasis', in the sense of 'after sending word to Amasis'.

αἴτεε ἰητρὸν ὀφθαλμῶν ὃς εἴη ἄριστος τῶν ἐν Αἰγύπτῳ: '[and] he asked for the best eye-doctor in Egypt' (lit. 'he asked for the eye-doctor whoever was the best of those in Egypt'). The verb in the relative clause is optative because it is indefinite.

1.2: ταῦτα δὴ ἐπιμεμφόμενος: explains the physician's motives. Herodotus gives a brief explanatory summary before moving on. ταῦτα links the motives just described to what is about to follow.

τῇ συμβουλῇ: 'in shared counsel'.

ἵνα ἢ δοὺς ἀνιῷτο ἢ μὴ δοὺς Καμβύσῃ ἀπέχθοιτο: A purpose clause sets up the dilemma that the physician's advice has created for Amasis. ἀνιῷτο is optative of the contracting verb ἀνιάομαι.

Τῇ δυνάμι τῶν Περσέων ἀχθόμενος καὶ ἀρρωδέων: Amasis' anxiety about Persian power is emphasized by the use of two verbs of similar meaning, further enhanced by the *assonance* of α in the phrase ἀχθόμενος καὶ ἀρρωδέων. Cambyses invaded Egypt in 526. It is entirely plausible that Amasis was afraid of the rapidly advancing power of Persia initially under Cyrus the Great, which then continued under Cyrus' son Cambyses II.

οὐκ εἶχε: 'he was unable' (lit. he had it not to ...). οὐκ ἔχω + infinitive.

οὔτε δοῦναι οὔτε ἀρνήσασθαι: The two infinitives explain the dilemma created. The consequences were grim either way. Amasis did not want to give his daughter up, since he was suspicious of Cambyses' real intentions, but feared the repercussions of refusing to give her up.

εὖ γὰρ ἠπίστατο ... ἀλλ' ὡς παλλακήν: εὖ is emphatically placed to stress Amasis' fears about Cambyses' true intentions for his daughter. The untrue and real intentions of Cambyses are contrasted in the parallel clauses οὐκ ὡς γυναῖκα ... ἀλλ' ὡς παλλακήν – 'not as a wife ...

but as a concubine'. παλλακήν is deliberately stressed at the end of the sentence to make Amasis' fears for his daughter's true fate more vivid. Such treatment would have also been insulting to the king. μιν: Amasis' daughter.

1.3: ταῦτα δὴ ἐκλογιζόμενος ἐποίησε τάδε: ταῦτα refers to the thoughts and worries of Amasis that Herodotus has just described. δὴ: the particle adds the sense of 'exactly' or 'precisely', so ταῦτα δὴ = these precise thoughts. ἐκλογιζόμενος: 'reflecting upon'. The present participle suggests Amasis was mulling over what to do carefully and for a while.

Ἀπρίεω τοῦ προτέρου βασιλέος: Amasis had succeeded Apries as pharaoh, after ousting him from the throne and having him murdered. Ἀπρίεω is an Ionic genitive singular (see Introduction, p. 29).

θυγάτηρ κάρτα μεγάλη ... ὡς ἑωυτοῦ θυγατέρα: Amasis plots to deceive Cambyses whilst appearing to satisfy his demand, and so avoid Persian wrath and protect his daughter. Instead of sending his own daughter, he dresses up the daughter of his predecessor. She was the lone survivor of Apries' family. Herodotus tells us that she was 'very/especially tall' (κάρτα μεγάλη) and 'beautiful' (εὐειδής). Presumably her fine appearance would make her a 'convincing' secret stand-in for Amasis' own daughter.

οἱ ἦν Νίτητις: ταύτην δὴ τὴν παῖδα: Herodotus' word order emphasises how it was 'Nitetis' whom he kitted out for Cambyses, as shown by the juxtaposition of 'Νίτητις' and 'ταύτην'. κοσμήσας: 'having dressed up/adorned [this girl]'. Nitetis is lavishly dressed so that she may be convincingly passed off as Amasis' own daughter. ὡς ἑωυτοῦ θυγατέρα: 'as his own daughter'.

1.4: δὲ: 'But'.

πατρόθεν ὀνομάζων: lit: 'addressing her after her father' or 'naming her from her father,' so, 'addressing her by her father's name' or 'addressing [her] as Amasis' daughter'.

ὦ βασιλεῦ: The direct address and direct speech add a sense of drama and variety to the text.

διαβεβλημένος ... οὐ μανθάνεις: 'you do not realize how you have been wronged'. Perfect passive participle from διαβάλλω. The participle is used in indirect statement after οὐ μανθάνεις.

τῇ ἀληθείῃ: 'in fact' or 'in truth', 'in reality'.

τὸν ἐκεῖνος ἐόντα ... ἐπαναστὰς ἐφόνευσε: 'the ruler against whom that man revolted along with the Egyptians and killed.' τὸν = Apries. ἐκεῖνος: 'that man' = Amasis.

1.5: τοῦτο δὴ τὸ ἔπος ... θυμωθέντα ἐπ' Αἴγυπτον: lit. 'it was this speech and this very reason grew and urged on Cambyses son of Cyrus furiously angry against Egypt', so 'And this speech was then the very reason that drove Cambyses son of Cyrus, since he was extremely angry, against Egypt.' τοῦτο δὴ τὸ ἔπος καὶ αὕτη ἡ αἰτίη: 'this speech was then the reason that...'

2

2.1: οἰκηιοῦνται: 'claim as their own'.

Κῦρον γὰρ εἶναι: the reported alternative version continues. Herodotus frequently relates more than one version of an event or explanation of an event. He does not always indicate the one he endorses, but here takes a sceptical approach to the Egyptian version (see §2.2 below).

τὸν πέμψαντα παρὰ Ἄμασιν ἐπὶ τὴν θυγατέρα: 'who had sent to Amasis (asking) for his daughter.'

2.2: λέγοντες δὲ ταῦτα οὐκ ὀρθῶς λέγουσι: the *polyptoton* of λέγω which frames the sentence draws attention to his rejection of the Egyptian account.

οὐ μὲν οὐδὲ ... ἐκ τῆς Αἰγυπτίης: Herodotus proceeds to explain his reasons for rejecting the Egyptians' claim that Cambyses was in fact son of a daughter of Apries and therefore half-Egyptian, not Cassandane's. εἰ γὰρ τινὲς καὶ ἄλλοι: 'for if any and others [do]'. The sense is 'they, if anyone does'. Herodotus asserts that the Egyptians know

Persian customs better than anyone. σφι: refers to the Persians., lit. 'it is not the custom to/for them'.

ὅτι πρῶτα μὲν ... βασιλεῦσαι γνησίου παρεόντος: an illegitimate child could not be king over the Persians when a legitimate one was alive.

ἀλλὰ παρατρέπουσι τὸν ... οἰκίῃ συγγενέες εἶναι: Herodotus argues that the Egyptians have twisted the story to claim kinship with the house of Cyrus. Although he does not explicitly say why, the story could be seen as an attempt by the Egyptians to lessen the humiliation of their defeat (see HW *ad loc.*). Later historians Dinon and Lyceas accepted the claim (see ALC *ad loc.*).

3

This story, like the one just rejected, had Cyrus as the one who requested Nitetis, but Cambyses remains the legitimate heir. This is a third version, which Herodotus also dismisses. The story is dramatic, the child who vows revenge and grows up to exact it.

3.1: ἐμοὶ μὲν οὐ πιθανός: Herodotus dismisses the story that follows, but includes it anyway. Why? It is quite a dramatic story, and one could argue that, although he does not endorse it, it does reveal something about the character of Cambyses, showing a vindictive streak early on. In this story, it was Cyrus who requested Nitetis.

ὑπερθωμάζουσα: a powerful choice of word, which conveys how impressed the Persian woman was upon observing the children of Cassandane.

3.2: ἐν ἀτιμίῃ ἔχει ... ἐν τιμῇ τίθεται: the parallel phrase and *variatio* stress the effect of Nitetis' arrival on Cyrus' regard for Cassandane.

3.3: ἐπεὰν ἐγὼ γένωμαι ἀνήρ: indefinite clause in primary sequence.

Αἰγύπτου τὰ μὲν ἄνω κάτω θήσω, τὰ δὲ κάτω ἄνω: Lit. 'I shall turn the affairs of Egypt upside down and downside up', so 'I shall turn the affairs of Egypt entirely upside down', or 'I shall thoroughly shake up the affairs of Egypt.'

4

4.1: ἄλλο τι τοιόνδε πρῆγμα: lit. 'another occurrence of the following sort'. The phrase highlights the significance of the involvement of mercenary Phanes, which Herodotus is about to explain.

γνώμην ἱκανὸς καὶ τὰ πολεμικὰ ἄλκιμος: adjectives with accusative of respect. Lit. 'capable as regards judgement and strong in matters of war', so a 'clever man and a skilled soldier'. ἄλκιμος is frequently used in the Homeric poems to denote physical and military prowess (see, for example, *Iliad*. VI.437 describing Diomedes – Τυδέος ἄλκιμον υἱόν: *the mighty son of Tydeus*; *Odyssey*, III.199-200 Nestor addressing Telemachus – γάρ σ' ὁρόω καλόν τε μέγαν τε, ἄλκιμος ἔσσ': *for I see you are a man both tall and handsome, and that you are mighty*').

4.2: μεμφόμενός κού τι Ἀμάσι: lit. 'because, I suppose, he blamed Amasis for something,' 'because he blamed Amasis for something or other'. This rather vague description of Phanes' motives could either suggest Herodotus is trivializing his motive or that he thinks the specific reason for his actions mattered less than the implications of the actions themselves.

ἐκδιδρήσκει: a vivid present and in this section; see also μεταδιώκει and αἱρέει, which Herodotus uses to depict the flight of Phanes alongside the urgent desperation of Amasis to recapture him. μεταδιώκει ὁ Ἄμασις ... μεταδιώκει δὲ: the repetition of the verb 'pursue' with difference subjects creates a sense of urgency. The verbs return to the aorist tense in the final sentence of this section (ἑλὼν ... ἀνήγαγε ... περιῆλθε).

οἷα: here used in the sense of 'since' or 'because'.

λόγου οὐ σμικροῦ: 'of no small account'. A *litotes*. σμικροῦ = μικροῦ. μιν = Phanes.

τῶν εὐνούχων: on the importance of eunuchs in the Persian royal court see note on §77.2.

σοφίῃ γάρ μιν περιῆλθε ὁ Φάνης: 'for Phanes surpassed him in intelligence/cleverness.' σοφίη is not wisdom in a philosophical sense here.

4.3: ὁρμημένῳ δὲ στρατεύεσθαι ... ἄνυδρον διεκπερᾷ, ἐπελθών: Phanes is the subject of ἐπελθών ('encountered', 'met'). The dative participles ὁρμημένῳ and ἀπορέοντι agree with Καμβύσῃ, dative because of ἐπελθών. ὅκως τὴν ἄνυδρον διεκπερᾷ is an indirect question introduced by ἀπορέοντι. τὴν ἄνυδρον: Herodotus will go on to explain the significance of this region and what happened to it following the Persian conquest of Egypt in §§5-7.

πέμψαντα παρὰ τὸν ... οἱ ἀσφαλέα παρασχεῖν: Herodotus explains the origins of the alliance between the Arabians and the Persians.

5

5.1: μούνη δὲ ταύτῃ ... ἐσβολαὶ ἐς Αἴγυπτον: Herodotus explains the importance of the desert region. μούνη is emphatically placed to stress that this is the only route by which the invaders could have entered Egypt.

ἀπὸ γὰρ Φοινίκης ... τῶν Παλαιστίνων καλεομένων: the region described has been identified as the Palestinian coast between the Casian Mountain and the southern border with Phoenicia and Gaza. See ALC for more on this region. Καδύτιος πόλιος: generally identified as Gaza.

5.2: Σαρδίων οὐ πολλῷ ἐλάσσονος: the phrase may suggest Herodotus' own familiarity with the region, as does ὡς ἐμοὶ δοκέει.

ἀπὸ δὲ Καδύτιος ... ἐστὶ τοῦ Ἀραβίου: identified as the Sinai peninsula. ἀπὸ δὲ Καδύτιος ... ἀπὸ ταύτης: *anacolouthon*. After pausing to give the relative size of Sardis, Herodotus resumes with ἀπὸ ταύτης. ταύτης refers to Cadytis. Cf. §5.3 ἀπὸ δὲ Σερβωνίδος λίμνης ... ἀπὸ ταύτης.

Ἰηνύσου πόλιος: identified with the city Khan Yunis.

μέχρι Σερβωνίδος λίμνης: for more on this lake and its identification, see ALC *ad loc*.

5.3: ἐὸν τοῦτο οὐκ ... ἄνυδρον ἐστὶ δεινῶς: Herodotus stresses the size of the region. Geography was an important part of the historical record for Herodotus and here, it is directly relevant to the main narrative, illustrating Cambyses' quandary as he was faced with crossing this vast desert region. The journey across was three days' worth. **οὐκ ὀλίγον:** *litotes.* **οὐκ ὀλίγον χωρίον ... ὅσον:** the repetition of the ending -ον (*homoioteletuon*) perhaps draws attention to the phrase. δεινῶς is emphatically placed and deliberately chosen to stress the excessive dryness of the place.

6

Herodotus tells of how wine jars imported from Phoenicia are taken to the region of the Syrian desert he is describing, where they are filled with water. He claims this is why not a single empty wine jar is to be found in Egypt.

6.1: τὸ δὲ ... τοῦτο ἔρχομαι φράσων: Herodotus uses a very similar correlating phrase at §103 (τὸ δὲ ... τοῦτο φράσω). He favours this balanced phrasing when signposting that he is about narrate a fact or story with which he assumes his audience is not familiar. τὸ = ὅ: see Introduction, p. 30 for the use of the definite article as the relative pronoun in Ionic Greek.

διὰ τοῦ ἔτεος ἑκάστου: 'throughout the year'. A variant reading of this phrase reads διὰ as δὶς, making it 'twice a year'.

καὶ ἓν κεράμιον ... κεῖνον οὐκ ἔστι: lit. 'and one cannot say, in short, that there is a single wine jar in number to see', so 'and it is not possible in short to count one single empty wine jar'. ἀριθμῷ is a *pleonasm* to emphasize the absence of wine jars in Egypt.

6.2: δῆτα: Chiasson notes that this is generally a colloquial usage and rare in Herodotus (1982: 156–61). εἴποι τις ἄν: Herodotus imagines a hypothetical questioner to introduce his explanation of this unusual phenomenon.

τοὺς δὲ ἐκ Μέμφιος: i.e., the demarchs of Memphis. δεῖ to be understood here.

ὁ ἐπιφοιτῶν κέραμιος: 'each jar that comes in' (lit. 'the habitually arriving jar').

ἐπὶ τὸν παλαιόν: to the old stock. κεράμιον must be understood here.

7

7.1: κατὰ δὴ τὰ ... τάχιστα παρέλαβον Αἴγυπτον: Herodotus explains the relevance of the jars story. This was how the Persians watered the dry region after they took Egypt.

7.2: τότε δὲ οὐκ: this marks the return to the main narrative, having left Cambyses at 4.3 wondering how to cross the desert region.

8

How the Arabians make their oaths. At §7.2 Cambyses, following Phanes' advice, sent to the Arabian king to achieve safe passage through the desert. Here we learn about the staunch commitment of Arabians to any oaths they make. On Arabia in Herodotus' time, see DGRG entry for an excellent and more detailed overview.

8.1: σέβονται δὲ Ἀράβιοι ... αὐτὰς τρόπῳ τοιῷδε: σέβονται is emphatically placed to stress Arabian reverence of oaths. This is presented as a practice still employed in Herodotus' day as the use of the present tense shows. ἀνθρώπων ... μάλιστα: Herodotus portrays the Arabians as particularly reputed for the honouring of pledges. ἀνθρώπων ὅμοια τοῖσι: this is very difficult to replicate comfortably in English. Literally it means, 'things similar to those of men [who do so]'.

τῶν βουλομένων τὰ ... ἐν μέσῳ ἑστεώς: this short section demonstrates Herodotus' ability for vivid and visual description. ἑστεώς

= ἑστώς (Attic). τῶν βουλομένων ... ἄλλος ἀνὴρ ἀμφοτέρων αὐτῶν: the enclosing word order of the presiding official by the genitives referring to the pledging parties imitates the scene of his standing in their midst. The *assonance* of alpha (highlighted in bold) draws attention to the central figure, the ἄλλος ἀνήρ.

τὸ ἔσω τῶν χειρῶν παρὰ τοὺς δακτύλους τοὺς μεγάλους: 'the inside of their hands along the large fingers.' The 'large fingers' are likely the thumbs, thus, the part cut by the stone traces the area of the palm nearest the thumb.

8.3: *Herodotus moves to discussing Arabian religious beliefs.*

καὶ τῶν τριχῶν ... ὑποξυρῶντες τοὺς κροτάφους: what is the significance of the hair-cutting practice?

τὸν Διόνυσον ... τὴν Οὐρανίην: 'Dionysus and the Heavenly Goddess.' These are the Greek gods that Herodotus identifies with the Arabian gods Orotalt and Alilat: 'ὀνομάζουσι δὲ τὸν μὲν Διόνυσον Ὀροτάλτ, τὴν δὲ Οὐρανίην Ἀλιλάτ'. The 'Heavenly Goddess' is generally identified with Aphrodite Ourania, as made clear at I.131. See ALC *ad loc.* for more on this goddess. Herodotus' practice of seeing non-Greek gods as equivalent to Greek gods rather than different was not unique, but rather reflects Greek practice. Herodotus suggests in Book II that Greek gods found their origins in the Egyptian pantheon. On Herodotus and religion see Harrison 2000: 208–22 (see also Lattimore 1939: 357–65; Griffiths 1955: 21–3).

9

9.1: ἐμηχανᾶτο τοιάδε: 'he contrived the following means'. This refers to the solution devised by the Arabian king to deal with the lack of water in the desert.

9.2: οὗτος μὲν ὁ ... δὴ λέγεται, ῥηθῆναι: Another example of how Herodotus 'considers it right also to relate the less trustworthy versions' (ALC, I.408). Here he expands briefly on why: 'but the less convincing must also be recounted, since they are told after all'. Reliable or not, they are still part of the deeds of human history.

τῷ: dative relative pronoun here.

Κόρυς: as there is no 'great' river in Arabia, it could be that Herodotus was mistaken or misinformed. See ALC (*ad loc.*).

ἐκδιδοῖ: flows out into.

τὴν Ἐρυθρὴν καλεομένην θάλασσαν: the Red Sea.

9.3: The alternative version is that the Arabian king created a pipe out of ox-hide and other skins to water the 'dry region'. Herodotus does not spell out why he considers this the less reliable version, but the distance of twelve days journey from the river to the desert region may be the reason.

10

Herodotus takes us back to the scene of the narrative of the war in Egypt.

10.1: ἐν δὲ τῷ ... τοῦ Νείλου ἐστρατοπεδεύετο: ALC note that this is the 'mouth of the Delta that marks the Eastern border of Egypt' (I.408).

Ψαμμήνιτος ὁ Ἀμάσιος παῖς: the throne has passed to Amasis' son, Psammenitus.

10.2: Ἄμασιν γὰρ οὐ ... ἐλάσας ἐπ' Αἴγυπτον: Cambyses did not capture the pharaoh, on whom he wished to take revenge, alive. This, however, did not stop Cambyses. He instead took revenge on the dead corpse of Amasis (see §16 for the grisly tale).

τέσσερα καὶ τεσσεράκοντα ἔτεα: Amasis reigned between 569 and 525, most likely dying 526. ALC note that he was Psamtik III, last pharaoh of the 26th dynasty of Egypt.

οὐδέν ... μέγα ἀνάρσιον πρῆγμα: §10.2 could be said to constitute Amasis' epitaph. Although he avoided any significant misfortune, upheaval and defeat followed shortly after his death. Herodotus may be noting Amasis' relatively uneventful reign as a point of contrast to what was about to befall Egypt and Psammenitus (see §15 for his gruesome death).

ταριχευθεὶς ἐτάφη ἐν ... τὰς αὐτὸς οἰκοδομήσατο: Herodotus is perhaps signposting the location of the tomb ahead of his account of Cambyses abuse of Amasis' corpse at §16. ἐτάφη ἐν τῇσι ταφῇσι: the *polyptoton* draws attention to the location. οἰκοδομήσατο : middle 'he had. ... built'.

10.3: φάσμα ... μέγιστον: Herodotus stresses the unusual nature of the natural phenomenon he is about to relate. ALC note that prodigies in Herodotus frequently foretell 'an imminent disaster', anticipating a contrast with the previously quiet rule of Amasis. μέγιστον perhaps deliberately echoes οὐδέν ... μέγα (§10.2) to emphasize the contrast.

οὔτε ... οὐδαμὰ ... οὔτε: the negatives stress the singularity of the rain falling on Thebes. Godley notes that there is very little rain in that region even now. More recent figures for rainfall in Egypt show the annual average to be less than 80mm. Some reports argue that this represents a decrease due to climate change.

§§11–12 *The battle at Pelusium.*

11.1: οἱ ἐπίκουροι: these were the mercenaries that Phanes had been a member of (§4.2). Mercenary troops were widely used in armies in the ancient world. μεμφόμενοι: here, 'feeling resentful towards.'

στρατὸν ... ἀλλόθροον: the *hyperbaton* and emphatic placement of ἀλλόθροον stress the resentment of the Greek and Carian mercenaries about a foreign army being led against Egypt.

μηχανῶνται: 'contrived'. The word reflects the deliberate and brutal plotting of the mercenaries.

11.2–3: ἦσαν τῷ Φάνῃ ... οὕτω δὴ συνέβαλον: the account of the gruesome slaying of Phanes' children in revenge, followed by the drinking of their blood from the mixing bowl by the resentful band of mercenaries, shows Herodotus' skill as a dramatic narrator. ἐς ὄψιν τοῦ πατρὸς reflects the horror of what they are about to do by making the children's father watch. κατὰ ἕνα ἕκαστον suggests the slaying is deliberately drawn out. ἔσφαζον: the imperfect shows the drawn-out process of the 'sacrifice'. διὰ παντῶν ... διεξελθόντες: 'having gone through them all' – a grim euphemism for 'having finished killing them all'. The passage shows that Herodotus does not shy away from showing Greeks as every bit as brutal as their non-Greek fellows. For the possible connection of this act to a blood rite, see ALC *ad loc*.

11.3: μάχης δὲ γενομένης ... ἐτράποντο οἱ Αἰγύπτιοι: Herodotus announces the occurrence of the battle in which the Egyptians were defeated, but returns to the aftermath at §13 after a digression at §12. πλήθεϊ πολλῶν the losses caused are stressed by the *pleonasm*.

12

Persian and Egyptian skulls compared. This is a fascinating passage. Thomas persuasively argued that this reflected the influence on Herodotus of fifth – century medical writings which prominently showed an interest in environmental causes and the relationship between nature versus nurture and its effect on human beings' health and physical development (2001: 29–32).

12.1: θῶμα δὲ μέγα ... παρὰ τῶν ἐπιχωρίων: Herodotus emphatically draws attention to the 'wonder' he is about to relate. The short phrase is very significant historiographically. εἶδον πυθόμενος παρὰ τῶν ἐπιχωρίων: '[thing] I saw, which I had also [also] learnt about from the natives'. Herodotus claims he learnt about this from the natives. He is thus making a claim to personal enquiry. He, nevertheless, goes further. He sought to verify what he learned. He appears an active historian, scientific in his enquiry.

τῶν γὰρ ὀστέων ... δὲ τῶν Αἰγυπτίων): 'For with the bones of those who fell in the battle on either side lying scattered separately, since those of the Persians lay in one place, as they had been separate at the start, and those of the Egyptians in a different spot'. This is a tricky passage. τῶν ... ὀστέων περικεχυμένων ... πεσόντων is a genitive absolute. χωρὶς is used adverbially twice. ἐχωρίσθη along with the repetition of χωρὶς further stresses the separation of the Persian and Egyptian bones, as does χωρὶς μὲν ... ἑτέρωθι δὲ ... ('apart ... in another place ...').

αἱ μὲν τῶν ... λίθῳ παίσας διαρρήξειας: Herodotus contrasts the weakness of Persian skulls with the strength of the Egyptians. The sentence switches construction (*anacolouthon*). Herodotus uses a result clause followed by indicative and open present condition (ἀσθενέες οὕτω ὥστε, εἰ θέλεις ψήφῳ μούνῃ βαλεῖν, διατετρανέεις) when discussing the Persians, but for the Egyptians, he uses a closed conditional *apodosis* stressing the impossibility, or extreme unlikelihood, of breaking the Egyptian skulls (μόγις ἂν λίθῳ παίσας διαρρήξειας) although the second οὕτω initially seems to expect a result clause. This emphasises the ease of breaking Persian skulls, with the near impossibility of cracking an Egyptian skull.

12.2: ἔλεγον ... ἔπειθον: Herodotus claims the reason was told to him.

12.2-3: Egyptian skulls are so strong because the skulls are exposed to the sun which thickens the bone. This is also given as an explanation for the lack of bald men among the Egyptians.

12.4: Persian skulls in contrast are weak because they wear caps that shield their heads from the sun, thus preventing the thickening of the bone evident in Egyptian skulls. We thus see nature and nurture (*physis* and *nomos*) both at play. The natural effect of the sun is encouraged by the Egyptians but shut out by the Persians with very different physical outcomes.

[εἶδον]· εἶδον: I favour keeping the bracketed εἶδον (excised by Godley), as does Wilson. It draws the passage nicely back to Herodotus' claim of enquiry at the start and is fittingly juxtaposed to the further supporting evidence he claims to have seen in the final sentence.

εἶδον δὲ καὶ ... Ἰνάρῳ τοῦ Λίβυος: 'heads' or 'skulls' needs to be supplied when translating. Herodotus claims he saw a similar phenomenon at Papremis, in the skulls of those killed along with Achaemenes son of Darius by Inaros the Libyan. Papremis was the site of a battle of 460, when Egypt revolted from Persia. Ἀχαιμένεϊ τῷ Δαρείου: this Darius is Darius II, not the successor of Cambyses.

13

We now return to the narrative of the Persian conquest of Egypt.

13.1: οἱ δὲ Αἰγύπτιοι ... ὡς ἐτράποντο: this echo of §11.3 returns us to events.

κατειληθέντων: 'when they were cut off (at Memphis)', i.e., the Egyptians.

ἐς ὁμολογίην προκαλεόμενος: 'calling [the Egyptians] to (make an) agreement.'

13.2: ἐκχυθέντες ἁλέες: the *pleonasm* shows the sheer number who streamed out of the walls.

οἳ δὲ: connecting relative. 'They', i.e. the Egyptians.

κρεουργηδὸν: a grim choice of word reflecting the savage butchery of the men on the ship. The savagery describes here makes an interesting comparison with Polybius' account of the savage Egyptian mob that rampaged through Alexandria in their anger at the conduct of corrupt minister Agathocles *c.* 203/202 (XV.30).

13.3: δείσαντες: the reaction of the Libyans and also the Cyreneans (§13.4: δείσαντες) to events illustrates the shockwaves sent out by the fall of Egypt. The reference to fear also recalls Amasis' own fear of the growing power of Persia at §1.2.

13.4: ὡς ἐμοὶ δοκέει: Herodotus often highlights when he is expressing his own opinion or judgement.

πεντακοσίας μνέας ἀργυρίου: this is roughly eight talents and twenty minas, not a large sum when one looks at the hundreds of talents assigned in tribute to provinces of the empire. Herodotus' conjecture that Cambyses showed contempt for so little an amount is plausible.

14

The torment of Psammenitus. ALC (ad loc.) note the positive traits in Herodotus' portrayal of Cambyses here (presumably before he goes mad) and clear parallels between his conduct and that of Cyrus in his exchange with Croesus on the pyre (I.86-90).

14.1: ἡμέρῃ δὲ δεκάτῃ ἀπ' ἧς: a time formula that Herodotus often uses (see also §155.5 for Zopyrus' instructions to Darius).

ἐπὶ λύμῃ: 'to cause outrage'. A powerful choice of word for what Cambyses will make Psammenitus endure – watching the degradation and suffering of his family.

14.2: ἐπ' ὕδωρ: 'to fetch water'. As ALC note, such an activity was treated in Greek poetry as being a task more proper for a slave. Thus, to watch one's daughter forced to fetch water was to watch her being forced into slavery. That this was clearly Cambyses' intention is confirmed by the fact the girl is dressed in a slave's clothing (ἐσθῆτι δουληίῃ). The scenario is a stark reminder of what the girl's future will be and valid comparison can be made with Andromache's fears of slavery and Hector's response in the *Iliad* (VI.414-65) and even Euripides' *Troades* as the various women of Troy lament their enslaved futures.

ἄλλας παρθένους... ἀνδρῶν τῶν πρώτων: 'other maiden daughters of the leading men.'

14.3: βοῇ τε καὶ κλαυθμῷ: stresses the pitiable reaction of the girls.

οἱ μὲν ἄλλοι ... ὁ δὲ Ψαμμήνιτος: Herodotus contrasts the laments of the fathers with the silence of Psammenitus. ἀντεβόων τε καὶ ἀντέκλαιον: the raising of audible lamentation was the normal mourning reaction. Psammenitus' is unusual and contrary to the usual practice.

14.4: οἱ = τῷ Translate here as 'his.'
ἔπεμπε: Cambyses is the subject.
τούς τε αὐχένας κάλῳ δεδεμένους καὶ τὰ στόματα ἐγκεχαλινωμένους: the appearance of the young men as slaves in chains and with their mouths bound by a bridle shows the humiliation of the Egyptians. Herodotus' detailed description is vivid and moving.

14.5: ἤγοντο δὲ ποινὴν ... σὺν τῇ νηΐ: see §12.1 for the butchery of the men on the ship.
ταῦτα γὰρ ἐδίκασαν ... ἀνταπόλλυσθαι: Herodotus explains that two thousand were chosen because of the decision of the Royal Judges. οἱ βασιλήιοι δικασταί: these judges are mentioned again at §31.3 when they are consulted by Cambyses about marrying his sister (see also V.25, VII.194; also on these officials, see Brosius 2021: 105–6).
ὑπὲρ ἀνδρὸς ἑκάστου δέκα Αἰγυπτίων τῶν πρώτων: this would mean two hundred men had been on the ship, as two thousand young men are paraded at §14.4. On the problems with these figures, see ALC a*d loc*.

14.6: τῶν ἄλλων Αἰγυπτίων ... ἐπὶ τῇ θυγατρί: Psammenitus again responds with silence. Herodotus reports that he did τὠυτὸ (= τὸ αὐτο – 'the same') as for his daughter in contrast to the lamentations of the other leading men, emphasizing his surprisingly subdued action.

14.7: ἐκπεπτωκότα ἐκ τῶν ... εἰ μὴ ὅσα πτωχός: lit. 'who had fallen from what he had having [now] nothing except as much as a beggar did'.
ὁ δὲ Ψαμμήνιτος ... ἐπλήξατο τὴν κεφαλήν: at the sight of his friend who has fallen on hard times, Psammenitus suddenly displays the more familiar demonstrations of mourning.

14.8: τὸ ποιεύμενον πᾶν ἐξ ἐκείνου: 'everything done by him [Psammenitus].'

θωμάσας: emphatically placed to show Cambyses' reaction.

14.9: Δεσπότης: 'Lord.'

14.10: Ὦ παῖ Κύρου: a common address in Herodotus (ALC, I.412).

μέζω ἢ ὥστε: 'too great to [weep].' Comparative adjective + ἢ + ὥστε = 'too *x* for *y*.'

ἐκ πολλῶν τε καὶ εὐδαιμόνων: a hendiadys for 'from many good fortunes.' The translation keeps the separation for emphasis.

ἐπὶ γήραος οὐδῷ: 'on the threshold of old age.' The phrase is used by Priam (*Iliad* XXII.60) as he begs Hector not to fight Achilles (see also XXIV.487 for the same phrase in Priam's plea to Achilles). The echo may well be deliberate. For more on the connection between Herodotus and Homer, see Introduction, pp.15-6.

καὶ ταῦτα ὡς ... δοκέειν σφι εἰρῆσθαι: 'When what he had said was reported back, they thought he [Psammenitus) had spoken well.' Translate δοκέειν as a main verb.

ὑπὸ τούτου: 'by this man' i.e., what had been said by Psammenitus.

14.11: ὡς δὲ λέγεται ὑπ' Αἰγυπτίων: according to ALC (*ad loc*) this is fictitious as the Egyptians knew nothing about Croesus. Has he made it up? Or did another source wrongly mis-attribute the story? It was also impossible chronologically as Croesus was no longer alive but had in fact died soon after the capture of Lydia (Brosius 2021: 44).

δακρύειν μὲν Κροῖσον ... δακρύειν δὲ Περσέων ...: the reaction of Croesus and the Persians affects Cambyses. This seems to show a clear parallel with Croesus' moment of understanding on his pyre and Cyrus' second thoughts (I.86-7). Just as Cyrus has a change of heart about executing Croesus, just so Cambyses decides to save the king's son, but alas, too late. Later in the book as his madness sets in, he becomes more hostile to Croesus.

ἐσελθεῖν ... κελεύειν: infinitives in indirect statement.

15

15.2: εἰ δὲ καὶ ἠπιστήθη ... ἀπέλαβε ἄν ... ὥστε ἐπιτροπεύειν αὐτῆς: past closed conditional followed by a result clause with the infinitive denoting the likely outcome (which in this case did not happen). ἠπιστήθη μὴ πολυπρηγμονέειν: '[if] he had known not to go meddling/interfering'.

διαιτᾶτο ἔχων: Psammenitus is the subject.

ἐπεὶ τιμᾶν ἐώθασι ... ἀποδιδοῦσι τὴν ἀρχήν: this was a common practice of Persian rulers following a conquest. Rather than directly annexing a place and imposing their own rule or system, its governance would be returned to the son or sons of the conquered ruler, as long as they toed the line, of course. See ALC *ad loc.* for examples. The practice is well-documented during Cyrus' reign, although see Waters on the 'superficial truth' of a so-called laissez-faire approach (2022: 110–12). τῶν, εἰ καὶ ... ἀποδιδοῦσι τὴν ἀρχήν: lit. 'to the sons of whom, even of they [the kings] have revolted, they give back power'.

15.3: πολλοῖσι ... καὶ ἄλλοισι: *hendiadys* stressing that this was common practice.

ἐν δὲ καὶ τῷ τε Ἰνάρῳ παιδὶ Θαννύρᾳ ... καὶ τῷ Ἀμυρταίου Παυσίρι: Inaros rebelled and was defeated in 455. His deportation to Persia and execution followed in 450. Amyrtaeus likely rebelled from the isle of Elbo in the western Delta. For more, see H&W *ad loc.*; ALC, I. 410, 413.

15.4: αἷμα ταύρου: Psammenitus allegedly committed suicide to avoid being captured by drinking bull's blood. It was widely believed in antiquity to be poisonous.

16

Cambyses and Amasis' body. H&W argue that Cambyses sought to reverse the religious policy of Amasis. This ran contrary to normal Persian practice, which was to allow already existing practices to continue.

16.1: βουλόμενος ποιῆσαι τὰ δὴ καὶ ἐποίησε: the use of βουλόμενος, the *polyptoton* of ποιῆσαι/ἐποίησε, and the emphatic particle δὴ all stress how Cambyses' actions were deliberate and premeditated.

τὸν Ἀμάσιος νέκυν: this marks Cambyses first act of sacrilege in Egypt. He may have been acting out of revenge. He could not take Amasis alive, as had been his intention, but he could still disturb his burial. By Cambyses' time defilement of an enemy corpse was not acceptable, which marked a significant change since the days of Homeric epics (see ALC, I.414).

μαστιγοῦν ... καὶ ... ἀποτίλλειν καὶ κεντοῦν τε καὶ ... λυμαίνεσθαι: the gruesome list of 'punishments' in *polysyndeton* is designed to shock and perhaps also to anticipate the slippery slope of religious outrage on which Cambyses was embarking.

16.2: κατακαῦσαι ... οὐκ ὅσια: the placement of ὅσια stresses how Cambyses' orders to burn the corpse violated Persian practice (see also I.131.2). This looks forward to Darius' experiment at §38 where the differing burial practices of the Greeks and Indians prove inconceivable and even horrifying to the opposite side.

16.2-3: Πέρσαι γὰρ θεὸν ... νέμειν νεκρὸν ἀνθρώπου: on the cult of fire in Persian religion, see also I.131.2. Fire had an important place in ancient Persian religion and is linked to Zoroastrianism, a central religion in the Persian empire. On Zoroastrianism, see Llewellyn-Jones (2022: 209–16; 216–20 on whether the Achaemenids were Zoroastrians). See also Brosius (2021: 93–4) and Waters (2022: 144–55).

16.3: οὐδαμῶς ἐν νόμῳ οὐδετέροισι ἐστί: the double intensifying negative shows how Cambyses was also violating Egyptian custom.

16.4: οὐκ οὖν θηρίοισι ... ὑπὸ εὐλέων καταβρωθῇ: Herodotus' explanation for the Egyptian practice of embalming is to prevent worms eating the body, since they believe it wrong to feed it to animals. Cf. Homeric threats to leave a body unburied for dogs and birds to eat (see for example, *Iliad*, XVI. 836-3; XXII.353-4).

οὕτω οὐδετέροισι νομιζόμενα... ποιέειν ὁ Καμβύσης: Herodotus reinforces his point that Cambyses' actions violated the practices of both sides.

16.5: ὡς μέντοι Αἰγύπτιοι λέγουσι: one detects a note of scepticism in Herodotus' tone, here. He is reporting it as a 'story told', but the way he prefaces the report suggests disbelief.

16.7: αἱ μέν νυν... αὐτὰ Αἰγύπτιοι σεμνοῦν: Herodotus confirms and explains his scepticism. He sees it as the Egyptians trying to gloss the affair more favourably. He does not believe that Amasis' preemptive orders were ever given.

§§17–25 *The ensuing expeditions of Cambyses and the 'embassy' to Ethiopia.*

17

17.1: μετὰ δὲ ταῦτα: this section introduces Cambyses' ventures after Egypt, all considerably less successful. On whether these were the failures that Herodotus makes them out to be, see ALC a*d loc*; Brown (1982) 387–403.

τε Καρχηδονίους καὶ ἐπὶ Ἀμμωνίους καὶ ἐπὶ τοὺς μακροβίους Αἰθίοπας: the *tricolon* with *polysyndeton* stresses Cambyses' ambition and his unrealistic aims in going against all three peoples at once.

τοὺς μακροβίους Αἰθίοπας: this was the traditional Greek epithet for the Ethiopians who were, as ALC note, 'wrapped in an aura of legend.' H&W regarded Herodotus' account of them as largely mythical. Herodotus mentions two other peoples he calls 'the Ethiopians', who are different (see §94.1 for the Ethiopians of Asia, §97.2 for the Ethiopians who border Egypt, whom Cambyses did conquer).

17.2: τοῦ πεζοῦ ἀποκρίναντα: 'chosen part of his land army'.

κατόπτας... ὀψομένους... κατοψομένους: the repetition of words relating to 'sight' underpin Cambyses' real intentions. ὀψομένους denotes the overt aim of ethnographic reconnaissance, but the clauses either side refer to his intention of spying. τῷ λόγῳ highlights that 'bringing gifts' is a mere pretext.

18

ἡ δὲ τράπεζα τοῦ ἡλίου: Herodotus seeks to explain his reference to the 'Table of the Sun' at §17.2, the survey of which he gives as an aim of Cambyses fact-finding mission. ALC link the 'legend' of the table to the Homeric accounts of the great hecatombs and banquets of the Ethiopians. Herodotus seems to be 'rationalizing' the myth. See H&W on a possible connection to an Egyptian tale of a 'meadow of offerings' where food was left for the souls of the dead.

λειμὼν ἐστὶ: the 'meadow' has been plausibly identified with land surrounding a Temple of the Sun discovered by Garstang at the beginning of the twentieth century. For more on the location, see ALC *ad loc*.

πάντων τῶν τετραπόδων: Herodotus depicts the richness of the land.

κρεῶν ἐφθῶν: 'boiled meat'. See §23.1 for the Ethiopian king's description of their diet.

τοὺς ἐν τέλεϊ: 'those in power'.

ἑκάστοτε... ἑκάστοτε: the repetition perhaps stresses that this is a routine practice and an important one.

προσιόντα τὸν βουλόμενον: 'anyone who wishes to can come'.

φάναι δὲ τοὺς... τὴν γῆν αὐτὴν ἀναδιδόναι: the natives believe that the riches spring spontaneously from the earth itself. Could this be why the feast is set out at night to maintain this illusion?

ἡ μὲν δὴ... λέγεται εἶναι τοιῇδε: Herodotus often rounds off an account by way of a conclusion, which verbally echoes his announcement of the account (cf. §12.1 and §12.4: θῶμα δὲ μέγα εἶδον... τοιαῦτα εἶδον). Such concluding phrases often mark a transition back to the main narrative.

19

19.1: ἐξ Ἐλεφαντίνης πόλιος ὢν Ἰχθυοφάγων ἀνδρῶν: the city of 'Elephants' or 'ivory' was the location of one of the three Persian garrisons in Egypt (see ALC *ad loc.* on this and also on the problem of identifying the 'Fish-eaters'). On the tendency of ancient writers to classify peoples by their diet and comparison with modern dietary stereotypes, see Clarke 2018: 13.

τοὺς ἐπισταμένους τὴν Αἰθιοπίδα γλῶσσαν: the pharaoh Psammetichus had apparently formed a 'class of interpreters' in Egypt to whom these Fish-eaters belonged (II.154.2, 164.1). For the use of interpreters in Herodotus, see also §38 (Darius and the Callatiae) and §140 (Syloson the brother of Polycrates at the Persian court). Elsewhere in the *Histories*, see I.78, 86; IV.24.

19.2: ἐπὶ τὴν Καρχηδόνα πλέειν ... οὐκ ἔφασαν ποιήσειν ταῦτα: the Phoenician mercenaries refuse to sail against fellow Phoenician city Carthage. Even though they are mercenaries, their refusal shows the strength of kinship and oaths as a tie between cities. Such relations did not always remain strong as the breakdown in relations between Corinth and its colony Corcyra show in at §49.

Φοινίκων δὲ οὐ ... οὐκ ἀξιόμαχοι ἐγίνοντο: this part of the army was very much dependent on the mercenaries for its strength. Thus, the planned campaign failed.

19.3: Καμβύσης γὰρ βίην ... ὁ ναυτικὸς στρατός: although three apparently simultaneous expeditions may have seemed overly ambitious, Cambyses was not completely devoid of prudence. The Phoenicians were too important to the fleet for him to risk upsetting them. He also recognized their voluntary surrender. Again, Herodotus shows a positive trait.

Κύπριοι: Cyprus was then a tributary of Egypt. At §91.1, it is listed in the fifth province of the Persian empire.

20

20.1: καὶ δῶρα φέροντας ... φοινικηίου οἴνου κάδον: the red robe is a symbol of monarchic power (see §139.2, where Darius wears the cloak given to him by Syloson, a foreshadowing of his own accession, and Syloson's recovery of his own kingdom). The necklace and bracelets are dismissed as symbols of slavery (§22.2). The king brands the ambassadors liars when they truthfully explain to him how the cloak and myrrh are made (§22.1, 3).

20.2: νόμοισι δὲ καὶ ἄλλοισι ... τοῦτον ἀξιοῦσι βασιληίας βασιλεύειν: ALC (*ad loc.*) argue that Herodotus is describing the 'mythical' Ethiopians, since the historical Ethiopians were 'thoroughly Egyptianized'. Herodotus has possibly conflated the real with the legendary. There are, however, later references to the Ethiopian practice of choosing the tallest of their male citizens to be king (Aristotle *Politics* 1290b6; see ALC a*d loc.* for other references).

21

21.1: αὐτῶν ἔλεγον τάδε: at §20.1 Cambyses had dispatched the Fish-eaters ἐντειλάμενος τὰ λέγειν χρῆν – 'ordering them to say whatever was necessary'. This is somewhat vague, but as we see, the purpose was to attempt to deceive the Ethiopian king as to the true aim of the visit. However, the king sees straight through the pretext, §21.2.

φίλος καὶ ξεῖνός: 'Guest-friendship' was a very common institution of ancient diplomacy in establishing cordial relations between peoples (see *Iliad* VI.119-211; on the significance of this passage, see Prestige-Jones (1999: 21–3).

διδοῖ: a present indicative active, despite appearances.

21.2: ὁ δὲ Αἰθίοψ μαθὼν ὅτι κατόπται ἥκοιεν: μαθών – 'having realized'. The king was not deceived. The short phrase contrasts with the effuse introduction made by the Fish-eaters. The normal construction after μαθών (as a verb of perceiving, learning, understanding, hearing) would be a participle, but Herodotus uses the ὅτι construction to illustrate the truth of the king's realization.

οὔτε ... οὔτε ... οὔτε: the *anaphora* and *tricolon* of negatives emphasises the king's total distrust of the Persian embassy and his moral condemnation of Cambyses' imperial ambitions. ἀληθέα and δίκαιος are morally laden terms. The Ethiopian king suggests Cambyses falls far short of what a true king should be. **ἐπεθύμησε:** ALC (*ad loc.*) note that the verb is 'loaded with moralistic warnings'.

εἰ γὰρ ἦν δίκαιος ... ὑπ' ὧν μηδὲν ἠδίκηται: the contrary to fact conditional continues the king's moral reproach.

21.2-3: νῦν δὲ αὐτῷ τόξον ... προσκτᾶσθαί τῇ ἑωυτῶν': the story of the bow's striking resemblance to that Odysseus' mighty weapon that could only be strung and fired by him reinforces the 'mythical' air that the Ethiopians are given by Herodotus. They appear untouchable and even unconquerable. The challenge belittles Persian strength and there is even a mocking tone suggesting that the king does not believe any Persian is up to the challenge and is directly attacking the famed Persian skill at archery. It is also ironic that the only Persian who capably handles the bow is Cambyses' brother Smerdis, whom he comes (wrongly) to fear as a challenger to his power (§30.1). On the recurring motif of the bow, see ALC *ad loc.*

22

22.1: πεποιημένον: '[how] it had been made'. εἴη must be supplied.

δολεροὺς μὲν ... δολερὰ δὲ: the king's reaction to the robes and the myrrh reflects an archaic Greek attitude to dress-like robes, ointment and perfume as deceitful.

22.2: πέδας: the king's reaction suggests he condemns the robe and jewellery as symbolic of Cambyses' true designs on Ethiopia, with the robe symbolizing his power, the fetters his aim to enslave. The king is also portrayed as having no taste for, even harbouring suspicion of, unnecessary luxury, not dissimilar to the famous fifth-century stereotype of the Spartans (see §46 for Spartan dislike of overly wordy appeals).

ὡς παρ' ἑωυτοῖσι ... ῥωμαλεώτεραι τουτέων πέδαι: a note of contempt is suggested as the king declares that Ethiopian chains are stronger.

22.3: τὸν αὐτὸν λόγον: the myrrh is also condemned as deceitful.

22.3-4: The passage may reflect the influence upon Herodotus of Ionian and fifth-century medical writings in the link asserted between diet and longevity. ὀγδώκοντα ... ἔτεα: ALC (*ad loc.*) note that this was a 'typical' figure given for a lifespan that was deemed longer than usual. σιτεόμενοι κόπρον: further shows the contemptuous attitude of the Ethiopian king towards the Persians. It is only the wine that he has a good word for. οὐδὲ γὰρ ἄν ...’Ἰχθυοφάγοισι τὸν οἶνον: present closed conditional.

23

23.1: ἔτεα μὲν ἐς εἴκοσι καὶ ἑκατὸν: 120 years often appears as the length of very long life in ancient texts, for example, Arganthonius (I.163.2) and also in the Old Testament. For more examples, see ALC (*ad loc.*). Attempts have also been made to explain this apparent longevity by positing a shorter year for the Ethiopian calendar (H&W *ad loc.*).

σίτησιν ... κρέα τε ἐφθὰ καὶ πόμα γάλα: see §18 on the Table of the Sun. It is to this diet that the king attributes Ethiopian longevity.

23.2: θῶμα: the emphatic placement emphasizes the amazed reaction of the Fish-eaters.

ἐπὶ κρήνην: the account of the spring is mostly likely a legendary feature. Springs and fountains are a common feature in quest for longevity myths in several cultures (see Gruman 2003: 29–42).

23.3: εἴ σφι ἐστὶ ... οἷόν τι λέγεται: a typical Herodotean phrase to distance himself from endorsing a fabulous report.

23.4: ἐν πέδῃσι χρυσέῃσι: gold was once produced abundantly in Ethiopia (H&W a*d loc.*). ALC (*ad loc.*) see it as a feature of Ethiopia's utopian aura in Herodotus, namely that the traditional symbol of greed is not valued as much as copper. Herodotus does not state this explicitly. He does, however, stress the great value placed on copper (χαλκὸς) in the superlatives σπανιώτατον and τιμιώτατον. σπανιώτατον καὶ τιμιώτατον: the adjectives are not in agreement with χαλκὸς, but are neuter, describing copper as the 'rarest and most prized thing'.

24

On the tale of the crystal tombs, H&W (*ad loc.*) amusingly comment: 'the marvels here described are as fictitious as Cinderella's "glass" slipper.'

24.1: ἐξ ὑάλου: 'from transparent stone'. This may refer to a naturally transparent crystal. ALC note that Herodotus may have been influenced by the Egyptian practice of mummification or glass production.

24.2: εὔεργος: lit. 'well-worked', so here 'malleable'.

24.4: πάντων ἀπαρχόμενοι: 'making a beginning of all the first things' (lit), so 'make offerings of all the first fruits to ...'

25

25.1: αὐτίκα ὁ Καμβύσης ... γῆς ἔμελλε στρατεύεσθαι: Herodotus makes clear that the planned Ethiopian expedition was doomed from the start. αὐτίκα ... ὀργὴν ποιησάμενος: the phrase emphasizes the impulsive and temperamental nature of Cambyses. οὔτε παρασκευὴν ... οὔτε λόγον: Herodotus emphasizes the lack of preparation and calculation, the ridiculousness of which is even further stressed by the description of Ethiopia as τὰ ἔσχατα γῆς – 'the ends of the earth'.

25.2: οἷα ... ἐμμανής τε ... καὶ οὐ φρενήρης: 'so mad and not in his right mind was he'. The *tautology* reflects the total lack of sense Cambyses showed.

Ἑλλήνων ... τοὺς παρεόντας: refers to the Greek mercenaries who were with him in Egypt. They did not participate in the campaign.

25.3: Ἀμμωνίους: see §17 on the expeditions planned following victory in Egypt.

τὸ χρηστήριον τὸ τοῦ Διὸς ἐμπρῆσαι: an aggressive and condescending disrespect of other peoples' religious monuments and practices comes to characterise Cambyses' strangest acts.

25.4: τὸ πέμπτον μέρος: the phrase denotes a very small portion, indicating the very short distance covered by the army before the expedition began to fall apart.

ἐπελελοίπεε: pluperfect tense, suggesting how completely food and resources had run out. They had even eaten the baggage animals.

25.5: εἰ μέν νυν ... ἐς τὸ πρόσω: the remote conditional, followed by the statement of what Cambyses actually did stresses the tragic and idiotic nature of his decision to proceed, illustrating the point Herodotus made at §25.2 that he was ἐμμανής. A rational mind would have stopped and limited the damage, but Cambyses, οὐδένα λόγον ποιεύμενος ('taking no rational thought') pressed on still further (ἤιε αἰεὶ ἐς τὸ πρόσω).

25.6: H&W note (see App. V, 395) that the account may betray an Egyptian bias in Herodotus' sources in its hostile portrayal of Cambyses.

ἀλληλοφαγίην: ALC suggest that the desperate hunger of the Persians in turning to cannibalism contrasts with the abundance of the Table of the Sun. Interestingly, when Herodotus reports the cannibalistic practice of an Indian tribe (§99) he shows no hostile judgement, he just reports it as their custom. Here, however, he is not reporting a cultural practice, but an ill-conceived expedition that led to starvation, which prompted desperate measures. That cannibalism would have shocked a Greek audience is suggested by the reaction of the Greeks to the notion of ancestor consumption at §38.3. In Greek mythology cannibalism, intentional or unwitting, generally brings retribution as in the story of Atreus serving up his brother's children as punishment for adultery.

26

26.1: ὁ μὲν ... στόλος οὕτω ἔπρηξε: 'this was how the expedition fared.'

ἀπικόμενοι μὲν φανεροί εἰσι ἐς Ὄασιν πόλιν: lit., 'clearly arrived at the city of Oasis', i.e., 'were known to have arrived at'. This was their last known movement. H&W (*ad loc.*) identifies the location as the 'Great Oasis' of Khargeh (see Thurston 2003: 204–6).

Σάμιοι τῆς Αἰσχριωνίης φυλῆς λεγόμενοι: this tribe could nothing to do with the Greek Samians, although H&W (*ad loc.*) note that 'Aeschrion' is found as a proper name at Samos, also noted by ALC (*ad loc.*). H&W suggest that Herodotus could have been confused by a similar sounding name.

ἀπέχουσι δὲ ἑπτὰ ἡμερέων ὁδόν: lit. 'they were away at a journey of seven days', so 'they were seven days' journey away from ...'

ὁ χῶρος οὗτος ... Μακάρων νῆσος: the place may refer to an 'island of the desert' (ALC a*d loc.*). H&W note that Herodotus may have been translating an Egyptian word.

26.2: λέγεται: Herodotus shrouds the whole account of the men allegedly wiped out by the sandstorm in mystery.

οὐδένες οὐδὲν ἔχουσι εἰπεῖν: 'no one can say anything.' The intensifying double negative stresses that no one can pronounce confidently on the fate of these men.

26.3: ἰέναι ... γενέσθαι: infinitives in continuing indirect statement after λέγεται, although one normally expects an indicative after ἐπειδή.

Commentary

That this is the version of the Ammonians is reinforced by the following verbal echo at the beginning and end of the account:

λέγεται δὲ κατὰ τάδε ὑπ' αὐτῶν Ἀμμωνίων (§26.2)
Ἀμμώνιοι μὲν οὕτω λέγουσι γενέσθαι (§26.3)

27

27.1: ὁ Ἆπις ... τὸν ... Ἔπαφον: see II.38 where Herodotus describes the Egyptian belief that bulls belong to Epaphus. On Epaphus and his identification in Greek culture with the son of Io, see Braund (2018: 143–4).

27.2: πρότερον μὲν ἐόντος αὐτοῦ ... τότε δὲ ἐπεὶ αὐτὸς παρείη: the phrase highlights Cambyses' mistaken perception that the Egyptians' celebratory mood has resulted from their delight at his disastrous expedition against the Ethiopians. πάγχυ ... καταδόξας: emphasizes how Cambyses jumps to conclusions and shows his paranoia. πρότερον μὲν ... τότε δὲ: in Cambyses' mind, the fact that they were not celebrating in this manner before means the actions must be against him.

27.3: οἳ δὲ: connecting relative.

οἳ δὲ ἔφραζον ... Αἰγύπτιοι κεχαρηκότες ὀρτάζοιεν: εἴη and ὀρτάζοιεν are optatives because the indirect statement is in historic sequence. ἐπεὰν φανῇ is an indefinite clause with the subjunctive.

The theme of Cambyses' disrespect for the religion of others continues. It has already appeared in the instructions given to the detachment to burn the oracle of Zeus Ammon (§25.3). Doubting and punishing the governors is just the beginning of his *hybris* against Apis.

28

28.1: οὐ λήσειν ἔφη ... εἰ ... εἴη Αἰγυπτίοισι: future open conditional in *oratio obliqua*. χειροήθης: 'tame'. The choice of word to represent

Cambyses' view of the god shows his disrespectful attitude toward the deity.

28.2: ἥτις οὐκέτι οἵη ... ἄλλον βάλλεσθαι γόνον: lit. 'Which is no longer able to cast another offspring into her womb' (translate: 'which is no longer capable of conceiving another offspring in its womb'). οἵη τε γίνεται is used here as an equivalent of οἷος τ' εἰμί.

28.3: Herodotus' very precise account of the appearance of the Apis calf has been confirmed by statues (H&W a*d loc.*).

29

ALC (ad loc.) give a good critique of the plausibility of this account. Was Cambyses really so mad, or does this reflect a resentful, anti-Cambyses Egyptian source?

29.1: ὑπομαργότερος: 'rather mad', as opposed to 'more mad'. Cambyses' madness seems to be accelerating and becomes a recurring theme of Herodotus' narrative. Some modern scholars remain sceptical about this crazy, tyrannical, irrational Cambyses (for example, see Brosius 2021: 39–40; Llewellyn-Jones 2022: 88–9). It is possible that Herodotus was rather too trusting of a very hostile Egyptian source. This is perhaps surprising, as he was perfectly aware of the embarrassment and resentment caused to the Egyptians by the Persian conquest and how this had spawned implausible alternative versions. For more on Herodotus' portrayal of Cambyses, see Introduction, pp. 26–7.

τὸν μηρόν: Herodotus' emphasis at the end of the sentence may well be deliberate in anticipation of the ironic, even providential, location of his wound to Apis, given his later incursion of his own fatal wound in the same place (§64.3-5). It is testimony to Cambyses' madness that he would even think of wounding an animal deemed sacred.

γελάσας: Cambyses' laughter in the context of religious practice or monuments recurs at §38.1-2.

θέλων τύψαι τὴν γαστέρα: Cambyses' aim was to kill Apis.

29.2: Ὦ κακαὶ κεφαλαί: lit. 'Oh, wicked heads!', so 'oh, you blockheads!'

ἔναιμοί τε καὶ σαρκώδεες καὶ ἐπαΐοντες σιδηρίων: *polysyndeton* stressing Cambyses' contemptuous dismissal of Apis.

ὑμεῖς γε οὐ . . . γέλωτα ἐμὲ θήσεσθε: Cambyses' paranoia is revealed. The fear of being laughed at by one's enemies was a key feature of Greek heroic thought. Hector angrily reproaches Paris for his feeble efforts, imagining that the Achaeans will mock the Trojans (*Iliad*, III.43-5). Medea's mind is finally made up about killing her sons because she cannot bear to be mocked by those who have insulted her (Euripides, *Medea* 1049-51). Laughter and humiliation are also major preoccupations of Sophocles' Ajax (*Ajax* 381).

τοῖσι ταῦτα πρήσσουσι: 'those who carry out (these things)', i.e., those who execute punishment.

τοὺς μὲν ἱερέας . . . Αἰγυπτίων δὲ τῶν ἄλλων: μὲν . . . δὲ intensifies the image of Cambyses' escalating aggression in ordering for the priests to be scourged, and also for any citizen taking part in the festivities to be killed.

τὸν ἂν λάβωσι: indefinite clause in vivid form. The subjunctive is normally used in primary sequence.

29.3: λάθρῃ Καμβύσεω: emphasizes their fear of Cambyses. However, see Brosius (2021: 41–2) on an inscription that mentions the burial and which even suggests it was in fact carried out at the behest of Cambyses.

30

30.1: ὡς λέγουσι Αἰγύπτιοι: may suggest scepticism.

τὸν ἀδελφεὸν Σμέρδιν . . . μητρὸς τῆς αὐτῆς: Herodotus emphasises that Smerdis was Cambyses' full brother, perhaps stressing the horror of his actions in having him murdered.

φθόνῳ ἐξ Αἰγύπτου ἀπέπεμψε: the phrase reveals clear personal grudge against his brother. ὅτι τὸ τόξον . . . οὐδεὶς οἷός τε ἐγένετο: this explains why. Only Smerdis could pull the bow given by the Ethiopian king. **δύο δακτυλους**: 'to a breadth of two fingers.' Accusative of extent of space or distance (for the challenge, see §21.3).

30.2: ἀποιχομένου ὡς ἐς ... τοῦ οὐρανοῦ ψαύσειε: the dream which Cambyses misinterprets. It is Smerdis the Magus in the dream, not his brother (see §61). This marks the arrival of Prexaspes into the narrative. He is very significant character, depicted essentially as a well-regarded man among the Persians caught up in an oppressive atmosphere first under Cambyses and then the Magi. He is a key figure in the theme of truth and deception.

μή μιν ἀποκτείνας ὁ ἀδελφεὸς ἄρχῃ: the *assonance* emphasises Cambyses' reaction to the dream.

30.3: οἱ μὲν λέγουσι ... οἱ δὲ: Herodotus reports two different versions. This could just be to show that he has researched thoroughly. Or he could be anticipating the air of mystery and secrecy that surrounded Smerdis' death, which facilitated the Magi's rebellion (see §61).

31

31.1: πρῶτον ... τοῦτο: notice the emphatic *hyperbaton* marking the start of Cambyses' terrors.

συνοίκεε: 'married'.

31.2: οὐδαμῶς ... ἐώθεσαν πρότερον: the emphatic placement of οὐδαμῶς stresses how Cambyses' desires were contrary to Persian custom. His violation of his blood ties in murdering his brother, then marrying his sisters, and ultimately killing one of them, too, is another feature of Cambyses' madness and tyrannical conduct.

τοὺς βασιληίους δικαστὰς: see §14.1 on the Royal Judges.

31.3: ἐς οὗ ἀποθάνωσι ... ἄδικον, μέχρι τούτου: 'Persians until the point when they either die or some wrongdoing of theirs is discovered'. ἐς οὗ correlates with μέχρι τούτου.

οὗτοι δὲ . . . ἐς τούτους ἀνακέεται: the judges guarded the ancestral laws. It is telling that Cambyses consulted the judges rather than pressing ahead regardless.

31.4: ἀσφαλέα: Godley translates as 'prudent', which also captures the implication that the judges knew they could not say anything which displeased Cambyses.

31.6: ἔσχε ἄλλην ἀδελφεήν: Atossa, who would become the wife of Darius.

τὴν νεωτέρην ἐπισπομένην: the one he first desired and whom he killed.

32

32.1-2: entirely in indirect speech dependent on λέγεται λόγος.

32.1: ὥσπερ περὶ Σμέρδιος: Herodotus refers back to the different versions that surround the death of Smerdis. The same is true for the wife/sister. The statement asserts personal enquiry and also suggests the mystery that surrounds some of Cambyses' actions, as well as being more entertaining for readers in presenting two different tales.

32.1, 3: Ἕλληνες μὲν λέγουσι (§32.1), Ἕλληνες μὲν . . . Αἰγύπτιοι δὲ ὡς: Herodotus notes that one version (the cub and the pups) is Greek and the other (the stripped lettuce) is Egyptian. Lettuce was prominent in the Egyptian diet (see ALC *ad loc*).

32.4: αὐτῇ ἐχούσῃ ἐν γαστρί: 'pregnant.' In this second version of the sister's death, Cambyses fatally injures her while she is pregnant. A similar tale was also told of the death of Melissa, wife of Corinthian tyrant Periander, whom he murdered. At §50.2, Herodotus mentions her murder, but does not say how.

33

ταῦτα μὲν ἐς τοὺς οἰκηίους ὁ Καμβύσης ἐξεμάνη: lit. 'these things Cambyses did while mad against his relatives.'

νοῦσον μεγάλην . . . τὴν ἱρὴν: most likely epilepsy, a disease often thought in antiquity to be divine in origin. The author of the Hippocratic text, *On the Sacred Disease*, dismissed this 'supernatural' cause and Herodotus also seems sceptical, as the phrase ὀνομάζουσι τινές ('some call') suggests.

οὔ νῦν τοι . . . τὰς φρένας ὑγιαίνειν: Herodotus makes a link between a healthy body and a healthy mind, an early nod to *sana mens in corpore sano* and a prominent strand of thought in Greek fifth century medicine, including the Hippocratic school (see Carrick 2001: 20).

34

34.1: τὸν ἐτίμα τε . . . ἀγγελίας ἐφόρεε οὗτος: *anacolouthon*. Prexaspes is the object of the relative clause and then abruptly becomes the subject (οὗτος) of ἐφόρεε

οἰνοχόος: the post of cupbearer was, as Herodotus, says 'no small honour' (τιμὴ δὲ καὶ αὕτη οὐ σμικρή). On this post, see Llewellyn-Jones 2022: 328–9.

34.2: Ὦ δέσποτα . . . φασὶ πλεόνως προσκέεσθαι: note how Prexaspes carefully pays Cambyses a compliment before adding his qualifying note about the king's drinking.

τῇ δὲ φιλοινίῃ σε φασὶ πλεόνως προσκέεσθαι: lit. 'but they say that you are excessively with the love of wine', so 'but they do say that you are rather too fond of your wine'.

34.3: Πέρσαι . . . προσκείμενον παραφρονέειν: the plosives perhaps suggest Cambyses' contempt for the opinion of the Persians.

34.4: πρότερον γὰρ δὴ: Herodotus now explains the οἱ πρότεροι λόγοι that Cambyses just referred to (§34.3). The explanation continues to

§35.1. Both their former lavish praise and current criticism of his drinking cannot, in Cambyses' mind, be true.

34.5: Κροῖσος δὲ παρεών . . . τὴν Κροίσου κρίσιν: Croesus' words are ambiguous. Is he praising Cambyses as a great son, who therefore needs to leave a son like himself? Or is he making a rather darker remark about just how unlike his father he really is? Godley translates ὅμοιος as 'equal', which perhaps captures the ambiguity even better. All that is clear is Croesus' disagreement with the Persians' judgement (οὐκ ἀρεσκόμενος τῇ κρίσι).

35

35.1: τούτων δὴ ὦν ἐπιμνησθέντα ὀργῇ: we are still in the *oratio obliqua* begun at §34.1. τούτων δὴ ὦν: Herodotus links Cambyses' angry reaction to the scene with Croesus and the leading Persians described at §34.4-5. ὀργῇ: we have already seen how quickly Cambyses is moved to anger in the Apis episode.

παραφρονέουσι: verbal echo of §34.4 (παραφρονέειν). The echo reappears at §35.3 as Cambyses confidently asserts how he has proved the Persians wrong.

35.2: εἰ μὲν γὰρ . . . με μὴ σωφρονέειν: The simple syllogisms expressed by the conditionals ironically betray Cambyses' madness. If he kills a boy with an accurate shot, he is not mad! Πέρσαι φανέονται λέγοντες οὐδέν: 'the Persians will seem to be talking nonsense'. φανέονται = uncontracted future.

35.3: γελάσαντα καὶ περιχαρέα: laughter once again reappears as evidence of Cambyses' madness and the choice of adjective περιχαρέα conveys his excessive pleasure in his 'achievement'.

νῦν δέ μοι εἰπέ . . . οὕτω ἐπίσκοπα τοξεύοντα: the theme of a 'bow' as a symbol of prowess. Herodotus probably intended readers to recall §30.1 where he described Cambyses' resentment of his brother's ability, alone of all the Persians, to draw the Ethiopian bow. It is not accidental that Cambyses asserts his accuracy to be superior and challenges Prexaspes, 'τίνα εἶδες ἤδη πάντων ἀνθρώπων οὕτω ἐπίσκοπα τοξεύοντα' ('who of all men have you seen shoot so precisely on the mark?').

35.5: τότε μὲν ταῦτα ἐξεργάσατο: Cambyses is the subject. **ἐπ' οὐδεμίῃ αἰτίῃ ἀξιοχρέῳ:** H&W note that being buried alive up to the neck was a punishment for very serious offences. Herodotus trivializes Cambyses' motives for doing so, thereby building a picture of his accelerating madness in inflicting so serious a punishment with little cause. At VII.114, Herodotus notes that live burial was a Persian religious practice, done to secure divine favour. Here, he recounts how nine local children are buried at the Nine Ways (Amphipolis), and Herodotus says he has also learnt that Amestris, wife of Xerxes, when old had fourteen sons of notable Persians buried as an offering to 'τῷ ὑπὸ γῆν λεγομένῳ εἶναι θεῷ' ('the god said to be beneath the earth'). H&W identify the god as Ahriman (cf. II.122.1), roughly the Persian equivalent of Hades.

36

36.1: ἡλικίῃ καὶ θυμῷ: *a hendiadys.* 'to your youth and anger' for 'to your youthful anger.' The translation maintains the separate terms in a bid to replicate the emphasis of the Greek.

ἀγαθόν τι πρόνοον εἶναι, σοφὸν δὲ ἡ προμηθίη: 'caution is a good thing, and forethought is wise'. This pithy phrase emphatically illustrates Croesus' point. Wilson's text has the minor variation ἀγαθόν **τοι** πρόνοον εἶναι, making the phrase more pointedly directed at Cambyses rather than a generalization.

σὺ δὲ κτείνεις ... κτείνεις δὲ παῖδας: the parallel clauses stress Cambyses' murderous deeds. The translation makes ἑλών a main verb but does not fully capture the stress of Herodotus' of the Greek on the killing, with ἑλών as a participle. ἀξιοχρέῳ lit. 'that can be deemed worthy,' so 'justifiable'. παῖδας is emphatically placed at the end of the sentence.

36.2: ὅρα ὅκως μή: clause of caution, here the indicative future is used for vividness. Croesus wishes to impress upon Cambyses that losing the loyalty of his own men is a very real possibility.

36.3: Σὺ: emphatic and sarcastic.

συμβουλεύειν ... συνεβούλευσας: the repetition of the verb highlights Cambyses' sarcastic mockery of Croesus and his advice.

ἀπὸ μὲν σεωυτὸν ὤλεσας ... ἀπὸ δὲ ὤλεσας Κῦρον: the parallel *tmeseis* balanced by μὲν ... δὲ ... reinforces the notion that Croesus' advice only brought about destruction first to himself and then to Cyrus.

οὔτι χαίρων: 'not rejoicing', i.e., 'you won't get away with it', 'not with impunity'.

κακῶς προστάς: lit. 'having led it badly'.

36.5: λάμψονται: Ionic form of λήψονται future middle indicative.

36.6: ἐπόθησέ τε δὴ: emphatic placement of ἐπόθησέ and use of δὴ, to convey that the attendants were correct in surmising Cambyses would change his mind, and also how erratic and volatile Cambyses' own thoughts and opinions were.

ἐκείνους μέντοι: anticipates Cambyses' ghastly punishment of the men, presumably because they had disobeyed orders.

37

37.2: ὡςδὲ δὴ ... τῷ ἀγάλματι κατεγέλασε: Cambyses' mockery of the statues is portrayed by Herodotus as symptomatic of his madness. δὴ and καὶ stress the depths to which he sunk, lightly engaging in impiety. On this temple see also II.101. κατεγέλασε: the laughter motif reappears.

τοῖσι Φοινικηίοισι Παταΐκοισι: not a great deal is known about the Pataeci. Newmyer suggests a connection between the name Pataeci and the Egyptian god Ptah. H&W note that Herodotus may have confused the image of Ptah (often identified with Hephaestus) with the 'sons of Ptah'.

ὃς δὲ τούτους ... ὄπωπε, ὧδε σημανέω: Newmyer argues that the phrase has the force of a conditional with a 'relative protasis'. ὅς correlates with ὧδε. ὧδε is Godley's reading '[I will explain it] to whomsoever'. Wilson reads ἐγὼ δὲ, which would emphasise Herodotus' announcement of the explanation he is about to give. The current text retains ὧδε. ὄπωπε is the perfect third person singular of ὁράω.

πυγμαίου ἀνδρὸς μίμησίς ἐστιν: the 'sons of Ptah' who were depicted as dwarves.

38

38.1: πανταχῇ: the emphatic placement stresses the level that Cambyses' madness has, in Herodotus' opinion (μοι δῆλα ἐστὶ), reached.

οὐ γὰρ ... ἐπεχείρησε καταγελᾶν: Herodotus uses the same verb for 'laugh' as he did at §37.2. This phrase anticipates Herodotus' argument that each race believes their own practices to be the best and that Cambyses, had he truly understood this and not been mad, could not have laughed at another people's religious practices.

εἰ γάρ τις προθείη ... ἂν ἑλοίατο: future remote conditional. The example Herodotus goes on to give (the enquiry of Darius) illustrates his point.

ἕκαστοι τοὺς ἑωυτῶν ... τοὺς ἑωυτῶν νόμους ἕκαστοι: the parallel repetition reinforces Herodotus' point that all people choose their own laws as the best even after consideration of other viewpoints (διασκεψάμενοι).

38.2: οὐκ ὢν οἰκός ἐστι ... γέλωτα τὰ τοιαῦτα τίθεσθαι: 'for it is not likely that anyone other than a madman would laugh at such things.' The phrase reinforces the point made in §38.1.

ὡς δὲ οὕτω νενομίκασι ... οἱ πάντες ἄνθρωποι: Herodotus generalises. All men 'have become accustomed' (νενομίκασι) to their own laws.

πολλοῖσί τε καὶ ἄλλοισι ... καὶ τῷδε: Herodotus now announces the proof of what he has asserted. πολλοῖσί τε καὶ ἄλλοισι τεκμηρίοισι: a *hendiadys* stressing the weight of evidence that supports his point.

38.3: Ἰνδῶν τοὺς καλεομένους Καλλατίας: it is not certain whether these are the same Indians referred to at §97.2, there spelt Callantiae.

38.4: εὐφημέειν μιν ἐκέλευον: emphatic phrase illustrating the horrified reaction of the Callatiae to the notion of burning their ancestors.

μοι δοκέει Πίνδαρος . . . νόμον πάντων βασιλέα: Herodotus rather dramatically concludes his discussion with a Pindar quotation to restate his point. He means 'king' in the sense that a people think their own customs to be supreme. The Pindar poem he is quoting now survives only as a fragment (fr.169.1-4). Pindar's meaning is rather different. He speaks of νόμος as a more general guiding force for good among men, rather than men's tendency to believe in the superiority of their own νόμοι. On both passages, see Humphreys 1987: 211–20.

§§39–60: *We now move to Samian affairs.*

39

39.1: Καμβύσεω δὲ ἐπ' Αἴγυπτον στρατευομένου: Herodotus moves to Samian affairs with a synchronic transition. The Spartan expedition against Polycrates occurred at roughly the same time as Cambyses' invasion of Egypt. The coincidence of timing may draw an implicit parallel between the Persian king and the most powerful Greek ruler at the time.

ἐπαναστάς: revolts are a recurring theme throughout Book III.

39.2: σχὼν δὲ ξεινίην . . . ἄλλα παρ' ἐκείνου: The formation of this connection closed Book II. *xenia* was a very important form of institutionalized friendship in the Greek world. On how *xenia* could be instrumental in securing military assistance, see Herman 2002: 97–105.

τὸν δὲ νεώτερον Συλοσῶντα: the son who will later be restored to power with Darius' support (see §§139–141 for Syloson, Darius and the cloak).

39.3: ἐν χρόνῳ δὲ ... τὴν ἄλλην Ἑλλάδα: χρόνῳ δὲ ὀλίγῳ αὐτίκα: a *tautology* emphasizing the rapid growth of Polycrates' power and his great success. βεβωμένα: 'loudly spoken of', from βοάω. The subject is τὰ πρήγματα, which puts the emphasis on what is being talked about, namely Polycrates' power. ὅκου γὰρ ἰθύσειε: the use of the indefinite construction stresses the apparently continuous nature of Polycrates' success.

39.4: τῷ γὰρ φίλῳ ... ἀρχὴν μηδὲ λαβών: 'for he said that he would receive greater benefit if he gave back to a friend what he had taken, than if he had taken it from the start'. ἀρχὴν: 'from the start', or 'in the first place'. Cf. §16.7. The adverbial use of ἀρχὴν is very common.

§§40–43 *are a flashback to when Amasis was on the throne with whom Polycrates had formed a tie of friendship. There is an irony in Amasis' advice concerning misfortune, given what has already befallen Egypt in the main narrative.*

40

40.1: πολλῷ δὲ ἔτι ... ἐπέστειλε ἐς Σάμον: lit. 'with still greater success by much having happened to him, having written the following into a letter he sent it to Samos.' The use of the genitive absolute puts the emphasis on εὐτυχίης and its extent, which, as we learn, is what worries Amasis (ἐπιμελές). πολλῷ stressed at the beginning of the sentence conveys the continued and increasing good fortune of Polycrates. βυβλίον: lit. 'little book' or 'strip of paper', so here 'note' or 'letter'.

40.2: ἄνδρα φίλον καὶ ξεῖνον: ALC note that this refers to a more personal diplomatic friendship rather than any kind of military alliance. See II.182.2 for the formation of this connection, described there as κατὰ ξεινίην.

τὸ θεῖον ... φθονερόν: the theme of divine envy lying behind the vicissitudes of human fortune is a recurring theme throughout the *Histories* (I.34.1, 86.6; II.120.5; IV.205). When discussing divine intervention in human affairs, Herodotus often refers to an unspecified divine higher power, τὸ θεῖον (or τὰ θεῖα; see also I.32.1, VII.16C.1-2, IX.100.2).

τὸ μέν τι εὐτυχέειν τῶν πρηγμάτων τὸ δὲ προσπταίειν: both τὸ μέν ... εὐτυχέειν and τὸ δὲ προσπταίειν go with τῶν πρηγμάτων. The enclosing word order emphasises Amasis' point that a mixture of success and failure is better than complete success.

40.3: πρόρριζος, εὐτυχέων: the jarring juxtaposition of 'in utter ruin' and 'successful' highlights the rather paradoxical link between great success and a miserable end, perhaps comparable to the English saying, 'the bigger they are, the harder they fall'.

40.4: φροντίσας τὸ ἄν ... τὴν ψυχὴν ἀλγήσεις: lit. 'having considered what you would find to be worth most which belongs to you and for the losing of which you will grieve most'. τὸ ἂν εὕρῃς indirect question in primary sequence ('consider what ...'). Notice how Herodotus switches to vivid construction for the second question with ἀλγήσεις in future indicative, perhaps emphasizing that it must be something that would truly upset Polycrates if he lost it. τὴν ψυχὴν ἀλγήσεις: lit. 'you will grieve in your soul', here translated with 'grieve deeply'.

οὕτω ὅκως μηκέτι ἥξει: result clause. Normally one would expect the infinitive for the intended or likely result, but the indicative is used here, stressing Amasis' urgency in telling Polycrates he must see to it that this comes about.

ἤν τε μὴ ... ἐμεῦ ὑποκειμένῳ ἀκέο: 'And conversely, if as a result of this your successes do not meet with sufferings, remedy the situation in the manner I set out.' The coniditonal clause is future open (ἤν = ἐαν), but the main clause contains an imperative.

41

41.1: ἦν οἱ σφρηγὶς ... τοῦ Τηλεκλέος Σαμίου: σφρηγὶς: the story of a lost and then found precious object, especially rings in fish, was a recurring feature of popular tales of many different cultures (see Introduction, pp. 13-4. A similar tale was related about Minos by Bacchylides in poem XVII. Note how Herodotus names the craftsman of the ring. Art and engineering works are often attributed in Herodotus. Theodorus is also mentioned at I.51.3. The ring was irreplaceable as its creator was dead by this period.

41.2: πάντων ὁρώντων τῶν συμπλόων: note how Polycrates is careful that the casting away of the ring be witnessed.

ῥίπτει: the vivid present creates a visual sense of immediacy as the sailors all watch Periander.

συμφορῇ ἐχρᾶτο: translate as 'mourned his loss' (lit. 'dealt with his misfortune').

42

42.1: ἔφη ἐθέλειν ἐλθεῖν ἐς: the *assonance* of ἐ and repeated aspirated consonants perhaps stress the fisherman's eagerness.

42.3: μέγα ποιεύμενος: lit. 'making a great thing' = 'being pleased/happy'.

ἐνεοῦσαν τὴν Πολυκράτεος σφρηγῖδα: Polycrates did not want the ring to be found. His name is emphatically placed between the ring and its agreeing participle to stress how he could not escape the fate he aimed to avoid.

42.4: ὡς δὲ εἶδόν ... ὅτεῳ τρόπῳ εὑρέθη: the reaction of the attendants who find the ring furthers the irony. ὡς δὲ εἶδόν τε καὶ ἔλαβον τάχιστα: they respond swiftly. κεχαρηκότες: Polycrates will not share in their rejoicing.

τὸν δὲ ὡς ... εἶναι τὸ πρῆγμα: τὸν = Polycrates. **θεῖον:** 'divinely sent'. This picks up on the fears Amasis expressed about the envious divine in his letter. Note that Wilson's text has ὁσία instead of οἷα. The current text keeps οἷα.

43

43.1: εἴη ἀνθρώπῳ ἄνθρωπον: the juxtaposition stresses the point. One man cannot protect another from whatever will happen to him.

ἐκ τοῦ μέλλοντος γίνεσθαι πρήγματος ... τελευτήσειν μέλλοι Πολυκράτης: the repetition of μέλλω reinforces the inevitability of the terrible end coming to Polycrates.

43.2: πέμψας δέ οἱ ... περὶ ξείνου ἀνδρός: Amasis' response seems odd in his decision to διαλύεσθαι ... τὴν ξεινίην (dissolve the friendship) to avoid personal grief. ALC note (*ad loc*) that he is an anti-heroic figure in Herodotus' portrayal, so this may be a further negative example of his behaviour. They also note that it could have been Polycrates who broke off the connection in the wake of the Persian invasion of Egypt, since this also seems to have coincided with Polycrates' alliance with Cambyses (§44.1-2).

44

44.1: ἐπὶ τοῦτον ... τὸν Πολυκράτεα: Herodotus resumes the narrative, explaining the Spartan expedition against Samos (begun at §39).

εὐτυχέοντα τὰ πάντα: 'fortunate in every way'. This echoes εὐτυχέων τὰ πάντα in Amasis' reaction (§43.2; see also εὐτυχέων, αἱ σαὶ μεγάλαι εὐτυχίαι, τὸ μέν τι εὐτυχέειν, εὐτυχέειν τὰ πάντα at §40 (Amasis' letter) stressing the impressively, but worryingly continuous fortunes of Polycrates).

ἐπικαλεσαμένων τῶν ... κτισάντων Σαμίων: the men who called in the Spartans. For their fate, see §§57-9.

πέμψας δὲ κήρυκα λάθρῃ ... Σάμον δέοιτο στρατοῦ: 'Polycrates, after secretly sending a herald to Cambyses son of Cyrus, who was gathering his army against Egypt, and asked him, after he (Cambyses) had sent to him at Samos, to request an army from him': Polycrates engineers a military arrangement with Cambyses to be rid of citizens that he suspects of fostering rebellion. λάθρῃ: ALC (*ad loc.*) note that such secrecy in diplomacy was 'normal' for tyrants.

44.2: ὁ δὲ ἐπιλέξας ... τούτους μὴ ἀποπέμπειν: Herodotus explains the grudge these men had against Polycrates. Because he is suspicious of them (ἀστῶν τοὺς ὑπώπτευε μάλιστα ἐς ἐπανάστασιν) he orders for them not to be sent back. ALC note that these may be a group who already had oligarchic and so pro-Spartan sympathies. Mitchell suggests that these men may also have had anti-tyranny and anti-Persian sympathies (1975: 75–9).

45

Herodotus reports three versions (οἱ μὲν δὴ λέγουσι ... οἱ δὲ λέγουσι [§45.1] ... εἰσὶ δὲ οἳ λέγουσι [§45.3] about the fate of the men sent away by Polycrates.

45.1: δοῦναι σφίσι λόγον: 'consulted with one another'.

45.2: ἐς μάχην κατέστη: 'engaged them in battle'.
δὲ ἐν αὐτῇ: resupply μάχη.

45.3: this is the third story surrounding what happened to the men – that they conquered Polycrates after leaving Egypt (τοὺς ἀπ᾽ Αἰγύπτου; see §44.2 for Polycrates' instructions to Cambyses not to send them back). Herodotus dismisses the story, but gives a clear argument for doing so.

εἰσὶ δὲ οἳ λέγουσι: 'There are those who say'. Herodotus draws attention to the third story variation by introducing with a different phrase.

ἐμοὶ δοκέειν οὐκ ὀρθῶς: cf. §2.2 'οὐκ ὀρθῶς λέγουσι' where Herodotus explains his reasons for refuting the Egyptian claim that Cambyses' was Apries' son.

οὐδὲν γὰρ ἔδει ... ἐπικαλέεσθαι: one might have expected a past closed conditional here, but Herodotus emphasizes the impossibility of the notion by saying, 'it was in no way necessary'.

οὐδὲ λόγος αἱρέει: lit. 'The story does not even persuade ..', so 'is not even convincing'. See also I.132.3 and VII.41.1 for this expression.

τῷ ἐπίκουροί τε μισθωτοὶ καὶ τοξόται οἰκήιοι ... πλήθεϊ πολλοί: τῷ and οἰκήιοι ('to whom/him' and 'his own') stress that Polycrates possessed his own manpower. Further emphasis is added by the *pleonasm* 'πλήθεϊ πολλοί – many in number'. The *tricolon* of troop types also lends support to Herodotus' claim about the implausibility of the expelled Samians defeating Polycrates by themselves.

45.4: ἐς τοὺς νεωσοίκους ... ὑποπρῆσαι αὐτοῖσι τοῖσι νεωσοίκοισι: Polycrates appears calculating and ruthless. Herodotus also seems to be making the point that it is unlikely any of the citizens would have joined the 'returning men' (τοὺς κατιόντας), therefore, making the alleged lone attempt on Samos seem even more implausible.

46

46.1: ἔλεγον πολλὰ οἷα κάρτα δεόμενοι: lit. 'they spoke at length such things as they were especially needing', so 'they spoke at length about their great need'.

46.2: Herodotus portrays the Spartans as men of very few words not impressed by long pleas for help, hence the modern 'laconic'. Even when the Samians give a visual representation of their request with a far shorter explanation, they are told that 'τῷ θυλάκῳ περιεργάσθαι' ('the sack was excessive'). Spartan distaste for wordy speeches was a very common stereotype of the fifth century. Thucydides remarks that Spartan general Brasidas was a skilled speaker 'for a Spartan' (IV.84.2). Another feature commonly associated with Sparta was physical endurance and strength (see Xenophon, *Anabasis*, IV.8.26).

47

47.1: εὐεργεσίας ἐκτίνοντες: 'in return for a benefaction'. εὐεργεσία was an important institution by which ties of obligation might be formed between peoples. The Samians seem to have assisted the Spartans in their wars against the Messenians, possibly those of the seventh century (see Figure 3).

ὡς μὲν Σάμιοι λέγουσι ... ὡς δὲ Λακεδαιμόνιοι λέγουσι ...: Herodotus draws attention to the two variant versions. The 'Samian' account suggests that Herodotus had a Samian source, which, he explains at §55, was a man named Archias whom he met at Pitane.

οὐκ οὕτω τιμώρησαι ... τίσασθαι: the Spartan version concerns the theft of a mixing bowl which they were taking to Croesus, and a breastplate sent to them as a gift by Amasis. H&W note (*ad loc.*) that Amasis may have been trying to entice the Spartans to an anti-Persian alliance or league.

47.2: ἐληίσαντο τῷ προτέρῳ ἔτεϊ ἢ τὸν κρητῆρα: the Samians are alleged to have stolen the breastplate a year before the bowl.

47.2-3: ἐόντα μὲν λίνεον ... πάσας φανεράς: Herodotus describes the elaborate decoration of the breastplate. ἐνυφασμένων τῶν: 'woven into'. **δὲ εἵνεκα θωμάσαι ἄξιον:** Herodotus seems to consider works of art of exceptional artistry and remarkable works of engineering to be part of the 'deeds' he promises to record in his preface. ἀρπεδόνας ἐν ἑωυτῇ τριηκοσίας καὶ ἑξήκοντα: the word order perhaps mimics the interweaving of the finer three hundred and sixty threads into each larger thread. πάσας φανεράς: 'each one visible'.

47.3: τοιοῦτος ἕτερος ... τῇ Ἀθηναίῃ Ἄμασις: the breastplate was one of a pair (see also II.182.1-2). Amasis had dedicated (ἀνέθηκε) the other to Athena at Lindus, one of Rhodes' three most important cities. The dedication is recorded in the Lindian chronicle, an inscription purporting to record dedications made at the temple before its destruction in 390. There is a debate among scholars about whether it represented a genuine temple record, a historical account, or lay somewhere between the two. It certainly reflects the genuine importance of this cult of Athena and not just for Rhodians (see Higbie 2003: 1-15).

§§48-53: *ALC note the 'novelistic' and 'anecdotal' nature of the stories in these sections, building up to Periander as a typically 'tragic' figure, whose world falls apart. The tyrant is portrayed favourably in Book I*

(I.20, 23-4), but here his actions set off the chain of events that leads to the disintegration of his household.

48

48.1: συνεπελάβοντο: lit. 'joined in taking part in'. The introduction of Samos into the narrative provides the opportunity to introduce the Spartans, Corinthians, and also the Corcyreans into the narrative. The unfortunate tale of Periander, tyrant of Corinth, and his younger son occupies the narrative in §49-53.

ὥστε γενέσθαι: lit. 'so that it took place/happened'.

καὶ Κορίνθιοι προθύμως: the new players are delayed to the end of the clause with extra emphasis on προθύμως, drawing attention to their enthusiastic participation in the expedition.

ὕβρισμα: the emphatic placement suggests that the fault lies with the Samians.

γενεῇ πρότερον τοῦ στρατεύματος v = ... τῇ ἁρπάγῃ γεγονός: '[which] occurred in the generation before this expedition, and about the same time as the theft of the bowl'. This seems to place the occurrence in the first third of the period 625-525. On the difficulties in the dating of this episode, see ALC *ad loc.*

48.2: Κερκυραίων γὰρ παῖδας ... ἱροῦ ἅψασθαι Ἀρτέμιδος: the Samians interfere in the conveyance of Corcyrean boys being sent by Periander to Alyattes (king of Lydia 635-585).

ἐπ' ἐκτομῇ: 'to be cut', i.e., made eunuchs.

τὸν λόγον, ἐπ' οἷσι: 'the reason, for which purposes', so 'the reason why'.

ἱροῦ ἅψασθαι Ἀρτέμιδος: the supplicant posture. A supplicant who clasped an altar and pleaded for sanctuary was considered sacrosanct and to disrespect this by their removal was considered shameful.

48.3: μετὰ δὲ οὐ ... χρέωνται κατὰ ταὐτά: ἐποιήσαντο οἱ Σάμιοι ὁρτήν: it was considered an outrage to invade a city celebrating a festival. τῇ καὶ νῦν ἔτι χρέωνται κατὰ ταὐτά: Herodotus is clear that the festival was a ruse to prevent the boys being snatched from the altar.

νόμον: here the sense is 'custom' or 'customary practice'.

ἁρπάζοντες: on ritual food thefts, see Xenophon, *Lacedaemonion Politeia* 2.9 for the practice at the sanctuary of Artemis Orthia. See also Calame 2001: 156–69.

48.4: ἐς τοῦτο δὲ τόδε ... ἐς ὅ: lit. '[this went on] until the precise moment when...', so 'this went on until'.

49

49.1: ταύτης εἵνεκεν τῆς αἰτίης: Herodotus says that had the Corinthians and Corcyreans been on better terms when Periander had died, the Corinthians would not have taken part, because the Corcyreans, out of gratitude to the Samians, would have persuaded the Corinthians, whose colonists they were, against taking part.

νῦν δὲ αἰεὶ ... διάφοροι, ἐόντες ἑωυτοῖσι: despite Corcyra being colonized by the Corinthians, relations between the two were always uneasy. The hostility between the two was instrumental in the early stages of the Peloponnesian War. Between 435 and 431, hostilities flared afresh. Feeling the pressure of Corinth's military response, the Corcyreans sought help from Athens (see Thucydides I.27-40).

49.2: τούτων ὦν εἵνεκεν: Herodotus emphasizes the account he has just given about Samian actions as the cause of Corinthian hostilities towards them.

πρότεροι γὰρ οἱ Κερκυραῖοι: 'For the Corcyreans first of all.' Herodotus moves again back in time from the main narrative to explain Samian hostility towards the Corcyreans.

50

50.1: ἐπείτε γὰρ: the digression about Periander and his family begins. Speeches are a recurring feature of the section, like the dramatic monologues of Greek tragedy, and there is a heavy moralizing tone.

τὴν ἑωυτοῦ γυναῖκα Μέλισσαν ... ἀπέκτεινε: Diogenes Laertius (I.94) records a version that says Periander kicked her to death while pregnant, as in the case of the second version of Cambyses' murder of his wife/sister (§32.4). See ALC (*ad loc.*) for more on this episode.

πρὸς τῇ γεγονυίῃ: 'in addition to the one that had already occurred.'

50.2: τούτους ὁ μητροπάτωρ ... εἶπε προπέμπων αὐτούς: ὁ μητροπάτωρ Προκλέης: the father of Melissa, the wife Periander murdered. What he goes on to say §50.3 will irremediably sour relations between Periander and his younger son.

ἐπείτε δὲ ... ἀπεπέμπετο, εἶπε προπέμπων αὐτούς: lit. 'when he was sending them away, before sending them away, he said...', or 'when he was about to send them away...'.

50.3: ὁ μὲν πρεσβύτερος: we learn at §53.1 that Periander considered his elder son to be rather 'dim-witted' νωθέστερος, and he thus pinned his succession hopes on younger son, Lycophron.

τοῦτο τὸ ἔπος ... ἐν οὐδενὶ λόγῳ ἐποιήσατο: lit. 'this speech, [the elder of the sons] held in no account', so 'to this utterance the elder of them gave no attention.'

τὸν πατέρα οὔτε ... λόγον οὐδένα ἐδίδου: a *tricolon*. The boy would neither address his father, talk with him, nor respond to him when questioned.

μιν περιθύμως ἔχων ... ἐξελαύνει ἐκ τῶν οἰκίων: vivid present. Anger and rash actions are a clear theme of the book (see §32 for Cambyses' murder of his sister/wife). Gould (1988: 52) notes that the 'story is one of non-communication'.

51

51.1: ἱστόρεε τὸν πρεσβύτερον: see §50.3, where Herodotus describes the older son as paying little attention to what his grandfather said.

σφεας φιλοφρόνως ἐδέξατο: the phrase contrasts with Periander's angry exiling of his younger son.

ἐκείνου δὲ τοῦ ... εἶπε καὶ τοῦτο: the scene here resembles a dramatic dialogue, although in indirect speech. Periander questions his son, who replies he cannot remember. Periander persists, and the boy remembers. ἐκείνου δὲ τοῦ ... οὐκ ἐμέμνητο: 'but what Procles said to them as he was sending them off he did not recall, because he had not taken it in/paid attention to it'.

οὐδεμίαν μηχανὴν ... ἐκεῖνον ὑποθέσθαι τι: '[he said] that there was no way that man did not make some suggestion to them'. The *litotes* emphasizes Periander's suspicion that Procles must have said something. οὐδεμίαν μηχανὴν: to be translated here with the adverbial sense 'in no way', 'by no means'.

ἐλιπάρεε ... ἱστορέων: the continuous imperfect stresses Periander's persistent questioning of his son.

51.2: νόῳ λαβών: echo of οὐ νόῳ λαβών in §51.1 which perhaps contrasts Periander's swift grasp of the meaning of Procles' utterance, compared to his dim elder son, who did not take on board its significance.

μαλακὸν ... οὐδέν: the *hyperbaton* stresses Periander's determination to maintain a strong appearance. Compare the silent treatment he continues to give his younger son versus the incessant badgering of the elder son.

τῇ: in the place where.

ἐς τούτους: 'to those [people]', i.e., those who had taken in Periander's son.

51.2-3: ὁ δὲ ὅκως ... ἔλθοι ἐς ἄλλην οἰκίην, ἀπηλαύνετ' ἄν: the indefinite stresses the son's relentless pattern of acceptance, expulsion, wandering.

ἐξελασθεὶς ... μὴ ... δέκεσθαι, ἀπελαυνόμενος ... ἀπηλαύνετ ... τοῖσι δεξαμένοισι, ἀπελαυνόμενος ... ἐδέκοντο: the ongoing rejection and acceptance that the younger son is forced to endure is stressed by the repetition and *polyptoton* of compounds of ἐλαυνω and parts of δέχομαι (δέκομαι).

52

52.1: τέλος δὲ ὁ... ὅσην δὴ εἴπας: indirect statement follows κήρυγμα ἐποιήσατο, hence the infinitive ὀφείλειν. ὅς ἄν ἦ... μιν ἢ προσδιαλεχθῇ is an indefinite clause following primary sequence, despite being in historic sequence. This is for vividness. ὅσην δὴ εἴπας: lit. 'having stated however much (this would be) i.e., the fine. Newmyer notes that the indefinite use of ὅσην δὴ is common in Herodotus. Did Herodotus not know the amount? Or is he putting the emphasis less on the fine than on Periander's extreme forced isolation of his son?

52.3: ἀλουσίῃσί τε καὶ ἀσιτίῃσι συμπεπτωκότα: lit. 'having fallen in with a lack of washing and lack of food.'

52.4-5: *Periander finally addresses his son.*
Κορίνθου τῆς εὐδαίμονος: Corinth was traditionally depicted as a wealthy city (see Salmon 1984).

A tricky section. Periander gives his son a choice. Carry on as he is, or inherit his father's power:

(1) **ταῦτα** <u>τὰ νυν ἔχων</u> **πρήσσεις**
lit. 'you carry on those things which you now have'
'You go carry on just as you are now/in your current state'

(2) **τὴν τυραννίδα καὶ τὰ ἀγαθὰ** <u>τὰ νῦν ἐγὼ ἔχω</u>, **ταῦτα** ... παραλαμβάνειν
lit. the tyranny and the good things which I now have, these things ... you take over 'that you take over the power and the good things which I now have'

The relative clauses are underlined, and the antecedents are highlighted in bold.
ἀντιστατέων τε καὶ ... σε ἥκιστα ἐχρῆν: lit. 'by being hostile to and using anger against whom you should least do so'.

52.5: φθονέεσθαι κρέσσον ἐστὶ ἢ οἰκτείρεσθαι: 'it is better to be envied than to be pitied'. The phrase recalls §52.3, where Periander is described as pitying his son in his current state. This was a familiar maxim of Greek fifth century thought, cf. Pindar, *Pythian* I.85 (κρέσσων οἰκτιρμοῦ φθόνος – 'envy is better than pity'). The envy men are wont to feel towards powerful rulers is a recurring theme of Xenophon's *Hiero* (1.9; 6.12; 11.6).

ἅμα τε ὁκοῖόν ... τοὺς κρέσσονας τεθυμῶσθαι: 'and at the same time [having learnt] what it is like to have been angry at your parents and your superiors'.

52.6: μιν ἱρὴν ζημίην ὀφείλειν τῷ θεῷ: the tragic irony of the boy's response quickly renders Periander's attempt to win him over as futile. The boy says Periander has violated his own proclamation and must now pay the fine (see §52.1 for the fine).

ἐς Κέρκυραν: Periander sends his son away to Corcyra. This anticipates their killing of the young man to avoid Periander coming to them (§53.7).

52.7: ἐστρατεύετο ἐπὶ τὸν πενθερὸν ... ἐόντα αἰτιώτατον: Periander takes revenge against Procles.

εἷλε μὲν τὴν Ἐπίδαυρον, εἷλε δὲ αὐτὸν: the clipped repetition highlights Periander's success.

53

53.1: προβαίνοντος ... Περίανδρος παρηβήκεε: the alliteration of π draws attention to Periander's advancing age and concern for his ability to govern.

οὔκων ἐνώρα: 'he certainly did not see anything.'

53.2: νεηνίεω = νεανίου

53.3: ALC note that 'the abundance of moral maxims, especially in the speech of Periander's daughter, re-creates well the flavour of archaic wisdom.' Sisters as intermediaries is a familiar motif of Greek tragedies, for example, Ismene in Sophocles' *Antigone* 531-70. On women in Herodotus more generally, see Dewald (1980: 11–18); Roberts (2011: 65–75).

Ὦ παῖ: this suggests that the sister was older. Periander was the father of both (ἑωυτοῦ δὲ θυγατέρα).

53.4: ἡ φιλοτιμίη: 'pride.'

μὴ τῷ κακῷ τὸ κακὸν ἰῶ: 'Do not cure an evil with an evil.' This is not so far from 'two wrongs don't make a right', and similar expressions can be found elsewhere. In Sophocles' *Ajax*, the Chorus caution the inconsolable, vengeful Ajax thus (362-3): 'μὴ κακὸν κακῷ διδοὺς ἄκος, πλέον τὸ πῆμα τῆς ἄτης τίθει' – 'Do not apply a wicked act as a cure for a wicket act. Do not make the pain of your mad ruin any greater.'

τυραννὶς . . . σφαλερόν: the vulnerability entailed by holding power was a recurring theme in fifth-century literature. The successful and powerful often emerge as the most vulnerable to plots, slanders and envy.

53.5: τὰ ἐπαγωγότατα: one cannot be certain whether this is Herodotus' opinion of the proposals, or how Periander wished them to be seen.

πυνθάνηται περιεόντα τὸν πατέρα: the alliteration may suggest the boy's enduring bitterness towards his father.

53.7: ἵνα μή σφι . . . τὴν χώρην ἀπίκηται: Herodotus hints once again at the poor relations between colony and mother city, and suggests that Periander was in part responsible for these sour relations, since the Corcyreans were anxious to prevent his arrival. Their aggressive response resulted in far worse.

ἐς τὴν χώρην ἀπίκηται, κτείνουσι τὸν νεηνίσκον: the *chiasmus* stresses the causal connection between Periander's impending arrival and the murder of Lycophron. 'The young man' is emphasized at the end of the sentence, evoking pity for the boy who had finally agreed to come home.

ἀντὶ τούτων . . . Κερκυραίους ἐτιμωρέετο: Herodotus brings the narrative back to §49, where he began the Corinthian digression, which aimed to explain why Corinth was seeking revenge against Corcyra.

54

54.1: Λακεδαιμόνιοι δὲ ... ἐπολιόρκεον Σάμον: Herodotus now resumes his narrative of Samian affairs.

προσβαλόντες δὲ πρὸς τὸ τεῖχος τοῦ μὲν πρὸς θαλάσσῃ ἑστεῶτος πύργου κατὰ τὸ προάστειον τῆς πόλιος ἐπέβησαν: note the heavy *alliteration* of π and τ. It is worth remembering that it is highly likely that Herodotus delivered his work as lectures of public readings. The sound created in this passage would have drawn attention to it and added a sense of building drama as the Spartans invade and mount the tower.

54.2: κατὰ δὲ τὸν ... αὐτῶν Σαμίων συχνοί: the mention of the location to which the troops swarmed, leaving the subject to the end of the clause, creates a vivid picture of the battle converging on the tower. **οἵ τε ἐπίκουροι καὶ αὐτῶν Σαμίων συχνοί:** stresses how many came out against the Spartans.

δεξάμενοι δὲ τοὺς Λακεδαιμονίους: 'having withstood the Spartans'.

οἱ δὲ ἐπισπόμενοι: the Spartans are the subject as shown by 'δὲ.' The Spartans pursue the fleeing Samians.

55

55.1: εἰ μέν νυν ... αἱρεθῇ ἂν Σάμος: Herodotus emphasises how close Samos came to being taken, using a past closed conditional and delaying 'Samos' until the end. Is Herodotus implying that the Spartans had lost their edge? Certainly, just two aggressively pursuing the runaways does not fit with the relentless determination that so often characterizes portrayals of the Spartans. **ὅμοιοι:** ALC suggest (*ad loc.*) that this may be a pun on the ὅμοιοι at Sparta, who were an elite group of full citizen Spartiates.

55.2: τρίτῳ δὲ ἀπ' ... γὰρ τούτου ἦν: a tricky sentence to render in English without it sounding confusing. τρίτῳ δὲ ἀπ' Ἀρχίεω τούτου γεγονότι ἄλλῳ Ἀρχίῃ: lit. 'another Archias born in the third generation from this Archias', i.e. grandson of the Archias who fought at Samos. The family tree is as follows:

Archias the Spartan who went in pursuit.
↓
Samius, his son.
↓
Archias, Herodotus' informant, son of Samius, and grandson of the first Archias.

Herodotus claims to have an account from personal enquiry (see H&W, *ad loc.*).

ταφῆναί ... δημοσίῃ: if true, public burial by Samians was a great honour indeed. Archias had become ἐθελοπρόξενος of Samos at Sparta. An ἐθελοπρόξενος was effectively a 'goodwill ambassador' (literally meaning, 'voluntary ambassador'). Cimon, the Athenian, acted as *proxenus* of Sparta at Athens. An ἐθελοπρόξενος or πρόξενος would generally advocate a policy that promoted good relations between his own city and the city on whose behalf he was acting. On this institution, see Mack (2015: 90–232. On the importance of the post of *proxenus* and the relationship between Samos and Sparta, see Jeffery and Cartledge (1982: 250–1, 259). They also note that the office was generally hereditary and so it is likely the first Archias' descendants continued in this role.

56

56.1: ἀπαλλάσσοντο ἐς Πελοπόννησον: the Spartans fail to take Samos and leave.

56.2: ὁ ματαιότερος λόγος: Herodotus does not always give his opinion of an alternative account, but here he brands it 'more foolish' or 'rather foolish'. The story goes that Polycrates bought off the Spartans with a fake currency, although it fits with the Spartan stereotype of their being unaccustomed to money and unfamiliar with the more widely circulating coinages of Greece.

ἐς τὴν Ἀσίην: it is interesting that Herodotus places Samos in Asia, not Greece, yet he counts Polycrates as a Greek tyrant. Samos is certainly closer to Asia Minor (see Figures 1 and 2). This shows that ethnic and geographical definitions and boundaries in Herodotus are not always equivocal. On the role of language as a mark of ethnicity in Herodotus, see Figueira 2020: 1–13, 43–71; on ethnographies in Herodotus, see D&M: 33–84).

§§57–8 *contain the account of the conduct of the Samian troops sent away by Polycrates upon their arrival at Siphnus, which fulfils a prophecy that the Siphnians failed to understand. The story began at §§45–6.*

57

57.1: ALC work out that the year reached is *c.* 518 (see *ad loc.* for their calculation).

Σίφνον: an Ionian island, which is part of the Cyclades.

57.2: χρημάτων γὰρ ἐδέοντο … χρήματα διενέμοντο: Herodotus describes the wealth of Siphnus, which he implies the exiles were well aware of. **οὕτως ὥστε:** the result clause stresses Herodotus' point that the Siphnians were so wealthy that their deposits in their treasury at Delphi were a mere tenth of their wealth. Many Greek cities possessed treasuries at Delphi. The frieze from the Siphnian treasury now resides in the Delphi Archaeological Museum.

57.3: ἐχρέωντο τῷ χρηστηρίῳ: 'they consulted the oracle.'

εἰ αὐτοῖσι τὰ παρεόντα … πολλὸν χρόνον παραμένειν: as we learn in §57.4, Siphnus' wealth was conspicuous in its public buildings, which H&W suggest could have made them an obvious target for raiders.

57.4: ἀλλ' ὅταν ἐν Σίφνῳ ... κήρυκά τ' ἐρυθρόν: cryptic oracles which baffle and ultimately trip up the enquirer are a recurring theme in Herodotus. Cf. Croesus (I.53.3), although one could argue his arrogant assumption that he would win blinded his interpretative powers.

ἦν τότε ἡ ἀγορὴ ... Παρίῳ λίθῳ ἠσκημένα: Herodotus explains part of the riddle. The 'turning white' refers to the colour of the Parian marble (known for its whiteness) that adorned the Siphnian public spaces.

58

58.1: τοῦτον τὸν χρησμὸν: the emphatic placement at the start of the sentence points to the oracle's significance.

οὔτε τότε εὐθὺς οὔτε τῶν Σαμίων ἀπιγμένων: Herodotus stresses how completely the Siphnians failed to understand the oracle.

58.2: μιλτηλιφέες: the truth of the oracle becomes apparent. H&W note that painting ships red began with Euxine trade.

58.4: πυθόμενοι δὲ εὐθὺς ... ἐσσώθησαν: the Siphnians grasp the oracle just a little too late as the exiles begin laying waste their land.

ἑκατὸν τάλαντα ἔπρηξαν: 100 talents would equate to over $1,000,000 in modern money, roughly £850,000, or a little less.

59

59.3: ἕκτῳ δὲ ἔτεϊ Αἰγινῆται ... ἠνδραποδίσαντο μετὰ Κρητῶν: the exiles' conduct brought them into conflict with the Aeginetans. Their 'purchase' of Hydrea and settlement at Cydonia on Crete would likely have been regarded by the Aeginetans as an encroachment into their sphere of influence. For more on Zacynthus, Hermione and Didyma, see the online Glossary of Peoples and Places.

59.4: ταῦτα δὲ ἐποίησαν ... ἡ μὲν αἰτίη αὕτη: historic grudges and human nature are the most common causative factor in Herodotus.

Indeed, the entire work opens with kidnappings and the blame game. Here, the Aeginetans, raw after their treatment at the hands of earlier Samian king Amphicrates, wreak their resentment on the exiles. ἔγκοτον ἔχοντες: 'bore spiteful feelings.' The *assonance* draws attention to the phrase.

60

60.1: ἐμήκυνα ... περὶ Σαμίων μᾶλλον: Herodotus explains his reasons for including the Samians. Their engineering achievements make them a worthy part of his record of the 'great and wondrous deeds' of men (I.*Pref*). It also forms part of his praise of Polycrates and his magnificence (see §125.2). For an excellent exploration of the importance of Samos in Herodotus' work, see Irwin (2009: 395–416) and see also Pelling (2011: 1–18).

ἐς πεντήκοντα καὶ ἑκατὸν ὀργυιάς: accusative of extent of space. The ancient Greek ὀργυιά equates to roughly six feet.

ὄρεός τε ὑψηλοῦ ... κάτωθεν ἀρξάμενον ἀμφίστομον: lit. a double-mouthed channel of this high mountain starting from below for one hundred and fifty *orugias* (nine hundred feet).

60.3: Μεγαρεὺς Εὐπαλῖνος Ναυστρόφου: just as with Polycrates' precious ring, Herodotus duly credits the architect of the tunnel, and also of the great temple at 60.4: Ῥοῖκος Φιλέω: Rhoecus son of Phileus.

60.4: τρίτον δέ σφι ... νηὸς μέγιστος πάντων νηῶν τῶν ἡμεῖς ἴδμεν: this splendid temple is probably the Heraeum mentioned at §125.1.

μᾶλλόν ... περὶ Σαμίων ἐμήκυνα: Herodotus ends this section with a pleasing ring composition, stating why he included the Samians.

§§61–88 resume the Persian narrative from the rebellion of the Magi to the accession of Darius. See H&W ad loc. and Appendix V for a detailed discussion of the issues with Herodotus' account. For Herodotus' account of these events and the Behistun inscription, see Introduction, p. 25.

61

61.1: Καμβύσῃ δὲ ... χρονίζοντι περὶ Αἴγυπτον ... παραφρονήσαντι: Herodotus moves back to Persian affairs with a chronological marker. We are also reminded of Cambyses' state of mind. Καμβύσῃ is dative because of ἐπανιστέαται (third person plural).

Μάγοι δύο ἀδελφεοί: the Behistun inscription mentions only one conspirator. However, the account does not preclude him having fellow conspirators and the following quotation from the inscription suggests that the Magus was indeed masquerading as Smerdis, Cambyses' brother (Smerdis may be a corruption of the name Bardiya given on the inscription): 'he lied to the people thus: 'I am Bardiya the son of Cyrus, the brother of Cambyses'' (*Column I*, §11: translation, Brosius 2021: 51).

μαθών τε τὸν ... ὡς κρύπτοιτο γενόμενος: lit. 'having learnt [about] the death of Smerdis, how it had been concealed'.

εἰδείησαν: 'believed' is the sense here. In a sense they 'knew' he was alive, as they had no reason to think otherwise.

61.2: οἰκὼς μάλιστα τὸ εἶδος ... ὅμοιος εἶδος: Herodotus repeats how like Cambyses' brother Smerdis the Magus was.

καὶ δὴ καὶ ... τὠυτὸ εἶχε Σμέρδιν: Herodotus stresses how the brother and would-be usurper even shared the same name. This surely recalls §30.2, where Cambyses dreamed about 'Smerdis' sitting on his throne and anticipates his realization that he had his brother murdered for no reason.

τὸν ὁ Καμβύσης ... ἀδελφεὸν ἀπέκτεινε: lit. 'whom Cambyses killed who was his own brother.' ἐόντα ἑωυτοῦ ἀδελφεὸν: compare Herodotus' phraseology at §53.2, 'ἑωυτοῦ δὲ θυγατέρα' (Periander's daughter and Lycophron's sister).

62

62.1: οἵ: connecting relative tying the ἄλλοι κήρυκες back to the κήρυκας of §61.3.

τῆς Συρίης ἐν Ἀγβατάνοισι: there is no Ecbatana in Syria according to H&W.

ἐς μέσον: lit. 'into the middle', 'into their midst', so 'openly', or 'in public'.

62.2: ἐλπίσας μιν λέγειν ἀληθέα: 'assuming/expecting that he [the herald] spoke the truth.'

αὐτός τε προδεδόσθαι ἐκ Πρηξάσπεος: further evidence of Cambyses' paranoia. He assumes he has been betrayed by Prexaspes.

γὰρ: 'since.'

Πρήξασπες . . . διεπρήξαο . . . πρῆγμα: the *alliteration* and *assonance* of η reinforces the play on the similarity between the words.

πρῆγμα: a euphemistic reference to the murder of Smerdis carried out by Prexaspes.

62.3: ἐκείνου τοῦ ἀνδρὸς: referring to Smerdis, Cambyses' brother.

χερσὶ τῇσι ἐμεωυτοῦ: emphatically placed. Prexaspes stresses that he did as Cambyses asked.

62.4: Ἀστυάγεα τὸν Μῆδον: Astyages was Cambyses' maternal great-grandfather who was deposed by Cyrus in 550.

νῦν ὦν μοι . . . Σμέρδιος βασιλέος ἀκούειν: Prexaspes advises a sensible course of action, perhaps intended to contrast with the paranoid Cambyses. ἐξετάζειν εἰρωτεῦντας: 'to thoroughly examine [him] by questioning'. Both words are not really needed, but the use of both emphasizes Prexaspes recommendation. Σμέρδιος βασιλέος ἀκούειν: lit. 'to listen to Smerdis as king'. The sense is 'to obey Smerdis as king'.

63

63.1: χαίρων: 'rejoicing' = 'unpunished,' the idea being that if you go away happy or in a good mood, you must have escaped punishment. Cf. §36.4 (οὔτι χαίρων).

63.2: τὸν ταῦτα ἐπιθέμενον εἶπαι πρὸς ὑμέας: 'that [Smerdis son of Cyrus] set down these orders and to relay them to you.'

64

64.1: ἡ ἀληθείη τῶν τε λόγων καὶ τοῦ ἐνυπνίου: *hendiadys*. 'The truth of the words and of the dream', so 'the truth of the words in the dream' (see §30.2). The *hendiadys* stresses the dawning of the message's truth on Cambyses, as does the emphatic word order of ἔτυψε and ἡ ἀληθείη. Truth, deception and lying are clear themes of Book III (§§17.2, 21.2, 35.1-2, 62.2-3, 63.1, 72.4-5, 75.2, 157.1). Interestingly, compare I.138, where Herodotus declares that Persians are taught not to lie or speak of things deemed unlawful. Deceit, however, is rife in Book III, for example, Cambyses' intrigues and secondly, his and Darius' declarations that deceit and cunning are permissible if justice is the end (§§65.6, 72.4-5). Is this an inconsistency, or rather a sign of a people in trouble with customs breaking down?

64.3: τοῦ κολεοῦ τοῦ ξίφεος ὁ μύκης: the curved Persian scimitar.

τρωματισθεὶς δὲ... καιρίῃ ἔδοξε τετύφθαι: Cambyses' act of sacrilege (§29.1) comes back to haunt him. κατὰ τοῦτο τῇ: emphasises how he ironically accidentally wounds himself, exactly where he deliberately struck the divine Apis calf. καιρίῃ: 'with a fatal wound'. This suggests Cambyses sees some sort of divine retributive act or fate in his injury.

64.4: ἐν τοῖσι ἐν Συρίῃ Ἀγβατάνοισι: lit. 'but the oracle in fact meant in Ecbatana in Syria', i.e., that 'he would die' there.

ἐκ Βουτοῦς πόλιος: a city in the Egyptian delta. The oracle located here was, according to Herodotus, considered to be Αἰγυπτίοισι ἐστὶ μαντήιον ἀψευδέστατον ('the most unerring among the Egyptians' II.152.3).

ἄρα: 'in fact'. ἄρα often stresses a fact that is true, but which has only just been realised. Here, Cambyses realizes he had been mistaken about which Ecbatana the oracle meant.

64.5: ὑπὸ τῆς συμφορῆς ... καὶ τοῦ τρώματος: a *hendiadys*. 'as a result of the misfortune and the wound', 'the unfortunate wound'.

ἐσωφρόνησε: recovery of one's senses or enlightenment at the point of death is a theme in Herodotus (cf. the late grasp of the Siphnians, §58.4). Cambyses is struck by the full truth of the prophecy, Croesus, although saved, understood the wisdom of Solon only when facing death (I.86.3).

65

65.1: τότε μὲν τοσαῦτα: lit. 'this much [he said] at that point'. A short emphatic phrase.

ἡμέρῃσι δὲ ὕστερον ὡς εἴκοσι: a 'stock' number. This number also reappears in Zopyrus' plan for taking Babylon §155.6.

καταλελάβηκέ με ... ἐς ὑμέας ἐκφῆναι: 'it has befallen me ... to show to you.' καταλελάβηκέ is used impersonally. τὸ ... τοῦτο: correlatives. 'something which ... this ...' ἔκρυπτον: 'I was trying to conceal.' The imperfect can have the sense of 'trying to'. Newmyer (*ad loc.*) calls it the conative imperfect.

65.2: μηδαμὰ ὤφελον ἰδεῖν: '[which] I wish I had never seen.'

Σμέρδις ἱζόμενος ἐς τὸν βασιλήιον θρόνον ψαύσειε τῇ κεφαλῇ τοῦ οὐρανοῦ: cf. the working at §30.2 and §64.2

65.3: ἀπαιρεθέω τὴν ἀρχὴν: 'I might be robbed of my kingdom.'

ταχύτερα ἢ σοφώτερα: 'with more haste than wisdom.' Cambyses has become wise after the fact.

ἐν τῇ γὰρ ... μέλλον γίνεσθαι ἀποτράπειν: 'For it is not in human nature to be able to turn away what is going to happen.' ἀποτράπειν is a gnomic aorist. The imperfect ἐνῆν functions like a gnomic aorist here. Cf. Amasis' realization upon reading Polycrates' letter about the recovery of his ring (§43.1).

μάταιος Πρηξάσπεα ἀποπέμπω: lit. 'I send Prexaspes in vain'. The striking historic present ἀποπέμπω gives a vivid and shocking air to Cambyses' rueful admission that he had his brother killed in vain.

ἐπιλεξάμενος μή: 'reckoning that'. The phrase takes a fearing clause as fear and anticipation are strongly implied in the verb.

65.4: οὐδὲν δέον: accusative absolute, 'when there was no need'.

τῆς βασιληίης οὐδὲν ἧσσον ἐστέρημαι: Cambyses emphasizes his agency not only in Smerdis' murder, but also in the loss of his power for failing to read the vision correctly.

65.5: οἱ δὲ ὑμῖν . . . κρατέουσι τῶν βασιληίων: 'the Magi rule as your masters over my kingdom'. ὑμῖν is possessive dative. One could also translate: 'The Magi are your masters and rule over my kingdom.'

τὸν μέν νυν . . . πεπονθότος τιμωρέειν ἐμοί: a tricky phrase. χρῆν is imperfect (augment omitted) expressing an unfulfilled obligation. ἐμεῦ αἰσχρὰ . . . πεπονθότος τιμωρέειν ἐμοί: 'to take revenge for me for my having suffered disgraceful things'.

65.5-6: τὸν μέν νυν . . . οὗτος μὲν . . . τούτου δὲ μηκέτι: Smerdis, Cambyses' brother. The construction stresses the contrast between what his brother should be doing, but cannot do because he killed him.

65.6: δεύτερα τῶν λοιπῶν: lit. 'the second things of those that remain, so 'in second place out of those who remain'.

θεοὺς τοὺς βασιληίους ἐπικαλέων: Cambyses' plea takes on the tone of a prayer and divine command. The royal Persian deities included Ahuramazda, with Mithra and Anakita as the next most important (Llewellyn-Jones 2022: 217, 91–93 on the gods and royal ideology in the Susa inscription; also Waters 2022: 152–6).

μὴ περιιδεῖν . . . περιελθοῦσαν: 'not to allow [the leadership] to pass'.

εἴτε δόλῳ . . . εἴτε . . . σθένεϊ τέῳ: 'either by trickery . . . or by your strength'.

65.7: ἐκφέροι . . . τίκτοιεν: optatives expressing a wish.

ἀρῶμαι ὑμῖν γενέσθαι: 'I pray that [the opposite] comes to you.' Cambyses calls down a curse upon the Persians if they fail to recover the kingdom, which is his dying wish Prexaspes echoes this curse before he hurls himself from the walls (§75.3).

ἀπέκλαιε: 'he was bewailing'. The same verb is used of his remorseful lament at §64.2.

66

66.1: Πέρσαι δὲ ὡς ... οἰμωγῇ ἀφθόνῳ διεχρέωντο: tearing clothing and wailing loudly were typical actions of mourning. οἰμωγῇ ἀφθόνῳ διεχρέωντο: 'engaged in unsparing lamentation'.

66.2: βασιλεύσαντα μὲν ... πέντε μῆνας: Herodotus, when narrating the death of a king or tyrant, often gives the length of time they ruled. τὰ πάντα: 'for a total of'.

66.3: ὑπεκέχυτο: 'spread over'. The choice of verb reflects the considerable distrust felt by the Persians towards Cambyses.

ἠπιστέατο: 'believed'.

67

67.1: ὁ Πρηξάσπης ἔξαρνος ἦν: Prexaspes knew well the danger of saying the wrong thing as his terrified silence after Cambyses' murder of his son showed.

ἐπιβατεύων τοῦ ὁμωνύμου: 'by usurping the name of him who shared his, Smerdis son of Cyrus'. Cf. §63.3.

μῆνας ἑπτὰ ... ἔτεα τῆς πληρώσιος: lit. 'for the remaining seven months that would have completed a full eight years for Cambyses.'

67.2: πάντας εὐεργεσίας μεγάλας: stresses the benefits the Magus Smerdis showed his subjects.

πόθον ἔχειν πάντας ... πάρεξ αὐτῶν Περσέων: 'all those in Asia longed for him, with the exception of the Persians.' This is perhaps suggestive of how Persian power was regarded.

ἀτελείην ... στρατιῆς καὶ φόρου: 'exemption from military service and tribute'. These privileges became standard features of grants of autonomy bestowed by rulers on subject cities. This section also shows that Darius was not the first to assign tribute, but rather the first, according to Herodotus, to reorganize the regions more systematically.

68

68.1: προεῖπε μὲν δὴ ... ἐνιστάμενος ἐς τὴν ἀρχήν: 'Such was the proclamation he made immediately upon coming to power.'

68.2: ὑπώπτευσε τὸν Μάγον ὡς οὐκ εἴην ... ὅς περ ἦν: lit. '[Otanes first] suspected the Magus, that he was not Smerdis son of Cyrus, who he really was.' The optative in 'ὡς οὐκ εἴην' reflects that this was the untrue option.

68.3: ἔσχε ... θυγατέρα: lit. 'had his daughter', i.e., as a wife.

τῇσι ἄλλῃσι πάσῃσι ... τοῦ Καμβύσεω γυναιξί: polygamy was customary among the Persians. Cambyses' harem passes to the Magus and then to Darius, for whom it becomes a ploy to legitimize his power and associate himself with the bloodline of Cyrus (see §88.2-3).

68.4: ὅστις εἴη: optative subordinate clause in *oratio obliqua*.

οὔτε γὰρ ... ἰδέσθαι οὐδαμὰ οὔτε ... αὐτῇ εἰδέναι: secrecy is a strong theme of §§68-9. The lack of public appearance first sparked Otanes' suspicions, as Herodotus described at §68.2; the Magus never left the citadel and never called the leading Persians to his actual presence (οὐκ ἐξεφοίτα ἐκ τῆς ἀκροπόλιος ... οὐκ ἐκάλεε ἐς ὄψιν ... οὐδένα). The intensifying double negatives throughout §68.2 and §68.4 reinforce the deliberate self-concealment of the usurper.

Ἀτόσσης ... ἑωυτῆς ἀδελφεὸν: Atossa is the 'other sister' (ἔσχε ἄλλην ἀδελφεήν) whom Cambyses married at §31.5.

69

69.1: Οὔτε Ἀτόσσῃ δύναμαι ... ἄλλην ἄλλῃ τάξας: this forced separation was unusual and reinforces the image of secrecy and concealment. Cf. §3.1, where one of the Persian women mingles freely among the wives of Cyrus, and also §130.4-5, where Atossa freely converses with Darius on his foreign policy. διέσπειρε ἡμέας ἄλλην ἄλλῃ τάξας: 'he dispersed us, assigning a different wife to a different place'.

ἀκούοντι δὲ ταῦτα ... κατεφαίνετο τὸ πρῆγμα: the splitting up of the wives confirms Otanes' suspicions, emphasised by the placement of ἀκούοντι, reinforcing the link between Phaedyme's revelation and Otanes' conviction. μᾶλλον κατεφαίνετο adds further emphasis and carries a tone of condemnation

δεῖ σε γεγονυῖαν ... πατὴρ ὑποδύνειν κελεύῃ: γεγονυῖαν εὖ 'of noble birth' (lit. 'having been born well'). κίνδυνον ... τὸν ἂν: 'whatever danger [your father commands]'.

οὔτοι μιν σοί ... δεῖ χαίροντα ἀπαλλάσσειν: οὔτοι a very emphatic negative. Otanes impresses upon Phaedyme the need to not let a suspected usurper get away unpunished (cf. §§29.3, 36.3, and 63.1 for χαίρων in the sense of 'unpunished').

69.3: νόμιζε: (here) 'know that'.

69.4: ἡ Φαιδύμη φαμένη ... ἢν ποιέῃ ταῦτα: future open conditional in indirect speech, but with the original subjunctive maintained for vividness.

εἰ γὰρ δὴ ... ὡς ἀιστώσει μιν: open conditional in *oratio obliqua*. The indicatives are maintained for vividness, perhaps stressing the very real danger Phaedyme faced in seeking to expose the Magus.

69.5: ἐπ' αἰτίῃ δή τινι οὐ σμικρῇ: maiming by cutting off the ears (and even nose as well) was a very serious, shaming punishment among the Persians (cf. Intaphrenes's punishment of the guards §118.2). It was a punishment for 'common offenders, rebels, and prisoners' (ALC, *ad loc.*). This is why Zopyrus' self-mutilation proved so convincing (see §§154.2,

155.2). See also §73.1, 'ὦτα οὐκ ἔχοντος' for Gobryas' contemptuous remark about the Magus' lack of ears. To say a man without ears is ruling the Persians, is effectively to say a criminal is ruling them. We are not told his crime, just that it was serious. Maybe there is even be a hint that the Magi were motivated by revenge for this affliction?

69.6: ἐν περιτροπῇ: on polygamy among the Persians see I.135.

οὐ χαλεπῶς ἀλλ' εὐπετέως: 'easily and without difficulty'. The *tautology* reflects how obvious it was that it was Smerdis the Magus and not the son of Cyrus. This explains the secrecy and why such intimate contact was necessary to expose the Magus, since in appearance the Magus was very like the real Smerdis in appearance (see §61.2).

70

70.1: ἐπιτηδεοτάτους ἐς πίστιν: Otanes emerges as careful in how he proceeds, carefully selecting whom he makes party to his suspicions and plans.

71

71.1: ἐδίδοσαν σφίσι λόγους καὶ πίστις: shows the care taken to secure loyalty among themselves.

71.2: ἥκω σπουδῇ ὡς συστήσων ἐπὶ τῷ Μάγῳ θάνατον: Darius is less cautious than Otanes and this suggests he would have been willing to act alone, which is perhaps a foreshadowing of his rise to sole power.

ποιέειν αὐτίκα ... μὴ ὑπερβάλλεσθαι: the chiastic arrangement stresses Darius' sense of urgency. They need to get a move on.

71.3: εἴς τε πατρὸς ἀγαθοῦ ... τοῦ πατρὸς οὐδὲν ἥσσω: comparison with a man's father as a way of judging character (here, favourable) appears elsewhere (see §34.4-5, where Cambyses asks how he compares to Cyrus).

οὕτω συντάχυνε ἀβούλως ... ἐπὶ τὸ σωφρονέστερον ... λάμβανε: the word order stresses that Otanes' recommendation is quite the opposite. He wants to proceed with caution.

δεῖ γὰρ πλεῦνας: Otanes believes they need more men to ensure success. Darius' objection that this only widens the risk of their being betrayed is, however, logical (§71.4: ἐξοίσει γάρ τις πρὸς τὸν Μάγον').

71.4: ἀπολέεσθε κάκιστα: 'you will perish most horribly.' The phrase is emphasized at the end of the sentence, stressing Darius' belief that Otanes is mistaken.

ἑωυτῷ κέρδεα: 'gain' or 'profit for himself'. Emphatically placed.

71.5: κατερέω πρὸς τὸν Μάγον: Darius puts the conspirators in an impossible dilemma. He will become the denouncer if they do not follow his advice to act straightaway. This threat emphatically ends his speech, leaving it ringing in the ears of the others. Sections §§71–2 somewhat resemble a tragic *agon* scene, with the debate creating dramatic tension as the narrative builds towards the action. The debate results in Darius taking charge and directing the group, a clear proleptic glance towards his future power.

ἰδίῃ περιβαλλόμενος ἑωυτῷ κέρδεα: the notion of personal gain being the undoing of a small powerful group anticipates Darius' argument against oligarchy in the debate (§82.3).

72

72.1: ἴθι ἐξηγέο: 'come, explain'. Otanes urges caution as far as he can. How will they get past the guards?

διεστεῶσας: 'stationed at regular intervals'.

γὰρ ... οἶδάς κου καὶ αὐτός: 'for you yourself also know, I suppose'. There is a rather sarcastic tone here. Otanes seems to be putting Darius on the spot by way of a challenge. If he is so keen to set things in motion, then how does he plan to gain entry to the palace. εἰ μὴ ἰδών, ἀλλ' ἀκούσας: 'if not because you have seen them but have heard'. Hearing is generally portrayed as the second-best way of knowing or learning something. Otanes implies that Darius must have heard about the guards and still needs to factor them into his plan, even if he has not seen them himself.

φυλακὰς ... τὰς: relative in agreement with φυλακὰς.

ὅτεῳ τρόπῳ πάριμεν ... τέῳ τρόπῳ περήσομεν: the *polyptoton* of the virtually repeated phrase reflects Otanes' concern that Darius' plan is too hasty.

72.2-5: Darius' reply has a highly rhetorical flavour and connects with the theme of secrecy and lying that recurs throughout the book.

72.2: πολλά ἐστι τὰ λόγῳ ... ἔργον δὲ οὐδὲν ... λαμπρὸν γίνεται: words do not necessarily match deeds and vice-versa. In other words, Darius is saying Otanes' fears are just talk, and it is time to act. The two sets of parallel clauses (λόγῳ μὲν ... ἔργῳ δέ; λόγῳ μὲν ... ἔργον δὲ) stresses the gulf between speech and action, a common idiom to emphasize this point.

72.3: τοῦτο μὲν ... τοῦτο δὲ: lit. 'on the one hand with regard to this matter ... on the other hand with regard to this matter'. Balanced accusatives of respect. This construction is used several times in Book III (§§78.1, 106.2, 115.2, 127.3, 132.2, 136.2, 159.1).

ἡμέων ἐόντων τοιῶνδε: lit. 'with us being such men'. Darius' point is that their status should ensure their admission to the palace.

βούλεσθαί τι ἔπος παρὰ τοῦ πατρὸς σημῆναι: Darius can use the ruse that he has come with a message from his father Hystaspes, whom Herodotus describes as a Persian governor or satrap (§70.3; on whether he was in fact a satrap of Parthia, see H&W *ad loc.*).

72.4: H&W class this section as 'an attempt at sophistry' in a bid to justify their actions in light of Herodotus' assertion at I.138 that Persian boys are taught not to lie. They argue that this actually reflects Greek thought rather than any Persian philosophy. Another interpretation might be that Herodotus is making a point about Darius and his ruthlessness rather than any more general point about Persian honesty.

λέγεσθαι, λεγέσθω: the *polyptoton* stresses that if lying is necessary, it must be done.

τοῦ γὰρ αὐτοῦ: the emphatic placement at the start stresses Darius' point that the goal is the key, not how it is achieved.

οἱ μέν γε ψεύδονται ... οἱ δ' ἀληθίζονται: whether men tell the truth or lie, they are usually hoping for something from it. **κερδήσεσθαι ... κέρδος:** the use of the verb and its cognate noun stress Darius' reasoning that the aim is always the same.

οὐ ταὐτὰ ἀσκέοντες τωὐτοῦ περιεχόμεθα: 'although we practise differently, we work for the same end'.

72.5: ὁμοίως ... ἀληθιζόμενος ψευδὴς ... ὁ ψευδόμενος ἀληθής: 'he who tells the truth would be as likely to be the liar, as the liar could become the truth teller'. ὁμοίως stresses that a liar can tell the truth and the normally truthful man can lie if need be.

ὃς ἂν μέν ... ὃς δ' ἂν: Darius points out the practicality of his approach. It will determine which of the guards is friend or foe.

73

These sections set up the main players of the seven (Otanes, Darius and Gobryas) and foreshadow the ultimate victory of Darius.

73.1: ὅτε γε ἀρχόμεθα ... καὶ τούτου ὦτα οὐκ ἔχοντος: Gobryas' statement reflects the shame of being ruled by a man punished by the Persian king (see §69.5).

73.2: μὴ πειρωμένοισι ἀνακτᾶσθαι τὴν ἀρχήν ... ἐπὶ διαβολῇ ... εἰπεῖν Καμβύσεα: Gobryas reminds the group of 'Cambyses' curse' and how they erroneously disbelieved his story about Smerdis' death.

74

74.1: ἐν ᾧ δὲ: the phrase marks a switch to a parallel scene.

ὅτι τε ... καὶ διότι: τε ... καὶ stresses the two reasons that the Magi resolve to try and win over Prexaspes. **πρὸς δ' ἔτι:** stresses Prexaspes' good reputation among the Persians.

ὅς οἱ τὸν παῖδα τοξεύσας ἀπολωλέκεε: see §34.1 and §35 for Cambyses' killing of Prexaspes' son.

74.2: προσεκτῶντο: 'they were trying to win him over'.

74.3-4: H&W find the 'declaration from the walls' episode implausible. Arguably it does seem like an unnecessary risk, given that at §61, Herodotus has stated that the Magi realized most Persians believed Smerdis son of Cyrus was alive.

75

75.1: ὁ δὲ τῶν ... μὲν ἑκὼν ἐπελήθετο: the relative clauses introduced by τῶν preceded the main clause. The antecedent of τῶν is τούτων. 'willingly forgetful of what that Magi demanded of him'.

ἀρξάμενος δὲ ἀπ' Ἀχαιμένεος: 'beginning from Achaemenes'. Achaemenes is depicted by Prexaspes (and also in the Behistun inscription) as ruler of the Persians in the seventh century and founder of the Persian Achaemenid dynasty. He was the great-great-grandfather of Cyrus the Great, father of Cambyses, and Darius sought to claim his own connection by lingeage to Achaemenes through Ariaramnes his own great-great grandfather. He further sought to strengthen his connection to the Achaemenid line, and thus also the legitimacy of his rule, through marriage to Cyrus' daughter Atossa (for the debate over the historicity of Achaemenes, see Introduction, pp. 23–5).

75.2: πρότερον μὲν κρύπτειν ... ἐν δὲ τῷ παρεόντι ... φαίνειν: the μὲν ... δὲ contrast emphasizes how Prexaspes felt formerly compelled to hide the truth, but now believes he must reveal all.

ἀναγκαίην μιν καταλαμβάνειν φαίνειν: 'necessity forced him to reveal [it]'. ἀναγκαίην .... καταλαμβάνειν is accusative + infinitive after φάμενος, and μιν ... φαίνειν follows ἀναγκαίην.

τοὺς Μάγους δὲ βασιλεύειν: stresses the reality through the emphatic placement of the phrase.

75.2-3: The parallels with Cambyses' speech just before his death are clear (§65). The death had formerly been concealed, now necessity means it must be revealed, and curses are called down should power not be recovered from the hands of the Magi. Note the following verbal echo:

§75.2:	§65.1:
ἀναγκαίην μιν καταλαμβάνειν φαίνειν	καταλελάβηκέ με ... ἐκφῆναι

Circumstances have overtaken them both and the truth must come out. This section constitutes Prexaspes' obituary, which is not unfavourable. Herodotus describes him 'ἐὼν τὸν πάντα χρόνον ἀνὴρ δόκιμος (lit. 'a man well-esteemed for his entire time'). His life is depicted as one fraught with walking a dangerous path of survival under oppressive rulers.

76

76.1: οἱ δὲ δὴ: we now turn back to the seven on their way.

76.2: ἐδίδοσαν αὖτις σφίσι λόγους: 'they again quarrelled/fell out'.

οἱ μὲν ἀμφὶ ... οἱ δὲ ἀμφὶ: 'those supporting [Otanes] ... those supporting [Darius]'.

κελεύοντες ὑπερβάλλεσθαι μηδὲ ... ἐπιτίθεσθαι ...

ἰέναι καὶ τὰ δεδογμένα ποιέειν μηδὲ ὑπερβάλλεσθαι: the word order reflects the opposing opinions and the deadlock the conspirators hit as a result of the news.

76.3: ὠθιζομένων δ' αὐτῶν ἐφάνη: the portent appears just in time to stop the quarrelling.

ζεύγεα: 'pair'.

ἰρήκων . . . αἰγυπιῶν: the seven pairs of hawks tear apart the two pairs of vultures. The seven are represented by the hawks, the Magi by the vultures. The omen thus portends the overthrow of the Magi. Birds bringing omens were important 'signs' to the ancient Greeks. The signs they brought could be both positive and negative (see *Iliad* XXIV.290-5, 314-21, where Hecabe bids Priam ask Zeus for a bird of good omen to ensure Priam's safe arrival at the Greek camp. Zeus answers with an eagle. A less positive example, is the eagles tearing apart the hare in Aeschylus' *Agamemnon*, 114-21, signifying Artemis' wrath at the Atreidae's intended destruction of Troy; more generally on divination and bird omens, see Dillon (2017: 139–77).

τήν . . . γνώμην: the *hyperbaton* reflects the renewed enthusiasm for and vindication of Darius' opinion in light of the ominous birds.

§§ 77-9 *The Seven victorious and the Magi put down. These sections show what a masterful and dramatic storyteller Herodotus can be. He captures a great sense of different simultaneous actions, building suspense, and conveys the rapidity of the of the eruption of the fighting.*

77

77.1: ἐπιστᾶσι: 'for them as they came to stand [at the gate]'. Dative participle.

οἷόν τι Δαρείῳ ἡ γνώμη ἔφερε: 'just as Darius' opinion stated'.

φύλακοι = φύλακες. An ionic form (also in Homer, see *Iliad* XXIV.566; elsewhere in Herodotus, I.84.2, 89.3).

καταιδεόμενοι . . . ἄνδρας τοὺς Περσέων πρώτους: verbal echo of §72.3 (καταιδεόμενος ἡμέας) where Darius confidently asserts that their status will ensure safe passage into the palace.

οὐδ' ἐπειρώτα οὐδείς: emphasizes the lack of suspicion they arouse initially.

77.2: ἥκοιεν: optative in indirect speech.

τοῖσι τὰς ἀγγελίας ἐσφέρουσι εὐνούχοισι: eunuchs occupied an important role in the Persian court. They were guardians of the royal harem and frequently possessed key administrative roles. Here, they are carrying the king's messages (see Xenophon, *Cyropaedia*, VII.5.60-4; Llewellyn-Jones (2022: 240–1, 345).

ἱστόρεον ... ἱστορέοντες: the repetition stresses the grilling the eunuchs gave the seven.

παρῆκαν, ἴσχον: the juxtaposition of the verbs shows how quickly the eunuchs act and the rapid escalation of the action.

77.3: οἱ δὲ: the seven.

τούτους ... τοὺς ἴσχοντας: referring to the eunuchs who are barring their path.

αὐτοῦ ταύτῃ: 'on that very spot', 'right there' (cf. §25.2).

ἐς τὸν ἀνδρεῶνα: it was not only in ancient Athens that houses were divided into women's and men's quarters.

78

78.1: ἔσω: the men's quarters.

ἐόντες ... ἔχοντες: both dependent on ἔτυχον.

τεθορυβημένους τε καὶ βοῶντας: the vivid present participles stress the commotion that erupted. The Magi hear the rumpus and react.

ἀνά τε ἔδραμον: *tmesis*. 'They ran back'.

πρὸς ἀλκὴν ἐτράποντο: 'turned to arms'.

78.2: ὁ μὲν ... ὁ δὲ: the contrast captures the different response of the Magi. One grabs his bow and arrow, the other his spear.

ἐνθαῦτα δὴ συνέμισγον ἀλλήλοισι: the emphatically brief phrase marks the moment they clash in battle.

τῷ μὲν ... ἀναλαβόντι ... ὁ δ' ἕτερος: the contrast reflects the varying fortunes of the Magi depending on their weapon choice.

78.3: οὕτερος = ὁ ἕτερος

τοῦτον: picks up τὸν ἀνδρεῶνα.

78.4: συμπλακέντος: the choice of word stresses how Gobryas and the Magus were locked at close quarters, making it difficult for Darius to land a clear blow.

προμηθεόμενος μὴ πλήξῃ: 'taking care not to strike'. Verb of precaution followed by subjunctive. The verb would normally be optative in historic sequence, but Herodotus uses the vivid subjunctive.

Ὤθεε τὸ ξίφος καὶ δι' ἀμφοτέρων: lit. 'thrust your sword even through us both'. Gobryas is portrayed as brave. Herodotus builds suspense as we fear he will be killed.

ἔτυχέ κως τοῦ Μάγου: 'somehow struck (only) the Magus'. The tension is released as quite fortuitously Darius stabs only the Magus.

79

79.1: ἔχοντες τῶν Μάγων κεφαλὰς: the parading of the decapitated heads signifies the humiliation of the Magi and conveys a public threat to the other Magi and any who supported them.

τοὺς μὲν τρωματίας: 'the wounded men'. This was Aspathines and Intaphrenes.

ἔθεον βοῇ τε καὶ πατάγῳ χρεώμενοι: 'ran shouting and making a clamour'.

καὶ ἅμα ἔκτεινον ... ἐν ποσὶ γινόμενον: 'and they were killing every single Magus who crossed their path' (see Newmyer *ad loc.*).

79.2: ἔκτεινον ὅκου τινὰ Μάγον: the verbal echo shows how the Persians willingly joined in the killing once they realized what had happened.

εἰ δὲ μὴ νύξ ... ἂν οὐδένα Μάγον: 'had nightfall not stopped them, they would have left not one Magus (alive).' This clipped closed conditional and emphatic placement of Μάγον stresses how nearly they came to annihilating the Magi.

79.3: ταύτην τὴν ἡμέρην ... μάλιστα τῶν ἡμερέων: emphatic placement at the start and end of the clause reflects the day's importance.

θεραπεύουσι: 'observe'.
ἐν τῇ: picks up ἡμέρην.

80

The constitutional debate. On the scepticism this section has met, see Introduction, pp. 22–3.

80.1: ἐπείτε = ἐπεί.

κατέστη: intransitive strong aorist of καθιστημι The sense here is 'subsided', 'died down'.

ἐκτὸς πέντε ἡμερέων ἐγένετο: best translated as '[when] five days had passed'.

ἐβουλεύοντο: the use of the imperfect tense may suggest that the deliberations were no easy task.

ἐπαναστάντες: 'the rebels' or 'the conspirators.' Intransitive strong aorist participle of ἐπανίστημι.

ἐλέχθησαν ... ἐλέχθησαν: the of the word reinforces Herodotus' assertion of the truth of the scene that he is about to relate.

ἄπιστοι μὲν ἐνίοισι Ἑλλήνων: why should the scene be 'unbelievable' to 'some of the Greeks'? Persians were often stereotyped as 'naturally slavish', governed by absolute rulers, whereas the Greeks were a 'free' people (see, for example, Aeschylus, *Persae*, 242). It may, therefore, have seemed unbelievable to some Greeks that the Persians had the political and philosophical awareness of different forms of government and also that they could choose what they saw as 'servitude' over democracy, or a government that shared power among more than one, or that there could be any notion of 'freedom' under a single ruler, as Darius will go on to argue.

80.2: ἐς μέσον: Liddell and Scott translate as 'in common to all'. The expression is also used at IV.97.5 and VI.129.2, where 'publicly' is given as a translation. Here the sense is '[affairs to be] publicly held by the Persians.

ὕβριν: this concept is a recurring theme in the debate in the speeches of Otanes and Megabyzus in particular. Whilst the term, as it often appears in Greek tragedy, can denote a crime of violence and/or arrogance that offends the god, a meaning frequently found in Herodotus and prose authors is that of excessive violence and aggression, often but not always by an individual or group in power, that results in unjust acts, which often demean and humiliate. Such is its primary meaning in the debate. Here, Otanes, describes the ὕβρις of the tyrannical ruler in acts of violence towards his own citizens, using Cambyses and the Magus as examples (on this episode and ὕβρις in Herodotus more generally, see Fisher 1992: 343–85).

μετεσχήκατε: perfect tense.

80.3: κατηρτημένον: perfect middle/passive participle of καταρτα/ω (*hang, suspend*). Here, it describes χρῆμα and is best translated as 'suitable', 'fitting', 'well-adjusted', fitting that is for Otanes' definition of just government, in which the ruler should be accountable, but a single ruler is normally not accountable ἀνευθύνος.

μουναρχίη: 'one-man rule', or 'monarchy'.

μουναρχίη, τῇ: 'one man rule, for which it is possible'. Dative + infinitive dependent on ἔξεστι. The use of the definite article as a relative was a feature of Homeric and Ionic dialect, see Introduction, p. 30.

ἀνευθύνῳ: 'without accountability'. A related term is εὐθυνη which refers to the Athenian procedure by which magistrates had to account for their conduct in office before the Athenian council βουλή.

καὶ γὰρ ἂν ... τῶν ἐωθότων νοημάτων στήσειε: Otanes' argument is that the nature of a single ruler's power would corrupt even the best man into thinking thoughts that he would not usually entertain.

ἐγγίνεται: 'is bred in' – the verb conveys the idea of arrogance being bred within human nature. Otanes argues that arrogance (ὕβρις) is stirred by wealth.

δύο δ' ἔχων ταῦτα ἔχει πᾶσαν κακότητα: the word order and *polyptoton* of εοξω reinforces the connection between ' δύο ... ταῦτα' and 'πᾶσαν κακότητα'. 'These two things' are arrogance (ὕβρις) and envy (φθόνος).

80.4: κεκορημένος: perfect middle participle of κορέννυμι.

πολλὰ καὶ ἀτάσθαλα: A *hendiadys*. 'many and reckless actions' for 'many reckless actions'. The device stresses the extent and nature of the single-ruler's actions.

τὰ μὲν ... ὕβρι ... τὰ δὲ φθόνῳ: the construction stresses how the ruler is motivated by both arrogance and envy in his actions, picking up on the earlier sentence about both being innate parts of human nature.

πέφυκε: perfect active of φυω (*bring forth, produce*). Otanes contrasts how the ruler should be (ἄφθονον – 'without envy') with how he actually behaves towards his citizens. The choice of verb stresses that this how he 'naturally' acts.

περιεοῦσί τε καὶ ζώουσι: 'those who surpass him and live', perhaps a *hendiadys* for 'the best men who surpass him while alive'. Herodotus may be playing on the sense περιεοῦσί can also have 'to survive', showing how some will not escape the tyrant's jealous guarding of power.

καίτοι ἄνδρα γε τύραννον ἄφθονον ἔδει εἶναι, ἔχοντά γε πάντα τὰ ἀγαθά. τὸ δὲ ὑπεναντίον: καίτοι and γε emphasise how an absolute ruler 'should' behave, given that he posses 'every good thing'. The positioning of τὸ δὲ ὑπεναντίον (quite the opposite) at the start of the following sentence stresses that the reverse is true.

τύραννον: 'absolute ruler'. The Greek word τύραννος did not initially carry the pejorative sense of our modern word 'tyrant'. It meant an absolute ruler and one who had come to power by an unconventional method, such as usurpation. However, it began to acquire less favourable connotations around this time, which is certainly detectable in Thucydides (see III.62.3; interestingly at II.63.2, Pericles likens the Athenian empire to a tyranny, and Creon, III.37.2 actually calls the empire a tyranny. It was not just a single ruler who could behave tyrannically).

φθονέει γὰρ τοῖσι ἀρίστοισι ... χαίρει δὲ τοῖσι κακίστοισι: the parallel structure highlights the contrast between the single ruler's attitude towards the best and worst citizens, and the fact that his reaction is the opposite to what it should be.

τῶν ἀστῶν: partitive genitive.

διαβολὰς δὲ ἄριστος ἐνδέκεσθαι: 'he is the best at giving his approval to slanders'. ἐστίν needs to be supplied.

80.5: ἀναρμοστότατον: 'most inconsistent'. I have adopted Godley's translation here, as 'inconsistent' best captures the capricious and unpredictable nature of the tyrant that Herodotus seeks to illustrate here. πάντων is somewhat hyperbolic, stressing the extreme 'inconsistency' of a monarchic ruler. The omission of the verb 'to be' from this phrase adds emphasis to 'ἀναρμοστότατον' and 'πάντων'.

ἤν τε γὰρ αὐτὸν μετρίως θωμάζῃς, ἄχθεται ὅτι οὐ κάρτα θεραπεύεται, ἤν τε θεραπεύῃ τις κάρτα, ἄχθεται ἅτε θωπί: Otanes explains 'ἀναρμοστότατον'. Moderate admiration displeases the ruler, because the flattery is not excessive, but if someone does heap excessive flattery upon him, he hates that as well, because the flatterer is 'false'. In effect, he is suspicious of the flatterer. This is a feature associated with the 'bad' single ruler, the tyrant in later political thought.

τὰ δὲ δὴ μέγιστα ἔρχομαι ἐρέων: Otanes pauses to signpost his 'most important' point. This is a common device in rhetoric, delaying the elaboration of a point by highlighting its significance.

νόμαιά τε κινέει πάτρια καὶ βιᾶται γυναῖκας κτείνει τε ἀκρίτους: the *polysyndeton* creates an accumulative effect in the *tricolon* of evils attributed to the tyrant. These were also features that became stock parts of the rule 'characteristic' of the tyrant in fourth-century political thought and beyond, and also in later portrayals of 'tyrannical rulers' in works of history (see, for example, Polybius, *Histories*, VI.6.11-7.8).

80.6: ἰσονομίην: a very difficult word to render in English, but 'equality in law' captures the sense, namely that all are bound the same laws, unlike the absolute ruler who acts as if above the law. The term does not necessarily refer to a full democratic government like Athens.

ἄρχει ... ἔχει ... ἀναφέρει: 'it appoints offices ... it possesses ... it refers' – the *tricolon* of verbs balances the previous *tricolon*. Three evils of the tyrant is capped by three positives of popular government. This sentence also contrasts with the previous in the absence of connecting 'ands' (*asyndeton*). πλῆθος is the subject. It is also an expanding *tricolon* of the advantages of democracy. πάλῳ ... ἀρχας ... (1), ὑπεύθυνον ... ἀρχη (2), βουλεύματα ... παντα (3) – 'election by lot ... power that is accountable ... all decisions': a crescendo to 'all decisions' being publicly debated is created, and this also underlines a key difference between one-man rule and popular power.

ἀέξειν: ἀεξω is a poetic form of αὐξάνω found only once in Herodotus (see Liddell and Scott, *ad loc.*). This perhaps suggests a deliberate choice of word to express the importance of the people in the new government envisaged by Otanes.

ἐν γὰρ τῷ πολλῷ ἔνι τὰ πάντα: 'for among the masses there is everything'. The phrase quite possibly means something very similar to the belief later expressed by Aristotle in the collective wisdom of the masses (*Politics* 1281b).

81

81.1: ὀλιγαρχίη: the term has not yet gained the sense of the degenerate rule of the few, and here simply refers to the numbers of the ruling power. It is notable, however, that in the debate as a whole there is an awareness of good and bad modes of rule within each form.

τὰ μὲν Ὀτάνης ... τὰ δ' ἐς: contrasts where he does and does not agree with Otanes. λελέχθω κἀμοὶ ταῦτα: lit. 'let these things be said also by me', in other words 'on these matters I also agree'.

γνώμης τῆς ἀρίστης ἡμάρτηκε: 'he has fallen short of the best opinion'.

ἀχρηίου: 'useless'. The word reflects a contemptuous attitude towards the masses that would have resonated with some Greeks (see, for example, ps. Xenophon ('The Old Oligarch'), *Athenaion Politeia*, 1.1). Not all approved of Athenian democracy, and one must be wary of equating Athenian with Greek.

οὐδέν ... ἀξυνετώτερον οὐδὲ ὑβριστότερον: 'nothing more senseless nor more arrogant'. The emphatic comparatives convey familiar objections to rule by the people. ὕβρις again appears as a human failing, characterised by excessive violence, fuelled by the possession of power. The masses, Megabyzus argues, would be even worse than the tyrant.

81.2: τυράννου ὕβριν ... δήμου ἀκολάστου ὕβριν: from one arrogant rule to another, or so Megabyzus argues democracy would be. His point, however, is that the mob cannot be punished or removed. **ἀνασχετόν:** 'intolerable' is emphatically placed at the end of the sentence.

οὔτ' ἐδιδάχθη οὔτε εἶδε καλὸν οὐδὲν οἰκήιον: the negatives stress Megabyzus' opinion that no fine deed can ever emerge from a democracy. **οὔτ' ἐδιδάχθη:** suggests he believes they are untaught and unteachable.

ὠθέει τε ἐμπεσών ... χειμάρρῳ ποταμῷ εἴκελος: Megabyzus likens democracy's tendency to act without sense to a swollen winter river.

81.3: οἵ Πέρσῃσι κακὸν νοέουσι: 'those who wish the Persians ill'. This may be an oblique reference to Athens.

ἀρίστων δὲ ἀνδρῶν οἰκός ἄριστα βουλεύματα: the ABAB word order stresses the logic of Megabyzus' argument in favour of oligarchy, namely that the best men normally yield the best counsels.

82

Darius is the last speaker and will be victorious in the debate, foreshadowing his accession to the role he advocates here.

82.1: τὰ μὲν ... ὀρθῶς λέξαι, τὰ δὲ ... οὐκ ὀρθῶς: Darius agrees with not turning to democracy, but opposes Megabyzus' advocacy of oligarchy.

τριῶν γὰρ προκειμένων ... ἀρίστων ἐόντων ... ἀρίστου καί: although separate terms for the good and bad varieties of each type had not yet crystallized (that began in fourth-century political philosophy), this passage reflects the notion that good and bad variants could exist within each type. **τῷ λόγῳ:** 'in word'. The sense here is that they have described in 'word' (I have used 'in theory' in the translation) the best types, as opposed to what would be the case in reality.

τοῦτο: i.e., monarchy.

82.2: ἀνδρὸς γὰρ ἑνὸς: the emphatic position stresses Darius' advocacy of monarchy.

ἐπιτροπεύοι ἂν ἀμωμήτως ... ἐπὶ δυσμενέας ἄνδρας: Darius' point is that the best monarch will guard against the flaws presented by democracy (unruliness) and oligarchy (plots, intrigue and rivalries).

82.3: ἐς τὸ κοινὸν ἔχθεα ἰδίᾳ ἰσχυρὰ: the juxtaposition of private rivalries and the common good highlights the key flaw in oligarchy that Darius points out – the rivalries among the ruling group. φιλέει: the sense here as 'is wont to' or 'it usually [arises]'.

αὐτὸς γὰρ ἕκαστος ... ἐστὶ τοῦτο ἄριστον: oligarchic rule is eventually torn apart through the factions that arise from personal aims and ambitions. βουλόμενος κορυφαῖος εἶναι γνώμῃσί: each individual is out to be the best. ἐξ ὧν στάσιες ἐγγίνονται, ἐκ δὲ τῶν στασίων φόνος: the parallel structure and *polyptoton* reinforce the link between the factions that break out and the bloodshed that follows. ἐκ δὲ τοῦ φόνου ἀπέβη ἐς μουναρχίην: the sentence opens with a parallel ἐκ δὲ τοῦ, which herald the inevitable emergence of monarchy from the disintegrated oligarchy. τοῦτο ἄριστον: emphasized at the end of the sentence. Darius concludes that monarchy is the best.

82.4: ἀδύνατα μὴ οὐ κακότητα: the *litotes* stresses that nothing good can come out of democratic rule. κακότητα here has the sense of inbred vice and evil, not cowardice.

κακότητα ἐγγίνεσθαι ... κακότητος τοίνυν ἐγγινομένης: the *polyptoton* again reinforces the notion of inbred evils within democracy, as does the triple *polyptoton* of ἐγγίνεσθαι ... ἐγγινομένης ... ἐγγίνεται which strengthens the image of evils arising from within.

θωμάζεται οὗτος ... θωμαζόμενος: the *polyptoton* emphasises the reaction that leads to the promotion of the individual who emerges to stop men who are corrupting public affairs (οἱ γὰρ κακοῦντες τὰ κοινὰ συγκύψαντες ποιεῦσι – 'For those who cause harm to the public good, do so by banding together'). He emerges with the willing support of the people. This became a key distinction between tyrant and king in later political philosophy, the latter was willingly supported by his citizens, the former by paid guards (see Aristotle, *Politics*, 1311a5-8; cf. Polybius, *Histories*, VI.52.4-9).

ἐφάνη μούναρχος ἐών ... ἡ μουναρχίη κράτιστον: Darius argues that monarchy is the inevitable result from the inherently divisive nature of oligarchy and democracy. Cf. Polybius on the violent descent of democracy into mob rule, whence monarchy returns (*Histories* VI.9.9-10).

82.5: ἑνὶ δὲ ἔπεϊ πάντα συλλαβόντα εἰπεῖν: 'and to sum up in a word so to speak.' Darius heralds the conclusion of his speech.

ἡμῖν ἡ ἐλευθερίη ... ἢ μουνάρχου ... ἡμέας ἐλευθερωθέντας διὰ ἕνα ἄνδρα: the notion that freedom could come from monarchy would certainly have seemed odd to Herodotus' contemporary Greek audience, especially any Athenian. But what is meant here by freedom? Freedom from harm by other powers, or a freedom to act in a political sense? The potential for the abuse of freedom without accountability became a theme in some authors' explorations of Athenian politics, for example, Xenophon's account of the Arginousae trial, *Hellenica* I.7.22.

πατρίους νόμους: the ancestral laws of a people could be a powerful appeal to tradition or against change in Greek politics and became a particularly powerful slogan at Athens during the late fifth and fourth centuries (Finley 1971: *passim*; Walters 1987: *passim*; Fuks 2013: 56).

οὐ γὰρ ἄμεινον: a pithy ending to Darius' powerful speech. The phrase is also a metrically perfect ending for a hexameter, giving a poetic air (see also, Hesiod, *Works and Days*, 737; in Herodotus, I.187.2). At §71.2 the phrase rounds off Darius' speech urging his fellow conspirators to act now. Here, as there, it is an emphatic rhetorical flourish to make it seem like his option is the only option.

83

83.1: ταύτῃ: i.e., Darius. The remaining four supported maintaining the monarchy.

ἰσονομίην: see note on 80.6 for the meaning of this term.

ἐς μέσον: 'publicly'.

στασιῶται: one could perhaps see a note or irony in Otanes' reference to the rebels with this term, given Darius' emphasis on the negatives of *stasis*.

83.2: κλήρῳ γε λαχόντα: 'after obtaining [it] by lot'. A method of choosing leaders strongly associated with the democratic process (see Plato, *Laws*, 765c; Isocrates, 7.22-3; Aristotle, *Politics* 1298b-1300b; see also Herodotus, VI.109).

ἐπιτρεψάντων ... ἂν ἐκεῖνο ἕληται: the two methods spelt out by Otanes are strikingly democratic compared to the one they agree in the end.

οὐκ ἐναγωνιεῦμαι: Otanes emerges as consistent. He does not want power, but he does not wish to be ruled either. He withdraws graciously.

οὔτε γὰρ ἄρχειν οὔτε ἄρχεσθαι ἐθέλω: the emphatic phrasing perhaps illustrates Otanes' commitment to rule by the people. He is not seeking power for himself, but neither does he wish to be ruled by a government he does not agree with.

οὔτε αὐτὸς ἐγὼ οὔτε οἱ ἀπ' ἐμεῦ αἰεὶ: Otanes asks that his wish be granted not just for himself but also for his descendants.

83.3: ἀλλ' ἐκ μέσου κατῆστο: as Newmyer notes, 'he withdrew himself from the debate'.

νόμους οὐκ ὑπερβαίνουσα: his wish was granted, but on the proviso he did not violate Persian laws, effectively granting the family an internal autnonomy as long as they repsected Persian constraints. καὶ νῦν suggests that this arrangement remained in place in Herodotus' own day.

84

84.1: καί σφι ἔδοξε ... ἀπὸ Ὀτάνεω αἰεὶ γινομένοισι: they agree to Otanes' terms.

ἐξαίρετα δίδοσθαι ἐσθῆτά ... ἐν Πέρσῃσι τιμιωτάτῃ: the grant of gifts indicates their great respect for Otanes and gratitude for exposing the Magus, as is stressed in the following sentence (τοῦδε δὲ εἵνεκεν ... ἐβούλευσέ τε πρῶτος ... καὶ συνέστησε αὐτούς).

84.2: παριέναι ἐς τὰ βασιλήια ... μετὰ γυναικὸς βασιλεύς: the condition that it was permitted for any of the seven to enter the palace unannounced unless the king was sleeping with a woman. We shall see how Intaphrenes' failure to respect this rule costs him dearly (§118.2).

84.3: ὅτευ ἂν ὁ ἵππος ... τοῦτον ἔχειν τὴν βασιληίην: the mode of appointment is agreed that the kingship will be held by whoever's horse first neighs at sunrise. On whether this story may find its origins in the sacred place of horses in Persian sun-worship, see ALC *ad loc.*

§§ 85–7 Darius' trick. *Some have accepted the anecdote-like story of Darius' ploy as historical, possibly supported by the mention Herodotus claims to quote of his groom Oebares on the inscription mentioned at §88. There is no mention of portents or favourable signs on the Behistun inscription, where Darius firmly grounds his claims to legitimacy in Achaemenid origins (see ALC ad loc.). Arguably, this would be more persuasive to Persians. H&W look rather less favourably on Herodotus here, saying that he 'is combining popular legend with a misunderstood inscription on the monument of Darius (ad loc.). On this episode and how Herodotus may be adapting Persian traditions, see Rollinger (2018: 125–48). See Waters (2022: 39) on Ctesias' portrayal of Oebares as Cyrus' right-hand man rather than Darius'.*

85

85.1: σοφός: here the sense is 'clever', rather than 'wise'. Cf. §4.2, 'σοφίῃ γάρ μιν περιῆλθε ὁ Φάνης' – 'For Phanes surpassed him in cleverness.'

ὅτευ ἂν ὁ ἵππος ... τοῦτον ἔχειν τὴν βασιληίην: an almost complete verbal echo of §84.3.

μηχανῶ: second person singular middle imperative. 'arrange it [so that]'.

μὴ ἄλλος τις: 'no one else.' The emphatic placement at the end of the sentence highlights Darius' ambition.

85.2: θάρσεε . . . θυμὸν ἔχε ἀγαθόν: Oebares emphatically reassures Darius.

ὡς . . . οὐδεὶς ἄλλος: echoes Darius' own words (μὴ ἄλλος τις).

τοιαῦτα ἔχω φάρμακα: used figuratively here to mean 'tricks' rather than 'drugs' or 'potions'.

μὴ ἀναβάλλεσθαι: a recurring trait of Darius at this point in the narrative is a sense of urgency. Cf. §71.2, where he advises his fellow conspirators not to put off (μὴ ὑπερβάλλεσθαι) removing the Magi.

85.3: ὡς ἐγίνετο ἡ νύξ: at once creates a scene of secrecy and intrigue.

86

86.1: κατὰ συνεθήκαντο: 'as they had agreed'.

ἵνα . . . ἐνθαῦτα: correlatives 'there . . . where . . .'

ἅμα δὲ τῷ ἵππῳ τοῦτο ποιήσαντι: ἅμα stresses the simultaneity of Darius' horse whinnying and of the thunder and lightning that followed.

ἀστραπὴ ἐξ αἰθρίης . . . βροντή: many ancient cultures saw thunder and lightning as signs of the gods. However, lightning was usually not a favourable sign, yet here it is taken as positive affirmation of Darius' 'victory' in the leadership 'contest' (see Dillon 2017: 178–83). The story may be part of a tradition suggesting Darius' rise to the kingship was fated and not merely due to the chance neighing of a horse.

86.2: ὥσπερ ἐκ συνθέτου: 'as if by agreement'.

87

87.1: οἱ μὲν δή φασι: an alternative version of Oebares' plan, where he rubs the genitals of the mare and uses the scent to provoke Darius' horse into whinnying first. Herodotus also tells us ἐπ' ἀμφότερα λέγεται ὑπὸ Περσέων – lit. 'for it is told on both sides by the Persians' ('both versions are told by the Persians). Herodotus does not tell us which he prefers. The argument could be made that Herodotus tells the earlier version (§85) as part of the narrative in the main flow of the story, and thus seems to support that one. τῶν ἄρθρων: 'genitals' here.

ἐν τῇσι ἀναξυρίσι: 'in his trousers'. Trousers were associated with the Orient by Greeks (see ALC on I.71.2).

88

88.1: πλὴν Ἀραβίων: 'except for the Arabians.' See note below.

Κύρου τε καταστρεψαμένου ... ὕστερον αὖτις Καμβύσεω: both added to the Persian empire.

ἀλλὰ ξεῖνοι ἐγένοντο ... Πέρσαι ἐς Αἴγυπτον: see §§8-9 for the establishment of Aegypto-Persian friendship, when Cambyses was seeking safe passage into Egypt.

88.2: τὴν μὲν Ἄτοσσαν ... αὖτις τῷ Μάγῳ: see §31.6 for Cambyses' marriage to Atossa, and §68.4-5 for reference to her as the wife of the Magus.

88.3: ἑτέρην ... Σμέρδιος τοῦ Κύρου θυγατέρα ἔγημε: 'as another wife he married the daughter of Smerdis, son of Cyrus.' This may well have been a political move to strengthen his legitimacy through connection to the ruling family.

τὴν τοῦ Ὀτάνεω θυγατέρα: Phaedyme. ἣ τὸν Μάγον κατάδηλον ἐποίησε: she was instrumental in exposing the Magus (see §69.4-6). Darius' move is in accordance with the agreement of the seven to keep their marriages between their households, but may also have been done in recognition of both Phaedyme's and Otanes' role in removing the Magus.

ἐπέγραψε δὲ γράμματα λέγοντα τάδε: lit. 'he wrote on it letters which said as follows'.

Δαρεῖος ὁ Ὑστάσπεος ... τὴν Περσέων βασιληίην: on the problems with identifying this statue and whether Herodotus really saw it or accepted reports about it, see H&W and ALC *ad loc*. Οἰβάρεος τοῦ ἱπποκόμου: the final acknowledgement given to Oebares may well lie behind the story of his agency in Darius' accession.

§§89-96 *The division of provinces and assignment of tribute. See Appendix I for a full table of the arrangement of tributes and provinces. See the online Glossary for more information about the peoples and places mentioned. See Figure 5 for a map of the Persian empire. The accuracy of this digression has been debated; see, for example, Armayor (1978b: 1-9).*

89

89.1: ποιήσας δὲ ταῦτα ... αὐτοὶ καλέουσι σατραπηίας: once he had taken power, Darius organized the revenues of the empire into twenty regions, here he calls them ἀρχὰς followed by the Persian name, σατραπηίας. This is the second instance of Herodotus usage of the term σατραπηία. Cf. I.192.2, where he qualifies it also with ἀρχή. Elsewhere he uses νομός for the administrative region and ὕπαρχος for the governor of the region. See H&W *ad loc* for Persian empire organizational terms in other authors.

καταστήσας ... τὰς ἀρχὰς καὶ ἄρχοντας ἐπιστήσας: *chiasmus* and *polyptoton*.

ἐτάξατο φορούς οἱ ... ἄλλα ἔθνεα νέμων: 'he drew up the tribute to be paid to him people by people, attaching together neighbouring peoples and as he went beyond those lands nearest, he assigned the more remote peoples to various regions'. ἐτάξατο ... προσιέναι: lit. 'he drew up [the tribute] ... to come in to him', so 'to be paid to him'. The infinitive is dependent upon ἐτάξατο.

89.2: τὸ δὲ Βαβυλώνιον τάλαντον: the Babylonian talent was equivalent to 78 Euboic minas. In modern money this equates to roughly $304,500, just under £240,000.

89.3: φόρου πέρι = πέρι φόρου

κατεστηκὸς οὐδὲν φόρου πέρι, ἀλλὰ δῶρα ἀγίνεον: Darius,, according to Herodotus, was the first systematically to organize the revenues of empire.

παραπλήσια ταύτῃ ἄλλα: 'other things very similar to this'. ταύτῃ: the arrangement made concerning revenue (τὴν ἐπίταξιν τοῦ φόρου).

λέγουσι Πέρσαι ὡς ... σφι πάντα ἐμηχανήσατο: the 'nicknames' given to Cyrus, Cambyses and Darius by the Persians.

ὡς Δαρεῖος μὲν ἦν κάπηλος, Καμβύσης δὲ δεσπότης, Κῦρος δὲ πατήρ, ὁ μὲν ὅτι ἐκαπήλευε πάντα τὰ πρήγματα, ὁ δὲ ὅτι χαλεπός τε ἦν καὶ ὀλίγωρος, ὁ δὲ ὅτι ἤπιός τε καὶ ἀγαθά σφι πάντα ἐμηχανήσατο.

The double *tricolon* in parallel structure stresses the very different characters of the kings. Notice how the two negative adjectives applied to Cambyses are balanced by two positive remarks about Cyrus. Darius is the 'shopkeeper' or 'businessman'. On this 'nickname' and its origins, see Ruffing (2018: 152–61).

90

90.1: ἀπὸ μὲν δὴ Ἰώνων: the catalogue begins with the Greek Asia Minor peoples and gradually moves further east. ἀπὸ .... οὗτός ... νομὸς: Herodotus punctuates using this formula like the modern bullet point until §94.

Μαγνήτων τῶν ἐν τῇ Ἀσίῃ: Magnesia on the Maeander here and Magnesia ad Sipylum who took their names from the Thracian Magnetes who founded both cities. They are mentioned in the Homeric catalogue of ships (*Iliad*, II.756-60).

90.3: ἀπὸ δὲ Κιλίκων ... τὴν Κιλικίην χώρην ἀναισιμοῦτο: in Herodotus the region of Cilicia stretches from the Halys (I.72) in the north, to Pamphylia in the West, and the Euphrates in the East. For more on this region and the two regions Cilicia comprised in Assyrian texts, see ALC *ad loc*. The Cilicians sent 360 horses as part of their tribute and the region seems to have been known for its horses. In the book of *Kings* (10:28) king Solomon's horses are recorded as being imported from Cilicia.

91

91.1: ἀπὸ δὲ Ποσιδηίου πόλιος ... ἀπὸ ταύτης μέχρι Αἰγύπτου: this is a vast stretch of the empire, running from Posideia on a promontory at the mouth of the Orontes, along the entire eastern Mediterranean coastline up to Egypt, excluding Arabia. The region came under Persian sway following the first fall of Babylon under Cyrus' leadership in 539.

πλὴν μοίρης τῆς Ἀραβίων: see §§8–9 and §88.1 for the establishment and nature of the connections between Persia and Egypt. **ταῦτα γὰρ ἦν ἀτελέα:** they did not pay tribute.

Κύπρος: ALC note that there is no confirmation in eastern sources that Cyprus was part of this satrapy. See §19.3 for the surrender of the Cypriots to the Persians.

91.2: ἀπ' Αἰγύπτου δὲ ... τὸν Αἰγύπτιον νόμον αὗται: 'The Egyptian Province.' This comprised the Libyans, Cyrene and Barca.

ἐκ τῆς Μοίριος λίμνης: located in the Fayum region of Egypt.

91.3: τούτου τε δὴ ... τοῦ ἐπιμετρουμένου σίτου: 'Apart from this silver and the grain that was measured out came seven hundred talents.'

ἐν τῷ Λευκῷ τείχεϊ τῷ ἐν Μέμφι: 'at the white wall in Memphis.' this palace became the base of the satrap or governor.

91.4: Σατταγύδαι δὲ: here we suddenly jump to the easternmost part of the empire, a region comprising modern central-western Pakistan and southern Afghanistan.

ἑβδομήκοντα καὶ ἑκατὸν τάλαντα: this represents the lowest tribute of the entire catalogue.

92

92.1: ἀπὸ Βαβυλῶνος ... τῆς λοιπῆς Ἀσσυρίης: Babylon was first conquered by Cyrus in 539. The rebellion and second conquest by Darius occupy the final ten chapters (§§150–60) of Book III.

παῖδες ἐκτομίαι: these boys would have become eunuchs in the royal court. See §48.2 for the boys sent by Periander to Persia, who were intercepted by the Samians. For the role of eunuchs in the royal court, see note on §77.2.

ἀπὸ δὲ Ἀγβατάνων καὶ τῆς λοιπῆς Μηδικῆς: this region had been conquered by Cyrus in 550. For Cambyses' Ecbatana confusion, see §§62.1 and 64.2.

92.2 and §93.3: note the different Caspians. See the online Glossary of Peoples and Places for more.

ἐς τὠυτὸ συμφέροντες: lit. 'gathering it together into the same thing', i.e., 'collectively contributed' or 'paid as their collective tribute'.

93

93.1: ἀπὸ Βακτριανῶν δὲ μέχρι Αἰγλῶν: a vast and very important satrapy, which ALC note was central to contacts with India and China.

ἀπὸ Πακτυϊκῆς: this is not the same as the region of India of the same name mentioned by Herodotus at §102.1.

τετρακόσια τάλαντα: Xenophon (*Anabasis* V.34) notes other forms of tribute from this region.

93.2: τοὺς ἀνασπάστους καλεομένους: the 'uprooting' of populations, usually rebellious ones, was one of Persia's harshest punishments. Ctesias records Cambyses as having deported *c.* 6,000 Egyptians to Susa (*Persica* 13.30).

93.3: Κάσπιοι: see note on §92.2.

Πάρθοι: the Parthians were a people to the east of Iran. The famous empire flourished from the third century. For more, see the online Glossary of Peoples and Places.

Ἄρειοι: for more on this people, see DGRG.

94

94.1: Παρικάνιοι δὲ: Herodotus switches his 'punctuating' construction (from ἀπὸ + genitive of people/place), partly to lend variety into what is essentially a series of lists. Here the Paricanians and Ethiopians are the subjects. In the following sentence the formula becomes *dative of people* dependent on ἐπέτετακτο.

Αἰθίοπες οἱ ἐκ τῆς Ἀσίης: different from the semi-legendary Ethiopians of §§17-25. Herodotus seems to refer to three different Ethiopians (see also §97.2).

94.2: πάντων τῶν ἡμεῖς ἴδμεν ἀνθρώπων: a similar phrase will be used at §122.2 (see note) on Polycrates' thalassocratic ambitions. There it distinguishes previous 'mythical' masters of the sea from those from 'what is called the human race'. Here, the sense may be similar, or Herodotus may be highlighting what is currently 'known', versus what may remain to be discovered in the distant corners of the world.

ψήγματος: the word is also found at I.93.1 Cf. IV.195.2 ψήγματος χρυσου.

95

95.1: τὸ μὲν δὴ ἀργύριον ... ἐξακοσίων καὶ τετρακισχιλίων: on the problems with the figures in this passage, see ALC a*d loc.*

95.2: τούτων ἔλασσον ἀπιεὶς: i.e., less than a talent. Herodotus implies the account of the financial divisions of the Persian empire could have been much longer, thus only further emphasizing the vast wealth flowing into Persia. For a more critical view of this final sentence, see

Wilson (2015: 61). One could argue that it would have taken too long to list all the more minor contributors if Herodotus were delivering this as a lecture.

96

96.1: οὗτος Δαρείῳ προσήιε ... προσήιε ἄλλος φόρος καὶ: the verbal echo stresses how the empire and its revenues were to grow still further.

96.2: τοῦτον τὸν φορὸν ... ἂν ἑκάστοτε δέηται: Herodotus explains how Darius stored the silver and gold as treasure. ALC note that the metals would likely have been test cut for forgeries with bases of less valuable metals. Cf. Croesus' melted casks at I.51.5. ἐς πίθους κεραμίνους ... ἂν ἑκάστοτε δέηται: 'After melting it down he pours it into clay jars, and having filled the vessel, he removes the clay around it. Whenever he needs money, he strikes has much as he needs for each occasion.' ἐπεὰν δὲ δεηθῇ ... ἂν ἑκάστοτε δέηται is an indefinite clause in primary sequence.

97

Herodotus moves on to lands assigned to bring 'gifts' rather than tribute.

97.1: ἀρχαί: Herodotus previously used the term νομοί for the administrative regions of the empire.

ἡ Περσὶς δὲ χώρη μούνη ... νέμονται χώρην: Herodotus notes that the Persian land is exempt from tribute. δασμοφόρος: 'tributary'. Brosius, however, cites Persian documents that prove this claim to be untrue (2021: 126).

97.2: οἱ δὲ φορὸν μὲν ... δῶρα δὲ ἀγίνεον: the income of the empire did not stop with tribute. The three peoples he discusses are the Ethiopians (the ones Cambyses attempted to make an expedition against), the Colchians and the Arabians.

οἵ τε περί…ἀνάγουσι τὰς ὀρτάς: Nysa was a semi-mythological and mountainous land associated by the Greeks with the Ethiopians. Interestingly, there is a city of the same name near the river Kunar in India, with a shrine to Dionysus that was allegedly discovered by Alexander the Great in 326 when he invaded Gandara. An account of this sanctuary survives in the *Life of Apollonius of Tyana* by Philostratus who described the life of first-century teacher and miracle worker, Apollonius (II.8). Whether there is any link with the Nysa here described, I cannot say.

[οὗτοι οἱ Αἰθίοπες…δὲ ἔκτηνται κατάγαια]: Godley rightly queries the presence of this remark at this point in the text. Herodotus returns to this theme at §101.2. But it does seem out of place here in terms of theme and content. The OCT keeps the passage. Here we highlight its difficulties by putting the word(s) in square brackets. On whether the Callantiae named here are the same as at §38.4, see note above.

97.3: διὰ τρίτου ἔτεος: Godley translates 'every other year', but this is actually the same as every three years in the Greek method of counting which counted the starting year inclusively.

χοίνικας: the *choinix* was a dry measure normally of corn, here referring to unmelted gold.

97.4: Περσέων οὐδὲν ἔτι φροντίζει: lit. 'as yet take no thought for the Persians', 'does not yet acknowledge Persian power', the regions north of the Caucasus were not as yet in the Persian empire.

98

98.1: τὸν δὲ χρυσὸν τοῦτον τὸν πολλὸν: a key theme of the digression from §§98–116 is the exotic and rich materials and substances of the lands beyond Europe.

98.2: ψάμμος: 'desert'. Herodotus claims that east of the Indian country, all land is desolate.

τῶν ... ἀνθρωπων τῶν ἐν τῇ Ἀσίῃ Ἰνδοί: the *hyperbaton* of τῶν at the start of the sentence and ἀνθρωπων τῶν at the end, sandwiching the details, stresses the peoples he now moves to, drawing attention to Ἰνδοί at the end of the sentence.

τῶν ... ἡμεις ἴδμεν ..., τῶν ... πέρι ἀτρεκές τι λεγεται: a variation on the phrase 'of those we [actually] know about', which Herodotus often uses to qualify the limits of his historical knowledge and what he deems certain or uncertain. ἀτρεκές τι: 'anything certain'. The adjective is used in a similar context in adverb form: ἔχω μὲν οὐκ ἀτρεκέως λέγειν (§115.1: 'I am not able to say anything certainly' on the lands far west of Europe) and οὐκ ἔχω οὐδε τοῦτο ἀτρεκέως εἶπαι (§116.1: 'I cannot say even this with any certainty' on the lands north of Europe).

98.3: πολλὰ ἔθνεα: Herodotus draws attention to the varied nature of the Indian peoples in their customs and also their languages (οὐκ ὁμόφωνα). Note however, how he does not mention specific place names, but broadly divides them 'οἱ μὲν νομάδες ... οἱ δε οὐ' and then goes on to discuss further differences of custom.

καλάμου δὲ ἕν γόνυ: 'one knee of reed'. This was the distance between the nodes on the stem of the reed. Newmyer (*ad loc.*) notes that this may be bamboo, making the 'knee' around seven feet.

98.4: φλοΐνην: 'made of rush'.

τὸ ἐνθεῦτεν ... ὡς θώρακα ἐνδύνοισι: τὸ picks up on φλοῦν ('the rush/reed'). φορμοῦ τρόπον: 'in the form/manner of a mat'.

99

99.1: Herodotus intends readers/listeners to recall how the starving Persian army resorted to cannibalism in the ill-planned and abandoned expedition against the Ethiopians. It is seen as shocking to the Persians and Greeks who do not practise it, but to the Callatiae of §38 and the tribes described here, it is established custom, and the view taken is quite different. One might conjecture a more shocked reaction of revulsion from his Greek audience.

99.1: ὅς ἂν κάμῃ τῶν ἀστῶν: Herodotus explains the κρεῶν ... ὠμῶν ('raw flesh') of the opening sentence.

φάμενοι αὐτὸν τηκόμενον ... τα κρεα ... διαφθείρεσθαι: 'because they claim that his wasting away is spoiling [their] meat'.

99.1-2: οἱ μάλιστά οἱ ὁμιλέοντες ... κατευωχέονται: the phrase is paralleled at §99.2: αἱ ἐπιχρεώμεναι μάλιστα ... κατευωχέονται, reinforcing the fact that men and women alike meet this fate among the Padaeans.

99.2: πρὸ ... τοῦ: 'before this point', i.e., old age. Many have been sacrificed and eaten before they get that far.

100

ἑτέρων ... ὅδε ἄλλος τρόπος: the framing word order stresses the difference between the tribe Herodotus will now describe compared to the Padaeans.

οὔτε ... οὐδὲν ... οὔτε ... οὔτε: the very different attitude of this tribe to eating flesh of any sort is stressed by the string of negatives. Again, the parallels with §38 cannot be denied. In effect, §§99–100 form a sort of supporting example – two different tribes with very different customs surrounding two issues: dealing with the sick and eating flesh. Herodotus makes no judgement about either, but as at §38, he highlights the differences.

κέγχρος ... ἐν κάλυκι: on the identification of this plant, see ALC a*d loc*. Newmyer translates: 'a grass with a seed about the size of a millet in the husk.' An ancient reference to a genuinely vegetarian tribe. Herodotus makes no adverse judgement, but it is worth noting that a vegetable or plant-based diet could be seen as a sign of primitivity or even unmanliness by Greeks (see Euripides, *Hippolytus*, 952-3 for Theseus' angry reproach of his son).

οὐδεὶς οὔτε ... οὔτε: 'no one gives any thought to whether he is dead or weary'.

101

101.1: μίξις ... ἐμφανής ἐστι κατά περ των προβάτων: a note of disapproval can be detected in Herodotus' likening the habit of sex in the open air to animals.

101.2: ἡ γονὴ δὲ ... ἀλλὰ μέλαινα: see note on §97.2 on the disputed passage where Herodotus apparently refers to the black semen of the Ethiopians (τοιαύτην ... Αἰθίοπες ... θορήν).

ἑκαστέρω τῶν Περσέων ... βασιλέος οὐδαμὰ ὑπήκουσαν: Herodotus reminds his reader/listener that we have now moved beyond the boundaries of the empire and its peoples.

102

Herodotus previously announced he would explain this at §98 but digressed into a brief account of the Indian peoples. Now having reached the most warlike group, he returns to the gold sand.

102.1: ἄλλοι δὲ ... τῶν ἄλλων Ἰνδῶν: these are the northern Indians, dwelling in the city of Caspytyrus (identified with modern Kabul) and that of Pactyae (identified with northeastern Afghanistan). πρὸς ἄρκτου τε καὶ βορέω ἀνέμου: Herodotus stresses the northern location of these places. ἄρκτου refers to the constellation of Ursa Major, which was considered a mark of the north as the most visible of the northern constellations. These Indians were part of the twentieth province of the Persian empire (see §94.2).

οἳ Βακτρίοισι παραπλησίην ... δίαιταν: the Bactrians inhabited northern Afghanistan and parts of Uzbekistan and Tajikistan.

102.2: τῇ ἐρημίῃ ταύτῃ καὶ τῇ ψάμμῳ: hendiadys. 'deserted and sandy area' for 'sandy desert area'.

μύρμηκες ... μέζονα: the giant ants who guard the gold dust. Has Herodotus made these up, or has he received a report that exaggerates their size, which he describes as μεγάθεα κυνῶν μὲν ἐλάσσονα ἀλωπέκων δὲ μέζονα: 'in size smaller than dogs, but larger than a fox'? μεγάθεα is accusative of respect.

κατά περ οἱ ... μύρμηκες κατὰ τὸν αὐτὸν τρόπον: Herodotus notes that these giant ants behave exactly as Greek ants (οἱ ἐν τοῖσι Ἕλλησι) do, introducing a point of familiarity for his audience.

ἡ δὲ ψάμμος ... χρυσῖτις: a reminder that this is the gold sand brought in tribute to the king. See §94.2.

102.3: ἀπὸ τέκνων ὡς νεωτάτων: the female camels are removed from newborn offspring but Herodotus does not explain why until §105.2.

αἱ γάρ σφι ... δυνατώτεραι πολλὸν φέρειν: 'For their female camels are no lesser in their speed than horses and are besides far more able to endure burdens.'

103

103.1: εἶδος ὁκοῖόν τι ... ἐπισταμένοισι Ἕλλησι: Herodotus assumes Greek familiarity with the appearance of camels, not implausible given dealings with Persia and Egypt.

τὸ μὲν δὴ ... τὸ δὲ μὴ ἐπιστέαται: Herodotus adds a little extra that he claims they do not know. Notice the emphatic phrasing: τὸ δὲ μὴ ... τοῦτο φράσω: lit. 'but a thing they do not know of, this I will explain', drawing the readers' or listeners' attention to the fact he is about to relate. Herodotus is asserting his authority as historian and enquirer. He has gone beyond the limits of typical Greek knowledge. The structure τὸ ... τοῦτο φράσω is one favoured by Herodotus for announcing a story or fact that he wishes to highlight (see §6.1 on the fate of wine jars in Egypt). On camels in Lydia, see I.80.2-5.

κάμηλος ἐν τοῖσι ... γούνατα τέσσαρα: ALC note that this error has resulted from the impression created by the animal bending down. Aristotle points out the mistake (*Historia Animalium* 499a20).

104

104.1: λελογισμένος ὅκως ... ἔσονται ἐν τῇ ἁρπάγῃ: the Indians have to calculate carefully how they time the retrieval of the sand. **καυμάτων τῶν θερμοτάτων ἐόντων:** the 'theft' (ἁρπάγη) must occur when the day is at its hottest.

μύρμηκες ἀφανέες ... ὑπὸ γῆν: Herodotus hints at the need to avoid the ants.

104.2: θερμότατος δὲ ἐστὶ ... οὗ ἀγορῆς διαλύσιος: the hottest part of the day is not at midday for the Indians, as it is for most peoples. This occurs at the closing of the marketplace, so before midday, c.10am.

καίει πολλῷ μᾶλλον ... ἐστι βρέχεσθαι τηνικαῦτα: the hottest time of day for the Indians is far more intense than midday in Greece. To illustrate his point, Herodotus notes the story told that they sprinkle themselves with water at that time.

104.3: μέσουσα δὲ ἡ ἡμέρα ... τὸ κάρτα ψύχει: Herodotus compares Greek and Indian temperatures to make his account more relatable to his audience. Midday temperatures are similar for both and the cooling off begins at this point for both, but the Indian regions cool to a far greater degree especially at around sunset. H&W dismissed Herodotus' claim here, stating that it was based on an erroneous view of the earth's shape and geographical ignorance. Cary (1919) takes a more nuanced approach, showing in fact that this earlier heat-peak can genuinely occur naturally, just not where Herodotus claims.

105

105.1: ἐπεὰν δὲ ἔλθωσι ... ταχίστην ἐλαύνουσι ὀπίσω: we return to the Indians setting off to gather gold dust with their camels.

αὐτίκα γὰρ μύρμηκες ... μαθόντες διώκουσι: 'for as soon as the ants sense them by smell ... they give chase.' Herodotus explains why they must collect the dust at the hottest part of the day (see §104.1). With the ants underground, they have more time.

ὡς δὴ λέγεται ὑπὸ Περσέων: it is interesting to note that Herodotus does not present the story as fact, but notes that this report comes from a Persian source. This suggests it was not perhaps familiar to a Greek audience. Fehling notes that Herodotus often quotes sources from within the empire as sources for places beyond the empire (or the 'ring' as he calls it, 1989: 101).

οὐδενὶ ἑτέρῳ ὅμοιον . . . οὐδενα ἂν σφέων ἀποσώζεσθαι: '[that] their speed is equal to no other so that, unless the Indians get a head start on their journey while the ants gather, none of them would be saved.' The sentence is in indirect statement after λέγεται. The result clause and open conditional 'if-clause' stress how dangerous the ants are and that the hunters would not survive if they planned any differently.

105.2: τοὺς μέν. . .ἔρσενας . . . τὰς δὲ θηλέας: Herodotus now comes to an explanation of the arrangement of the camels that he described at §102.3.

ἐνδιδόναι μαλακὸν οὐδέν: the females do not yield in any way because they are racing to get home to the young they have been torn from.

ὡς Πέρσαι φασί: Herodotus inserts a reminder that this is a report (see §105.1).

106

On the riches of the remote lands.

106.1: αἱ δ' ἐσχατιαί . . . κεκρημένας ἔλαχε: Herodotus argues that the most remote lands hold the richest materials, but they Greece enjoys the finest seasons by far. The parallel clauses reinforce the contrast:

<u>αἱ δ' ἐσχατιαί</u> . . . τὰ **κάλλιστα ἔλαχον**,
κατά περ <u>ἡ Ἑλλας</u> . . . ὥρας . . . **κάλλιστα** κεκρημένας **ἔλαχε**

τῆς οἰκεομένης: 'the inhabited world.'

106.2: πρὸς τὴν ἠῶ: 'towards the dawn', i.e., towards the east.

ἐσχάτη τῶν οἰκεομένων ἡ Ἰνδική: Herodotus places India at the furthest limits of inhabited places (see Figure 5).

τοῦτο μὲν τὰ ἔμψυχα: Herodotus gives three reasons for his claim that the furthest lands have the finest possessions, the first is the wildlife. The four-footed and winged creatures (τετράποδά τε καὶ τὰ πετεινά) are bigger by far (πολλῷ μέζω). He qualifies this statement noting that Indian horses are surpassed by the Nasaean horses of the Medes (οὗτοι δὲ ἑσσοῦνται ὑπὸ τῶν Μηδικῶν Νησαίων δὲ καλευμένων ἵππων).

τοῦτο δὲ χρυσὸς ἄπλετος: the second justification is the boundless gold of the area. This is gathered by mining, dragging from rivers, and the ant theft. ὥσπερ ἐσήμηνα: recounted at §102 and §105.

106.3: τὰ δὲ δένδρεα: the third justification is the produce of the wild trees that bear a wool, which he emphatically describes as far superior in beauty and quality to that of sheep (καρπὸν εἴρια καλλονῇ τε προφέροντα καὶ ἀρετῇ τῶν ἀπὸ τῶν ὀίων). The material referred to is flax or cotton.

§§107–13 *deal with the ways the Arabians gather frankincense, myrrh, ledanon, cassia and cinnamon.*

107

107.1: πρὸς δ' αὖ μεσαμβρίης ... τῶν οἰκεομενέων χωρέων: we now swing to the southern limits of the known world according to Herodotus. ἐσχάτη Ἀραβίη: is classed as the furthest point to the south.

ἐν δὲ ταύτῃ ... τε ἐστὶ μούνη: λιβανωτός is framed in the middle of this phrase stressing that this, according to Herodotus, is the only place where it can be found.

καὶ σμύρνη καὶ κασίη καὶ κινάμωμον καὶ λήδανον: the *polysyndeton* stresses the sheer number of exotic substances to which Arabia is home.

ταῦτα πάντα ... δυσπετέως κτῶνται: Herodotus announces the theme of these chapters. The arduous task of obtaining these substances, except for the myrrh (πλὴν τῆς σμύρνης).

§§107.2–108.1: ὄφιες ὑπόπτεροι: the tale of the flying snakes. It would be very easy to dismiss this as mythical nonsense, but having been told (by an eyewitness) that the alarming leap of the desert-dwelling sand viper very much gives the effect of a flying snake, I do wonder whether this is the creature behind the story told to Herodotus.

107.2: τὴν ἐς Ἕλληνας Φοίνικες ἐξάγουσι: evidence of trade between the Phoenicians and the Greeks. Frankincense was important in Greek cleansing rituals (see Petrovic and Petrovic 2016: 90, 103-5, 108).

σμικροὶ τὰ μεγάθεα, ποικίλοι τὰ εἴδεα: the pithy phrasing gives a vivid description of these creatures.

πλήθεϊ πολλοὶ περὶ δένδρον: the plosives convey the sheer number that throng each tree, guarding the frankincense.

οὗτοι οἱ ... ἐπ' Αἴγυπτον ἐπιστρατεύονται: the military language (lit. 'march against') paints the snakes as aggressive. Another hypothesis about the creature behind the flying snakes is that they are locusts.

οὐδενὶ δὲ ἄλλῳ ... τῆς στύρακος τῷ καπνῷ: burning the storax, the stem of the plant, is the only way they can drive the snakes from the trees, and so obtain the frankincense. The emphatically placed οὐδενὶ δὲ ἄλλῳ stresses the hazard.

108

108.1: λέγουσι δὲ καὶ ... ἠπιστάμην γίνεσθαι: Herodotus explains the reason the Arabians give why they are not overrun with these snakes. λέγουσι δὲ καὶ τόδε Ἀράβιοι, ὡς: lit. 'and the Arabians tell the following thing, that...'

ἂν ... ἐπίμπλατο ... εἰ μὴ γίνεσθαι: past closed conditional in indirect speech. εἰ μὴ γίνεσθαι κατ' αὐτοὺς οἷόν τι κατὰ τὰς ἐχίδνας: 'unless similar occurred among them, as I know happens among vipers'.

108.2: τοῦ θείου ἡ προνοίη: Herodotus sees a divine wisdom in the natural order of natural processes.

ὅσα μὲν ψυχήν . . . καὶ ἀνιηρά, ὀλιγόγονα: a neat parallel structure highlights the contrast between the prolific animals and those which bear fewer offspring.

(1) **ὅσα μὲν** ψυχήν τε δειλὰ καὶ ἐδώδιμα, <u>ταῦτα μὲν πάντα πολύγονα</u> πεποίηκε

ἵνα μὴ ἐπιλίπῃ κατεσθιόμενα,

(2) **ὅσα δὲ** σχέτλια καὶ ἀνιηρά, <u>ὀλιγόγονα</u>

Essentially, the hunted are more prolific, so they do not die out through being eaten, the hunters, less so.

108.3: ὁ λαγὸς . . . καὶ ἀνθρώπου: the hare is the example of the edible, hunted animal, and Herodotus uses a *tricolon* to convey how it is hunted from all quarters.

τὸ μὲν δασὺ . . . τὸ δὲ ἀναιρέεται: these super-pregnancies or parallel pregnancies (namely that the hare can conceive while carrying already developing unborn young) is perfectly possible, it seems.

108.4: ἡ δὲ δὴ λέαινα . . . λείπεται αὐτέων ὑγιὲς οὐδέν: this story about the reproduction of the lioness is a 'stupid tale' (Aristotle's words not mine, *Historia Animalium* 579a2), possibly made up to support the point Herodotus made at §108.2 about predators being less prolific than typical prey animals.

109

109.1: ὡς δὲ καὶ . . . ἦν βιώσιμα ἀνθρώποισι: the flying snakes and the vipers do not lay eggs as most snakes do (ὡς ἡ φύσις αὐτοῖσι ὑπάρχει – 'as is natural for them/their kind'). Were they more prolific, life would be possible for men in these regions, so Herodotus tells us.

109.1-2: νῦν δ' ἐπεὰν θορνύωνται ... τὴν ἔκδυσιν ποιέεται: one cannot help but be reminded of Agamemnon by this story with the murderous female mate receiving due retribution from her offspring, especially in Herodotus' usage of the vocabulary of revenge (ἀποτίνει, τιμωρέοντα; cf. Orestes' interpretation of Clytemnestra's dream in Aeschylus' *Choephori* 540-50).

109.3: κατὰ τοῦτο δοκέουσι πολλοὶ εἶναι: the snakes only 'seem' numerous because of their concentration in one place.

110

In this short passage, Herodotus creates a surprisingly engaging little account of this peculiar ritual.

τὸν μὲν δὴ λιβανωτὸν ... τὴν δὲ κασίην ὧδε: Herodotus moves from the frankincense to the cassia, a spice not dissimilar to cinnamon (see II.86.5 for the usage of this substance in Egyptian embalming).

ἐπεὰν καταδήσωνται βύρσῃσι ... καὶ τὸ πρόσωπον: Herodotus explains the 'dressing up' first and the reason for it second, enticing the curious listener/reader to want to learn more. πᾶν stresses the complete covering created by the various skins.

περὶ δὲ αὐτὴν καὶ ἐν αὐτῇ: 'and around it and in it', namely the lake from which they gather the cassia.

θηρία πτερωτά: now the reason for the protective clothing is revealed as Herodotus mentioned the 'winged beasts' that inhabit the lake and its *environs*. He gives a grim picture of these squealing (τέτριγε δεινόν) and strong (ἐς ἀλκὴν ἄλκιμα) bat-like creatures (τῇσι νυκτερίσι προσείκελα).

τὰ δεῖ ἀπαμυνομένους ... δρέπειν τὴν κασίην: 'they have to keep these away from their eyes in order to get the cassia' (lit. 'they have to get the cassia thus, keeping these [creatures] away from their eyes').

111

111.1: κιναμώμον: whether this is cinnamon as we know it nowadays is debated. At §111.2, Herodotus refers to τά κάρφεα τα ἡμεῖς ἀπὸ Φοινίκων ... κινάμωμον ('those sticks from Phoenicia which we call cinnamon'; cf. Pliny, *Natural History*, X.50). Herodotus was wrong that cinnamon comes from Arabia, but he was not the only ancient observer to be mistaken and he himself notes the difficulty in pinpointing its origins (ὅκου μὲν γὰρ γίνεται καὶ ἥτις μιν γῆ ἡ τρέφουσα ἐστί, οὐκ ἔχουσι εἰπεῖν; see also Theophrastus, *Opinions of Natural Philosophers* IX.4.5). On the confusion, see Dalby (2000: 37).

ἔτι τούτων θωμαστότερον: Herodotus has organized his tales of exotic item-gathering rituals in order of the wondrousness, each more amazing than the previous. A similar phrase appears in in his account of the collection of the *ledanon* §112.1 (ἔτι τούτου θωμαστότερον). This repetition creates a kind of crescendo to the next tale about exotic produce.

ὅκου μὲν γὰρ ... οὐκ ἔχουσι εἰπεῖν: 'for whichever land it is that rears them, they are not able to say'. Herodotus qualifies his account about the cinnamon collection, by highlighting the uncertainty surrounding its provenance.

πλὴν ὅτι λόγῳ ... ὁ Διόνυσος ἐτράφη: the lands in which Dionysus was reared Newmyer (*ad loc.*) takes to be India. ALC (*ad loc.*) note that Arabia is a possibility (see §8.3 on the Arabian oath to Dionysus/Orotalt and the shaving of the hair in the manner attributed to Dionysus). ALC also note that Herodotus prefers the identification with Nysa in Ethiopia, the one Cambyses went against (see §97.2 and note). λόγῳ οἰκότι ... φασί τινὲς: Herodotus takes no stance, but merely notes the version's plausibility.

ὄρνιθας δὲ λέγουσι ... ἀνθρώπῳ οὐδεμίαν εἶναι: note the parallel structure of:

ὄρνιθας δὲ λέγουσι ... φορέειν ταῦτα ...
φορέειν δὲ τὰς ὄρνιθας

Herodotus slightly digresses in the first clause to explain the plant he is talking about and then resumes the story, continuing the *oratio obliqua* after λέγουσι. ἐς νεοσσιὰς: Herodotus' story is that the cinnamon sticks are carried by large birds to their high nests which are inaccessible to men. The Arabians set out meat which the birds retrieve and take to their nests, causing the cinnamon to fall to the ground for collection (§111.3). Pliny the Elder has a story about a bird in Arabia that builds its nests with sprigs of cinnamon, which the natives knock down with arrows (*NH*, X.50). However, Pliny denies that Arabia produced cinnamon and locates its origins elsewhere (XII.41-2, 82-94). Of Herodotus' version, he cynically notes that such tales are told merely to drive the prices up (XII.42.85).

111.3: βοῶν τε καὶ ὄνων ... τὰ μέλεα διαταμόντας: Herodotus is quite fond of structuring his more unusual tales in this way. He explains an unusual aspect of the story, here the setting out of chunks of meat, but giving the reason second as if to pique his reader's curiosity.

τοὺς δὲ ἐπιόντας: i.e., 'the Arabians'.

112

Λήδανον ... λάδανον: black balsam.

ἔτι τούτων θωμαστότερον: see note §111.1.

ἐν ... δυσοδμοτάτῳ γινόμενον εὐωδέστατον ἐστί: the word order stresses the rather paradoxical contrast between the balsam's provenance versus its most pleasant scent. This story seems, in fact, to be true, showing that the bizarre is not always fantastical (cf. Pliny, *Natural History* XII.37).

113

113.1: ἀπόζει δὲ τῆς ... θεσπέσιον ὡς ἡδύ: 'there breathes on the Arabians from their land a divine aroma, so sweet'. θεσπέσιον is

Homeric (see *Odyssey* IX.210). Pliny (*NH*, XII.42.86) mentions the story, but brands it 'falsa'. Note how the repeated aspirates of ὡς ἡδύ imitate the sweet breath of the spices.

113.2: ἐπέλκειν, ἕλκεα: the pun stresses the connection between the *sores* the sheep would have if they were allowed to *drag* their long tails around. It is easy to dismiss this as cute nonsense, but for an interesting argument that these carts may have been real see Goodridge 2006: 229–39.

§§114–116 *More remote lands and exotic items.*

114

καὶ ... καὶ ... καὶ ... καὶ ... καὶ ... καὶ ...: the lengthy *polysyndeton* stresses the richness of the Ethiopian land (here the long-lived people of §§17–25), listing gold, ivory, wild trees of every kind, ebony (see §97.3) and the tallest, fairest and most long-lived men.

μεγίστους καὶ καλλίστους καὶ μακροβιωτάτους: Herodotus has already noted these features of the Ethiopians (see §§17.1, 20.1, 97.2). The expanding *tricolon* stresses the impressive height, appearance and longevity of the Ethiopians.

115

115.1: περὶ δὲ τῶν ... οὐκ ἀτρεκέως λέγειν: Herodotus' little 'tour' of the world's extreme regions now swings west. ἐσχατιαί ... ἐσχατιέων: the *polyptoton* shows that we are at the limits of the earth (§115.1 transitions us from the eastern and southern extremes to the west) and, as we shall see, we also arrive at the limits of knowledge, as 'ἔχω μὲν οὐκ ἀτρεκέως λέγειν' shows. A similar phrase appears at §116.1 (οὐκ ἔχω οὐδὲ τοῦτο ἀτρεκέως εἶπαι).

οὔτε γάρ ἔγωγε ... κασσίτερος ἡμῖν φοιτᾷ: Herodotus indicates that he does not accept stories about a river Eridanus nor about the Tin Islands. τὸ ἤλεκτρον: this is not *electrum*, the gold/silver alloy native to Lydia and the region around it, and used for the earliest coins by the Lydian and Persian kings. Here, in fact, the word refers to amber, which certainly can be washed down from the Baltic region. The Eridanus was identified with the Po by some writers, which ALC note (*ad loc.*) might explain the flourishing amber crafts in northern parts of Italy in the sixth century. Later ancient authors identified the Tin Islands as Britain or islands in what we now call the English Channel, or even the Scilly Isles. Cornwall, famed for its tin mines, is another possibility.

115.2: τοῦτο μὲν γάρ ... αὐτὸ κατηγροέει τὸ οὔνομα: 'for by its very name the Eridanus shows that it [is Greek].' Herodotus seems more to be criticizing historians who accept this claim without any verification, rather than the poet he mentions. For more on this passage, see ALC *ad loc.*

οὐδενὸς αὐτόπτεω γενομένου: as Herodotus cannot find an eyewitness to corroborate the accounts he has received, he does not refute them entirely, but remains sceptical. He carefully points out, however, that he has done his best.

ἐξ ἐσχάτης δ' ... καὶ τὸ ἤλεκτρον: he does, however, conclude that tin and amber certainly come from a remote region.

116

116.1: πρὸς δὲ ἄρκτου: we now move north.

πολλῷ τι πλεῖστος χρυσός: the *polyptoton* of πολύς stresses the apparent abundance of gold to the north.

116.1-2: λέγεται δὲ ὑπὲκ ... τοῖσι ἄλλοισι ἀνθρώποισι: these gold-stealing one-eyed men and the gold guarding griffins reappear at IV.13.1, where Herodotus similarly mentions them following a 'there is a story' opening rather than giving any kind of authorial sanction of their actual existence. In the later passage, he relates the story as an alternative explanation of the flight of the Cimmerians from the

Scythians. Here, he declares that he is 'not convinced' by the notion that there exist one-eyed men of the same nature as other human beings. φύονται, φύσιν: the juxtaposed cognates stress the point of the argument: that one-eyed men of a like nature are alleged to exist.

116.3: ἐσχατιαί οἴκασι, περικληίουσαι ... χώρην and περικληίουσαι ... χώρην ... ἐντὸς ἀπείργουσαι: the double *chiasmus* mimics the encircling of other lands by these remote regions.

αὐτά: note that Wilson's OCT reads πάντα here, which would stress the great abundance of rare and splendid items found in the furthest lands.

117

This passage forms a thematic transition back to the main narrative of the Persian empire. ALC aptly note that the passage 'seems to have been inserted here in order to recall the reader from the fabulous boundaries of the world to the administrative realities of the Persian empire and the story of Darius.

117.1: περιεκληιμένον ὄρεϊ πάντοθεν: the word order mimics the meaning – the plain is surrounded on all sides. The Chorasmian plain was in the region that is now modern Uzbekistan.

ἦν μέν κοτε ... ἐπείτε δὲ Πέρσαι: the contrast stresses the difference between the situation before and then under Persian rule that Herodotus is about to narrate.

Χορασμίων ... Ὑρκανίων ... Πάρθων ... Σαγγέων ... Θαμαναίων: five peoples corresponds to the διασφάγες...πέντε that Herodotus mentioned at the start of the section. The *polysyndeton* (τε ... καὶ ... καὶ ... καὶ ... καὶ) emphasizes the number of peoples dependent on these passes. Four out of the five are mentioned in Herodotus' digression on the Persian empire's tribute (Χορασμίων: 16th province, §93.3; Πάρθων: 16th province, §93.3; Σαραγγέων: 14th province, §93.2; Θαμαναίων: 14th province, §93.2).

ἐστὶ τοῦ βασιλέος: the emphatic placement shows the power of the Persian king over this region.

117.2: ποταμὸς μέγας... Ἄκης: ALC (*ad loc.*) note that this river can possibly be identified with the Oxus.

ἄρδεσκε: 'used to water'. Ionic imperfect of ἄρδω ('irrigate').

διαλελαμμένος: 'divided'. Perfect passive participle of διαλαμβάνω.

διὰ διασφάγος... ἑκάστης ἑκάστοισι: Herodotus is exploiting the sound echoes here to stress how each people was formerly adequately supplied by the river.

πρότερον μὲν ἄρδεσκε... ἐπείτε δὲ ὑπο: μέν... δέ in phrasing that parallels §117.1 stresses the contrast between before and during Persian control.

117.3: τὰς διασφάγας: emphatically placed. These are what the king blocked up, further reinforced by the repetition ἐπ' ἑκάστῃ διασφάγι at the end of the sentence – 'at each channel'.

117.4: οὐκ ἔχοντες αὐτῷ χρᾶσθαι: 'no longer having it to use', or 'no longer being able to use it'.

συμφορῇ μεγάλῃ διαχρέωνται: 'They meet with great misfortune.' Herodotus illustrates the rather grim realities of Persian rule for these peoples.

τὸν μὲν γὰρ... τοῦ δὲ θέρεος: the contrast highlights that the difficulties are more severe in the summer. σφι ὁ θεὸς... τοῖσι ἄλλοισι ἀνθρώποισι: 'when the god rains for them as for the rest of mortals'. ὁ θεὸς could imply Zeus as god of weather, or may be a symbol for the natural order of things. Herodotus stresses how the king's meddling costs these people dearly and he depicts the motive as being purely material (§117.6).

τοῦ δὲ θέρεος... χρηίσκονται τῷ ὕδατι: 'when they sow their millet and sesame seed, they are greatly in need of water'. χρηίσκονται is frequentative showing the ongoing nature of their need.

117.5: κατὰ τὰς θύρας τοῦ βασιλέος: the palace at Susa. On the 'King's Gate', see ALC a*d loc*. At §119.3, this is where Intaphrenes' wife comes to plead with Darius for mercy. τὰς πύλας refers to the river gates.

117.6: ὡς δ' ἐγὼ οἶδα ἀκούσας: again, Herodotus mentions how he got his information. He qualifies that this has been learnt from hearsay, and, therefore, not by his own observations.

Χρήματα μεγάλα … πάρεξ τοῦ φόρου: an emphatic statement about the king's coldly material motives for inflicting such suffering.

§§118 *A loosely thematic connection brings us back in medias res to the aftermath of the overthrow of the Magi. Intaphrenes gets it wrong.*

118

118.1: κατέλαβε: used impersonally here ('it befell').

ὑβρίσαντα τάδε ἀποθανεῖν αὐτίκα μετὰ τὴν ἐπανάστασιν: the strong *assonance* of 'α' draws attention to the fact of Intaphrenes' swift demise following the rebellion.

ὁ νόμος οὕτω … τυγχάνῃ μισγόμενος βασιλεύς: for the rule that the any of the other six could enter the palace unannounced unless the king was sleeping with one of his wives, see §84.2.

118.2: σπασάμενος τὸν ἀκινάκεα … καὶ τὰς ῥῖνας: a deeply humiliating punishment for any Persian, which Intaphrenes has inflicted on mere suspicion (see note on §§69.5 and 73.1).

καὶ ἀνείρας περὶ … ἔδησε καὶ ἀπῆκε: Intaphrenes did not stop with the mutilation but displayed the severed parts to add to the humiliation he had inflicted.

119

119.1: Δαρεῖος δὲ ἀρρωδήσας … πεποιηκότες ἔωσι ταῦτα: Darius' immediate reaction is to fear a common plot (κοινῷ λόγῳ) by the other six against him.

ἕνα ἕκαστον: this implies he questioned them separately to root out any conspiracy.

119.2: εἴη ... πεποιηκώς: optative after ὡς in indirect statement in historic sequence.

αὐτόν τε τον ... τοὺς οἰκηίους πάντας: fearing conspiracy, Darius has the entire household arrested, as stressed by the *polysyndeton* (τε ... καὶ ... καὶ).

ἐλπίδας πολλὰς ἔχων: 'strongly believing' (lit. 'having many expectations'). For this sense of ἐλπίζω (and ἐλπις) as 'being suspicious' or 'believing', rather than 'hoping' in the usual sense of the term, see §62.2 on Cambyses' reaction to the herald bringing the Magus' announcement (see also §151.2, where the sense is 'expecting' or 'suspecting' rather than 'hoping').

119.3: ἐπὶ τὰς θύρας τοῦ βασιλέος: Intaphrenes' wife comes to the palace to plead with Darius (see note on §117.5).

κλαίεσκε ἄν καὶ ὀδυρέσκετο: the frequentative forms demonstrate her repeated and relentless lamentation at the palace.

αἰεὶ τώυτὸ τοῦτο: the emphatic little phrase stresses his wife's determined protest at the doors.

Δαρεῖος διδοῖ ἕνα ... τὸν βούλεαι ἐκ πάντων: 'Darius grants that you save whichever one you choose from all of your imprisoned relatives.' The antecedent of τὸν is ἕνα.

119.5: θῶμασας: Darius is surprised by her choice of her brother.

ὅς καὶ ἀλλοτριώτερος ... καὶ ἧσσον κεχαρισμένος: Darius' argument is that a brother is not as close to her as her sons and less dear to her than her husband, at least this how he sees it.

119.6: ἀνὴρ μέν μοι ... οὐδενὶ τρόπῳ γένοιτο: Intaphrenes' wife argues that whilst she could still remarry and have more children, with her parents dead, she will never have another brother. A sibling could even be considered a stronger blood tie than a son, a notion powerfully reflected in the words of Antigone in her tomb (Sophocles, *Antigone* 909-13; see Ovid, *Metamorphoses* VIII.445-532 for this theme in the story of Althaea and Meleager). See also §124.2 on the notion of blood ties being stronger than those of marriage (Polycrates' daughter's plea). It was a strong theme in fifth-century thought.

ταύτῃ τῇ γνώμῃ ... ἔλεξα ταῦτα: the framing word order with the *polyptoton* creates an assertive tone in Intaphrenes' wife's speech.

119.7: ἡσθεὶς: being impressed with her words, Darius releases her eldest son as well. The story and his pity can be compared to Cambyses', sadly too late, sense of pity for Psammenitus (§14.10-11) when he declares his family's suffering too great for tears and also Cyrus' amazed admiration at Croesus' 'enlightenment' on his pyre (I.88-9).

§§120-8 *These sections deal with Oroetes' murder of Polycrates and Darius' swift visiting of revenge on him for his crimes.*

120

120.1: κατὰ δέ κου ... νοῦσον ἐγίνετο τάδε: Herodotus now gives some background to Oroetes' hostility towards Polycrates, dating its origins to around the time sickness befell Cambyses, i.e., his diseased wound rather than his madness (see §§64.3-4, 66.2).

Σαρδίων ὕπαρχος Ὀροίτης: Oroetes' post was hardly insignificant, and we learn he had been appointed by Cyrus. ὕπαρχος here denotes the post of *satrap*. For its other meanings, see ALC *ad loc.*

πρήγματος οὐκ ὁσίου: '[he desired] a thing/matter that was not pious.' Herodotus offers authorial judgement on Oroetes' aims, and they are not favourable. Polycrates' obituary ends with the note that the manner of his death was: οὔτε ἑωυτοῦ ἀξίως οὔτε τῶν ἑωυτοῦ φρονημάτων – 'a manner worthy neither of him nor of his aims' (§125.2). Such comment on the injustice of a ruler's demise is rare in Herodotus, and one wonders whether it may reflect the sentiment of his Samian source.

οὔτε ... τι παθὼν οὔτε ἀκούσας μάταιον ἔπος: 'for he had neither suffered anything [at his hands] nor been insulted' (μάταιον ἔπος ἀκούω = 'hear a unfounded rumour (*against oneself*)' hence 'I am insulted').

The *chiasmus* stresses the lack of any justifiable reason for Oroetes' actions.

οὐδὲ ἰδὼν πρότερον: Herodotus adds that Oroetes had never even seen Polycrates before.

ὡς μὲν οἱ πλεῦνες λέγουσι: Herodotus does not directly endorse either version that he gives. This is balanced by οἱ δὲ ἐλάσσονες λέγουσι at §121.1.

120.2: κατήμενον τόν τε Ὀροίτεα ... οὔνομα εἶναι Μιτροβάτεα: accusative + infinitive after λέγουσι.

νόμου ἄρχοντα τοῦ ἐν Δασκυλείῳ: 'governing the province in Dascyleium'. This was located on the south coast of Lake Manyas.

τούτους ἐκ λόγων ἐς νείκεα συμπεσεῖν: 'they were quarrelling'.

κρινομένων δὲ περὶ ἀρετῆς: 'comparing themselves in terms of their prowess'.

εἰπεῖν τὸν Μιτροβάτεα τῷ Ὀροίτῃ προφέροντα: 'Mitrobates reproachfully said to Oroetes'.

120.3: Σὺ γὰρ ἐν ἀνδρῶν λόγῳ: 'you are a man in word only' (lit. for you are of men in word). The sense is, 'you're not a real man'. Mitrobates was allegedly goading Oroetes into proving himself during their exchange.

ἐοῦσαν εὐπετέα: referring to νῆσον Σάμον.

τῶν τις ἐπιχωρίων: a dismissive and derogatory way of referring to Polycrates. Mitrobates argues that Oroetes has no excuse for not adding Samos to the empire, because 'some native' conquered it with only 'fifteen' hoplites. This is clearly an exaggeration. Herodotus narrates elsewhere that Polycrates was very well equipped militarily (§§39.3, 45.3).

120.4: οἱ μὲν δή μιν φασὶ: Herodotus reminds readers that this is only one alleged reason.

τοῦτο ἀκούσαντα καὶ ἀλγήσαντα τῷ ὀνείδεϊ: Mitrobates' taunting worked. Oroetes was provoked into proving himself.

ἐπιθυμῆσαι οὐκ οὕτω ... δι' ὅντινα κακῶς ἤκουσε: the verbal echoes with §120.1 are evident and deliberate, reinforcing the point made about the unjust nature of Oroetes' designs against Polycrates. He was insulted, but not by Polycrates.

§120.1	§120.4
ἐπεθύμησε ... ἐπεθύμεε	ἐπιθυμῆσαι
αὐτὸν ἀπολέσαι	Πολυκράτεα...ἀπολέσαι
οὔτε ἀκούσας μάταιον ἔπος	ὅντινα κακῶς ἤκουσε

121

121.1: οἱ δὲ ἐλάσσονες λέγουσι: 'fewer say that ...'. Herodotus now presents the alternative version to the one given at §120.2-4.

Ἀνακρέοντα τὸν Τήιον: Anacreon of Teos was a famous Greek lyric poet. He was particularly known for his drinking songs. He was music teacher to the sons of Polycrates. Teos was a city in Asia Minor in Ionia, north of Samos.

122

122.1: αἰτίαι μὲν δὴ αὗται διφάσιαι ... τις βούλεται αὐτέων: Herodotus' remarks on the alternative stories show a clear awareness of the difficulty in discovering exactly what happened. Here he acknowledges and has related both, stating that it is perfectly possible to be convinced by either.

ἐν Μαγνησίῃ τῇ ὑπὲρ Μαιάνδρου ποταμοῦ οἰκημένῃ: Magnesia on the Maeander in Ionia was a city of significant strategic importance, located between Priene, Ephesus and Tralles (see Figure 1).

Μύρσον τὸν Γύγεω ἄνδρα Λυδόν: this Gyges is not the Gyges of I.7.1, but he was likely from the dynasty.

μαθὼν τοῦ Πολυκράτεος τὸν νόον: Polycrates' 'intention' was apparently supremacy by sea. This phrase is echoed at §122.3 (μαθὼν ὢν ταῦτά μιν διανοεύμενον).

122.2 *This section is highly revealing about Herodotus' attitude towards myth as history, showing that he is not the credulous accepter of tales he has sometimes been portrayed as.*

Πολυκράτης γὰρ ... πρῶτος ... θαλασσοκρατέειν ἐπενοήθη: Polycrates has been highly successful and now he seeks mastery over the seas. τῶν ἡμεῖς ἴδμεν Ἑλλήνων: '[first] of the Greeks who we know about'. There is a palpable note of scepticism here. Herodotus clearly suggests that one cannot without caution accept traditions about previously reported would-be thalassocrats.

πάρεξ Μίνωός τε: Minos, who famously according to tradition was powerful over the seas surrounding Crete.

τῆς δὲ ἀνθρωπηίης λεγομένης γενεῆς: 'of the race that is called human'. Herodotus shows a further note of caution towards the stories from earlier times. On this passage, see Introduction, p. 5.

Ἰωνίης τε καὶ νήσων: Ionia and the islands near it were strategically central for controlling the Aegean.

122.3: καὶ χρήματά τοι ... κατὰ τὰ φρονήματα: 'and that your resources do not match your plans' (lit. 'that your money is not in accordance with your designs').

σύ νυν ὧδε ... δὲ καὶ ἐμέ: the parallel structure of ὀρθώσεις μὲν ... σώσεις δὲ emphasises Oroetes' strategy – appeal to Polycrates' ambition and play the 'we can help each other out' card to make his feigned argument more convincing. It works, and in the end the always successful Polycrates becomes another figure of the *Histories* tripped up by his own ambition.

ἐμοὶ γὰρ ... καί μοι τοῦτο ...: Oroetes paints himself as being in a desperate situation and, arguably, such a claim about Cambyses was credible given his track record for removing perceived threats. However, one might be surprised Polycrates bought into this, as he had sent troops to help Cambyses previously (see §44.2).

122.4: σύ νυν ἐμὲ ἐκκομίσας ... τὰ μὲν αὐτῶν ... ἔχε, τὰ δὲ ἐμὲ ἔα: the near juxtaposition of σύ and ἐμὲ in the opening clause followed by parallel imperatives reinforces Oroetes' clever tactic in twinning Polycrates' ambition with a pretence of mutual benefit in his bid to persuade him.

ἁπάσης τῆς Ἑλλάδος: emphasised at the end of the sentence as Oroetes pretends to depict Polycrates' aim as within his grasp.

πιστότατος: the superlative reinforces Oroetes' apparent willingness to demonstrate the veracity of his offer and strengthens the reliability of his claim, encouraging Polycrates into his trap.

123

123.1: ἥσθη τε καὶ ἐβούλετο: the pithy phrase and τε καὶ stress how easily Polycrates was persuaded.

ἱμείρετο γὰρ χρημάτων μεγάλως: this shows that Oroetes' assessment of Polycrates' need was right.

Μαιάνδριον Μαιανδρίου ἄνδρα τῶν ἀστῶν: this is the Maeandrius who will reappear as governing affairs at §142 with his vain attempt to set up democracy at Samos. On the possibility that Maeandrius may have played a more sinister and instrumental role in Polycrates' demise than Herodotus suggests, see Roisman (1985: 259–263).

γραμματιστής: just as the satraps do, Polycrates has a scribe. A scribe would be in a position of trust, explaining why Polycrates sent him as πιστότατος.

ἀνέθηκε πάντα ἐς τὸ Ἥραιον: quite possibly the temple described at §60.4.

123.2: λάρνακας ὀκτὼ πληρώσας . . . λάρνακας εἶχε ἑτοίμας: Oroetes creates an impression of great wealth, which proves sufficient to persuade Polycrates.

124

124.1: πολλὰ μὲν τῶν μαντίων . . . πολλὰ δὲ τῶν φίλων: Herodotus stresses just how many sought to dissuade Polycrates from going to Oroetes, but in vain. He even ignored the words of soothsayers. The ruler who ignores the wise adviser or wise words of caution, but who then has a wise 'enlightenment', is a recurring motif in Herodotus: Croesus ignores Solon, I.31-3; Xerxes ignores Artabanus, VII.10-16; see Shapiro (1994: 349–55).

ἐστέλλετο αὐτόσε: 'was getting ready to go there'.

πρὸς δὲ: emphatic introduction to the vision of Polycrates' daughter, which also fails to dissuade him.

ὄψιν ἐνυπνίου τοιήνδε: prophetic dreams are a clear theme in Herodotus and portend momentous events, as the dream of Cambyses about Smerdis showed. In that case, it was ironically not ignored, but fatally misread.

πατέρα ἐν τῷ ἠέρι μετέωρον ... λοῦσθαι μὲν ὑπὸ τοῦ Διός, χρίεσθαι δὲ ὑπὸ τοῦ ἡλίου: how the cryptic dream manifests itself in events is explained at §125.3.

124.2: παντοίη ἐγίνετο μὴ: 'tried everything (to persuade him) not ...' (lit. 'she was in every form that he not ...').

βούλεσθαι γὰρ παρθενεύεσθαι ... τοῦ πατρὸς ἐστερῆσθαι: the notion that blood ties were stronger than those of relation by marriage was a feature of ancient Greek thought. Cf. §121 on Intaphrenes' wife.

125

125.1: πάσης συμβουλίης ἀλογήσας: ignoring wise advice and caution because of ambition is a recurring theme in the *Histories* and ultimately it will prove to be Polycrates' downfall, too, reinforcing the point made at §124.1 that his ambitions blinded his ability to heed objections.

ἅμα ἀγόμενος ἄλλους τε πολλούς: the phrases stresses how many Polycrates took with him.

ἐν δὲ δὴ ... Δημοκήδεα: ἐν δὲ δὴ: 'among whom in fact'. Democedes will reappear at §129.3 where he is called in to help cure Darius' injured foot. This passage explains how he came to be among the slaves of Oroetes. He will be a highly significant figure in events §§129.3-137.5.

ἰητρόν τε ἐόντα ... τὴν τέχνην ἀσκέοντα ἄριστα τῶν κατ' ἑωυτόν: the nature of his future role in events is hinted at here in the reference to his surpassing skill as a physician. Κροτωνιήτην: Croton was a powerful city in Magna Graecia in southern Italy, settled by the Achaeans *c*. 710 in the Tarentine Gulf (see Figure 4).

125.2: Μαγνησίαν: Magnesia on the Meander in Ionia (see Figure 1), where Oroetes settled before sending Myrsus to Samos (§122.1). It was part of the first province of the empire (§90.1).

Πολυκράτης διεφθάρη κακῶς ... τῶν ἑωυτοῦ φρνημάτων: the injustice of Polycrates' demise is re-emphasized, further reinforced by the following: οὔτε ἑωυτοῦ ἀξίως οὔτε τῶν ἑωυτοῦ φρνημάτων. See note on §120.1.

ὅτι γάρ μὴ ... μεγαλοπρεπείην συμβληθῆναι: the obituary continues. Herodotus argues that no other Greek tyrant, bar those of Syracuse, can even be compared with Polycrates in magnificence. οἱ Συρηκοσίων γενόμενοι τύραννοι: Herodotus is probably thinking of Gelo and Hiero I. Gelo defeated the Carthaginians, driving them out of Sicily until *c*. 411/410, at the Battle of Himera 480, and Hiero was victorious at the naval Battle of Cumae in 474, defeating an army of invading Etruscans. They were key patrons of Pindar and odes *Olympian* 1 and *Pythians* 2 and 3 are dedicated to their victories. Bacchylides also wrote his fifth ode to Hiero, *c*. 476. Hiero has also been blessed with a role in *Assassin's Creed* in rather more recent popular culture.

μεγαλοπρεπείην: what does Herodotus mean by magnificence? He does not mean that Polycrates was always morally praiseworthy. He could be brutal as shown by his readiness to torch the wives and children of the men he exiled (§45.5). Rather, he seems to be referring to his success, ability and prosperity (cf. Aristotle, *Nichomachean Ethics* 1107b). Isocrates's usage of the term in describing honours given to Cypriot tyrant Evagoras suggests capacity for lavish outlay and splendour (9.2). See Clarke (2018: 174–7) on how Herodotus' portrayal of Polycrates reveals a more nuanced attitude to tyrant rulers than he is sometimes given credit for. He does not simply polarize tyrants as eastern and freedom as purely Greek.

125.3: μιν οὐκ αξίως ... Ὀροίτης ἀνεσταύρωσε: οὐκ ἀξίως ἀπηγήσιος refers to the ghastly manner of Polycrates' death. Herodotus does not go into details; he leaves it to the reader/listener's imagination. H&W note (*ad loc.*) that, 'H., like a true Greek, gives here no details of Asiatic barbarity'. The current author thinks, nevertheless, that Herodotus' purpose here is primarily dramatic to emphasize the injustice of what happened to Polycrates. He is less sparing elsewhere (§159.1 on the punishment of the Babylonians; IV.202 on Cyrenean queen Pheretime's punishment of the Barcaeans). ἀνεσταύρωσε: 'he crucified him'.

τῶν δὲ οἱ ἑπομένων ... δοῦλοι τῶν ἑπομένων: the ring composition of the sentence stresses Oroetes' very different treatment of the native Samians in Polycrates' party compared to the slaves and foreigners, further stressed by ὅσοι μὲν ἦσαν Σάμιοι ... ὅσοι δὲ ἦσαν ξεῖνοί τε καὶ δοῦλοι. ἑωυτῷ χάριν εἰδέναι ἐόντας ἐλευθέρους: 'that they acknowledge their gratitude to him for their being free'. Oroetes attempts to bind the Samians he releases by obligation. The implication is that he is binding them to himself rather than the Persian king, thus buying personal loyalty.

Πολυκράτης δὲ ἀνακρεμάμενος ... ἐκ τοῦ σώματος ἰκμάδα: the fulfilment of his daughter's vision that failed to dissuade him (§124.1). The rain fulfilled the 'washing' by Zeus, his sweating, the anointment by the sun.

125.4: αἱ πολλαὶ εὐτυχίαι ... Αἰγύπτου βασιλεὺς προεμαντεύσατο: Herodotus is good at cross-referencing earlier relevant sections of his work. Here, Amasis' fears for Polycrates' grim demise have come to pass (§43.2).

126

Oroetes' gruesome deeds.

126.1: χρόνῳ δὲ οὐ πολλῷ ... Πολυκράτεος τίσιες μετῆλθον: Herodotus stresses how quickly Oroetes' actions recoil upon him in the form of revenge.

μετά...Καμβύσεω θάνατον... Μάγων τὴν βασιληίην: this dates these events to *c.* 522.

ὠφέλεε μὲν οὐδέν... Μήδων ἀπαιρημένους τὴν ἀρχήν: this seems to confirm the self-serving motivations of Oroetes.

126.2: ὁ δὲ ἐν... ἐν Πέρσῃσι δοκίμους: Oroetes murders Mitrobates and his son, who we are told were esteemed among the Persians. ἐν ταύτῃ τῇ ταραχῇ: namely, the period of uncertainty that followed the overthrow of the Magi. The implication is that Oroetes was taking advantage.

κατὰ μὲν ἔκτεινε... κατὰ δὲ: *tmesis.* ἔκτεινε is not repeated after κατὰ δὲ but must be resupplied – 'he killed Mitrobates... and (he killed) the son of Mitrobates, Carnaspes'.

ὅς οἱ ὠνείδισε... ἐς Πολυκράτεα ἔχοντα: lit. 'who had hurled the reproaches at him by referring to Polycrates' (see §120.3).

ἄλλα τε ἐξύβρισε παντοῖα... ἠφάνισε αὐτῷ ἵππῳ: Oroetes emerges as vindictive. The verb 'kill' appears twice in this passage and has become like a refrain in this section. ἐλθόντα Δαρείου παρ' αὐτόν: referring to the messenger who came to him from Darius. This foreshadows that it is Darius who will set in motion reprisals against Oroetes.

κτείνει μιν ὀπίσω... ἠφάνισε αὐτῷ ἵππῳ: he killed the messenger who brought it, after laying a trap for the men on their return journey, and having killed him, he concealed him along with his horse. ἄνδρας: shows that Oroetes killed more than one. μιν... μιν picks up on τινα.

127

127.1: Δαρεῖος δέ ὡς... τὸν Ὀροίτα τίσασθαι: this echoes §126.1, where Herodotus signposts that revenge will come upon Oroetes. It is tempting to see ἐπεθύμεε as a deliberate and ironic echo of Herodotus' usage of this verb for Oroetes' own malicious designs at §125. His own 'desire' was going to come back to haunt him.

ἐκ μὲν δὴ... πυνθανόμενος ἔχειν: Darius sees he has to proceed with caution. οἰδεόντων ἔτι τῶν πρηγμάτων: the period following the overthrow of the Magi and early on in Darius' reign. Herodotus implies a clear connection between the unsettled state of politics and Oroetes deeds.

A   B   B   A
νεωστὶ ἔχων τῇ ἀρχὴν καὶ τὸν Ὀροίτεα μεγάλην τὴν ἰσχὺν πυνθανόμενος ἔχειν

The chiastic word order and *polyptoton* of ἔχω stresses Darius' reasons for being careful. He has only lately come to power and Oroetes has considerable forces (including, of course, those of Polycrates) at his disposal.

τὸν χίλιοι μὲν ... Λύδιον καὶ Ἰωνικόν: the sentence begins with a connecting relative, which then switches to a fresh main clause (εἶχε δὲ νόμον) with Oroetes as the subject. The sentence also details Oroetes' resources, explaining Darius' actions. χίλιοι ... Περσέων ἐδορυφόρεον: Oroetes had a native Persian bodyguard, as well as his provinces' forces. νόμον τόν τε Φρύγιον καὶ Λύδιον καὶ Ἰωνικόν: the *polysyndeton* illustrates his power. These are the third, second, and first provinces respectively (see Figure 5).

127.2: πρὸς ταῦτα: 'in response to these things'.

τάδε ἐμηχανήσατο: 'he [Darius] made the following plan'.

τίς ἄν μοι ... βίης ἔργον οὐδέν: τίς ἄν μοι ... μὴ βίῃ τε καὶ ὁμίλῳ: 'which of you would undertake to carry this out for me by means of your cleverness, and not by means of force or numbers' (τίς ἄν μοι τοῦτο ὑμέων ὑποστὰς ἐπιτελέσειε (lit. 'which of you having undertaken this for me would carry t out'). ἔνθα γὰρ σοφίης δέει, βίης ἔργον οὐδέν: 'for where this is need for cleverness, there is no place for force'. Darius' speeches often contain typically sophistic generalizations or contrasts. Herodotus may use these to reflect his cleverness and shrewdness. On this meaning of σοφίη, see §4.2 (on Phanes) and §85.1 (on Darius' astute groom Oebares).

127.3: ὑμέων: emphatically placed. Darius is placing his hopes on this group.

ὃς ὠφέλησε μέν ... κακὰ δὲ μεγάλα ἔοργε: ὅς: connecting relative. 'A man who...'.

ὠφέλησε μέν... οὐδέν... κακὰ δὲ μεγάλα ἔοργε: the chiastic word order emphasizes Darius' point that Oroetes has not brought anything good to the Persians, quite the opposite in fact.

ἠΐστωσε: lit. 'he made unseen', so 'he destroyed'. Note how Darius is made to use a different verb for what Oroetes did to Mitrobates and his son, stressing his particular anger over these murders (see §127.1: ἐπεθύμεε... τίσασθαι... μάλιστα Μιτροβάτεω καὶ τοῦ παιδός).

ὕβριν οὐκ ἀνασχετὸν: Darius conveys the seriousness of Oroetes' crimes. This also recalls ἄλλα τε ἐξύβρισε παντοῖα (§126.1).

καταλαμπτέος ἐστὶ ἡμῖν θανάτῳ: 'we must take him down by death', so 'we must arrest him and put him to death'. καταλαμπτέος is the gerundive form of καταλαμβάνω.

128

128.1: αὐτὸς ἕκαστος ἐθέλων ποιέειν ταῦτα: 'each wanting to carry it out himself'. The phrase suggests the strong loyalty Darius has inspired in the men.

κελεύων πάλλεσθαι· παλλομένων δὲ λαγχάνει: decision by lot was associated primarily with democracy in Greek political thought (see Otanes' argument for democracy, §80.6).

Βαγαῖος ὁ Ἀρτόντεω: an Achaemenid nobleman. He may have been rewarded with the post of satrap after getting rid of Oroetes.

128.2: βυβλία γραψάμενος πολλὰ... ταῦτα ἐς τὰς Σάρδις: we are not told immediately what Bagaeus' plan is and Herodotus leaves the reader intrigued. In this short section, Herodotus shows how well he can build up suspense. σφρηγῖδά σφι ἐπέβαλε τὴν Δαρείου: 'he stamped on them the seal of Darius'. This would carry great authority for those to whom these notes would be given. βυβλία: 'notes', or 'documents' (see §40.1).

128.3: ἐδίδου τῷ γραμματιστῇ... πάντες ὕπαρχοι ἔχουσι: each of the satraps had a royal scribe. They were in theory loyal to the king rather than the governing satrap.

ἀποπειρώμενος δὲ τῶν δορυφόρων: Bagaeus tests the loyalty of the bodyguards. The first letter asks if they will revolt from Oroetes.

128.4: σεβομένους μεγάλως: the guards' loyalty is evident. They 'greatly respect the letters', undoubtedly aided by the presence of the king's seal. **τὰ λεγόμενα ἐκ τῶν βυβλίων ἔτι μεζόνως:** they respect the content of the letters even more greatly.

βασιλεὺς Δαρεῖος ἀπαγορεύει ... μὴ δορυφορέειν Ὀροίτεα: a clause of prevention. The plan unfolds gradually. First, they are barred from being Oroetes' bodyguards, and so from showing him any loyalty.

128.4-5: οἱ δὲ ἀκούσαντες ... ὡς ἤκουσαν ταῦτα: the repetition conveys how swiftly the guards followed the letters' commands.

128.5: ἀκινάκεας: a short straight Persian sword (see also §118.2).
οὕτω δὴ Ὀροίτεα ... τοῦ Σαμίου τίσιες μετῆλθον: this verbal echo of §126.1 brings the Oroetes episode to a close with an emphatic ring composition.

§§129-38 *Darius' foot and a determined physician.* ALC (ad loc.) brand it a 'novelistic story' but note that it is 'well incorporated'.

129

129.1: χρόνῳ οὐ πολλῷ ὕστερον: Herodotus gives an approximate chronology.
ἐν ἄγρῃ θηρῶν: beast hunts are frequently depicted in Persian art, especially with the king in combat with a wild beast.

129.2: κως ἰσχυροτέρως ἐστράφη ... ἐκ τῶν ἄρθρων: Darius' injury was likely a dislocation.
νομίζων δὲ καὶ ... τούτοισι ἐχρᾶτο: 'Because he thought previously that the Egyptians around him seemed to be the best regarding

medicine, he employed them'. Quite a tricky sentence grammatically. Indirect statement after νομίζων with infinitive ἔχειν. Αἰγυπτίων τοὺς δοκέοντας: 'those of the Egyptians.' τοὺς δοκέοντας is the object of ἔχειν and εἶναι is dependent on the participle. τὴν ἰητρικήν is accusative of respect dependent on πρώτους.

στρεβλοῦντες καὶ βιώμενοι: 'by twisting and forcing'. The violence of the treatment does not improve Darius' injury, but rather κακὸν μέζον ἐργάζοντο ('they made it worse'). The Egyptians were renowned physicians long before Herodotus (see Gabriel 2012: 69–86, 118–19 on Darius' regard for them). Although Democedes will succeed here, 'it is clear that the Egyptians are the standard against which medical skill is measured at the court of the great king' (Moyer 2011: 61)).

129.3: ἐπ' ἑπτὰ ... ἡμέρας καὶ ἑπτὰ νύκτας: the number seven is typical in ancient accounts both mythical and historical.

ἔχοντί οἱ φλαύρως: 'to him while he was in distress'.

τοῦ Κροτωνιήτεω Δημοκήδεος ... ἐν τοῖσι Ὀροίτεω ἀνδραπόδοισι: this occurred at 125.3, where Oroetes freed the Samians in Polycrates' entourage, but enslaved everyone else. Democedes' presence was noted at §125.1.

πέδας τε ἕλκοντα καὶ ῥάκεσι ἐσθημένον: Democedes is a sorry sight when he is led in.

130

130.1: ἀρρωδέων μὴ ἑωυτὸν ... Ἑλλάδος ἦ ἀπεστερημένος: Democedes fears that he will never see Greece again. There is a parallel with the grudging Egyptian physician, whom Amasis sent to Persia away from his wife and children (see §1.1-2).

130.2: τεχνάζειν ἐπιστάμενος: 'to apply his skills', here in the sense of 'to be cunning', this echoes and plays on Darius' question τὴν τέχνην εἰ ἐπίσταιτο (§130.1), stressing that Democedes is not willing to play along at that point (§130.1: ὁ δὲ οὐκ ὑπεδέκετο).

μάστιγάς τε καὶ κέντρα: sensing that Democedes is deliberately being evasive, Darius resorts to force.

130.3: ἤπια μετὰ τὰ ἰσχυρὰ: contrasts Democedes' gentle approach with the harsh force of the Egyptians.

οὐδαμὰ ἔτι ἐλπίζοντα ἀρτίπουν ἔσεσθαι: 'in no way still hoping that his foot would recover'.

130.4: δωρέεται δή μιν ... μιν ὑγιέα ἐποίησε: δωρέεται δή μιν 'he presented him with...'. Darius' gift of two golden fetters to Democedes for curing him may seem odd, as Democedes himself notes – ὁ δέ μιν ἐπείρετο ... μιν ὑγιέα ἐποίησε: 'he asked him whether he was awarding him a double evil for making him well'. Cf. §23.4 on the Ethiopian king's view of the bracelets.

ἡσθεὶς: 'being pleased with/impressed by' (see also §§42.2, 119.7).

130.5: ὑποτύπτουσα δὲ αὐτέων ἑκάστη: this implies that the wives mixed freely, showing that the separation enforced by the Magus was not the norm, and hence why it confirmed Otanes' suspicions (see note on §69.1).

οὕτω ... ὡς ... ἀνελέγετο: result clause.

οὕτω δή τι ... τι χρυσοῦ συνελέχθη: so much that an attendant accompanying him, whose name was Skiton, collected a considerable quantity of gold for himself once he had gathered for himself the staters which fell from the bowls' (lit. 'collected for himself the staters which fell from the bowls and gathered for himself a considerable quantity of gold'). The double gathering phrase is like a *hendiadys* stressing the sheer quantity Skiton gathered as mere fallen 'crumbs', leaving the even greater amount that Democedes must have been granted to the imagination. By extension, Herodotus hints at the wealth of Persia. **Σκίτων:** ALC (*ad loc.*) note that this is an Attic name, meaning 'worthless'. The name was used for a stock character in Attic comedy. Herodotus uses the name as a paradoxical jest at his unexpected good fortune.

131

Background of Democedes.

Κρότωνος: on Croton, see note on §125.1.

πατρὶ συνείχετο ... ὀργὴν χαλεπῷ: 'In Croton, he quarrelled with his father who had a harsh temper' (lit. 'in Croton, he was at odds with his father who harsh with regard to his anger'). ὀργὴν is accusative of respect.

131.1-2: καταστὰς δὲ ἐς ... Κροτωνιῆται ἰητροὶ εὐδοκίμησαν: the glittering career of Democedes. πρώτῳ ἔτεϊ: in his first year on Aegina, Democedes surpassed the other physicians there. δευτέρῳ ἔτεϊ: in his second, the Aeginetans paid him a talent at public expense (δημοσίῃ), a considerable sum. δημοσίῃ μισθοῦνται: ALC (*ad loc.*) note that Herodotus places a fifth-century Athenian practice in the sixth century. τρίτῳ δὲ ἔτεϊ: in his third, the Athenians paid him one hundred minas, which is over a talent (1 talent = 60 minas). τετάρτῳ δὲ ἔτεϊ: in his fourth, Polycrates paid him two talents. ἀπὸ τούτου τοῦ ἀνδρός: Herodotus attributes the great reputation of the Crotonian physicians principally to Democedes.

131.3: δεύτεροι δὲ Κυρηναῖοι: the Cyreneans, according to Herodotus, were reputed throughout Greece to be the second best physicians (cf. Pindar, *Pythian* 5.85-6).

[κατὰ τὸν αὐτὸν ... εἶναι Ἑλλήνων πρῶτοι]: the comment on the Argives' musical talents seems out of place here.

132

132.1: ὁμοτράπεζος: the fact that Democedes sat at the table with the king shows the great favour he enjoyed (cf. συνέστιος καὶ ὁ ὁμοτράπεζος: IX.16.2; see also, Xenophon, *Cyropaedia* VII.1.30, where it is used as a

Persian term of honour for certain favoured courtiers; cf. Xenophon, *Anabasis* I.8.25).

πλήν τε ἑνὸς ... πάντα τἄλλά οἱ παρῆν: Herodotus stresses the great favours Democedes enjoyed compared to the one thing he really wanted, to return to Greece.

132.2: ἰῶντο: 'treat' here, rather than 'heal'.

ἐσσώθησαν ... ἐρρύσατο: Democedes achieved mercy for the Egyptian physicians who failed to cure Darius.

μάντιν Ἠλεῖον ... ἐρρύσατο: Elean soothsayers were particularly famous, especially the Iamidae family, who claimed descent from Apollo (see Pindar, *Olympian* 6).

ἦν δὲ μέγιστον πρῆγμα ... παρὰ βασιλέϊ: 'For Democedes possessed very great influence with the king'. Herodotus ends his account of Democedes' status by repeating the great influence Democedes enjoyed with Darius.

133

133.1: Ἀτόσσῃ τῇ Κύρου: Atossa, who had been married to her brother Cambyses (§31.6) the Magus (§68.4), and then to Darius (§88.2).

ἐπὶ τοῦ μαστοῦ ... φῦμα: the precise condition is debated, but the swelling was probably a benign tumour or a form of mastitis.

ἐξορκοῖ μιν ἦ ... ἂν αὐτῆς δεηθῇ: 'but exacted from her an oath that she would repay him whatever he requested from her'. δεηθῇ· δεήσεσθαι: the *polyptoton* emphasizes how Democedes sees a chance to effect his return to Greece.

δεήσεσθαι δὲ οὐδενὸς ... αἰσχύνην ἐστὶ φέροντα: 'But he said that it would be nothing that would bring her any shame (lit. '[he said that] he would ask for not any of all those things that led to shame (for her).' ἐς αἰσχύνην: He reassures Atossa he will ask for nothing shameful. ALC link this expression to the ethics of the doctor–patient relationship formulated by the Hippocratic school (see also Carrick 2001: *passim*).

134

134.1: ὑγιέα ἀπέδεξε: 'made her healthy', 'restored her to health' (see also §130.3: ὑγιέα μιν ἀπέδεξε).

ἔχων δύναμιν τοσαύτην ... οὔτε δύναμιν Πέρσῃσι: 'despite having such great power you are sitting about and not adding any additional race or power for the Persians'.

134.2: οἰκὸς δὲ ἐστὶ ἄνδρα ... ὑπ' ἀνδρὸς ἄρχονται: Darius needs to prove he is truly a man. Atossa's speech reflects the notion the masculinity should be proven through martial prowess, expansion and acquisition. There are overtones of Homeric τιμὴ with the importance laid on public perception of power. One is also reminded of Mitrobates' alleged taunting of Oroetes with his lack of imperial success, also reproaching Oroetes with not being a true man (§120.3). **ἐπ' ἀμφότερα:** lit. 'on both sides', so 'from both angles'. **ἵνα καὶ ... καὶ ἵνα ... καὶ ἵνα:** the *anaphora* and *tricolon* of purpose clauses (although the second is variation on the first) gives urgency to Atossa's exhortation. **ἵνα τρίβωνται πολέμῳ ... ἄγοντες ἐπιβουλεύωσί τοι:** the notion that war keeps the people occupied and prevents them from revolting was a common principle of Greek political thought. Polybius depicts the Romans as using war as a way of keeping citizens sharp and battle-ready, such is the partial motive he gives for the senate voting for war against the Dalmatians 155 (*Histories* XXXV.7). Aristotle, *Politics* 1313b19-32, cynically argues that great works serve a similar purpose for the tyrant who cannot rely on his citizens' trust and support. Note, however, that tyranny had become a more pejorative term by Aristotle's time.

134.3: αὐξομένῳ γὰρ ... συναύξονται, ... γηράσκοντι δὲ συγγηράσκουσι: the parallel phrasing stresses the connection between mental and physical aging.

134.4: βεβούλευμαι ζεύξας γέφυραν ... ἐς τὴν ἑτέρην ἤπειρον: for Xerxes' bid to 'bridge' the Hellespont, see VII.155.1.

134.5: Ὅρα νυν ... τὴν Ἑλλάδα στρατεύεσθαι: Atossa's speech takes on an authoritative tone (Ὅρα νυν – 'now, look...'). μὲν τὴν πρώτην ἰέναι ἔασον lit. 'in the first instance, allow to let it go against the Scythians', so 'allow yourself to give up your plan against the Scythians for the present'. οὗτοι γάρ, ἐπεὰν ... βουλῇ, ἔσονταί τοι: Atossa implies that the Scythians are far too easy a target. σὺ δέ μοι: she adds a personal note, asking Darius to 'make an expedition against Greece' for her.

λόγῳ πυνθανομένη Λακαίνας ... μοι γενέσθαι θεραπαίνας: it is perhaps significant that Atossa highlights Spartan women as her desired attendants first, the Greek women whose lifestyle and education were very different from the rest of Greece.

ἄνδρα ἐπιτηδεότατον ἀνδρῶν πάντων: Democedes. The phrase is a subtle euphemism, so that he can be mentioned without being directly named, thereby avoiding any suggestion of overfamiliarity. τοῦτον ὅς ... τὸν πόδα ἐξιήσατο: continues the indirect highlighting of Democedes as the man for the task.

134.6: κατασκόπους: for the Persian use of spies, see §§17–25 on the spies sent by Cambyses against Ethiopia (see also I.100.2 on the spies of Median king Deioces; on Greeks using spies, see VII 146.1).

135

135.1: ἅμα ἔπος τε καὶ ἔργον ἐποίεε: 'he acted at once upon what he said' (lit. 'and made word and deed at the same time'). Darius swiftly follows his spoken intent with action.

ὅκως τε μὴ ... πάντως ὀπίσω ἀπάξουσι: the implication could be that Darius does not fully trust Democedes and suspects that he could seize the opportunity to escape. It is not clear whether Darius had any inkling that Democedes was manipulating Atossa for his own ends. However, μιν πάντως ὀπίσω ἀπάξουσι ('so that they would bring back him especially'), may simply suggest that he was an important figure for Darius, who wanted to ensure he returned.

135.2: ἐδέετο αὐτοῦ ὅκως ... Πέρσῃσι ὀπίσω ἥξει: 'he asked him to come back once he had explained and shown all of Greece to the Persians.' (lit. 'he asked him (to take care) that he would come back'), a somewhat elliptical clause of precaution.

δῶρα δέ μιν ... τὴν ἅμα οἱ πλεύσεσθαι: Darius' lavish promises seek to secure Democedes' loyalty. πάντα ... πολλαπλήσια ... παντοίων: stress the richness of Darius' promised gifts.

135.3: δοκέειν ἐμοί ... οὐδενὸς δολεροῦ νόου: Herodotus does not think Darius did this as a trick or out of suspicion.

δείσας μὴ εὖ ἐκπειρῷτο Δαρεῖος: Democedes, however, feared he was being tested. εὖ = reflexive.

ἐπιδραμὼν: 'rush into, 'hasten to', or 'greedily run after'.

τὰ μὲν ἑωυτοῦ ... σφέα ἀπελθὼν ἔχοι: Democedes says he will leave his belongings as he will need them when he returns, in a bid to divert what he sees as Darius' suspicion.

136

136.1: Φοινίκης ἐς Σιδῶνα πόλιν: Sidon was one of Phoenicia's most important ports (modern Saida in Lebanon). Homer notes the skill of Sidonian embroidery (*Iliad* VI.289-91) and refers to 'Sidon, rich in bronze' (ἐκ μὲν Σιδῶνος πολυχάλκου: *Odyssey* XV.426).

παντοίων ἀγαθῶν: recalls §135.2.

γαῦλον μέγαν: a Phoenician merchant vessel.

ἐς Τάραντα: Tarentum (modern Taranto), a Doric settlement in Magna Graecia.

136.2: ἐκ ῥηϊστώνης τῆς: 'out of friendly feeling'. On this word, see ALC *ad loc.*

τῶν Μηδικέων νεῶν: the distinction between Median and Persian is not always a clear one in Herodotean usage.

ὡς κατασκόπους ... ἐόντας: 'because they were spies.'

ἀπικνέεται· ἀπιγμένου: Aristophilides bought Democedes time to get to Croton, and then released the ships.

καὶ τὰ παρέλαβε . . . νεῶν ἀπέδωκέ σφι: 'and he gave back the items he had seized from the ships'. τὰ relative pronoun picking up on τὰ πηδάλια from earlier.

137

137.1: ἀγοράζοντα: 'wandering about in public'.
ἅπτοντο: imperfect.

137.2: Κροτωνιητέων οἱ μὲν . . . οἱ δὲ ἀντάπτοντο: the Persian arrival divides the Crotonians. Some want to let the Persians take Democedes out of fear, others try and seize him back. The latter group resort to physical attack to retrieve him.

προϊσχομένους ἔπεα τάδε: 'spoke out as follows' (lit. 'put forth the following words').

δρηπέτην: 'runaway slave'.

137.3: κῶς ταῦτα βασιλέϊ . . . ἀνδραποδίζεσθαι περιησόμεθα: the four rhetorical questions aim to scare the Crotonians into letting Democedes' go with the threat of a Persian backlash looming. It fails. **περιυβρίσθαι:** '[when he has been] so insolently insulted'. Here, the ὕβρις lies in the betrayal of trust and disrespect of Darius' orders. **ἐπὶ τίνα δὲ . . . πόλιν; τίνα δὲ προτέρην:** the final two questions show a parallel structure to stress that Croton will surge straight to the top of Darius' invasion list if they do not release Democedes. The second προτέρην picks up on πόλιν.

137.4: ἀπέπλεον ὀπίσω ἐς . . . ἐστερημένοι τοῦ ἡγεμόνος: the planned *reconnaissance* of Greece comes to a very abrupt end. The loss of Democedes shows that the Persians were, according to Herodotus, not sufficiently familiar with Greece to continue without his insight. The whole episode may also be sowing the seeds of a theme that emerges more strongly in the later books – that Greece was not going to be an easy conquest (see especially, Artabanus' warning to Xerxes VII.49), as the stout resistance of the Crotonians subtly suggests.

137.5: τοσόνδε μέντοι ἐνετείλατο ... κελεύων εἰπεῖν σφεας: an *anacolouthon*. κελεύων explains ἐνετείλατο, but starts a new construction.

τὴν Μίλωνος θυγατέρα ... γυναῖκα: Milon was a famous wrestler from Croton. Strabo records a story about Milon being eaten by beasts while his hand was stuck in a tree which he was trying to split (VI.1.12).

Μίλωνος ἦν οὔνομα πολλὸν παρὰ βασιλέϊ: this explains why Democedes asks the retreating spies to tell Darius about his marriage. It is not entirely clear why the name carried such weight with Darius but may simply have been down to the wrestler's fame.

κατὰ δὲ τοῦτο ... τῇ ἑωυτοῦ δόκιμος: Herodotus takes a somewhat cynical view of Democedes' motives, namely that he was ensuring a good reputation with both his home citizens and with Darius. See ALC (*ad loc.*) for his later exile and death at the hands of the democratic party of Croton. H&W brand his conduct unscrupulous (see their note on §138.1 and the comparison with Gillus).

138

The fate of Tarentine exile Gillus.

138.1: ἐς Ἰηπυγίην: the region of Iapygia stretched from Tarentum up to Brundisium (modern Taranto and Brindisi, see Figure 4 – Taras is marked), including the Salento promontory. The story here suggests that relations between the Iapygian peoples and the ruling party of Tarentum were hostile. The Iapygians are mentioned again, where he refers to the Messapians who were of the peoples inhabiting that region (VII.170.2).

ἐκπίπτουσι: (*here*) 'were wrecked'.

σφεας δουλεύοντας ἐνθαῦτα: presumably they were enslaved after being shipwrecked.

σφεας δουλεύοντας ... Ταραντῖνος φυγὰς ῥυσάμενος: Gillus rescued them and led them back to Darius.

ἀντὶ τούτων ἕτοιμος ... διδόναι τοῦτο ὅ τι βούλοιτο: the indefinite clause stresses Darius' gratitude.

138.2: ἵνα δὲ μὴ ... κάτοδόν οἱ ἔσεσθαι: this short passage offers an insight into the complexity of relations between Greek cities. ἵνα δὲ μὴ συνταράξῃ τὴν Ἑλλάδα: Gillus may partly have feared that if his return was perceived as being assisted by a major external power, it would cause uproar. Like H&W, ALC (*ad loc.*) see a moralizing tone in this passage, with Gillus showing a respect for Greek interstate relations which Democedes did not. He shows a sense that uneasy relations need to be delicately handled. He asks for the Cnidians as escorts, fearing the reaction of the Tarentines if anyone else were involved. Κνιδίους μούνους ... τούτων ἐόντων τοῖσι Ταραντίνοισι φίλων: the connection seems to have been one of kinship, as the Cnidians were, like the Tarentines, a Spartan colony. On the revolutionary connotations that the phrase φυγάδων καθόδος later came to have, see ALC *ad loc.*

138.3: πειθόμενοι δὲ Δαρείῳ ... Ταραντίνους οὔκων ἔπειθον: the *polyptoton* and framing word order shows the contrasting reaction. ALC note the irony of the fact that the Cnidians are persuaded by Darius, but that they, supported by the king, cannot persuade the Tarentines at all.

βίην δὲ ἀδύνατοι ἦσαν προσφέρειν: the phrase reflects the careful, if uneasy, maintenance of peaceful relations between cities. The episode marks a beginning of uneasy Persian relations with the Greeks beyond Asia. 'Firsts' in the development of relations between east and west is a recurring theme in the *Histories*, as seen in Book I with Croesus' conquests (I.6).

§§139–50 *We now swing briefly back to Samos.*

139

139.1: Σάμον βασιλεὺς Δαρεῖος ... πολίων πασέων πρώτην Ἑλληνίδων: Darius' first conquest in Greece brings us back to Samos and Herodotus first shares the rather charming story of this venture's origins (διὰ τοιήνδε τινὰ αἰτίην).

Καμβύσεω ... στρατευομένου ἐπ' Αἴγυπτον: we now glance back to the reign of Cambyses. **ἄλλοι τε συχνοὶ ... Αἴγυπτον ἀπίκοντο Ἑλλήνων:** Herodotus gives an idea of the number of Greek visitors to Egypt: οἱ μέν, ὡς οἰκός, κατ' ἐμπορίην ... οἱ δὲ τινὲς ... θεηταί: they came for trade and sightseeing. κατ' ἐμπορίην στρατευόμενοι: 'came with an army for trade'.

τῶν ἦν καὶ Συλοσῶν ὁ Αἰακέος: one of these many Greek visitors was Syloson, then exiled from Samos by his brother Polycrates (§39.2). His other brother Pantagnotus had been murdered by Polycrates.

139.2: τοῦτον τὸν Συλοσῶντα ... εὐτυχίῃ τις τοιήδε: the emphatic phrasing stresses the chance nature of the occurrence that will prove so beneficial to Syloson. It is tempting to see in εὐτυχίῃ a verbal echo of the many εὐτυχίαι of Polycrates, now by an ironic twist of fate about to pass to the brother he drove out.

λαβὼν χλανίδα καὶ περιβαλόμενος πυρρὴν: 'having taken his red cloak and put it on'. The *hyperbaton* of χλανίδα and πυρρὴν highlights the cloak as a key element in this story.

ἠγόραζε: 'was wandering in the open' (cf. §137.1).

δορυφόρος τε ἐὼν ... λόγου οὐδενός κω μεγάλου: 'who was [then] the bodyguard of Cambyses and as yet of no great note'. There was back then no clue that Darius would rise to the supreme post.

προσελθὼν ὠνέετο: 'he approached him and tried to buy it'. ὠνέετο is conative imperfect.

139.3: θείῃ τύχῃ χρεώμενος: '(as if) employing divine fortune'. Herodotus does not mean this literally, he simply emphasizes the incredible good luck this would bring Syloson. It could be argued that there was an element of divine justice in the return of Samos to the exiled brother.

δίδωμι δὲ ἄλλως: lit. 'I give it to you otherwise', 'I give it you free.'

τὸ εἷμα: emphatic placement of the significant and well-omened garment.

140

140.1: Συλοσῶν ἠπίστατο τοῦτό ... ἀπολωλέναι δι' εὐηθείην: Syloson reflects that he might have been naïve simply to give his cloak away 'on account of his good nature' (δι' εὐηθείην).

Καμβύσης τε ἀπέθανε ... τὴν βασιληίην ἔσχε: *polysyndeton* stressing the dramatic turn of events since Syloson gave Darius the cloak.

ἐς τοῦτον τὸν ἄνδρα τῷ: 'to the very man to whom ...'. This emphasizes the dramatic twist that the mere bodyguard asking for the cloak was now king of the Persians. A cloak for a kingdom.

Δαρείου εὐεργέτης εἶναι: Syloson calls himself Darius' benefactor, a carefully chosen word which contains the expectation of reciprocity.

140.2: Καὶ τίς ἐστὶ ... τῷ ἐγὼ προαιδεῦμαι: 'And who of the Greeks is the benefactor to whom I am obliged...'. Darius is well aware of the obligations of the benefactor.

ἀναβέβηκε δ' ἤ τις ἢ οὐδείς: 'hardly anyone has come up to see us yet' (lit. 'either someone or no one has come up (to see me)'). H&W (*ad loc.*) note that the idiom ἤ τις ἢ οὐδείς (for 'hardly any') is a colloquialism.

ἵνα εἰδέω τί θέλων λέγει ταῦτα: there is a possible hint of suspicion here.

140.3: καὶ τί ποιήσας ... φησί εἶναι βασιλέος: 'and for what deed he claimed to be the king's benefactor' (lit. 'having done what he said that he was benefactor of the king').

140.4: σὺ κεῖνος εἶς ... εἰ καὶ σμικρά: Darius is impressed by Syloson and the fact that he kindly gave him his cloak to him back when he was a relative nobody.

ὡς μή κοτέ ... Ὑστάσπεος εὖ ποιήσαντι: 'so that you may never regret that you treated Darius son of Hystaspes well'.

140.5: ἀνασωσάμενός: used previously by Herodotus for the recovery of rightful power (see §65.7).

ἔχει δοῦλος ἡμέτερος: Maeandrius, whose story begins at §142 and ends with his somewhat cowardly departure from Samos at §146.3 and eventual expulsion from Sparta at §148.2. The reference to Maeandrius as δοῦλος arguably reflects Syloson's tyrannical ambitions.

ἄνευ τε φόνου καὶ ἐξανδραποδίσιος: Syloson wishes for a peaceful recovery of Samos.

141

στρατηγὸν Ὀτάνεα ἀνδρῶν τῶν ἑπτὰ γενόμενον: Otanes re-enters the story as commander of this expedition.

καταβὰς δὲ ἐπὶ ... ἔστελλε τὴν στρατιήν: similar to the expression used for the dispatch of any army at §135.3.

142

142.1: Μαιάνδριος ὁ Μαιανδρίου: the name was common in Ionia and Samos, quite likely because of the river. This Maeandrius first appeared at §123, sent by Polycrates to assess Oroetes' state of affairs. See note on §123 for a more hostile version of Maeandrius' intentions.

τῷ δικαιοτάτῳ ... οὐκ ἐξεγένετο: Maeandrius wished to be just in his plans for Samos, but it was not possible. Herodotus credits Maeandrius with honourable intentions, initially at least, but disapproval of his treatment of leading citizens following the failure of his plans is palpable (§143.1).

142.2: Διὸς Ἐλευθερίου βωμὸν ... τῷ προαστείῳ ἐστί: the establishment of the altar to Zeus the Liberator coheres with his avowed aim to offer the Samians freedom from tyranny. ALC (*ad loc.*) note that this cult is attested elsewhere and came particularly strongly to be associated with political freedom following the fall of various Greek tyrannies between 472 and 461 (see Pindar, *Olympian* 12.1-2, where he entreats Fortune as the child of Zeus the Liberator (or 'Deliverer' as in some translations). τοῦτο τὸ νῦν: the phrase hints at Herodotus' personal familiarity with Samos.

142.3: ἐμοὶ...σκῆπρτον καὶ δύναμις ... μοι...ἄρχειν: Maeandrius wishes to stress the power that he could potentially wield, but does not, he claims, wish to.

μοῖραν: the word can mean 'lot' as in one's life and the length of time one lived for, or something stronger, akin to destiny. There is a hint that Polycrates, in Maeandrius' view, got what was coming to him.

ἰσονομίην: Otanes uses the term §80.6, where he is advocating a 'democratization' of government. On whether Maeandrius envisaged similar: see Roisman 1985: 264–6). The term also appears at V.37.2, where tyrant Aristagoras lays down his power and gives the citizens 'ἰσονομίη'. A key strand in all three references is that ἰσονομίη is incompatible with tyranny. On how the term came closely to be associated with democracy, see Lombardini (2013: 393–420).

142.4: γεγονώς τε κακῶς καὶ ἐὼν ὄλεθρος: the Samian citizen mocks only Maeandrius' claim to rule on grounds of his birth. No apparent desire for freedom is voiced.

λόγον δώσεις: ALC (a*d loc.*) note that this is not the same as democratic accountability, for example, the famous εὐθύνη associated with Athens, but the account expected of a regent ruler during a period of transition. This should not be read as any argument against tyranny by the vociferous Telesarchus.

143

143.1: Μαιάνδριος δὲ νόῳ ... εἶχε μετιέναι αὐτήν: Maeandrius realizes that tyranny will continue, and if he does not rule, someone else will.

ἀνεχώρησε ἐς τὴν ἀκρόπολιν: tyrants in retreat. One might compare Maeandrius to the Magus in his retreat to his seat of power (see §66).

μεταπεμπόμενος ἕνα ἕκαστον ... συνέλαβέ σφεας καὶ κατέδησε: 'having summoned each one individually ... he arrested and imprisoned them'. Maeandrius effectively becomes the tyrant he did claimed he did not want to rule Samos any longer. ὡς δὴ λόγον τῶν χρημάτων δώσων: the sense is here 'on the pretext that he was going to give account of the money'.

143.2: οἱ μὲν δὴ ... ταῦτα κατέλαβε νοῦσος: one can see a thematic parallel with Cambyses here: an increase in/acquisition of power and the beginning of madness/sickness. For κατέλαβε in the sense of some state of sickness or fortune befalling a mortal, see §149 on Otanes after his devastation of Samos.

ἐλπίζων .... ἀποθανέεσθαι: 'hoping that he would die'. ἐλπίζων: the case could be made to translate as 'expecting that he would die', depending on how maliciously the intentions of Lycaretus are interpreted. I favour 'hoping' here.

οἴκασι: 'as is likely'.

144

ἐπειδὴ ὦν ἀπίκοντο ... Πέρσαι κατάγοντες Συλοσῶντα: the Persians now enter this somewhat unsettled state of affairs.

οὔτε τίς σφι ... ἐκ τῆς νήσου: Maeandrius' readiness to leave and relinquish power may suggest his desire to grant them freedom was genuine. Or he was simply sensible enough to know he was no match for the Persians. ὑπόσπονδοί: 'under treaty', i.e., they would be granted safe passage out of Samos to elsewhere.

τῶν Περσέων οἱ ... τῆς ἀκροπόλιος κατέατο: this rather arrogant vaunting of an apparently easy victory was rather mistaken and led to a more violent takeover than Syloson desired.

145

145.1: Μαιανδρίῳ δὲ τῷ τυράννῳ: there is perhaps an implied judgement of Maeandrius' conduct in Herodotus' use of τυράννῳ.

ὑπομαργότερος: 'rather mad.' The term is used of Cambyses at §29.1, where he laughs at Apis and stabs him in the thigh. Charileos will show himself to be a similarly rash figure.

διακύψας διὰ τῆς γοργύρης: 'having glanced through the prison window'.

ὡς εἶδε τοὺς Πέρσας εἰρηναίως κατημένους: the brother was angered by the sight of the Persians on their thrones (see §144).

145.2: λοιδορέων τε καὶ κακίζων: 'railing and cursing'.

ὦ κάκιστε ἀνδρῶν: 'oh most cowardly of men'.

ὁρέων δὲ τοὺς ... ἐόντας εὐπετέας χειρωθῆναι: whilst the grammar is not overly tricky here, smooth rendition in English is harder. 'But upon seeing the Persians throwing you out and making you homeless, you do not dare to take revenge, even though they are thus easy to subdue.' οὕτω δή τι ἐόντας εὐπετέας χειρωθῆναι, lit. 'even them in fact being easy to overcome'. Does Charileos believe they are easy to overcome because he is mad, or because he foolishly sees just those few Persians and think they are alone?

146

146.1: ὡς μὲν ἐγὼ δοκέω ... ἀκέραιον τὴν πόλιν: Herodotus qualifies the judgement he gives as his own opinion. οὐκ ἐς τοῦτο ἀφροσύνης ... ὡς δόξαι: result clause. ἀλλὰ φθονήσας μᾶλλον ... ἀκέραιον τὴν πόλιν: 'but more because he refused to make it possible for Syloson to recover the city intact without difficulty' (lit. 'but more because he begrudged Syloson that he should be about to recover the city in tact without difficulty'). φθονέω + dative followed by εἰ means 'resent that', 'take it badly that' (see also Xenophon, *Hellenica* II.4.29; Lysias, 3.9).

146.2: ἤθελε ὡς ἀσθενέστατα ... καὶ οὕτω παραδιδόναι: 'he wanted to make Samian affairs as weak as possible and hand them over in this state.'

εὖ ἐξεπιστάμενος ὡς ... ἔμελλον τοῖσι Σαμίοισι: Maeandrius' calculation proves correct. He knows that if the Persians are angered, strong reprisals will come back on the Samians. His reasoning is the reverse of that of Croesus in book I (I.89.1–3) who recommends that Cyrus does not destroy Sardis and to avoid reprisals, whereas Maeandrius wants the opposite. προσεμπικρανέεσθαι: 'get even more angry with'. An unusual choice of word and not a common one, chosen to reflect the violent reaction of the Persians that follows.

ἐκ τῆς νήσου... φέρουσα ἐπὶ θάλασσαν: this perhaps suggests that Charileos' accusation of cowardice was fair. Maeandrius sets in motion events that will wreak havoc on Samos but will quietly escape so that they do not affect him.

146.3: ἀναπετάσας τὰς πύλας ... πλείστου ἐόντας ἔκτεινον: Herodotus gives a vivid picture of the viciousness of Charileos' attack. He 'bursts out of the gates'. οὔτε προσδεκομένους τοιοῦτον ... οὐδὲν δοκέοντάς... συμβεβάναι: the phrase emphasizes the completely unexpected nature of the attack and also contains a subtle moral judgement in the mention of the agreement that the Persians believed had been reach, which Charileos' attack now shatters.

146.4: ἡ δὲ ἄλλη στρατιὴ: Charileos had clearly failed to anticipate the arrival of the rest of the army.

147

πάθος... πεπονθότας: the *polyptoton* stresses what spurred on Otanes.

μεμνημένος ἐπελανθάνετο: 'remembering [these orders] he forgot them'. It is not entirely clear whether Otanes 'deliberately' forgot the orders, or whether he genuinely forgot them the instant he saw what was happening, despite remembering them previously.

πάντα τὸν ἂν λάβωσι... ὁμοίως κτείνειν: the indefinite emphasises the indiscriminate nature of the slaughter that Otanes unleashes on Samos.

ὁμοίως ἔν τε ἱρῷ καὶ ἔξω ἱροῦ: the angry Otanes does not even spare those inside the temple. A clear link between his conduct here and his later illness is implied (§149).

148

Maeandrius at Sparta.

148.1: ὅκως ποτήρια ἀργύρεά ... ὅκως δὲ ἴδοιτο: 'whenever he set out his silver and gold drinking cups ... whenever Cleomenes saw '. Cf. §51.3. The parallel phrasing puts the focus on the cups and Maeandrius' attempt to use them to bribe Cleomenes.

148.2: ὁ Κλεομένης δικαιότατος: Cleomenes does not rise to the bait. This also reflects the famous Spartan ethos that rejected luxury.

μαθὼν δὲ ὡς ... εὑρήσεται τιμωρίην: 'after learning that he would find vengeance after offering them [the cups] to other citizens.' Cleomenes rightly fears corruption.

τοὺς ἐφόρους: a board of five magistrates elected annually at Sparta who had to swear their loyalty to the state. They had a significant range of powers, including religious and military, and could be instrumental in foreign policy. Their name means 'overseer' (see Xenophon, *Lacedaemonion Politeia* 15.2; see Aristotle, *Politics* 1265b on whether the ephors reflect an oligarchic or democratic aspect of Spartan government).

ἄλλον τινὰ Σπαρτιητέων: Spartiates referred specifically to Spartan citizens who met the property qualification and manned the citizen army.

149

σαγηνεύσαντες: 'having swept Samos clean'. The use of this word has been disputed here; it normally refers to the sweeping of a drag-net when fishing. It reappears at IV.9.6. However, the current commentator thinks that a metaphorical usage of the term fits well here in conveying the depletion inflicted on Samos by the angry Otanes. See §147 for Otanes' violent reprisals against the Samians.

ἔκ τε ὄψιος ὀνείρου ... νοσῆσαι τὰ αἰδοῖα: there is a clear connection between the depletion of Samos and Otanes' disease of the genitals. The vision and the sickness in combination suggest some kind of warning from a higher power. But Herodotus leaves this as an implication.

§§150–60 *Babylon revolts.*

150.1: ἐπὶ δὲ Σάμον . . . ναυτικοῦ οἰχομένου: the implication is that the Babylonians picked their moment while the fleet was absent at Samos. Cyrus had conquered Babylon in 539.

ἐν ὅσῳ γὰρ . . . ἐν τούτῳ παντί: this confirms that the Babylonians took advantage of the turmoil in Persian political affairs during the rule of the Magus and then the revolt of the seven. ἐν τούτῳ παντὶ τῷ χρόνῳ καὶ τῇ ταραχῇ: a *hendiadys*. Lit. 'and during that entire period and in the confusion', for 'in that entire period of confusion'.

καί κως ταῦτα ποιεῦντες ἐλάνθανον: 'they also managed to escape being noticed as they did this'.

150.2: ἁπάσας συναγαγόντες ἀπέπνιξαν . . . ἀπέπνιξαν δὲ αὐτάς: the repetition of the verb 'they strangled' stresses the cold brutal logic of the Babylonian siege preparations. ἀπέπνιξαν δὲ αὐτάς, ἵνα μή . . . τὸν σῖτον ἀναισιμώσωσι: the negative purpose clause also reinforces this.

151

151.1: πᾶσαν τὴν ἑωυτοῦ δύναμιν: the fact that Darius gathers his entire force shows he realizes that retaking Babylon is not going to be easy.

ἐπολιόρκεε φροντίζοντας οὐδὲν τῆς πολιορκίης: the *polyptoton* stresses the confidence of the Babylonians in their preparation.

κατωρχέοντο καὶ κατέσκωπτον: mockery and being laughed at by one's enemies was considered a great source of shame, a theme that is important in Homer and which recurs throughout Greek tragedy. See §37.3 where κατασκώπτω is used for Cambyses' mockery of the statues of Hephaestus in the temple of the Cabeirians (κατασκώψας). At §155.2,

Zopyrus shows his anger at someone mocking the Persians. See note on §29.2 for parallels.

τοῦτο τὸ ἔπος: the phrase perhaps draws attention to what the Babylonian goes on to say, since it will come back to haunt them later.

151.2: ἐπεὰν ἡμίονοι τέκωσι: in other words, the bold citizen is saying that the Persians will never conquer Babylon, as mules cannot breed.

οὐδαμὰ ἐλπίζων ἂν ἡμίονον τεκεῖν: 'in no way expecting that a mule would give birth'. By adding this, Herodotus hints that the taunt will somehow be proven wrong.

152

ἑπτὰ δὲ μηνῶν καὶ ἐνιαυτοῦ διεληλυθότος: over a year passes without any progress in the capture of Babylon.

Δαρεῖός τε ἤσχαλλε ... ἡ στρατιὴ πᾶσα: Darius and the army are bitter at their lack of success.

οὐ δυνατὴ ἐοῦσα ἑλεῖν ... οὐδ' ὣς ἐδύνατο ἑλεῖν ... οὐδὲ...οἷός τε ἦν ἑλεῖν: the lack of success becomes like a refrain in this section, reinforced by Herodotus' use of *variatio*. Despite Darius' efforts, he is thwarted at every turn.

πάντα σοφίσματα καὶ πάσας μηχανὰς ... ἄλλοισί τε σοφίσμασι πειρησάμενος...: the verbal echoes in these phrases emphasize Darius' strenuous efforts.

καὶ δὴ καὶ τῷ Κῦρος εἷλε ... καὶ τούτῳ ἐπειρήθη: even the way Cyrus managed to capture the city does not work for Darius. Cyrus had one hundred and eighty canals laboriously dug by which he was able to approach Babylon across the Gyndes river (see I.189-92 for Cyrus' success).

153

153.1: ἐνθαῦτα εἰκοστῷ μηνὶ: 'then, in the twentieth month'. The emphatic phrase creates a sense of anticipation.

Ζωπύρῳ τῷ Μεγαβύζου ... Μεγαβύζου παιδὶ Ζωπύρῳ: note the repetition of the name, stressing the connection between Zopyrus and the Megabyzus of the seven conspirators. It is hard to replicate in English without sounding awkward.

ἐγένετο τέρας τόδε ... ἡμιόνων μία ἔτεκε: the scenario used by the Babylonian citizen to taunt the Persian army actually happens. τέρας: 'portent', a sign from the gods. Pregnancy in mules is rare, but not impossible. Cf. VII.57, where a mule giving birth is similarly read as ominous but is ignored by Xerxes.

ὑπὸ ἀπιστίης: Zopyrus at first does not believe what he has been told.

ἀπείπας τοῖσι ἰδοῦσι ... τὸ γεγονὸς ἐβουλεύετο: Zopyrus orders those who have witnessed the birth to keep quiet.

153.2: οἱ πρὸς τὰ ... ῥήματα ... πρὸς ταύτην τὴν φήμην: lit. 'with regard to the words..., with regard to this report *anacolouthon*. Herodotus, after reminding his readers/listeners of what the Babylonian said, effectively restarts his sentence.

ἁλώσιμος ἡ Βαβυλών: 'Babylon could be taken'.

σὺν γὰρ θεῷ: Zopyrus sees the workings of the divine in the matter.

154

154.1: ἐδόκεε μόρσιμον εἶναι ... τῇ Βαβυλῶνι ἁλίσκεσθαι: 'it seemed to him that it was now fated for Babylon to be taken'.

εἰ περὶ πολλοῦ κάρτα ποιέεται ... πολλοῦ τιμῷτο: the verbal echo reinforces the importance of capturing Babylon to Darius. It was a wealthy city, as the tribute assigned to Babylon and the rest of Assyria at §92.1 reveals.

ὅκως αὐτός τε ἔσται ὁ ἑλὼν αὐτὴν καὶ ἑωυτοῦ τὸ ἔργον ἔσται: a *tautology* which illustrates that Zopyrus has his sights on glory and honour.

Πέρσῃσι αἱ ἀγαθοεργίαι ... πρόσω μεγάθεος τιμῶνται: Zopyrus has his sights on future glory if his plan is successful. It is recognized by Darius at §160.1 (ἀγαθοεργίην).

154.2: αὐτομολήσειε: optative because it is a future open conditional in indirect speech.

λωβησάμενος... λωβᾶται λώβην: the *polyptoton* of words relating to his self-mutilation stresses the extreme lengths he is going to. The passage is very effective when read aloud. **ἀνήκεστον:** a powerful choice of word emphatically placed, showing that these injuries are irremediable.

ἐν ἐλαφρῷ ποιησάμενος: 'having made light of it'. Zopyrus emerges as brave and determined, and just a little ruthless.

ἀποταμὼν γὰρ ἑωυτοῦ ... περικείρας καὶ μαστιγώσας: the harsh alliteration of τ and κ conveys the grim nature of Zopyrus' self-inflicted suffering. See §155.1 for Darius' reaction.

155

155.1: κάρτα βαρέως ἤνεικε: Darius is shocked when he sees Zopyrus.

ἄνδρα δοκιμώτατον λελωβημένον: the reader/listener is surely intended to recall §69.5 where we learn that it was Cyrus who had mutilated the Magus. Cutting off a man's ears and nose was a profound mark of shame as a punishment among the Persians, hence Gobryas' remark about the shame of Persians being ruled by a Mede without ears at §73.1. The anger of the other conspirators at Intaphrenes' treatment of the gate guards at §118.2 also reflects this stigma.

ἀναπηδήσας ἀνέβωσέ: the swift rhythm of this phrase in ἀνα- and ἀνέ- perhaps imitates the speed with which Darius leaps up in horror from his throne.

155.2: δεινόν τι ποιεύμενος Ἀσσυρίους Πέρσῃσι καταγελᾶν: the humiliating taunt of the Babylonian citizen spurred Zopyrus on (see §151.2).

155.3: τί δ', ὦ μάταιε ... οἱ πολέμιοι παραστήσονται: Darius understandably does not follow Zopyrus' reasoning immediately. He has not fully explained. Darius just sees his appalling state.

κῶς οὐκ ἐξέπλωσας τῶν φρενῶν: 'how have you not taken leave of your senses?' lit. 'how have you not sailed out of your senses?'

155.4: ἢν μὴ τῶν σῶν δεήσῃ, αἱρέομεν Βαβυλῶνα: 'if you do not neglect what you need to do, we will take Babylon,' or 'if you are not wanting on your part'.

155.5: τὸ τεῖχος: a *metonymy* for the 'city', Babylon is symbolically represented by its famous, strong wall.

τῆς οὐδεμία ἔσται ὤρη ἀπολλυμένης: lit. 'for which there will be no care in [their] being destroyed'.

ἐᾶν infinitive used as an imperative. See also κελεύειν at §155.6.

ἐχόντων δὲ μήτε ... ἐτῶν ἀμυνεύντων μήτε: 'Let neither the previous group nor these men have any means of defending themselves.'

The plan is as follows (the section references in brackets are to the sections where the plan is played out):

- 10 days later: send one thousand men that Darius does not care about losing to the gate of Semiramis (§157.2).
- 7 days after that: send two thousand expendable men to the gates of the Ninevites (§157.3).
- 20 days after that again: send four thousand to the gates of the Chaldaeans (§157.4).
- (§155.6) straight after the twentieth day, surround the wall and draw up the Persians at the Belian and Kissian gates (§158.1).

155.6: μεγάλα ἔργα: the phrase is of course ironic. The Babylonians will see the defeats and believe Zopyrus is achieving great defeats on their behalf.

156

156.1: ἐντειλάμενος ἤιε ἐπὶ τὰς πύλας: Zopyrus departs straight to his task.

ἐπιστρεφόμενος: 'turning back'. Zopyrus plays his part well, looking cautiously behind him to make his 'desertion' convincing.

ὀλίγον τι παρακλίναντες: 'opening [the other gate] just a little.' The Babylonians show great caution at first.

156.2: ἐπὶ τὰ κοινὰ τῶν Βαβυλωνίων: Zopyrus is led to the assembly of the Babylonians. This would have been a Council of Elders (on the government of Babylon, see Beaulieu 2018: 60–96).

φὰς ὑπὸ Δαρείου πεπονθέναι τὰ ἐπεπόνθεε ὑπ' ἑωυτοῦ: Herodotus reminds the reader of Zopyrus' own agency to show how the Babylonians are being tricked.

συμβουλεῦσαι: Hude and Wilson in their OCT texts make this an Ionic third person aorist optative singular, which fits with διότι, but Godley makes it an infinitive συμβουλεῦσαι, the only difference being the accent on the upsilon. The current text follows the OCTs.

ἀπανιστάναι τὴν στρατιήν: Zopyrus pretends that he was punished for advising the army to leave.

156.3: Δαρείῳ δὲ καὶ τῇ στρατιῇ καὶ Πέρσῃσι μέγιστον κακόν: an expanding *tricolon*, suggesting Zopyrus is emphasizing how much he wants revenge on all the Persians to convince the Babylonians.

μέγιστον ἀγαθόν . . . μέγιστον κακόν: parallel word order stresses the contrast, and κακόν is saved for the end of the sentence, he has come to benefit the Babylonians and disadvantage Darius. Of course, the irony is that his plan is the other way round.

ἔλεγε: the imperfect suggests he said this on more than one occasion.

157

157.1: οἱ δὲ Βαβυλώνιοι . . . τῶν ἐδέετο σφέων: the Babylonians are completely taken in. δοκιμώτατον ῥινός τε . . . καὶ αἵματι ἀναπεφυρμένον: seeing a man of Zopyrus' status and esteem mutilated and scourged convinces them. πάγχυ ἐλπίσαντες λέγειν μιν ἀληθέα: 'entirely believing that he spoke the truth'.

157.2 ἐποίεε τά περ τῷ Δαρείῳ συνεθήκατο: the short phrase stresses how Zopyrus does exactly what he agreed with Darius.

157.3: μαθόντες δέ μιν ... ἕτοιμοι ἦσαν ὑπηρετέειν: Herodotus gives a vivid picture of the increasing faith that the Babylonians place in Zopyrus. **πάγχυ περιχαρέες:** the short alliterative phrase stresses their delight at the 'victory.' **τοῖσι ἔπεσι τὰ ἔργα παρεχόμενον ὅμοια:** the irony of this is unmistakeable. Zopyrus is making his deeds match his words, but not as the Babylonians think.

οἱ Βαβυλώνιοι πάντες ... ἐν στόμασι αἰνέοντες: 'the Babylonians all held words of praise for Zopyrus on their lips' (lit. 'all the Babylonians held Zopyrus on their lips praising him'). We see how their faith and admiration increases with each 'battle'.

157.4: κυκλωσάμενος κατεφόνευσε: Herodotus creates an accumulative impression of Zopyrus' success and variations on this phrase have been repeated throughout the section (§157.2: κυκλωσάμενος τοὺς χιλίους ... τούτους κατεφόνευσε; §157.3: κατεφόνευσε).

πάντα δὴ ἦν ... τοῖσι Βαβυλωνίοισι Ζώπυρος: the Babylonians, just as Zopyrus predicted (§155.6), have total faith in him.

στρατάρχης τε οὗτός ... τειχοφύλαξ: Zopyrus has all he needs, having been appointed to the top posts of 'commander of the army' and 'guardian of the wall.' One cannot help but see a similarity to the Trojan Horse, Zopyrus being the living horse. It is interesting also to compare the similarity of Livy's account of Sextus Tarquinius' feigned desertion to the Gabii (*AUC*, 1.53), but with no mutilation involved. The pre-battles form an ascending *tricolon* as a prelude to the final storming of the city.

158

158.1: πύλας ἀναπετάσας ἐσῆκε ... ἐς τὸ τεῖχος: Zopyrus fulfils his promise and the Persians are admitted.

158.2: οἱ μὲν εἶδον ... οὗτοι μὲν ἔφευγον ... οἱ δὲ οὐκ εἶδον ... οὗτοι ἔμαθον προδεδομένοι: Herodotus skilfully conveys the ensuing confusion and dawning of the reality of their betrayal upon the Babylonians. There is an element of the irony one finds in Greek tragedy as the unsuspecting protagonist(s) hurtle towards their own downfall, realizing the truth too late.

159

159.1: τὸ τεῖχος περιεῖλε … πύλας πάσας ἀπέσπασε: Darius learns from Cyrus' error in not tearing down the walls and ripping up the gates.

ἀνεσκολόπισε: 'he impaled'. This method of torture was associated with the Persians. Xerxes gruesomely ordered for the head of Leonidas to be impaled (VII.238.1). At §132, the Egyptian physicians who failed to heal Darius' foot were about to be impaled, but for the influence of Democedes.

τοῖσι δὲ λοιποῖσι Βαβυλωνίοισι ἀπέδωκε τὴν πόλιν οἰκέειν: this seems to have been Achaemenid procedure, not to take over directly, but allow the people or previous leader's son to continue to live in or govern a place, perhaps as a way of securing loyalty and obligation (cf. §15 on how Psammenitus could similarly have retained Egypt).

159.2: ὡς δ' ἕξουσι γυναῖκας … οἱ νῦν Βαβυλώνιοι γεγόνασι: the replenishing of Babylon's female population, most of whom had been strangled to conserve food supplies (§150.2). **ἐπέταξε τοῖσι περιοίκοισι … ὅσας δὴ ἑκάστοισι ἐπιτάσσων:** Darius sets in place a kind of 'tribute' arrangement for women to be sent from the neighbouring peoples.

οἱ νῦν Βαβυλώνιοι γεγόνασι: Herodotus connects the aftermath of Darius' conquest with the Babylonians of his own day.

160

160.1: Ζωπύρου δὲ οὐδεὶς … παρὰ Δαρείῳ κριτῇ: Herodotus highlights the great gratitude Darius felt to Zopyrus. **οὔτε τῶν ὕστερον γενομένων οὔτε τῶν πρότερον:** this further stresses how Zopyrus has become the greatest of Persians to Darius. **ὅτι μὴ Κῦρος μοῦνος:** 'except for Cyrus'.

Δαρεῖον λέγεται γνώμην ... τῇ ἐούσῃ προσγενέσθαι: Herodotus relates that it is said that Darius often expressed the opinion that he would prefer an un-maimed Zopyrus to twenty Babylons.

ἐτίμησε δέ μιν μεγάλως: shows Darius' great regard for Zopyrus.

160.2: Ζωπύρου δὲ τούτου ... ηὐτομόλησε ἐκ Περσέων: this may seem a rather flat ending, but it in fact contains a rather nice twist of irony. This Zopyrus had a son named Megabyzus, named after his father, who like the Megabyzus of the seven, served the Persians. Naming a child after the grandfather was a Greek practice (see §55.2 for Archias grandson of Archias). Yet this later Megabyzus' son, who was also called Zopyrus, truly did desert the Persians, unlike his grandfather of the same name who had only pretended to do so. Even more ironically, he deserted to the Athenians.

Bibliography

Abbreviations

ALC   Asheri, D., Lloyd, A., and Corcella, A. (2007), *A Commentary on Herodotus*: Books I–IV vol.1 (Oxford University Press).

H&W   How, W., and Wells, J. (1990 edition), *A Commentary on Herodotus in Two Volumes*, vol.1 (Oxford University Press).

D&M   Dewald, C., and Munson, R. V. (2022), *Herodotus Histories Book I* (Cambridge University Press).

DGRG   Smith (1854), *A Dictionary of Greek and Roman Geography* (Walton and Maberley).

Works cited

Further editions, texts, commentaries

Godley, A. D. (1921), *The Histories of Herodotus: A Translation. Loeb Library* vol.II (Harvard University Press).

Hude, C. (1906), *Herodoti Historiae I–IV: Tomus 1* (Oxford University Press).

Newmyer, S. T. (1986), *Herodotus Book III* (Bryn Mawr Classical Press).

Rawlinson, G. (1875), *The Histories of Herodotus: A Translation.* (J. M. Dent & Sons).

Wilson, N. G. (2015), *Herodoti Historiae I-IV: Tomus* 1 (Oxford University Press).

The Histories

Alberge, D. (2019), 'Nile shipwreck discovery proves Herodotus right – after 2,469 years', *The Guardian* 17 March. https://www.theguardian.com/science/2019/mar/17/nile-shipwreck-herodotus-archaeologists-thonis-heraclion (accessed 09/12/2023).

Armayor, O. K. (1978a), 'Did Herodotus ever go to Egypt?', *Journal of the American Research Center in Egypt* 15: 59–73. https://www.jstor.org/stable/40000131 (accessed 04/06/2023).

Armayor, O. K. (1978b), 'Herodotus' Catalogues of the Persian empire in light of the Monuments and Greek literary Tradition,' *Transactions of the American Philological Association* 108: 1–9.

Baragwanath, E. (2008), *Motivation and Narrative in Herodotus* (Oxford University Press).

Baragwanath, E., and de Bakker, M. (2012), 'Introduction: Myth, Truth, and Narrative in Herodotus' *Histories*', in E. Baragwanath and M. de Bakker (eds), *Myth, Truth, and Narrative in Herodotus* (Oxford University Press): 1–57.

Brown, T. S. (1982), 'Herodotus' Portrait of Cambyses', *Historia Zeitschrift für alte Geschichte* 31.4: 387–403. http://www.jstor.org/stable/4435820 (accessed 01/03/2024).

Cary, M. (1919), 'Herodotus III.104', *Classical Review* 33.7–8: 148–9.

Chiasson, C. C. (1982), 'Tragic Diction in Herodotus: Some Possibilities', *Phoenix* 36.2: 156–61. https://doi.org/10.2307/1087674 (accessed 04/06/2023).

Clarke, K. (2018), *Shaping the Geography of Empire* (Oxford University Press).

Dewald, C. (1980), 'Biology and Politics: Women in Herodotus' "Histories"', *Pacific Coast Philology* 15: 11–18. https://www.jstor.org/stable/1316610 (accessed 28/11/2023).

Dewald, C. (1987), 'Narrative Surface and Authorial Voice in Herodotus' "Histories"', *Arethusa* 20.1/2: 147–70. https://www.jstor.org/stable/44578852 (accessed 04/06/2023).

Fehling, D. (1989), *Herodotus and His 'sources': Citation, Invention and Narrative Art* (Francis Cairns).

Fehling, D. (1994), 'The Art of Herodotus and the Margins of the World', in Z. R. W. M. von Martels (ed.), *Travel Fact and Travel Fiction: Studies on Fiction, Literary Tradition, Scholarly Discovery, and Observation in Travel Writing* (Brill): 1–15.

Goodridge, J. (2006), 'The case of John Dyer's fat-tailed sheep and their tail-trolleys: "a thing to some scarce credible"', *Agricultural History Review* 54.2: 229–39. https://www.bahs.org.uk/AGHR/ARTICLES/54n2a3.pdf (accessed 03/12/2023).

Gould, J. (1989), *Herodotus* (Bloomsbury Academic).

Houliang, L. (2022), 'Herodotus on Persia and Its Historical Value', in Q. E. Wang, O. Michihiro and L. Li (eds), *Western Historiography in Asia: Circulation, Critique, and Comparison* (de Gruyter): 53–79.

Humphreys, S. (1987), 'Law, Custom, and Culture in Herodotus', *Arethusa* 20.1/2: 211–20. https://www.jstor.org/stable/44578858 (accessed 04/06/2023).

Immerwahr, H. R. (1956), 'Aspects of Historical Causation in Herodotus', *Transactions and Proceedings of the American Philological Association*: 241–80. https://doi.org/10.2307/283883 (accessed 04/06/2023).

Irwin, E. (2009), 'Herodotus and Samos: Personal or Political?', *The Classical World* 102.4: 395–416. https://www.jstor.org/stable/40599875 (accessed 30/11/2023).

Lateiner, D. (1989), *The Historical Method of Herodotus* (University of Toronto Press).

Marincola, J. (1997), *Authority and Tradition in Ancient Historiography* (Cambridge University Press).

Matijašić, I., et al. (2022), *Herodotus: The Most Homeric Historian? Histos* Supplement 14. https://histos.org/documents/SV14Matija%C5%A1i%C4%87HerodotusMostHomericHistorian.pdf (accessed 04/06/2022).

Munson, R. V. (1991), 'The Madness of Cambyses (Herodotus 3.16-38)', *Arethusa* 24.1: 43–65. http://www.jstor.org/stable/26309412 (accessed 01/03/2024).

Munson, R. V. (2009), 'Who are Herodotus' Persians?', *The Classical World* 102.4: 457–70. https://www.jstor.org/stable/40599878 (accessed 06/12/2023).

Munson, R. V. (2012), 'Herodotus and the Heroic Age: The Case of Minos', in E. Baragwanath and M. de Bakker (eds), *Myth, Truth, and Narrative in Herodotus* (Oxford University Press): 193–212.

Pelling, C. B. R. (2006), 'Homer and Herodotus', in M. J. Clarke, B. F. G. Currie, and R. O. A. M. Lyne (eds), *Epic Interactions: Perspectives on Homer, Virgil, and the Epic Tradition Presented to Jasper Griffin by Former Pupils* (Oxford University Press): 75–104.

Pelling, C. B. R. (2019), *Herodotus and the Question Why* (University of Texas Press).

Raaflaub, K. A. (2002), 'Philosophy, Science, Politics: Herodotus and the Intellectual Trends of his Time', in E. J. Bakker, I. J. F. de Jong, and H. van Wees, *Brill's Companion to Herodotus* (Brill): 149–86.

Roberts, J. T. (2011), *Herodotus: A Very Short Introduction* (Oxford University Press).

Rollinger, R. (2018), 'Herodotus and the Transformation of Ancient Near Eastern Motifs: Darius I, Oebares, and the Neighing Horse', in T. Harrison and E. Irwin (eds), *Interpreting Herodotus* (Oxford University Press): 125–48.
Ruffing, K. (2018), 'Gifts for Cyrus, Tribute for Darius', in T. Harrison and E. Irwin (eds), *Interpreting Herodotus* (Oxford University Press): 149–61.
Shapiro, S. O. (1994), 'Learning through Suffering: Human Wisdom in Herodotus', *The Classical Journal* 89.4: 349–55.
Thomas, R. (2001), *Herodotus in Context: Ethnography, Science, and the Art of Persuasion* (Cambridge University Press).
Wainwright, G. A. (1953), 'Herodotus II, 28 on the Sources of the Nile', *The Journal of Hellenic Studies* 73: 104–7. https://doi.org/10.2307/628240 (04/06/2023).
Williams, B. (2004), *Truth and Truthfulness* (Princeton University Press).
Wilson, N. G. (2015), *Herodotea: Studies on the Text of Herodotus* (Oxford University Press).

Historical and cultural context

Abe, T. (2014/15), 'Herodotus' First Language: The State of Language in Halicarnassus', *Talanta* XLVI-XLVII: 145–64. https://www.talanta.nl/wp-content/uploads/2017/08/Abe.pdf (10/12/2023).
Beaulieu, P-A. (2018), *A History of Babylon 2200 BC – AD 75* (Blackwell).
Braund, D. (2018), *Greek Religion and Cults in the Black Sea Region: Goddesses in the Bosporan Kingdom from the Archaic Period to the Byzantine Era* (Cambridge University Press).
Brosius, M. (2021), *A History of Persia* (Wiley-Blackwell).
Calame, C. (2001), *Choruses of Young Women in Ancient Greece: Their Morphology, Religious Role, and Social Functions* (Rowman and Littlefield).
Carrick, P. J. (2001), *Medical Ethics in the Ancient World* (Georgetown University Press).
Dalby, A. (2000), *Dangerous Tastes: The Story of Spices* (University of California Press).
Dillon, M. (2016), *Omens and Oracles: Divination in Ancient Greece* (Routledge).

Figueira, T. (2020), 'Language as a Marker of Ethnicity in Herodotus and Contemporaries', in T. Figueira and C. Soares (eds), *Ethnicity and Identity in Herodotus* (Routledge): 43–71. (See also Figueira's 'Introduction':1–13.)

Finley, M. I. (1971), *The Ancestral Constitution* (Cambridge University Press).

Fisher, N. (1992), *Hybris: A Study in the Values of Honour and Shame in Ancient Greece* (Aris and Phillips, reprinted. Liverpool University Press).

Fuks, A. (2013), *The Ancestral Constitution* (Routledge).

Gabriel, R. A. (2012), *Man and Wound in the Ancient World: A History of Military Medicine from Sumer to the Fall of Constantinople* (Potomac Books).

Griffiths, J. G. (1955), 'The Orders of Gods in Greece and Egypt According to Herodotus', *Journal of Hellenic Studies* 75: 21–3. https://www.jstor.org/stable/629164 (accessed 21/11/2023).

Gruman, G. J. (2003), *A History of Ideas About the Prolongation of Life* (Springer).

Hall, E. (1989), *Inventing the Barbarian: Greek Self-Definition through Tragedy* (Oxford University Press).

Harrison, T. (2000), *Divinity and History: The Religion of Herodotus* (Oxford University Press). See especially chapter 8: 208–22.

Herman, G. (2002), *Ritualised Friendship and the Greek City* (Cambridge University Press).

Higbie, C. (2003), *The Lindian Chronicle and the Greek Creation of Their Past* (Oxford University Press).

Jeffery, L. H., and Cartledge, P. (1982), 'Sparta and Samos: A Special Relationship', *The Classical Quarterly* 32.2: 243–65. http://www.jstor.com/stable/638563 30/11/2023).

Lattimore, R. (1939), 'Herodotus and the Names of Egyptian Gods,' *Classical Philology* 34.4: 357–65. https://www.jstor.org/stable/264098 (accessed 12/12/2023).

Llewellyn-Jones, L. (2022), *Persia: The Age of the Great Kings* (Headline).

Lombardini, J. (2013), '*Isonomia* and the Public Sphere in Democratic Athens', *History of Political Thought*, 34.3: 393–420. (http://www.jstor.org/stable/26225837).

Mack, W. J. B. G. (2015), *Proxeny and Polis: Institutional Networks in the Ancient Greek World* (Oxford University Press).

Mitchell, B. M. (1975), 'Herodotus and Samos', *Journal of Hellenic Studies* 95: 75–91. https://www.jstor.org/stable/630871 (accessed 30/11/2023).

Moyer, I. S. (2011), *Egypt and the Limits of Hellenism* (Cambridge University Press).

Pelling, C. B. R. (2011), 'Herodotus and Samos', *Bulletin of the Institute of Classical Studies* 54.1: 1–18. https://www.jstor.org/stable/43693964 (accessed 30/11/2023).

Petrovic, A., and Petrovic, I. (2016), *Inner Purity and Pollution in Greek Religion Volume I: Early Greek Religion* (Oxford University Press).

Prestige-Jones, C. (1999), *Kinship Diplomacy in the Ancient World* (Harvard University Press).

Roisman, J. (1985), 'Maiandrios of Samos', *Historia: Zeitschrift für Alte Geschichte* 34.3: 257–77. https://www.jstor.org/stable/4435928 (accessed 30/11/2023).

Salmon, J. B. (1984), *Wealthy Corinth: A History of the City down to 338 BC* (Clarendon Press).

Walters, K. R. (1987), *Ancestral Laws and the Ancestral Constitution in the Oligarchic Movements of Late Fifth Century Athens* (University Microfilms).

Waters, M. (2022), *The Life of Cyrus the Great: King of the World* (Oxford University Press).

The Tribute Digression – Appendix I

The names given by Herodotus seem overall tally with the Persian sources, but not all regions can be identified (see Figure 5 for a map of the empire). The table below lists the areas as given by satrapy and the tribute according to Herodotus. See ALC §95.2 for difficulties with the total amount given by Herodotus.

Province	Reference in Text	Places/Peoples Included	Tribute Assigned
I	§90.1	Ionians, Magnesians in Asia, Aeolians, Carians, Lycians, Milyans, Pamphylians	400 talents (silver)
II	§90.1	Mysians, Lydians, Lasonians, Cabalians, Hytennians	500 talents
III	§90.2	Hellespontine peoples, Phrygians, Thracians in Asia, Paphlagonians, Mariandynians, Syrians	360 talents
IV	§90.3	Cilicians	500 talents of silver 360 white horses
V	§91.1	Posideia, Phoenicia, Palestine, Cyprus	350 talents
VI	§91.2-3	Egypt, Libyans, Cyrene, Barca	700 talents Silver from Lake Moeris 120,000 measures of grain
VII	§91.4	Sattagydae, Gandarii, Dadicae, Aparytae	170 talents
VIII	§91.4	Susa, the Cissians	300 talents
IX	§92.1	Babylon, Assyria	1,000 talents 500 castrated boys
X	§92.1	Ecbatana, Media, Paricanians, Orthocorybantians	450 talents
XI	§92.2	Caspians, Pausicae, Dareitae	200 talents
XII	§93.1	Bactria	360 talents
XIII	§93.1	Pactyae, Armenians, their neighbours up to the Euxine	400 talents

The Tribute Digression – Appendix I

Province	Reference in Text	Places/Peoples Included	Tribute Assigned
XIV	§93.2	Sagariti, Saranges, Thamanaei, Outii, Mycii, islands in the Red Sea	600 talents
XV	§93.3	Sakae, Caspians	250 talents
XVI	§93.3	Parthians, Chorasmians, Sogdi, Areii	300 talents
XVII	§94.1	Paricanians and Ethiopians of Asia	400 talents
XVIII	§94.1	Matieni, Saspeiri, Alarodii	200 talents
XIX	§94.2	Moschi, Tibareni, Macrones, Mossynoeci, Marsi	300 talents
XX	§94.2	Indian peoples	360 talents of gold dust
			TOTAL: 14, 560 euboic talents (§95.2)

Non- Tribute Extras

1. The Ethiopians (whom Cambyses conquered, not the long-lived people)	§97.2-3	2 *choinixes* of unsmelted gold 200 ebony logs 5 Ethiopian boys 20 large elephant tusks
2. The Colchians	§97.4	100 boys, 100 virgins every five years
3. The Arabians	§97.5	1,000 talents of frankincense

Index Locorum of Greek and Latin Authors

References to Herodotus' Histories outside of Book III are included.

Aeschylus
Agamemnon 114-21: 275

Choephori 540-55: 306

Persae 242: 278

Aristophanes
Acharnians 69-89: 3

Aristotle
Historia Animalium
    499a20: 300
    579a2: 305

Nichomachean Ethics
    1107b: 321

Politics 1265b: 344
    1281b: 282
    1290b6: 225
    1298b-1300b: 286
    1311a5-8: 285
    1313b19-32: 331

Bacchylides
    XVII 60-3: 244

Ctesias
Persica 13.30: 293

Euripides
Hippolytus 952-3: 298

Medea 1049-51: 233

Herodotus (outside Book III)
I   31-3: 320
    32.1: 243
    34.1: 14, 242
    51.3: 244
    72: 291
    78: 224
    84.2: 275
    86: 224, (86.2) 14, 242
    89: 275, 343
    93.1: 294
    131: 211, 221
    132.3: 246
    187.2: 285
    189-92: 346
II   28: 6
    38: 231
    86.5: 306
    101: 239
    120.5-6: 14, 242
    122.1: 238
    152.3: 263
    154.2: 224
    164.1: 224
    182.1-2: 242, 248
IV   9.6: 344
    13.1: 310
    16: 6–7
    24: 224
    97.5: 278
    195.2: 294
    202: 322
    205: 14, 242
V   25: 218
    37.2: 340

Index Locorum of Greek and Latin Authors

VI	109: 286	
	129.2: 278	
VII	10-16: 320	
	16C.1-2: 243	
	41.1: 246	
	49: 335	
	57: 347	
	114: 238	
	137: 3	
	155.1: 331	
	170.2: 335	
	194: 218	
	238.1: 352	
IX	16.2: 329	
	100.2: 243	

Hesiod
Works and Days 737: 285

Homer
Iliad

II	756-60: 291
VI	119-211: 225
	289-91: 333
	437: 207
XVI	836-3: 221
XXII	60: 219
	353-4: 221
XXIV	487: 219
	566: 275

Odyssey

III	199-200: 207
IX	210: 309
XV	426: 333

Isocrates
(*Areopagiticus*) 7.22-3: 286

(*Evagoras*) 9.2: 321

Livy
Ab Urbe Condita (AUC)
1.53: 351

Lysias
3.9: 342

Ovid
Metamorphoses
VIII.445-532: 314

Philostratus
Life of Apollonius of Tyana
II.8: 296

Pindar
Olympians
I: 321
6: 330
12.1-2: 340

Pythians
I.85: 254
2: 321
3: 321
5.85-6: 329

Fragments
169.1-4: 241

Plato
Laws   765c: 286
Republic
  359a-260d: 14

Pliny
Naturalis Historia

X	50: 307, 308
XII	37: 308
	41-2: 308
	82-94: 308
	42.85: 308
	42.86: 309

Polybius, *Histories*

VI	6.11-7.8: 281
	9.9-10: 285
	52.4-9: 285
XV	30: 216
XXXV	7: 331

Ps. Plutarch
Placita Philosophorum
    2.13: 19

Sophocles
Ajax   362-3: 255
          381: 233

Antigone 531-70: 254
            909-13: 314

Strabo
Geographica VI.1.12: 335

Theophrastus
Opinions of Natural Philosophers
    IX.4.5: 307

Thucydides
I   27-40: 250
II   63.2: 280
     67: 3
III 37.2: 280
     62.3: 280
IV 84.2: 247

Xenophon
Anabasis
I   8.25: 330
IV 8.26: 247
V   34: 293

Cyropaedia
VII 1.30: 329
     5.60-4: 276

Hellenica
I   7.22: 285
II 4.29: 342

Hiero 1.9: 254
        6.12: 254
        11.6: 254

ps. Xenophon
Lacedaemonion Politeia
    2.9: 250
    15.2: 344
Athenaion Politeia ('The Old Oligarch')
    1.1: 282

Index

Places and Peoples named only once in the tribute digression (§§89–96) will not be included in the Index. More detail about these peoples is contained in the online Glossary of Peoples and Places. Page numbers in italics indicate a reference in the translation.

Achaemenes (founder of
 Achaemenid dynasty) 24, *109*,
 152, 216, 273
Achaemenids 23–5, *146*, 221
Aeaces (father of Polycrates and
 Syloson) *128*, *190*
Aegina viii, *141*, *184*, 329
Aeginetans
 conflict with Samian exiles *141*,
  220
 and Democedes *184*, 329
Aeschrione *119*
Aeschrion (name at Samos) 230
Alilat (Arabian equivalent to the
 Heavenly goddess) *106*, 211
Alyattes (king of Lydia 635–585) *133*,
 249
Amasis *passim*
 breastplate dedicated by *133*
 predicts Polycrates' grim end
  129
amber *174*, 310
Ammon (oracle of Zeus) 231
Ammonians *113*, *119*, 231
Amphicrates *141*, 260
Amphilochus (son of Amphiareus)
 163
Anacreon (of Teos) *178*, 317
Aphrodite Ourania (equivalent to
 Alilat) 211
Apis 26, *120–1*, *123*, *144*, 231–3, 237,
 263
Apries 26–7, *102–3*, *204–5*, 246
Arabia ix, *105–7*, *163*, 212, 292,
 307–8

Arabians
 the Arabian king 10, *105–7*, *163*,
  170–1, *172*, 211
 Arabian reverence of oaths *106*,
  210–11
 Arabians and exotic produce
  170–3, 303–9
 relationship to Persian power *161*,
  166, 208, 289, 295–6, 361
Araxes (river crossed by Cyrus)
 126
Archias
 grandson of the above and
  Herodotus' source *138*, 248,
  257, 353
 who fought at Samos *138*, 257
Ariaramnes, great-great grandfather
 of Darius 273
Aristophilides, king of the Tarentines
 188, 334
arrogance
 and the downfall of Oroetes *181–2*
 and the tyrannical ruler *156*, *182*,
  278–80
Artemis
 Artemis Orthia 250
 temple of, refuge of Corcyrean
  boys *133–4*
Artontes, father of Bagaeus *182*
Artystone
 daughter of Cyrus and wife of
  Darius 24, *161*
Asia *161–97 passim*, 360–1
 Dorian Spartans first expedition
  139

first Persians to arrive in Greece
    from *189*, 336
  peoples subject to Persia *161*,
    162–3, *164–5*, 222
  Samos as part of 257–8
  tribute from *165*
Aspathines *149*, *155*, 277
Assyria *164*
  part of wealthy province 347
Astyages 13, *143*, 262
Athena
  cult at Lindus *133*, 248
  temple at Aegina *141*
Athens x, 257, 285
  Corcyra seeks help from in 431 250
  democratic government of 21,
    279, 281, 283, 340
  Herodotus and 2, 3
  and intellectual culture 16
  and Persia 26, *201*, 353
Athenians 353
  and Democedes *184–5*, 329–30
  versus Persian in Herodotus 26
Atossa
  daughter of Cyrus 330
  and Democedes *186*, 330
  married to Cambyses *161*
  married to Darius 24, *161*, 289
  married to the Magus *148*, *161*
  rebukes Darius *148*, *186*, 331, 332

Babylon 7, 15, 72, *195–201 passim*,
    264, 345–53 *passim*
  first taken by Cyrus 24 (on Cyrus
    Cylinder), 292–3
  in wealthiest province 164, 360
Babylonian
  conversion to Euboic talent *165*,
    290
  talent, value of *162*
Bactria *164*, 360
  Bactrians *168*, 299
Bagaeus *182–3*, 325
Barcaeans 14, *109*, 322
  in Persian empire *163*, 292, 360

Bardiya
  name of usurper on Behistun
    inscription 261
Behistun, inscription 24–5, 261, 273,
    287
benefaction
  between Samos and Sparta *132–3*,
    247
  Syloson and Darius *190–1*, 338
Bisitun *see* Behistun
Bisotun *see* Behistun
burial
  of Apis 233
  customs 11, *112–13*, 220–2
  live 237–8
  as public honour *138*, 257
Buto *144*, 263

Cadytis *105*, 208
Callantiae *166*
  possibly same as Callatiae 241,
    296
Callatiae 21, 23, *127*, 224, 241, 297
Cambyses
  and the Achaemenid dynasty 24,
    273
  actions against Persians and
    Croesus *124–6*, 236–9, 293
  allegedly Nitetis' son *103*, 204–6
  allegedly plotting against Oroetes
    179, 318
  alliance with Polycrates *131*,
    245–6
  and Amasis' body *112–13*, 220–1
  and Apis *120–2*, 231–3
  atrocities against wife and
    Smerdis *122–4*, 232–5, 251
  Darius former bodyguard of *190*,
    337
  deceived by Amasis *102–3*, 204
  disrespect towards religious
    practice 21, *126–7*, 239–41,
    345
  as example of tyrannical rule 22,
    156, 279

expeditions after Egypt 18, *113–19 passim*, 222–3, 225–30, 295, 307, 332
Herodotus' portrayal of 26–7, 222
injury, illness and death of *146–7, 177–8, 181*, 263–4, 265–6, 293, 315
invades and conquers Egypt 4, 9–11, *103–14 passim, 128, 166, 189*, 203, 209–10, 213–19, 244–5, 289, 337
madness 19, *123–4, 126*, 219, 232–3, 234–5, 237–40, 315, 341 (compared to Charileos)
and the Magi rebellion *142–4, 148–9, 151–3*, 261–2, 314
marries sisters *122–3, 161*, 289, 330
misinterprets dream *121–2, 144–5*, 234–5, 261–2, 320
plea to Persians *145–6*, 264–5, 272
reputation among Persians *162 passim*, 266, 291
tests, then shows pity for Psammenitus 15–16, 315
vows revenge *103–4*, 206–7
Candaules, Gyges and 13–14
cannibalism
in army of Cambyses 18, *119*, 229–30, 297
Greek view of 229–30
Carian
language spoken in Halicarnassus 2, 28
Carians
as mercenaries in the Egyptian army *108*, 213
in Persian empire *162*, 360
Carnaspes, son of Mitrobates *181*, 323
Carthage xiii, *114*, 224
Carthaginians
defeated by Gelo of Syracuse 321
expedition against by Cambyses *113–14*

Cassandane
allegedly son of Apries' daughter 205
children admired *103*, 206
mother of Cambyses 103
wife of Cyrus *104*, 206
cassia
produced in Arabia *171, 172*, 303, 306–7
Caucasus *166*, 296
Charileos *193–4*, 341–2, 343
choinix 166, 296, 361
Chorasmians
and the plain 11, 17, 18–19, *175*, 311
and tribute *164*, 361
Cilicia *163*, 291–2
Cilicians *163*, 291, 360
cinnamon *171, 172–3*, 303, 306–8
Cleomenes, king of Sparta *195*, 344
Cnidians, Cnidus *189*, 336
Corcyra *133–4, 138*
poor relations with mother city Corinth *134*, 224, 255
Corcyreans 249–50
anger Periander *134, 138*
Corinth x, *133–4, 135, 136–8 passim*
anger against Samos *133*
poor relations with colony Corcyra *134*, 224, 250, 255
wealthy *136*, 253
Corinthians *133–4*, 248–9
Corys, river in Arabia according to Herodotus *107*, 212
Cretans
assist Aeginetans against Samians 141
Crete xiii
and Minos 318
Samian exiles settle on *140*, 259
Croesus
adviser to Cyrus 343
enlightened then facing death (I.86–90) 16, 217, 219, 264, 315

presence with Cambyses in Egypt
    219
relationship with Cambyses *111*,
    124–6, 237, 238–9
Croton ix, 20, *180*, *183–4*, *188–9*, 321,
    329, 334–5
Crotonians
    renowned physicians *185*, 329
    some defend Democedes *188*, 334
Ctesias 24, 287, 293
customs (general) 23, 27, *103*, *112–13*,
    115, *127–8*, *167*, 206, 229–30,
    234, 240–1, 250, 263
    Cambyses' violation of *122–3*, 234
    Hecataeus' interest in 17
    Herodotus' interest in and
        treatment of 4, 11, 17–18
    and *nomos* versus *physis* 20–1, 215
    varied nature of among Indians
        297
Cydonia
    foundation angers Aeginetans 259
    founded by Samian exiles *131*,
        140, 259
Cyprus ix, *163*, 224, 292, 360
    Cyprians, surrender to Cambyses
        114
Cyrene ix, *163*, 202, 292, 360
Cyreneans *109–10*, 216, 329
    reputation as physicians *185*
Cyrus
    and the Achaemenid dynasty 24,
        152–3, 267, 273
    angers Cambyses *103*, 205, 206–7
    background 7, 13
    in Ctesias' account 24, 287
    deposed Astyages 262
    Egypt claims kinship with *103*,
        206
    father of Cambyses *passim*
    father of Smerdis *142*, *143*, *145–9*
        passim, *152–3*, *161* (on
        Behistun inscription), 261,
        269, 273
    Herodotus' attitude to 27

ill-advised by Croesus *126*, 239
mutilation of the Magus *148*, 348
Oroetes appointed by *177–8*, 315
spared Croesus 217, 219, 315,
    342–3, 345–6
success and reputation 7, *152*, *161*,
    162, *200*, 203, 291, 352–3
successfully captured Babylon
    196, *200*, 292, 293, 352

Darius
    and the Achaemenid dynasty 24,
        267, 273
    agrees to help Syloson *190–1*, *194*,
        241, 338
    and Babylon *196–7* (fails to take),
        293, 345–8
    becomes king 7, *161*
    and the Behistun inscription 25
    burial customs debate 21, *127–8*,
        221, 223, 240
    and constitutional debate 22–3,
        157–9, 278, 283–6
    deals with Intaphrenes *176–7*,
        314
    and Democedes 20, *183–5*, *198–9*,
        320, 327–8, 330, 332–5
    and Gillus *189*, 335–6, 338
    gives cloak to Syloson *189–90*,
        225, 335–6
    goes to palace *153–4*
    honours Zopyrus *201*, 352–3
    joins the rebellion *149–50*
    kills Magus *154–5*, 276–7
    marriages after becoming king
        161, 289, 330 (Atossa)
    persuaded by Intaphrenes' wife
        177, 314
    plans expedition against Greece 7,
        26, *186*, 331–2
    plots with Oebares *160*, 287–8,
        290
    portrayal in Herodotus 26–7, 263,
        269–72
    punishes Babylon *200–1*, 352

General Index

reorganizes tribute *162*, *165*, 267,
    290–1, 295
supported by fellow conspirators
    151, *157*, 274–5
takes revenge on Oroetes *181–2*,
    323–6
wounded and cured *183*, 326–7
and Zopyrus *197–200*, 348–9, 350
Darius (II) *109*, 216
Dascyleium *178*, *181*, 316
date, of the *Histories* 2–3
deities
    Arabian deities and their Greek
        equivalents 17, *106*, *146*,
        307–8
    Persian royal deities 265
    statues of mocked by Cambyses
        11, *127–8*, 239–40
Delphi
    Pythia of *139*
    treasuries at ix, *139*, 258
Demarchs *105*, 210
Democedes *180*, *183–9 passim*,
    320–1, 326–35 *passim*
democracy
    lot associated with 325, 341
    offered to Samos by Maeandrius
        191–2
    topic of Persian debate 22–3,
        278–85
    topic of political debate 21
dialect, Ionic 28–31, 204, 209, 239,
    279, 312, 350
Dionysus
    equivalent to Arabian Orotalt *106*,
        211
    and Nysa *166*, 296, 307–8
    and places where cinnamon
        grows *173*, 307–8

Ecbatana *142*, *144*, *164*, 262, 263, 293,
    360
Egypt ix
    allied with Polycrates 14, *128*
    betrayed by Phanes *104–5*, *106*

in Book II 7, 211
Cambyses' resentment towards 9,
    103–4, 205, 206–7
Herodotus' sources from 20, 26–7,
    205, 229–30
invaded and defeated by
    Cambyses 10, 15, 26, 27, *102–3*,
    107–8, *114*, *124*, *128*, *131*, *142*,
    143, *161*, *162*, *189*, 203, 208,
    360
mercenaries of *108*, 213–14
not given back to Psammenitus
    112
rain in Thebes *107–8*, 213
Samian exiles sent to *131–2*
visited by Herodotus 2
and wine jars *105–6*, 209–10
Egyptian, Egyptians
    aggression of *109*, 216
    Apis and Cambyses *120–2*, *144*,
        231–3
    attacked by winged serpents *172*
    burial customs 21, *112–13*,
        117–18, 228
    defeated at Memphis *109–10*,
        216–17
    doctors 20, *184*, *185–6*, 203
    knowledge of Persian customs 27,
        103, 205–6
    leading men with Psammenitus
        110–12, 218
    religion mocked and disrespected
        by Cambyses 11, 21, *112–13*,
        220–1
Elephantine *114–15*, 224
envy *121*, *156*, 242, 254–5, 279
Epaphus *see above entry on Apis*
ephors *195*, 344
epic, influence on Herodotus 15–16
Epidaurus *134*, 136
Eridanus 9, *174*, 309–10
Ethiopia 18, *174*, 222, 226–8, 307, 332
Ethiopians (1), long-lived 15, 20,
    113–19 passim, *166*, *168*, 222,
    226, 231, 297, 299, 309

Ethiopians (2), conquered by
    Cambyses 166, 295–6, 361
Ethiopians (3?) of Asia 164, 294, 361
Euboic
    minas 290
    talent 162, 165, 361
eunuchs 104, 154, 184, 207, 249, 276,
    293
Eupalenus, designer of Samian tunnel
    141
Europe 6, 165, 174–5, 296–7

Fish-eaters 115–17 passim, 121, 224,
    225, 227
folktales
    influence on Herodotus 13–14
frankincense 166, 170–1, 172, 304,
    306, 361

geography 2, 16–19
Gillus 189, 335–6
Gobryas 149, 151, 154–5, 269, 272
gods, see above deities
government, Persian debate about
    22–3, 278–86
Greeks (general) 3, 5, 120, 141, 169,
    179, 190, 318, 338
    Aeolian Greeks 102, 202
    in burial customs debate 21, 23,
        127, 221, 230, 231, 297–8
    Greek mercenaries in Egyptian
        army 108, 118–19
    Herodotus' portrayal of 28, 214
    Herodotus seeks to inform 18
    importance of omens for 274–5
    interest in geography and
        ethnography 2, 16–17
    interest in medicine and science
        19–20, 236
    Ionian Greeks 16, 102, 202
    not all fans of democracy 282
    in Persian army 118
    relations with Persia 336
    sceptical about constitutional
        debate 22, 155, 278, 282
    stereotyping of non-Greeks 278,
        289
    trade with Phoenicians 304
    and versions of events 123
    view of Nysa 296
    view plant diets as unmanly 298
    visitors of Egypt 189–90
guest-friends/friendship 128, 129,
    138, 225
gum-mastic (ledanon) 171, 173, 303
Gyges, father of Maeandrius 179, 317
Gyges, murderer of Candaules 13–14

Halicarnassus
    and Herodotus 1–2, 6
    and Ionic dialect 1, 28
    Phanes from 104, 106
Hecateus of Miletus 16–17, 28
Hephaestus
    identified with Ptah 127, 239, 345
Hermione 140, 259
Herodotus passim
    as historian
    interest in geography,
        ethnography 2, 11, 16–19, 209,
        257–8
    interest in science and medicine
        19–21
    and Persia 23–8
    politics and human nature in
        21–3, 259–60, 279, 280
Hippocratic
    school of medicine 330
    writings 19, 236
Homer, Homeric 207, 219, 221, 223,
    275, 291, 309, 331, 333, 345
    influence on Herodotus 13,
        15–16
    Ionic forms in 30, 279
hubris/ὕβρις (and related words) 249,
    279, 282, 313, 323, 325, 334
Hydranes 149
Hydrea 140, 259
Hystaspes, father of Darius 24, 149,
    150, 161, 191, 271, 339

General Index

Iapygia *189*, 335
Inaros *109*, *112*, 216, 220
India 293, 296, 303, 307
Indians 18, *[166]*, *168-74 passim*, 221, 241, 229, 301-2
Intaphrenes 27, *149*, *154*, *176-7*, 277, 287, *312-13 passim*
Ionia 2, 5, *128*, *179*, 317, 317-18, 321, 339
Ionian Greeks
   and intellectual culture 16, 226
   in Persian empire *102*, *162-3*, *181-2*, 202, 361
Ionic, forms and dialect 28-31, 204, 209, 239, 275, 279, 312, 350
Italy 7, *188*, *189*, 310, 321

Judges, Persian Royal *110*, *122*, 218, 234

kingship
   Ethiopian method for choosing *115*, 225
   Persian *145*, *159-60 passim*, *190*, 287-8, 331

Libya, Libyans *109*, *113*, *163*, *165*, *174*, 216, 292, 360
Lycaretus 192, 341
Lycopas, Spartan soldier at Samos 138
Lycophron, son of Periander *135-7 passim*, 251, 255
Lydia, Lydians 219, 249, 300, 310
   under Persian rule *162*, *182*, 360

Maeandrius
   and Chaerileos *193-4*
   holds on to power *192*, 340, 341
   offers to lay down tyranny *191-2*, 339-40
   in power at Samos *191*, 347
   quietly facilitates destruction of Samos *194*, 342-3
   ready to leave Samos *193*, 341
   sent by Polycrates to Oroetes *179-80*, 319
   at Sparta *195*, 344
Magna Graecia ix, 321, 333
Magnesia on the Maeander vii, ix, 291, 317
Magi
   beheading and humiliation of *155*, 277
   Massacre of, festival 155
   rebel *142*, *144-6 passim*, *153*
   rebellion against and overthrow 22, 25, *153*, *154*
   take Prexaspes into their confidence 152
Magus
   Cambyses prepares to attack 144
   many killed by the seven 155
Mede, Medes *143*, 146, *151*, *170*, *181*, 303, 348
Median
   clothing 159
   difference to Persian not always clear 333
Megabyzus
   conspirator 22-3, *149*, *157*, *196-7*, 278, 282-3, 347, 353
   grandson of (also Megabyzus) *201*, 353
Melissa *134*, 235, 251
Memphis *105*, *109-10 passim*, *112*, *119-20*, *163*, *190*, 210, 216
   seat of the satrap 292
mercenaries
   in Egyptian army 28, *104*, *108*, 213
   in Polycrates'/Samian army *132*, *193-4*
Messenians *133*, 247
Milon of Croton *189*, 335
Minos 5, *179*, 244, 318
Mitrobates *178*, *181*, 316-17, 323, 325, 331
monarchy 22-3, *157-8*, 279, 283-5
myrrh *115*, *116*, *171*, 225, 226-7, 304

Naustrophus *141*
Nile 6, *107*
Nitetis *102*, *104*, 204, 206

Oasis, city of *119*, 230
Oebares *160–1*, 287–90 *passim*, 324
oligarchy 22–3, *157–8*, 270, 283–5
omens 274–5
oral tradition 13, 15, 25
    delivery of the *Histories* 31
Oroetes 5, 10, *177–83 passim*, *191*, 315–26 *passim*, 327, 331, 339
Orotalt, Arabian equivalent of Dionysus *106*, 211, 307
Otanes
    argues against tyranny 26, *156*, 279–81
    argues for democracy 22–3, *156–7*, *279–82 passim*, 286, 325, 340
    asks for freedom from kingly rule *158–9*, 286–7
    disagrees with Darius over when to act *150*, *153*, 269–71, 274
    forgets instructions and suffers *194–5*, 341, 343, 344–5
    forms the rebellion 22, *149*, 269, 289
    leads expedition against Samos *191*, *193*, 339
    suspects the Magus *147–9*, 267–8, 328

Padaeans, Indian tribe *167*, 298
Pantagnotus, brother of Polycrates *128*, 337
Papremis, battle site *109*, 216
Parthia, Parthians *164*, 294, 361
Patizeithes, the Magus *142*, *144*
Peloponnese vii, viii, *139*, *140*, 195
Pelusium 107
    battle at 213–14
Periander *133–8 passim*, 235, 244, 248–55, 261, 293

Persia 3, 7, 11, 17, 20, 23–6, *104*, *121–2*, *146*, *162*, *166*, *175*, 202–4, 216, 220, 292–3, 295, 300, 327–8
    customs 18, 21, *103*
    Persian empire ix, 2, 7, 11, 17, 18–19, 25–7, *102*, *106*, *166*, *175–6*, 216, 221, 224, 289–92, 294–6, 299, 301–2, 316, 321, 360–1
    Persian versions of events *103*, *161*, *169–70*, 289
    Persians, Herodotus' attitude to 25–8
Phaedyme *147–8*, 268, 289
Phanes 28, *104–5*, *108*, 207–10, 213–14, 287, 324
Phoenicia, Phoenicians *105*, *114*, *127*, *163*, *171*, *173*, *187*, 208–9, 224, 304, 307, 360
Polycrates
    ambitions of 5, 14, *179–81*, 294, 317–19, 320
    death of *180–1*, *183*, *191*, 315, 322
    and Democedes *180*, *184–5*, 327, 329
    excessive good fortune 11, 13–14, *128–31*, *241–6 passim*, 337
    and Maeandrius *179–80*, *191–2*, 319, 339–40
    power 9, 13–14, 28, *128–39*, 246–7, 260, 316, 321, 324
    ruthlessness of (towards brothers), 28, *128*, *190*, 337; (towards citizens), *132*, 247
    sends men away as exiles *131–2*, *139*, 246
    Spartans make expedition against *131*, *132–3*, *138–9*, 241, 245–6, 257–8
    targeted by Oroetes 10, *177–9*, *181–2*, 315–16, 316–17, 322–3

polygamy 267–8
Prexaspes 24, *122–5 passim*, *142–6*, *152–4*, 234, 236–8, 262, 264–6, 273–4
Procles *134–6 passim*, 252, 254
Psammenitus 15, *107*, *110–12*, 212–13, 217–18, 352

Rhoecus *141*, 260

Samius, son of Archias *138*, 248, 257
Samos vii, viii, 28, *128–34 passim*, *138–41*, *178–9*, *183*, *185*, *189–96 passim*, 202, 230, 242, 245, 247, 249, 256–60 *passim*, 316–17, 319, 321, 336–45 *passim*
Samians, of Samos
  exiles of 9, *131–2*, *139–41*, 247, 258, 259–60
  outrage against Corinthians *133–4*, 249–50, 293
  Persian anger with and reprisals against *194–5*, 342–3, 344
  reject Maeandrius' offer of freedom *192*, 339–40
  relations with Sparta *132–3*, 241, 247–8
  released by Oroetes *181*, 322, 327
  resist the Spartans *138*, 256
  Samian source of Herodotus 2, *138*, 248, 257, 315
  splendid engineering of 10, *141*, 259–60
Samians, of the Aeschrione *119*, 230
Sardis 14, *105*, *133–4*, *177*, *181–3*, 208, 343
Scylax 16
Scythians *186*, 311, 332
Siphnus, Siphnians *139–40*, 258–9, 264
skulls, Egyptian and Persian compared 19–21, *108–9*, 214–16

Smerdis
  on Behistum inscription (Bardiya) 261
  brother of Cambyses and son of Cyrus 26, *121–3*, *142–9 passim*, *152–3*, *161*, 226, 233–5, 261–3, 265–6, 272–3, 289, 320
  comparable to Maeandrius 340
  in dream of Cambyses *145*, 234
  example of tyrannical rule 22, *156*, 279
  exposed by Otanes and Phaedyme 148–9, 268, 287, 289
  the Magus *142*, *144–5*, *147–9*, 261–3, 266, 267–9
  married Atossa *161*, 289, 330
  mutilated by Cyrus *148*, 348
  overthrown 22, *155*, *196–7*, 276–7
  Patizeithes *142*, 144
  ruling Persia 16, *142*, *145*, *149*, *196*, 266, 268–9, 345
  separates royal wives *148*, 328
  suspected by Otanes *147–9 passim*, 267
  the seven rise against *150–1*, *152*, *176*, *190*
  very like Smerdis son of Cyrus *142*, 261, 269
Solon 14, 16
Sparta vii, viii, *132*, *195*, 247, 256–7, 339, 344
Spartans 9, *128*, *132–3*, *138–9*, 227, 245, 247–8, 249, 256–8
spies
  Cambyses
    Fish-eaters sent as to Ethiopia by *114*, *116*, *117–18*, 332
  Greek use of 332
  sent by Darius to Greece *187*, *188*, *189*, 332, 333, 336
Syloson *128*, *190–5*, *224–5*, 241, 337–42 *passim*
Syracuse *180*, 321
Syria, Syrians *105*, *142*, *144*, *163*, 209, 262, 263, 360

Tarentum, Tarentines *188, 189*, 321, 333, 335–6
Telesarchus, citizen of Samos *192*, 340
Teos *178*, 317
Thannyras *112*
Thebes, Thebans *108, 118–19*, 213
Theodorus *130*, 244
tragedy, Greek
    elements of in Herodotus 15–16, 250, 279, 345, 352
tribute, paid to Persian king 27, *109, 147, 162–6 passim, 176, 201*, 217, 267, 290–5 *passim*, 300, 307, 311, 347, 360–1

women as tribute to repopulate Babylon 352
tyranny 26, *137, 157*, 246, 253, 280, 331, 339–40

xenia 241
Xerxes 238, 320, 331, 335, 347, 352

Zopyrus
    grandson of (called Zopyrus) *201*, 353
    pretend deserter 15, 27, *196–201*, 217, 264, 268, 346–51 *passim*, 352–3
Zoroastrianism 221

www.ingramcontent.com/pod-product-compliance
Lightning Source LLC
Chambersburg PA
CBHW071757300426
44116CB00009B/1109